watercolor boot camp

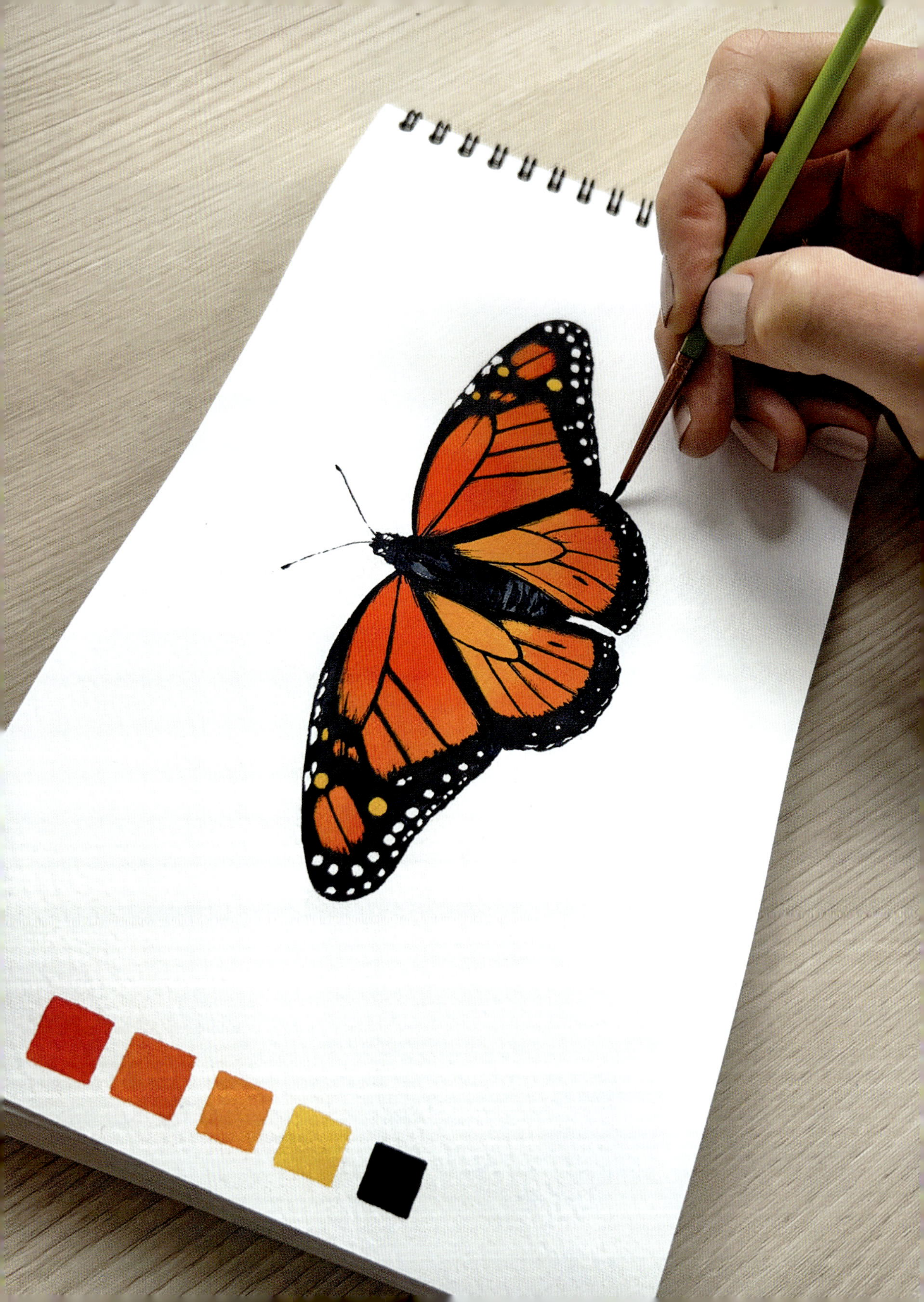

watercolor boot camp

Strengthen Your Skills and Create Beautiful Paintings in One Month

Hannah M. Pickerill

Author of *Watercolor Wanderlust*

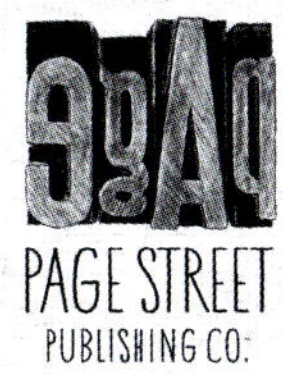

PAGE STREET
PUBLISHING CO.

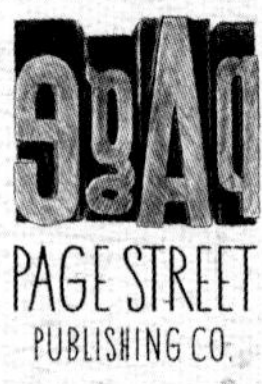

First published in 2026 by
Page Street Publishing Co.
27 Congress Street, Suite 1511
Salem, MA 01970
www.pagestreetpublishing.com

Distributed by Macmillan, sales in Canada by The Canadian Manda Group.

30 29 28 27 26   3 4 5

ISBN-13: 979-8-89003-421-2

Library of Congress Control Number: 2025940447

Edited by Sadie Hofmeester
Cover and book design by Emma Hardy for Page Street Publishing Co.
Photography by Hannah M. Pickerill with the exception of the author photo on page 233 by Grace J. Zielinski and select reference photos: Rule of Thirds (bottom on page 33) by Ariel Gazarian, Fluffy Clouds (page 81) by Ch Photography, Cherry Bomb (page 113) by Quaritsch Photography, Butterfly Fly Away (page 123) by Allec Gomes, Pumpkin Spice (page 134) by Marius Ciocirlan, Nocturne (page 139) by Mijail Pari, Making Waves (page 147) by Anuk De Fonseka, Limited Palette (page 153) by Valen Gorordo, Let the Sunlight In (page 171) by Anne Nygård, Ink and Wash (page 200) by Getty Images, Painting Water with Water(color) (page 213) by Geoffrey Baumbach, No Brushes Allowed! (page 218) by Jack Ward

Printed and bound in the United States of America

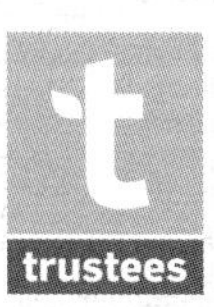

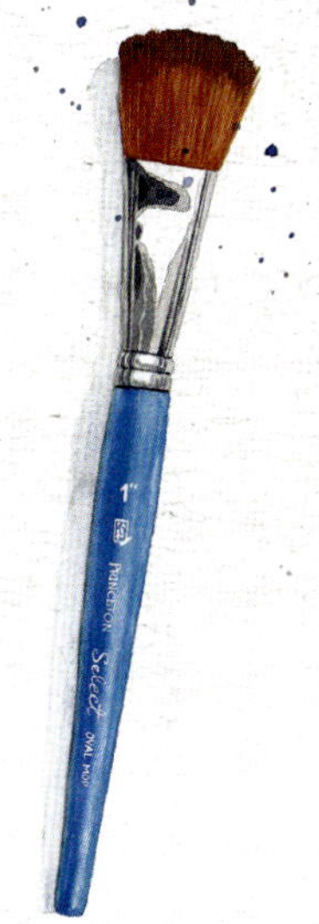

Dedication

This book is dedicated to my family. None of this would have been possible without you. I love you to infinity and back.

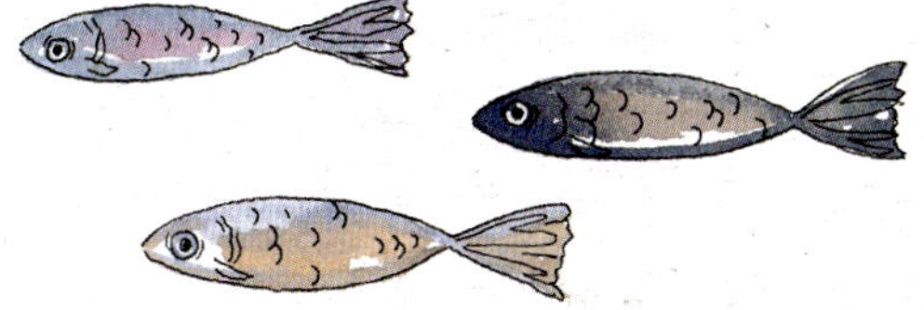

Table of Contents

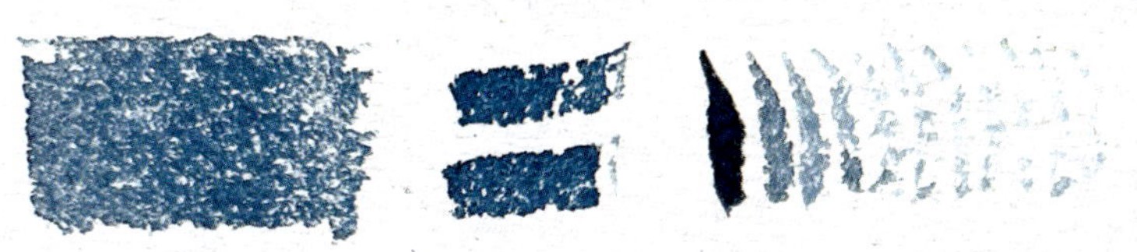

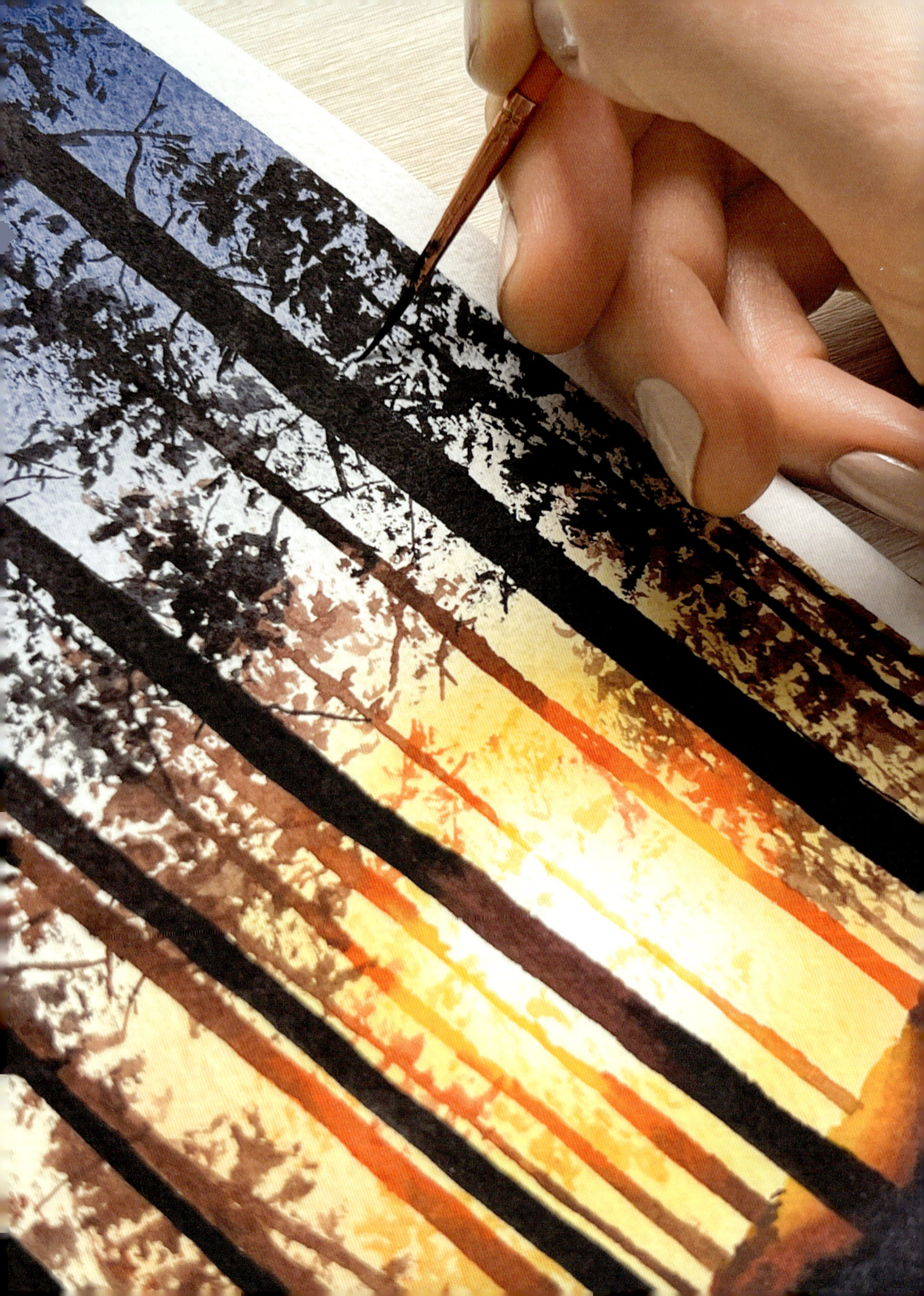

Introduction

Welcome, my friends, to *Watercolor Boot Camp*! I have been an artist all my life; I've loved drawing and painting since before I can remember. I loved taking art classes in school, and a lot of my free time was spent painting at a disastrously messy art desk at home, headphones in and dead to the world. Growing up, I never thought of it as a potential career, since adults always seemed to discourage it in favor of a "real job." I got lucky for sure, but I also worked hard to make it into my full-time career in October of 2021.

Since then, I've filled my time (and paid my bills) creating and selling my own original paintings and prints, making custom paintings for clients, publishing my first instructional book, *Watercolor Wanderlust,* in 2024, and cultivating a community on social media where I share my work and my hard-earned art knowledge with the world. I'm still learning and growing as an artist, but passing along my current knowledge and inspiring others to pick up a paintbrush (both on social media and in book form) has been an unexpected and gratifying aspect of my career. I have always loved to teach, and I am so grateful to get to help thousands of people with the thing I am most passionate about.

I am very fortunate to have had access to an art education during my school years. Art and creativity are significant defining characteristics of being human, and the arts are an incredibly important, and often underfunded, component of a good education. I was able to take art classes throughout grade school, where I learned about different mediums, styles and techniques, and had dedicated time to practice. In college, I added an art minor to my course schedule just so that I could continue to learn.

I learned a lot on my own as well; I've made tons of mistakes and bad paintings and learned from them, and we are so lucky to live in a time where basically all the knowledge in the world is available on the internet. But learning a new skill solely from the internet is like drinking from a fire hose—there's too much, too fast and it can feel scary and overwhelming. That's where this book comes in—I've provided you with a condensed version of the art lessons I had growing up, plus the best of what I've learned from my own trials and errors. We'll cover a lot of information together, but if the art world is a vast ocean of knowledge, we'll be splashing around in the shallow waves on the beach. My hope is that this book will provide you with a good base of skills that will launch you with confidence into your independent art journey.

HOW TO USE THIS BOOK

Watercolor Boot Camp is composed of five chapters, each with six individual lessons. This means if you complete one lesson per day, you'll dramatically improve your art and watercolor skills in just one month! I've created each lesson so that they can be completed in approximately 30 to 60 minutes. Of course, this depends on how fast you work and how comfortable you are with watercolor to begin with. If you need to work slower, or you don't have large chunks of uninterrupted time, don't hesitate to break up each lesson over a couple days. You *can* work through this book in one month, but that's not the actual goal. Your goal is to get through this book, however long that takes, and improve your art skills along the way.

I've grouped the five chapters into two larger parts: Part 1 (page 18) contains the first two chapters, where each lesson focuses on a different fundamental principle of art and watercolor. Each lesson contains two or three accompanying exercises, which are quick studies or experiments to help you grasp each concept. Part 2 (page 118) contains Chapters 3, 4, and 5, where you'll apply the knowledge you learned in Part 1 to one complete painting per lesson. Throughout the lessons in Part 2, I will make callbacks and references to concepts from Part 1, so don't be afraid to flip back through the book (and your own work) to remind yourself of those concepts.

The most important factors for success throughout this book (and with art in general) are your dedication and consistency. Find a schedule that works for you, stick to it and I'll have you in your best artistic shape by the time you reach the end!

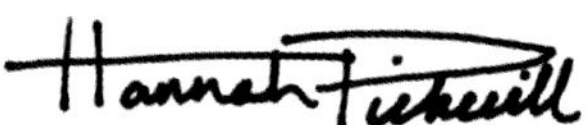

Know Before You Go

BEGINNING YOUR BOOT CAMP JOURNEY

Before we get into this book, let's talk about expectations. This book is organized in such a way that the information builds on itself through each chapter. If you are already a seasoned artist (or just a merchant of chaos), feel free to flip through this book to find whatever inspires you. You may already feel comfortable with the more fundamental lessons in this book, but they are always there for you as a reminder, a warm-up, or a way to break out of artist's block.

For my little hatchling artists, I recommend working through this book in order. This way you'll be able to build up your skills logically throughout the book, and build a great starter portfolio along the way! As you work, you might find yourself struggling with certain techniques. Even though it feels icky, this is such a good sign. Learning and growing as an artist requires you to step outside your comfort zone, struggle and fail a few times. It happens to me all the time, and any artist who has ever lived has had to do exactly the same. Art is a skill that can be learned just like anything else—there are no shortcuts and it requires dedication and practice, but if you stick with it, I can guarantee you'll end up with paintings you're proud of!

One powerful (though slightly traumatic) aspect of art classes is Critique. If you've never had the pleasure, Critique is an exercise that takes up at least one entire art class on the due date of a project. Each student hangs their work on the wall, and the entire class plus the teacher migrates as a group to each person's piece and tells them, to their face and in front of everyone, what they like and what they don't like about it.

Of course, since you're working through this book on your own, I can't subject you to this particular form of torment. However, there is a ton of value in an honest critique of artwork, looking past the knee-jerk reactions of "I like this painting" or "This painting sucks" and actually figuring out what worked and what didn't. Throughout this book, I will prompt you to take a step back and analyze your painting once you've finished it. Take note of what specifically went well; maybe you mixed exactly the right color for one part of the painting, or maybe you accurately depicted light hitting a subject. And while it may be a

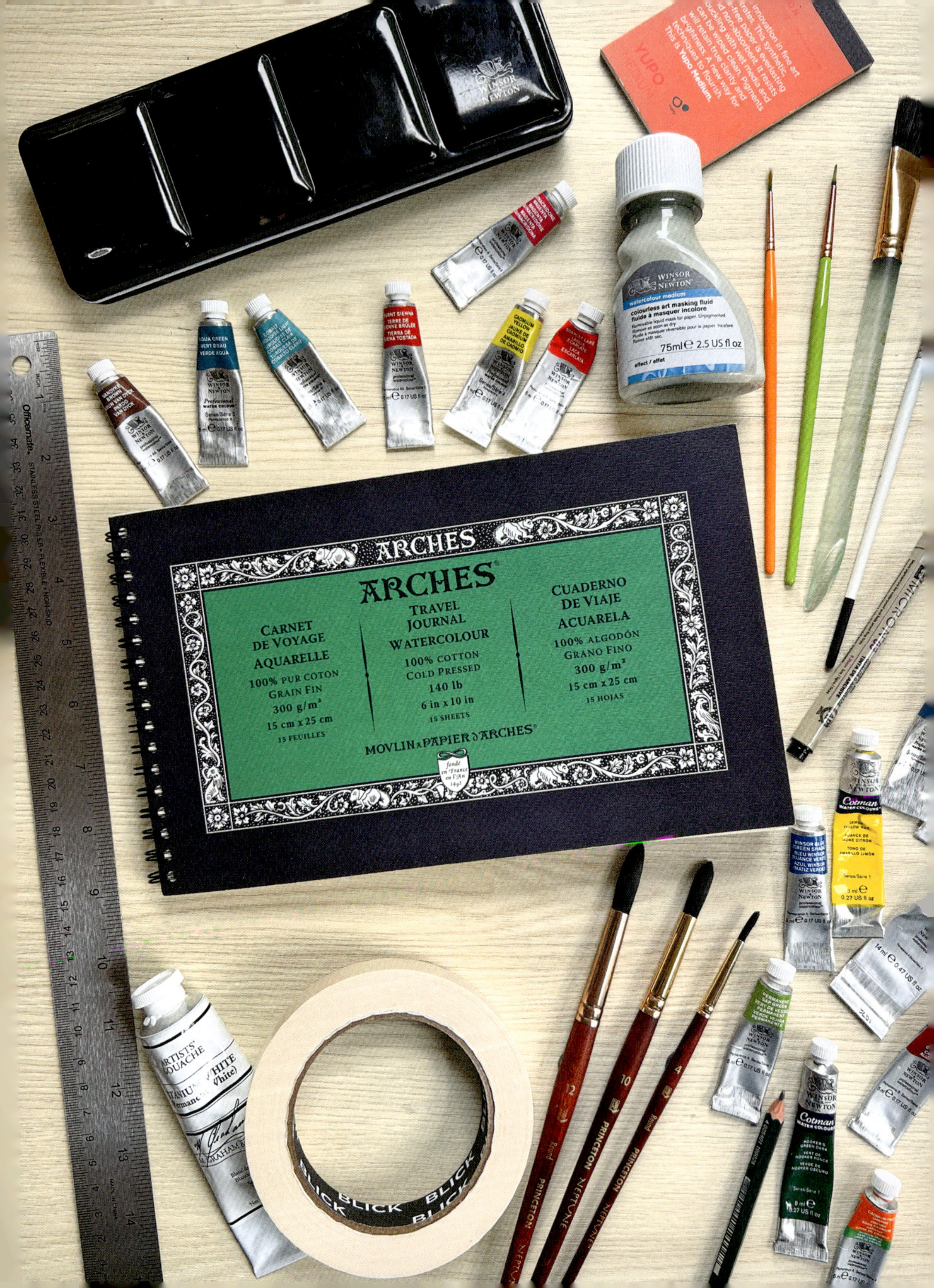

little uncomfortable, also take note of what didn't go well; maybe you had a hard time adding details to something, or used the wrong color somewhere.

I highly recommend taking physical notes about each painting either right there on the paper, or on a sticky note or separate notepad. If you're feeling brave, you could even have a friend or family member critique your work, or if you're feeling even more brave (borderline psychotic) you could post your work on the internet and get critiques from strangers. Regardless of how you do it, analyzing your work in a mindful and constructive way can really help you improve next time you pick up a brush.

I have one last note/plea for you before we jump into the content of this book. I will provide you with directions as clear as I can make them, along with step-by-step photos to guide you through each lesson. However, there will likely still be times where you will have to make an executive decision about things like the exact tone of a color you're mixing, where exactly to put it on the paper, small things like that. There will also be times, especially with a hard-to-control medium like watercolor, where you'll follow my directions exactly and end up with something that looks significantly different from my painting. This is where I want to encourage you to be your own artist,

be confident in your own decisions and focus more on learning the techniques and completing the painting in front of you rather than worrying about copying mine exactly.

MATERIALS

Let's talk about the materials you'll need to acquire in order to get through this book. All of them can be found at your local art store or online, and you can find options that will fit within your budget. As you might expect, more expensive supplies will yield better results to a certain point, but you can still get great results from student-grade or less expensive supplies. Throughout this section, I'll do my best to give you some different options, what you can compromise on and what might be worth the splurge. The three most important materials are watercolor paints, watercolor paper and watercolor brushes, so let's talk about those first.

Watercolor paints: I use 16 colors of Winsor & Newton™ professional watercolor paints, which you can see swatched and listed on page 14. These paints are quite nice, and I've used them for many years, but they are expensive. There are tons of options out there for watercolor paints depending on your budget, and most will have colors that are similar to these. Winsor & Newton has a student-grade line

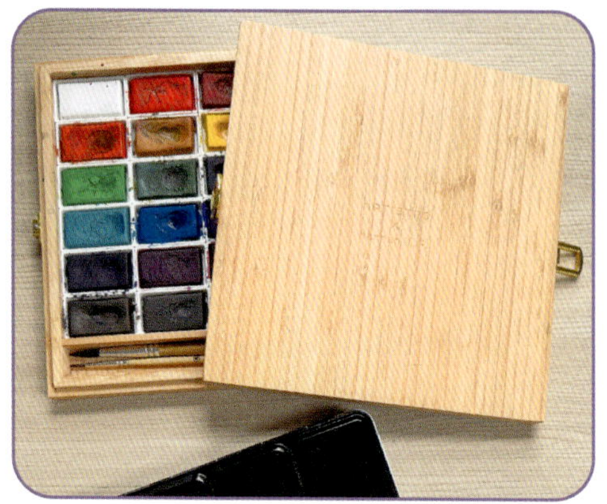

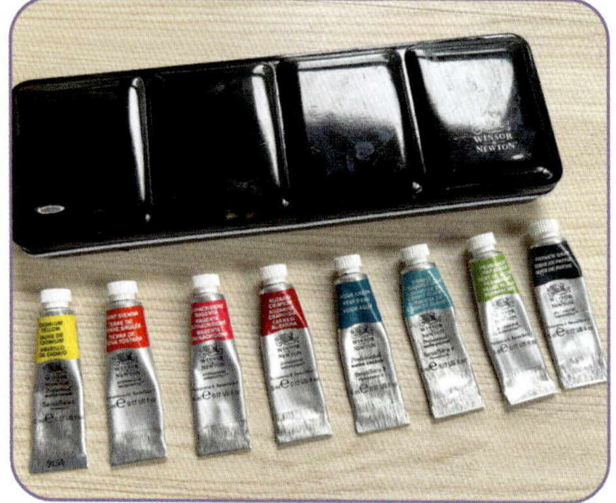

called Cotman, Etchr® has a good set of 24 watercolors, and I've even helped design a watercolor set with Artistro®, which you can find on Amazon by searching Artistro x Hannah M. P. (while supplies last). Take a moment to locate the colors in your palette most similar to the swatches below so that you can easily follow the color-mixing directions in this book.

> **NOTE:** Watercolor paints can come in hard pans or as a thick liquid in small tubes. The hard pans are a little bit more concentrated, but they tend to be more expensive. I personally use tube watercolors and simply squeeze paint from each tube into its designated half-pan container in my palette when that color is running low. You can work with the tube watercolors while they are still in liquid form, or reactivate them with water after they dry. Either one works fine, though for one project (No Brushes Allowed! [page 218]) you'll need at least a couple tube watercolor paints.

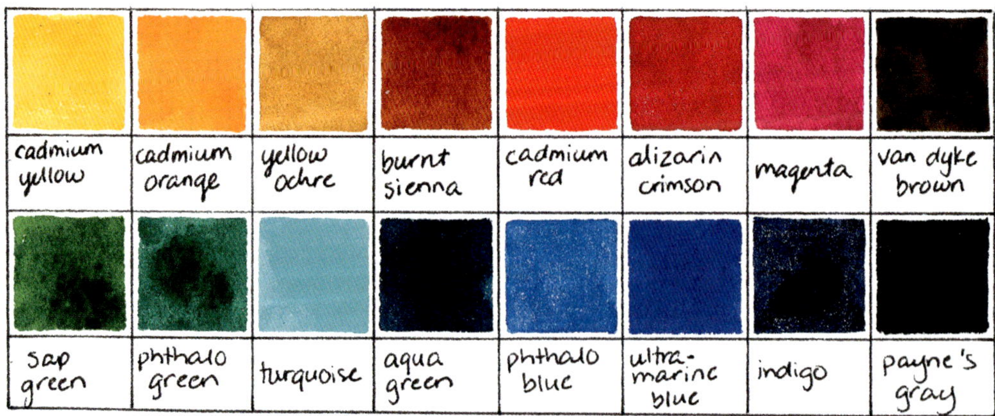

cadmium yellow	cadmium orange	yellow ochre	burnt sienna	cadmium red	alizarin crimson	magenta	van dyke brown
sap green	phthalo green	turquoise	aqua green	phthalo blue	ultra-marine blue	indigo	payne's gray

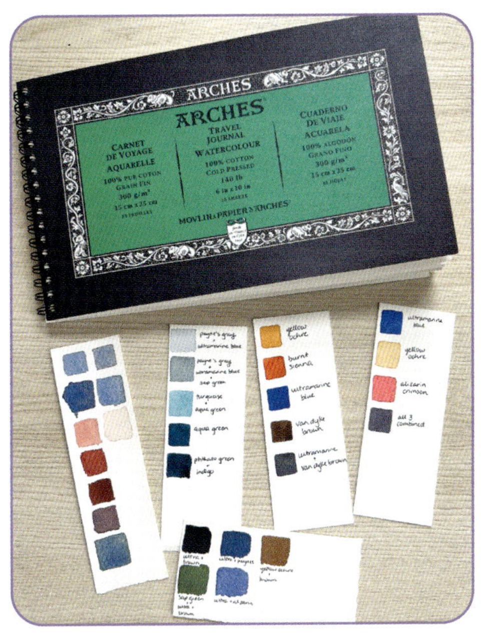

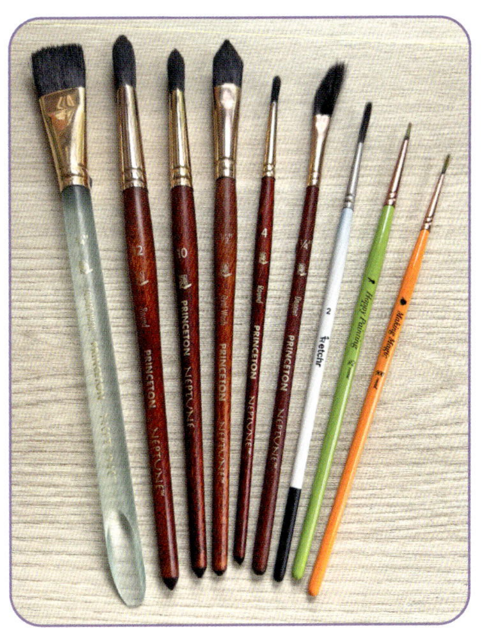

Watercolor paper: I used the Arches® Watercolor Travel Journal sketchbook for this entire book, which measures just under 6 x 10 inches (15 x 25 cm). Arches paper is fantastic, but again, there are plenty of options out there: Fluid® 100 and Baohong® are also good budget-friendly paper brands, and Etchr makes my favorite watercolor sketchbooks. The one thing I highly recommend looking for from any brand is 100 percent cotton watercolor paper—it will perform SO much better for you! You'll also notice that watercolor paper is labeled either hot press or cold press. Cold press tends to have more texture or "tooth" on the surface of the paper, while hot press tends to be smoother. I personally prefer cold press, but either option works!

Watercolor brushes: Most of my brushes are from Princeton Neptune, which is my favorite brand, as their brushes aren't overly expensive and hold up so well over years of constant use. In this book, I used a ¾-inch (2-cm) flat, a 12 round, a 10 round, a ½-inch (1.27-cm) oval, a 4 round, and a ¼-inch (0.63-cm) dagger brush from Princeton Neptune. My detail brushes are a 2 round and a 000 round from Kristy Rice's brush sets, and for one project, I used a #2 liner brush from Etchr.

If you're looking to start your brush collection, you can get a lot done with only three brushes. I'd recommend starting with round brushes as they are the most versatile. Grab a large brush (size 10–20), a medium brush (size 4–8) and a detail brush (size 0 or 2), and you're good to go!

Now let's talk about some other art supplies mentioned in this book. Several of the projects in this book do require a couple extra materials you may or may not already have. I did my best to keep extra supplies to a minimum or provide alternatives because I know many of us are ballin' on a budget, but here are the things I would suggest grabbing from your local art store when you get a chance:

Masking fluid: Liquid latex that covers your paper with a waterproof seal, which can be removed later to reveal the painting underneath.

White gouache: Good to have a small tube on hand for adding highlights to a finished painting. My favorite brand is M. Graham®.

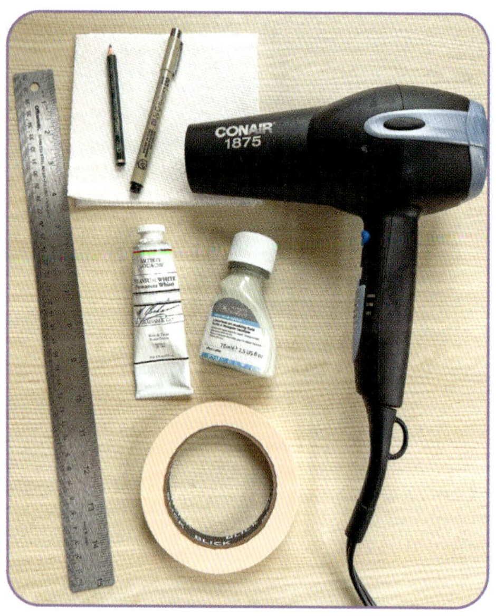

Masking tape: Great for taping your paper down and creating a nice border. I get mine from Blick®, but your local hardware store will have some too. Just make sure you test it on your watercolor paper because sometimes it will rip the paper. You can always use a hair dryer to heat up the masking tape for a few seconds before you peel it to reduce the chance of ripping.

Waterproof pen: Any alcohol-based pen will work and you may already have one around the house! Just test it first by scribbling on a piece of scrap paper, then brush some water over it. If the pen marks stay put, it's waterproof. I use Micron pens, but there are tons of options out there.

Household materials: Finally, gather a cup you don't care about for water, a hair dryer to speed up drying time, paper towels, a pencil, an eraser, a phone camera and a ruler. If your watercolor set doesn't come with a mixing area, grab a ceramic plate to serve as your palette.

This should have you covered for most of the lessons in this book, but please note that some lessons have unique materials you may need to collect. Carefully read the materials list in each lesson before starting, so you don't have to pause your watercolor workout to race around the house grabbing needed items like table salt or plastic wrap (see page 101 if I've piqued your interest!).

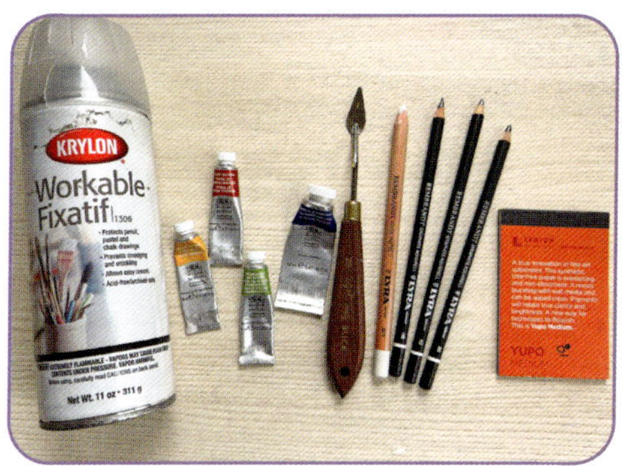

Chapter 5 (page 192) of this book goes into some watercolor experimentation, which requires a few extra materials. We'll discuss these in more detail in Chapter 5, but I'll list them here so you can include them in your next art store run:

» At least 1 watercolor graphite pencil, 8B graphite softness

» White charcoal pencil

» Tube watercolors in Yellow Ochre, Burnt Sienna, Sap Green and Ultramarine Blue

» A small palette knife, or similar flat object like a used gift card

» YUPO® paper (more commonly found in art stores) or stone paper (from the brand Karst®)

» Optional: fixative spray to keep pencil drawings from smudging

REFERENCE PHOTOS

Lastly, let's discuss reference photos. Many of the reference photos I've used in this book are photos I've taken myself, but some are from a royalty-free photo website called Unsplash. The reference photos are printed with every project of the book, but sometimes it can be nice to have access to the actual photo, so I've compiled all of the photos in a single folder on Unsplash (with the exception of one from Upon Further Reflection, page 160, which was taken many years ago and was unfortunately too low quality to be uploaded). You can access the folder by following this website link, or by scanning this QR code with your phone:

https://unsplash.com/collections/ZZ3yNZ40KSk/book-references

PART 1

The Fundamentals

If I asked you to run a marathon tomorrow without any training, could you do it? Maybe you could, if like me you're stubborn and can't resist a challenge, but it would be painful and frustrating; you could injure yourself and you likely wouldn't be motivated to ever try again. Now, if I asked you to run a marathon in a year, and gave you a personal trainer, a private chef and time off work to train and properly recover, you'd probably have a much better chance of completing that marathon and enjoying it (as much as one can possibly enjoy running 26 miles [42 km]).

Just like a marathon, or any skill or hobby, creating art is best experienced if you start at the beginning and build a foundation of skills and knowledge that you can bring forward into larger and more complex creations. I started drawing and painting at a very early age, which has given me the advantage of many years of trial and error throughout my childhood and young adult life. If you are an adult picking up watercolor (or any hobby for that matter) for the first time, you'll need to build that foundation of skills on your own. Enter *Watercolor Boot Camp*.

In Part 1 of this book, I'll give you the quick and dirty essentials that I think will benefit you the most in your art journey. In Chapter 1 (page 20), we'll talk about some art basics that can apply to any medium you'd like to work with. We'll discuss topics like light, color, perspective and value, and you'll solidify your new knowledge with a few hands-on exercises. In Chapter 2 (page 68), we'll transition to watercolor-specific knowledge, going over several different ways to apply paint to paper to produce different effects. With these two chapters under your belt, you'll be ready to tackle the more complex lessons further on in this book. The key (and I cannot stress this enough) is consistency, so embrace both the failure and success that come with learning a new skill, stick with me through it all and let's make some art!

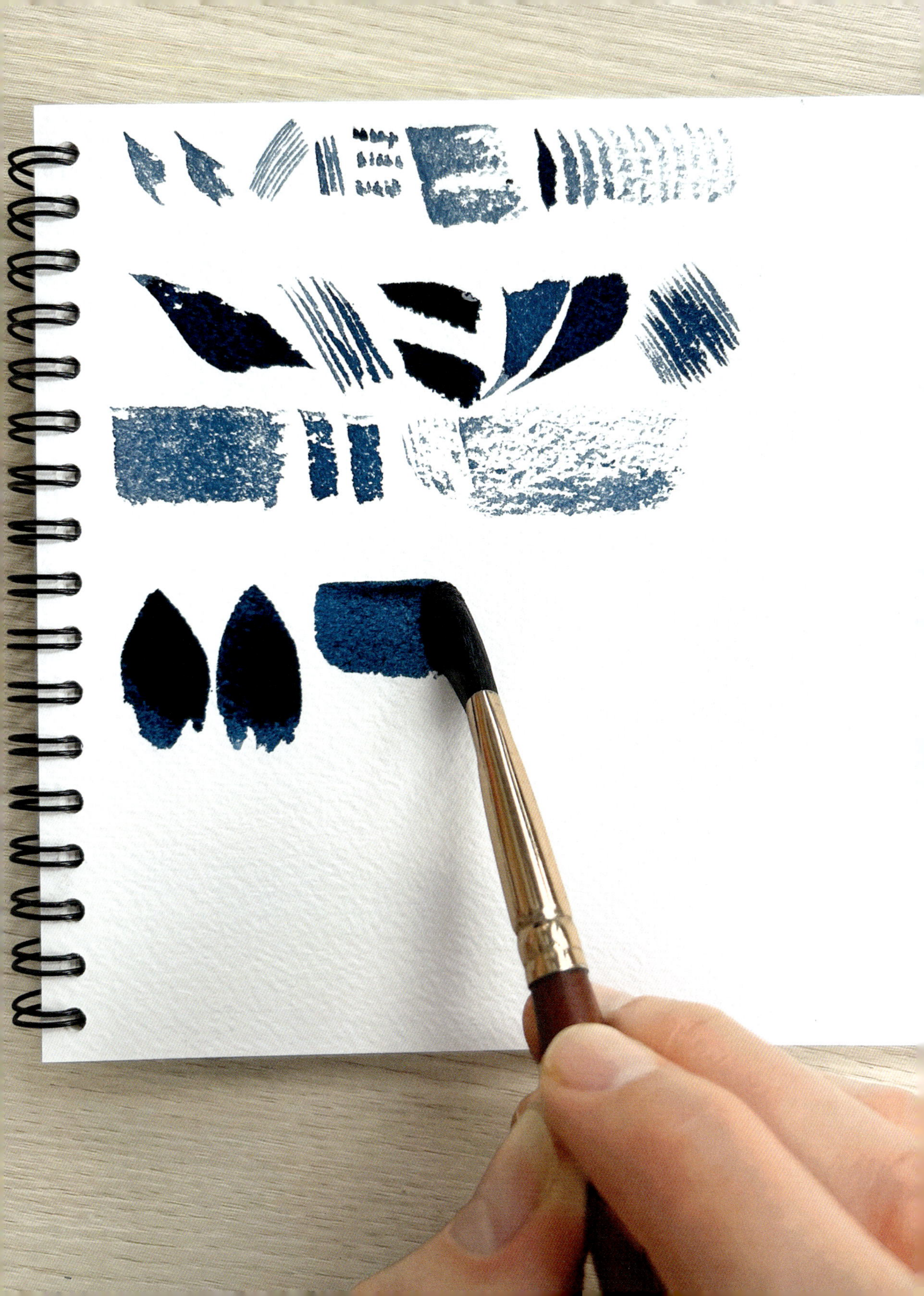

Art Essentials

Key Techniques to Build Your Foundation

We'll kick off *Watercolor Boot Camp* with some foundational principles. As in music or sports, it's very important to understand the fundamentals of art before jumping into more complicated projects. Musicians learn notes and scales before full songs, gymnasts learn handstands and cartwheels before flips, and artists must learn about things like color and composition before creating a masterpiece painting.

Chapter 1, we're warming up: The following six lessons will help you develop your foundation in a hands-on way. This is the art equivalent of learning to walk before you can run, luckily without the actual running. We will talk about composition, perspective, light and color, and with these lessons, you'll start to unlock the true magic behind art!

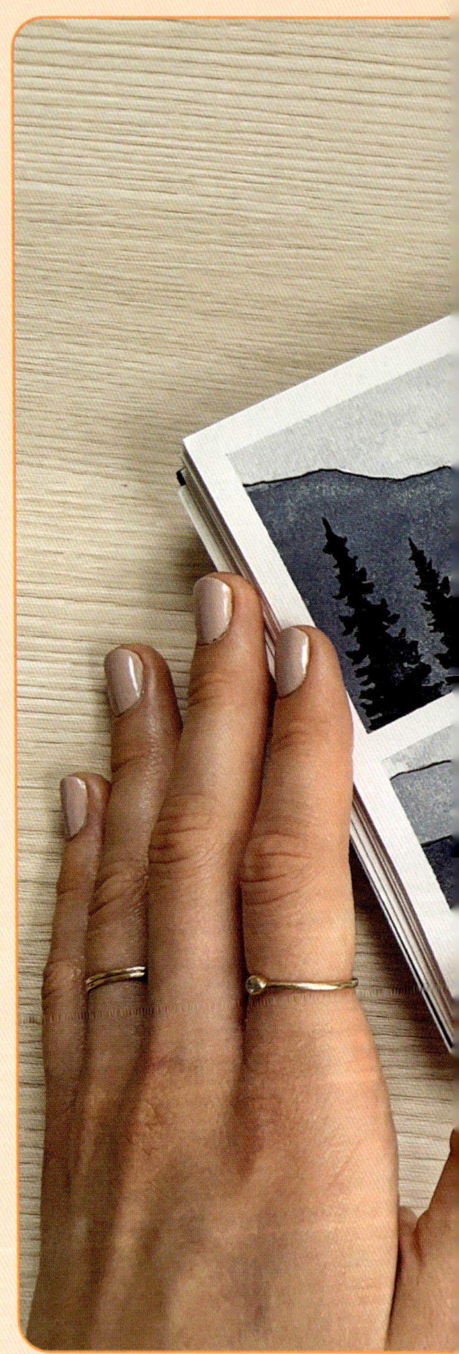

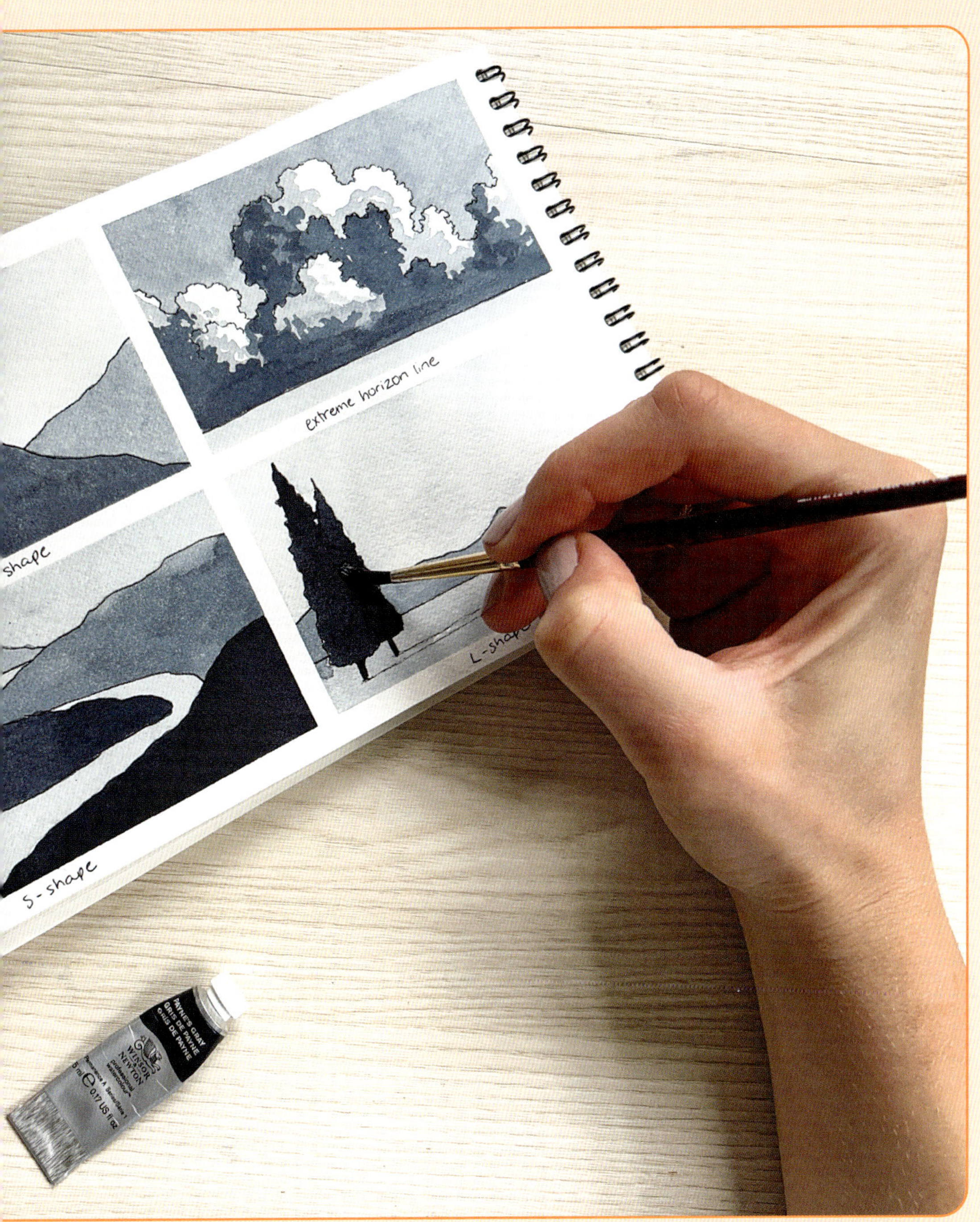

extreme horizon line
L-shape
shape
S-shape

See the Light . . . Source

Fun fact: Art, when you boil it down, is simply the study of light. Light waves bounce off everything around you, and each object absorbs certain wavelengths of light and reflects others back to your eyes to create the colors, shapes, textures, shadows and highlights that you can see. Painting is the science of observing that light closely, then translating it into a two-dimensional form using paint. Light is one of the most important factors in a compelling painting.

All of this is not to say that you *have to* translate the light from a scene to your painting exactly as you see it. There are so many ways to play with color and light to create paintings that range from hyper-realistic to completely abstract. It is very important, however, to recognize the role that light plays in any art form. Our very first lesson in *Watercolor Boot Camp* will walk you through the basics of light.

Light can come from many different sources—the sun, the moon, stars, flashlights, indoor lights or a fire. All of these light sources can be sorted into two categories:

» **Natural light:** light coming from the sun or moon

» **Local light:** light originating from a nearby source like a fire, flashlight or light bulb

Regardless of the light source, it can shine at many different angles on your painting subject. For example, the sun can be in different positions compared to a landscape you're looking at, or a local light source can be held or positioned at different angles around an object you want to paint. I like to call the angle of the light on a subject a "lighting scheme," and once you've identified the lighting scheme, you can figure out exactly where all of your shadows and highlights need to be placed.

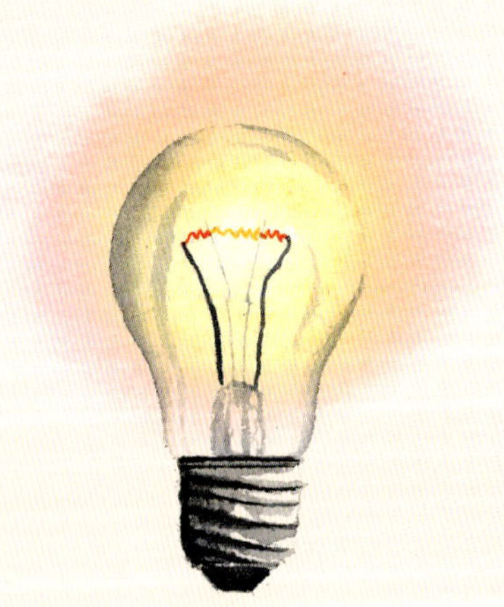

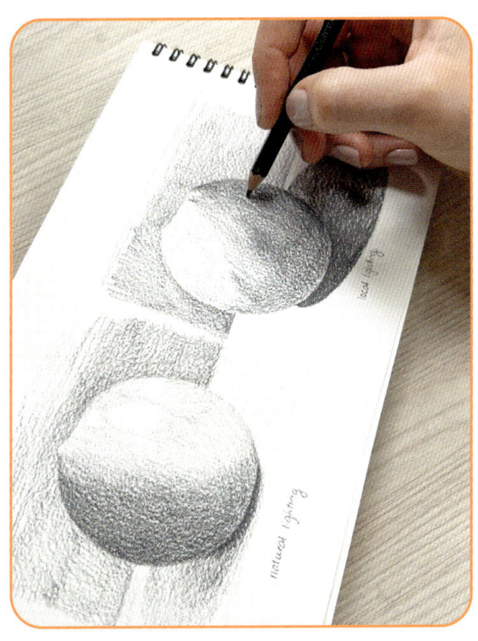

EXERCISE 1: PLAYING WITH LIGHT SOURCES

For our first little exercise, you are going to play around with some different lighting schemes. You'll need:

» A round object of any kind (I used an orange, but you could use any round fruit, a baseball or tennis ball, a ball of yarn, etc.)

» A phone camera or regular camera

» A flashlight

1   Once you have your objects ready, head to a room with less sun exposure so you can really see your local light source.

2   Set up your round object in front of you. Hold your camera in one hand and your flashlight in another.

3   Shine your flashlight on your round object and take a picture.

4   Move your flashlight around to different angles and take a picture at each one. Try holding your flashlight directly above your round object, or behind it, or shining directly at it. Also try shining it diagonally down at your object from different directions.

5   Take four or five photos of your object with different lighting angles.

6   Move to a location where the sun can shine on your object (either inside by a window or outside) and take a few more photos with natural lighting. You can move to different locations around your object so that the sun is shining on it at different angles in the photos. Take four or five photos in this way.

NOTE: If you're taking these photos on a cloudy or rainy day, the lighting scheme won't be as obvious. Take them anyway, but make a note to take more on a sunny day if you can!

Now that you have your photos, let's discuss which lighting schemes are more effective than others.

» Generally, the best lighting schemes are those where the light is originating from above and slightly to the side, so it's shining down diagonally on the object. This allows the viewer to see both the highlighted and shaded areas of the object, as well as the cast shadow of the object on the table.

» A lighting scheme that is less ideal is one where the light originates directly overhead. The viewer can still see the highlights, shaded areas and cast shadow of the object, but these elements are stacked on top of each other, which can produce a very dramatic effect. This lighting scheme can still be used, but proceed with caution!

» Other lighting schemes I'd generally recommend avoiding (unless you're making an intentional stylistic choice) are those where the light originates directly in front of the object or directly behind the object. These lighting schemes cause the object to look flat, as you won't be able to see both the highlights and shaded areas of the object. The cast shadow will also be nearly invisible with front lighting, or take up a ton of space with back lighting.

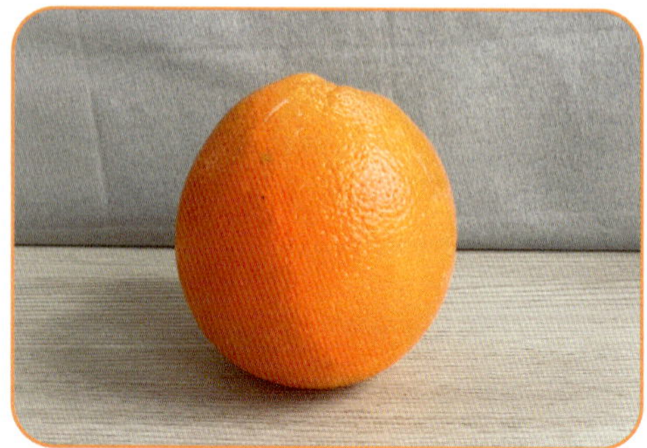

Ideal natural light scheme: sun shining diagonally down on the orange.

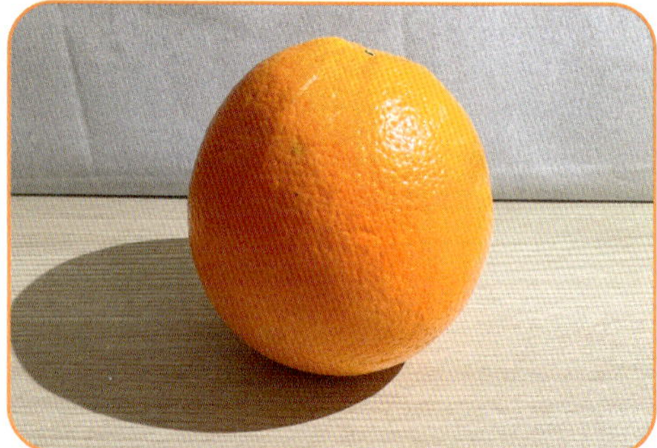

Ideal lighting scheme: local light shining diagonally down on the orange.

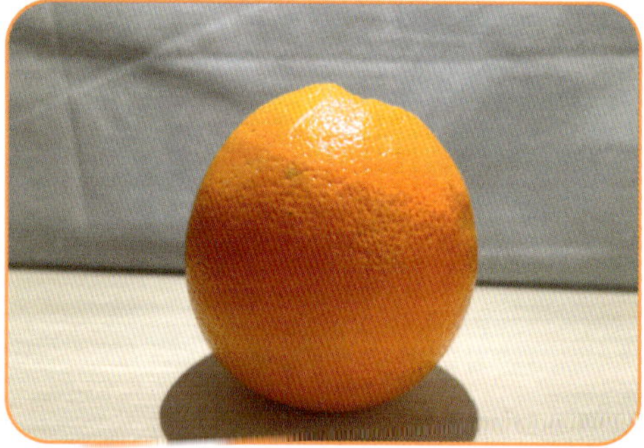

Less ideal lighting scheme: local light shining directly on top of the orange.

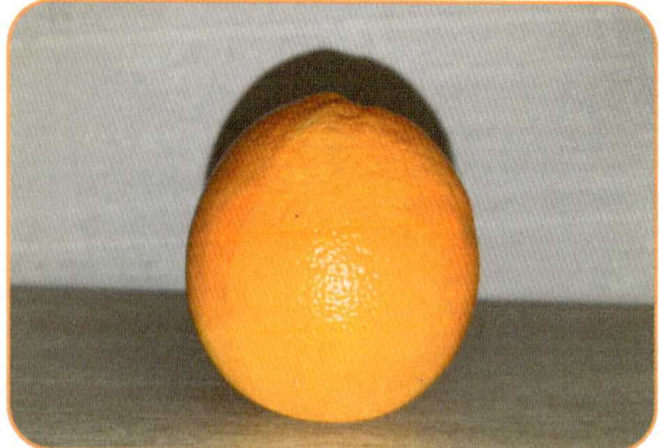

Not an ideal light scheme: local light shining directly in the front of the orange.

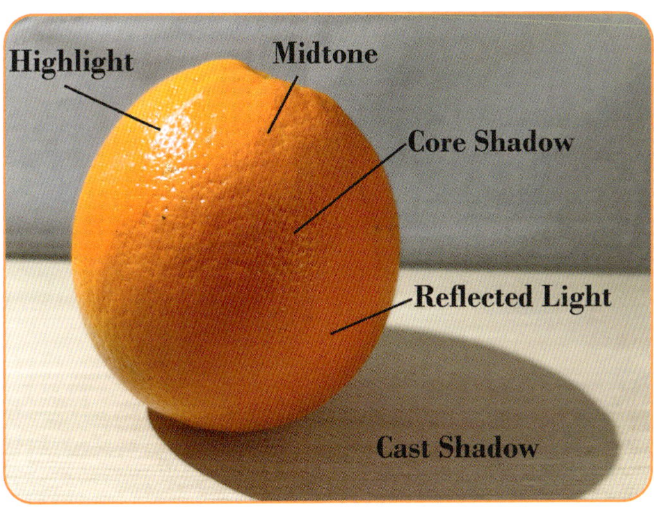

EXERCISE 2: LIGHT SOURCE ANATOMY

Now that we understand which lighting schemes are more favorable for painting, let's do a little sketching to start to get familiar with the anatomy of the light source. For this project, you'll need:

» The photos of your round object

» Paper to sketch on (I used a page of my Arches sketchbook, but any paper will work if you don't want to use up a piece of watercolor paper)

» A pencil and eraser

First, select one of your photos with a favorable light source–one where the light is coming from diagonally above the round object and shining down on it diagonally. In the photo, identify the following regions:

Highlight: the lightest point of the object, faces the light source

Midtone: the most saturated (area with the brightest color) spot on the object, usually located right at the edge between the light and dark sections of the object

Core shadow: the dark area of the object shaded from the light

Reflected light: the slightly lighter area within the shaded section, usually at the opposite end from the highlight, where light from the surrounding environment bounces up to lighten this spot

Cast shadow: the shadow created on the table or floor by the object, always extends in the opposite direction from the light source

Once you've identified these areas, it's time to sketch! This process is much easier with a black and white photo, so if you're able, I'd recommend editing the photo you've chosen to make it black and white. If using a smartphone, you can either use one of the preset black and white filters, or toggle the saturation to zero.

1   Start by lightly sketching the shape of your object. Don't worry about it being perfect, just get the general shape down.

2   Next, start filling in the core shadow area. Notice the angle of the shadow across your object in your photo and try to imitate it in your sketch. Also notice that the core shadow is often not one uniform shade—there are darker areas and lighter areas within it, especially around where the reflected light is. Try to include these nuances in your sketch.

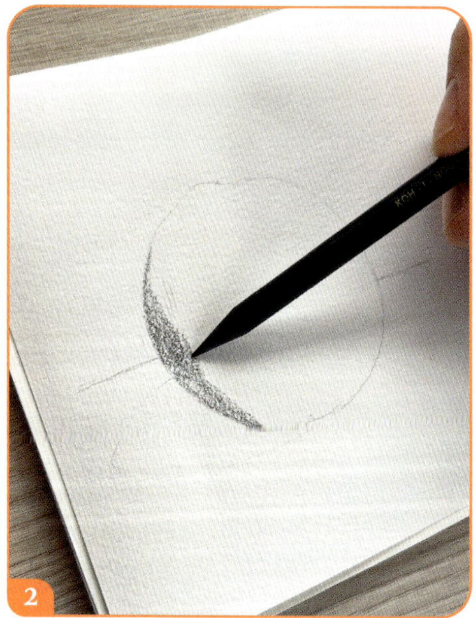

3   *Super* lightly outline the highlighted area of your object. This is the lightest spot on your object, and you won't be filling it in with any shading, so it's good to know where it is.

4   With lighter pressure, shade in the rest of the lighted section of your object.

5   Use a medium amount of pressure to create a smooth transition between the lighted and shaded areas of your object.

6   Finally, sketch the shape of the cast shadow and fill it in. If you had a strong light source, your cast shadow may be much darker than the object itself. If you had a weaker light source, or used natural light, your cast shadow may be darkest underneath the object, then transition to lighter shades farther away from the object.

7   Optional: Sketch in a midtone (not too dark and not too light) background to really make your object pop.

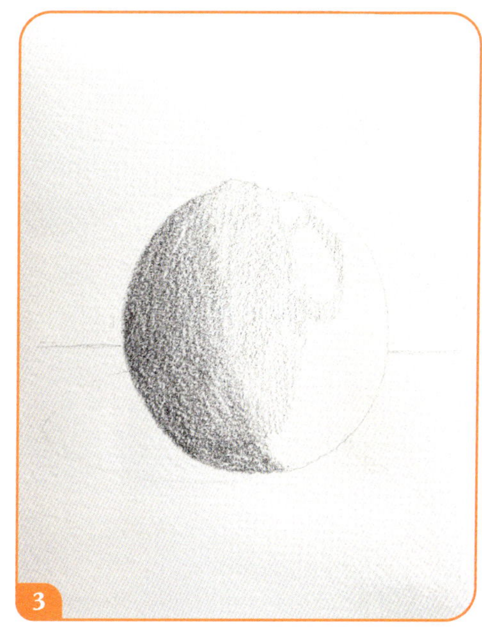

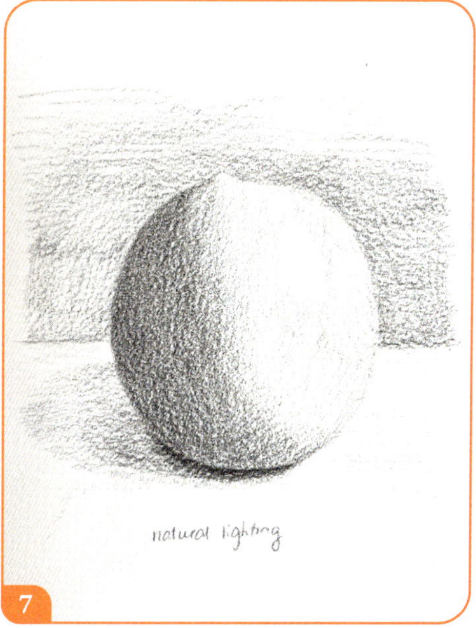

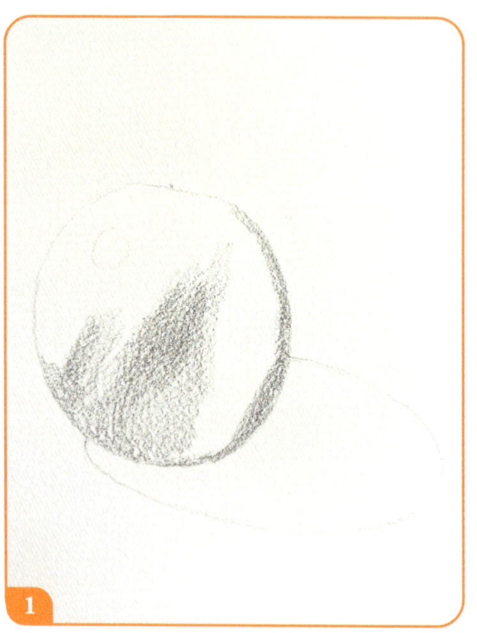

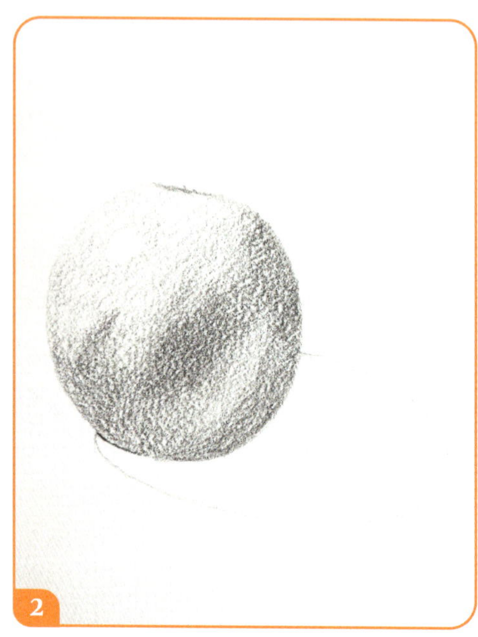

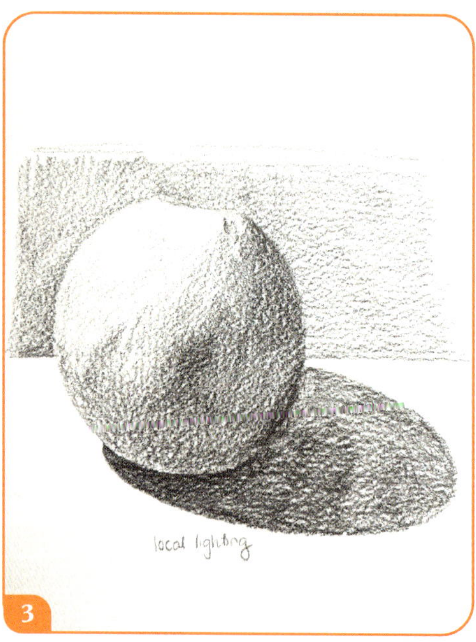

Take It Up a Notch: Repeat this process with as many photos as you like (I repeated the same process using a photo of my orange under local lighting)! Choose one with a different lighting scheme, or if you used a natural light reference in your first sketch, choose a local light reference for your second, or vice versa! You could also choose a uniquely shaped household object to repeat this exercise with and get familiar with how light behaves on subjects that aren't perfectly round.

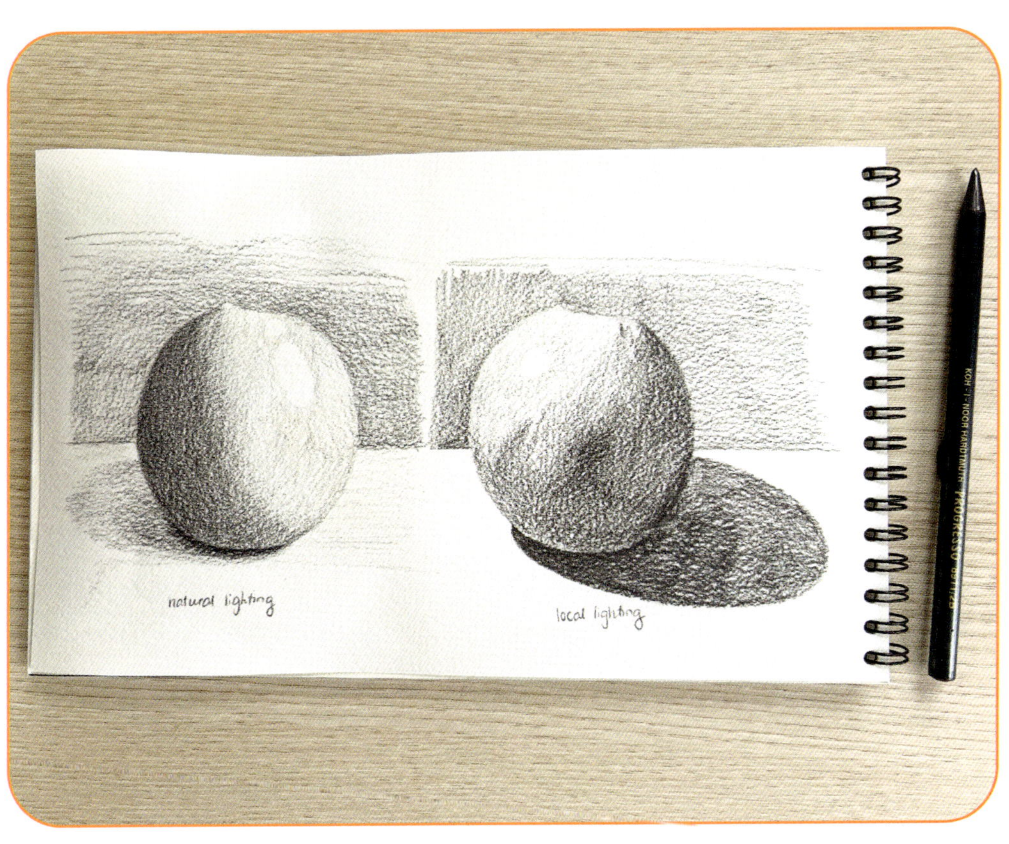

natural lighting
local lighting

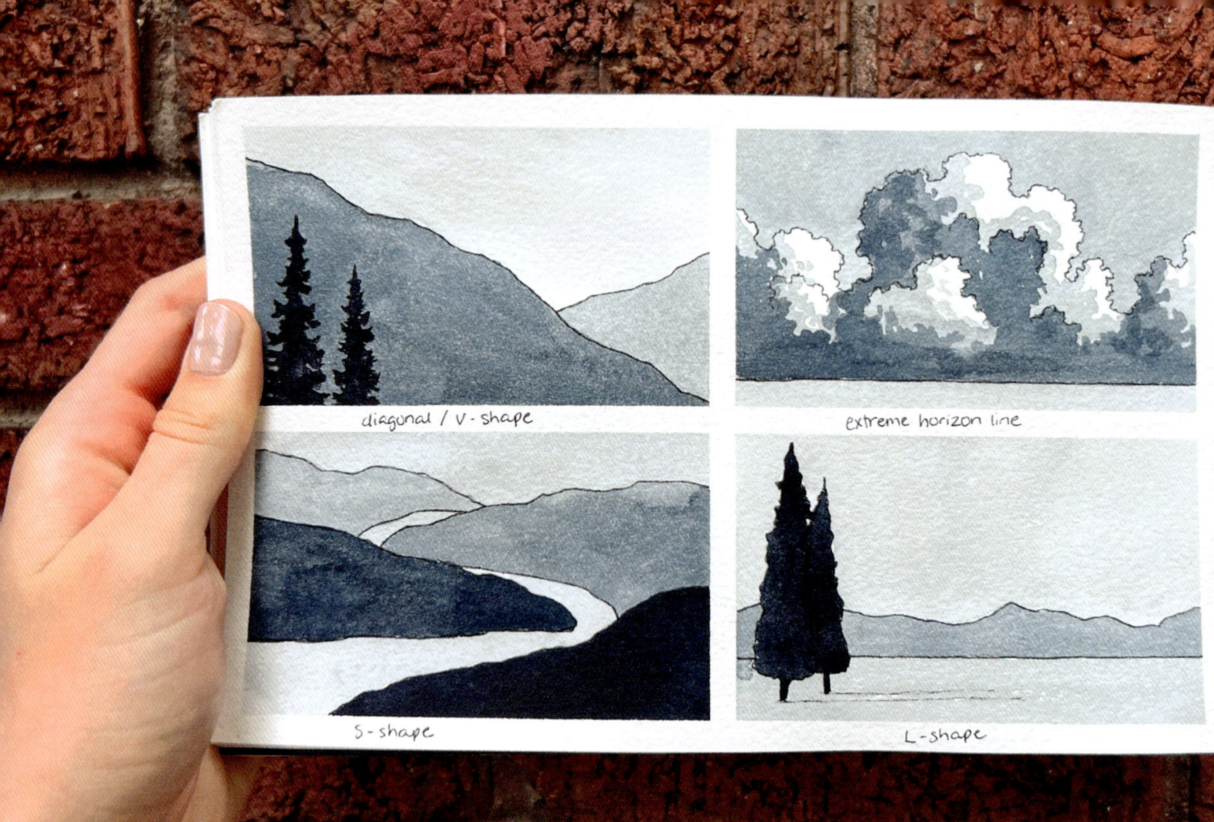

Compose Yourself

Composition is a factor that can really make or break a painting. You can be painting the coolest thing in the world with all the right colors and techniques, but if it isn't composed in a pleasing or interesting way on the page, the whole thing can feel off. Composition is simply the position of the focal points of a painting on the page, along with the balance of light and dark areas throughout the painting.

Now, you may be asking: What the foc-al is a focal point? Let's talk about that, along with the other compositional elements you'll need to consider briefly before diving in.

A focal point is any element in a painting that draws the viewer's attention to itself and through the painting. A painting may have only one focal point, or it can have several and they can be obvious or quite subtle.

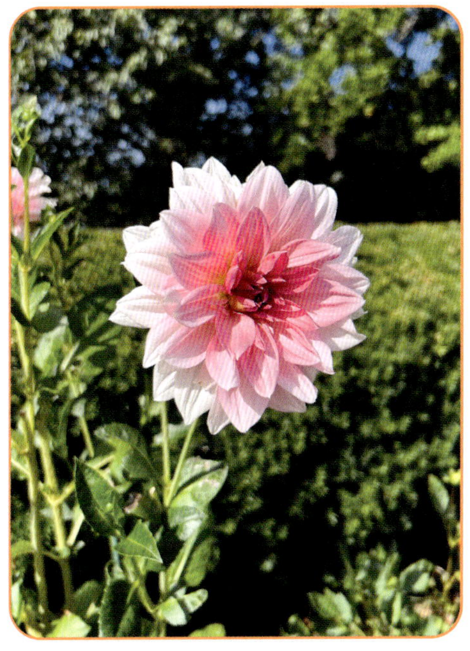

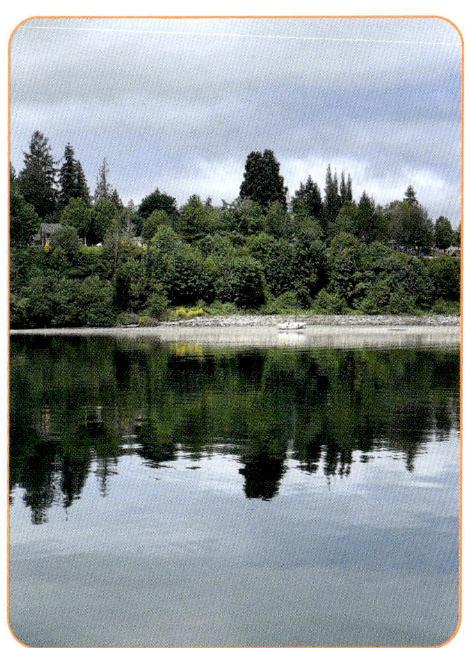

For example, this photo of a flower has a pretty clear focal point—the flower takes up a large portion of the photo, and it is lighter in value and contrasting in color to the surrounding environment.

In this photo of Niagara Falls, the brightest white area of mist at the center of the painting grabs your attention, then leads you along the waterfall to the right. The

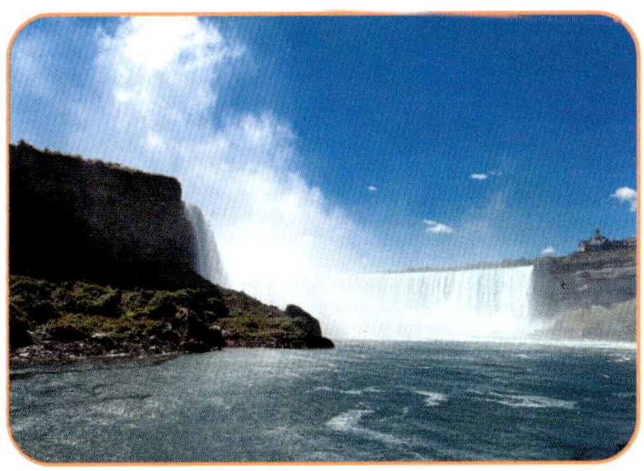

waterfall is the main focal point, but it is so eye-catching because it has the contrasting focal point of the dark cliff in shadow on the left. These two elements balance each other in this photo and make for an effective composition.

But what if there's no obvious focal point, like in the photo of the ocean above? Yes, there's a small beached sailboat if you look closely, but because it is so small and similar in value to its surroundings, it's not eye-catching at all. You might not have even noticed it until I pointed it out. In this case, the horizon line is actually the main focal point because it's so much lighter in value than the surrounding trees. Your eye is drawn there immediately; then you notice the secondary focal points of the trees and reflections of the trees. The light and dark areas are also nicely balanced, especially with the symmetry in the reflection.

Focal points are easy to identify when they're obvious, but when they are more subtle, you'll have to rely more on your instincts. What is your eye drawn to first when you look at the composition? Is it the horizon line? The lightest spot in the composition? The darkest? The spot with the most unique shape, texture or color? Then, once you've identified your focal points, pay attention to the large areas of light and dark in the composition. It can help to squint your eyes as you look at the composition to blur out the details and only see the main light and dark shapes. Do they seem balanced in a pleasing way throughout the composition? Is the scene too dark with not enough light spots? Or too light with not enough contrasting dark spots? Asking yourself all of these questions as you take reference photos or compose a painting will really help you stay mindful of your composition!

EXERCISE 1: RULE OF THIRDS REFERENCE PHOTOS

The first and easiest composition guideline is the rule of thirds. If you divide your paper up into thirds vertically and horizontally, you'll end up with four points where those lines intersect. The goal is to have at least one focal element (if not more) land on or near those lines or their intersections. You can see some examples of reference photos taken with the rule of thirds in mind here.

TIP: Most smartphone cameras have an option to overlay a rule of thirds grid onto your screen when you're taking a picture. You can find how to do this with your specific phone with a quick internet search. This makes it really easy to follow the rule of thirds when you take reference photos.

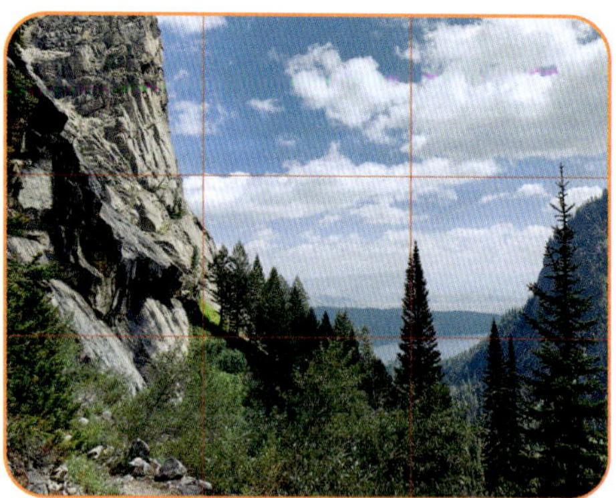

The cliff on the left ends almost exactly at a third line, the dark tree in the middle lands at an intersection, and the horizon line in the distance lands at a third line.

Our first exercise for today is to take a couple reference photos using the rule of thirds. You can do this anywhere—in your home, right outside your home or any place you like to visit. You'll need:

» Your phone camera or a regular camera

1 Grab your camera and turn on the grid feature if desired.

2 Look around in your chosen location and pick out an area with at least one focal point. Remember, the focal point can be a specific object, or an area with a strong value, color or texture. Point your camera at it, then shift the camera so that at least one of your chosen focal points is either on a line or at an intersection. Take the picture!

3 Repeat this process with a few different objects or scenes to practice taking reference photos using the rule of thirds.

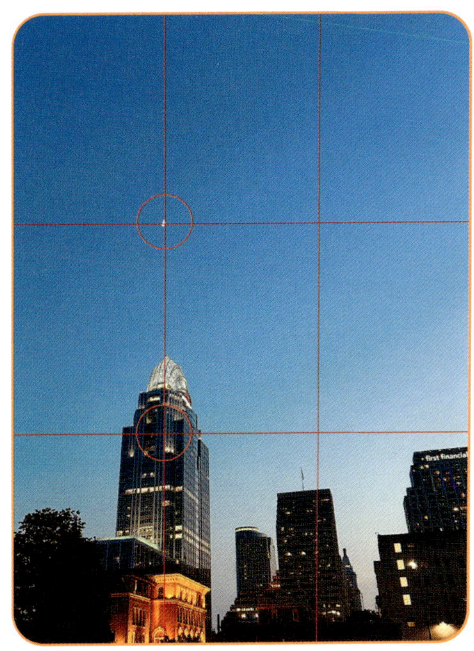

The moon and the focal point building both land on intersecting third points (circled).

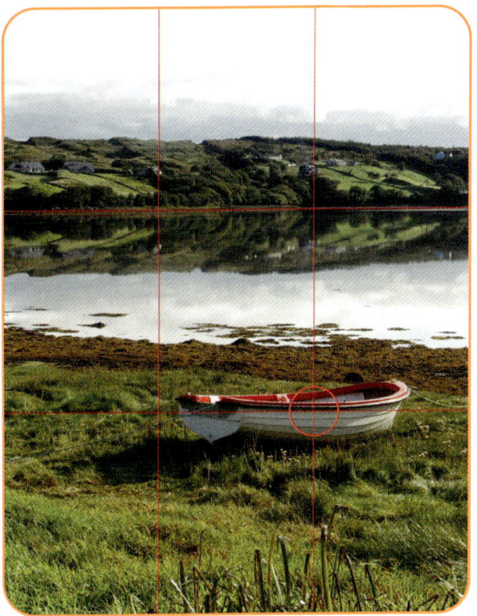

The horizon line lands at a third line, and the rowboat is centered on an intersection point (circled).

EXERCISE 2: COMPOSITION SHAPES

The rule of thirds is not always applicable—if your scene only has one major focal point, you may want to have it front and center in your painting. Or maybe the elements of your painting won't fit neatly into the rule of thirds. This is where different composition shapes can come into play. Knowing these different composition shapes can help you place elements in a reference photo or a painting so that it feels balanced and leads the viewer's eye through the composition. An artist named Edgar Payne wrote an incredible book called *Composition of Outdoor Painting*, which covers a ton of different potential composition shapes common in landscape paintings. We'll talk about a few common ones today, but I highly recommend checking out his book either from a bookstore or a local library if you want more information about landscape composition!

Let's get into four common composition shapes. We'll talk about these in the context of landscape painting, but these shapes are applicable in almost any kind of art!

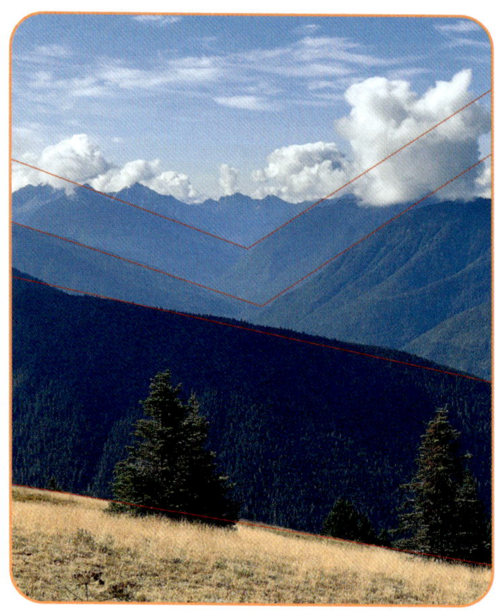

Diagonal or V-shape: Elements of the composition form strong, opposing diagonal lines.

Extreme horizon line: Placing the horizon line very low in the composition emphasizes the vastness of the sky, while placing the horizon line high in a composition will emphasize the elements on the ground.

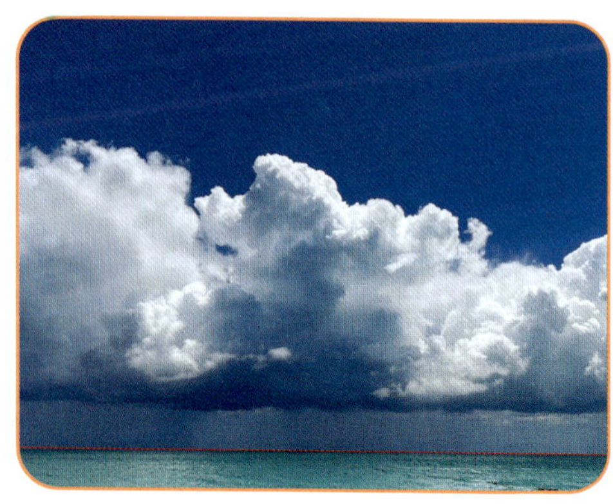

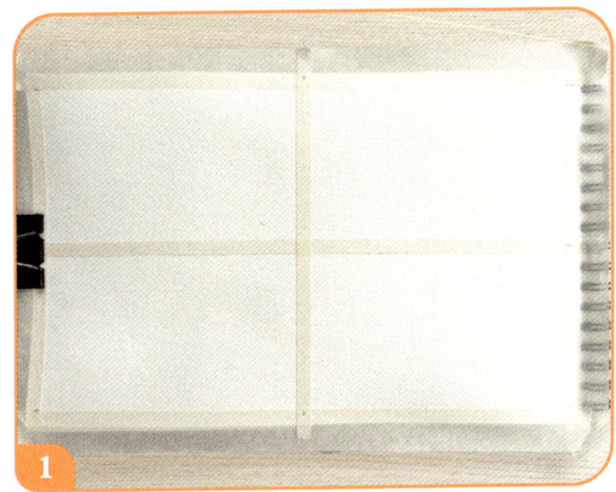

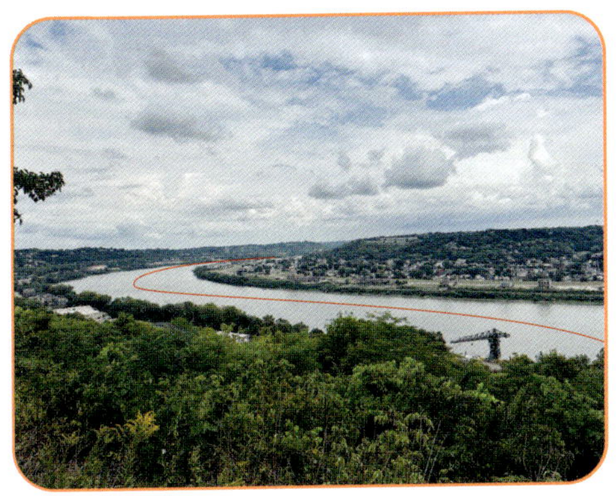

S-shape: Rivers and valleys often form S-shapes, and the flowing shape draws the eye of the viewer through the composition.

L-shape: A strong focal element is on one extreme side of the composition, balanced by a horizontal element crossing the composition.

Get out your pen and paper; it's time to do a little practice! For this exercise, you'll need:

» Watercolor paper (I used a page of my Arches sketchbook)

» Pencil

» Optional: masking tape

» Pen (ideally waterproof)

1   Divide your paper into four rectangular sections, using either pencil lines or masking tape to mark the boundaries.

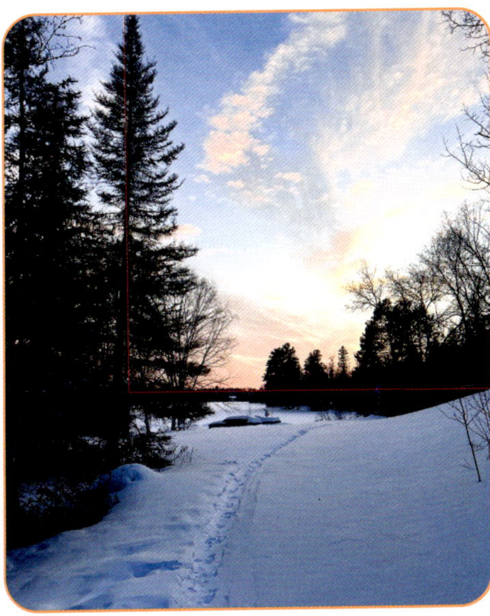

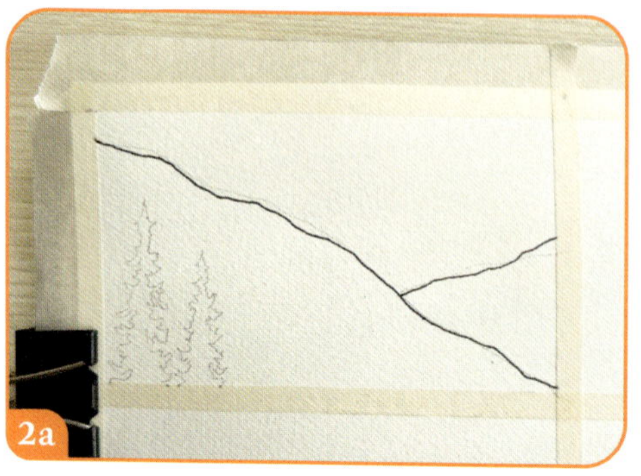

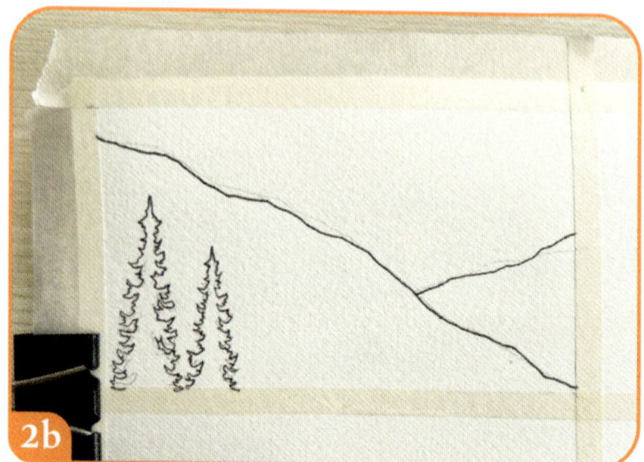

2   In section one, create a V-shape com-position by sketching in a diagonal textured line that starts in the top left corner and ends in the bottom right, then add a second textured line behind it in the opposite direction. Add a few trees at the bottom or a few birds in the sky for extra elements. Go over your lines with a pen once you're happy with the pencil sketch.

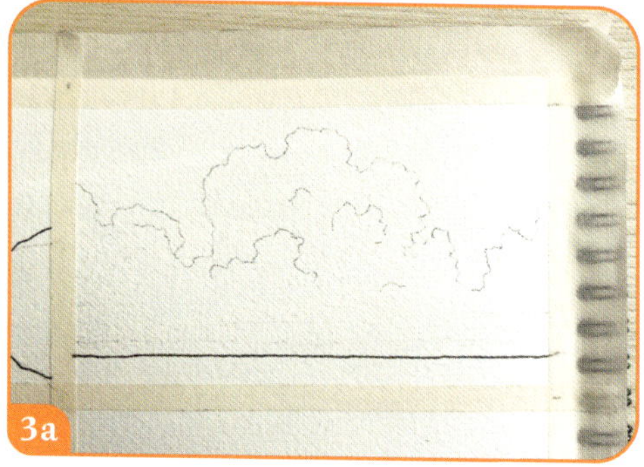

3   In section two, sketch a flat horizon line just slightly above the bottom of the section. Then add some fluffy cloud shapes that take up the major-ity of the section above the horizon line. Go over your lines with a pen once you're happy with the pencil sketch.

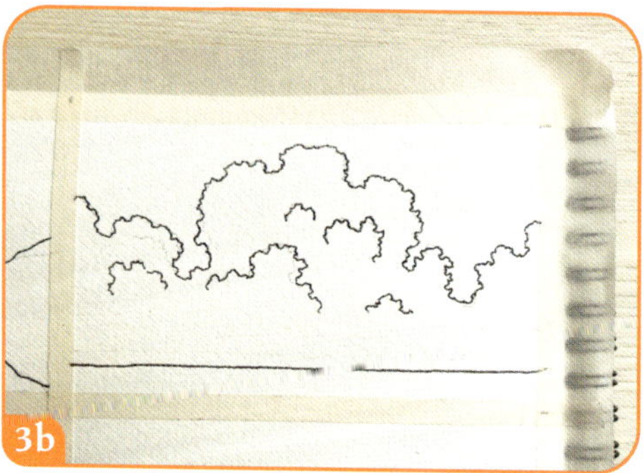

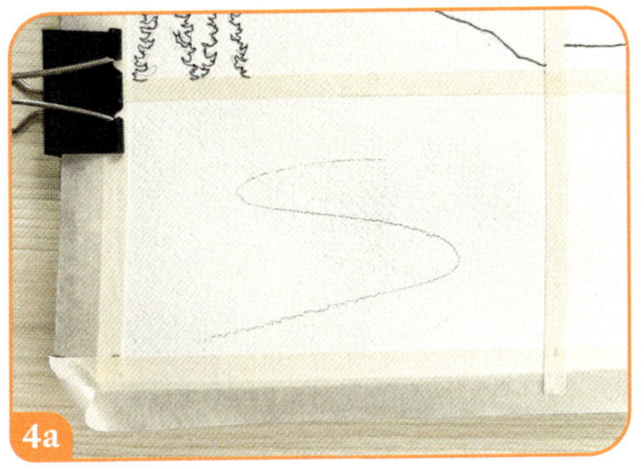

4a

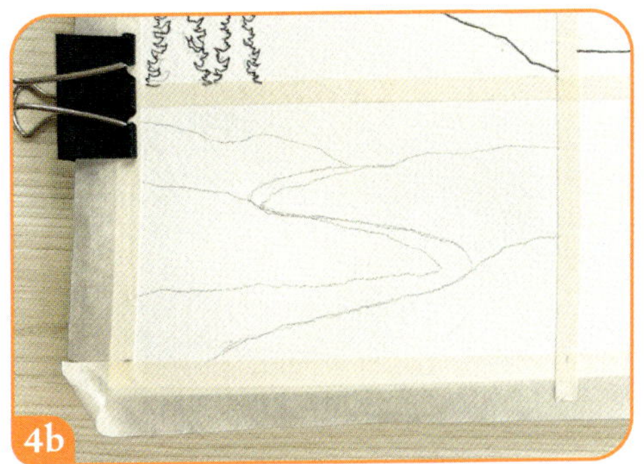

4b

4 In section three, sketch a light S-shape on your page that starts a bit below the top of the section and extends to the very bottom of the section. Add in land sections extending from each curve of the S-shape to create a simple river scene. Go over your lines with a pen once you're happy with the pencil sketch.

5 In the fourth and final section, sketch a horizon line about one-third of the way up the section (hello again, rule of thirds!), then add a small mountain range above the horizon line. Then sketch two simple tree shapes on the extreme left side of the section. Go over your lines with a pen once you're happy with the pencil sketch.

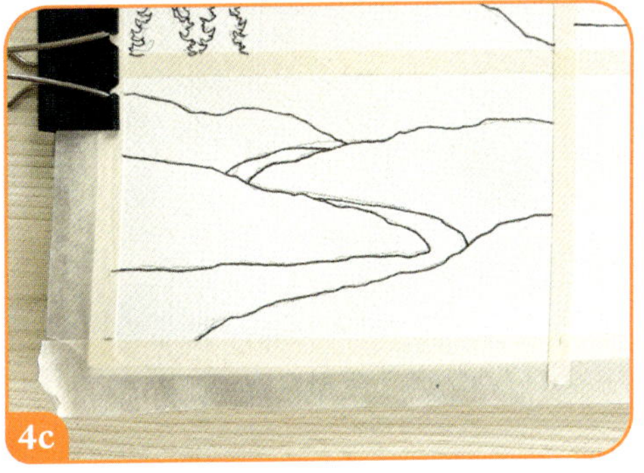

4c

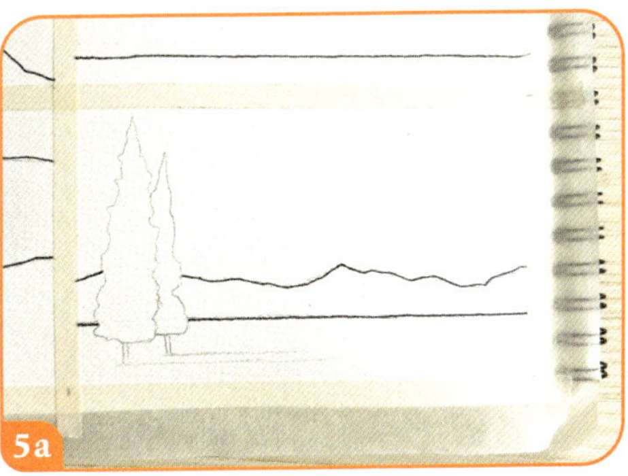

5a

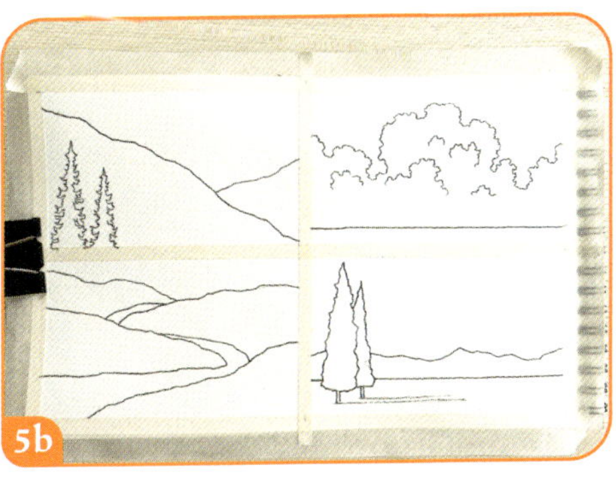

5b

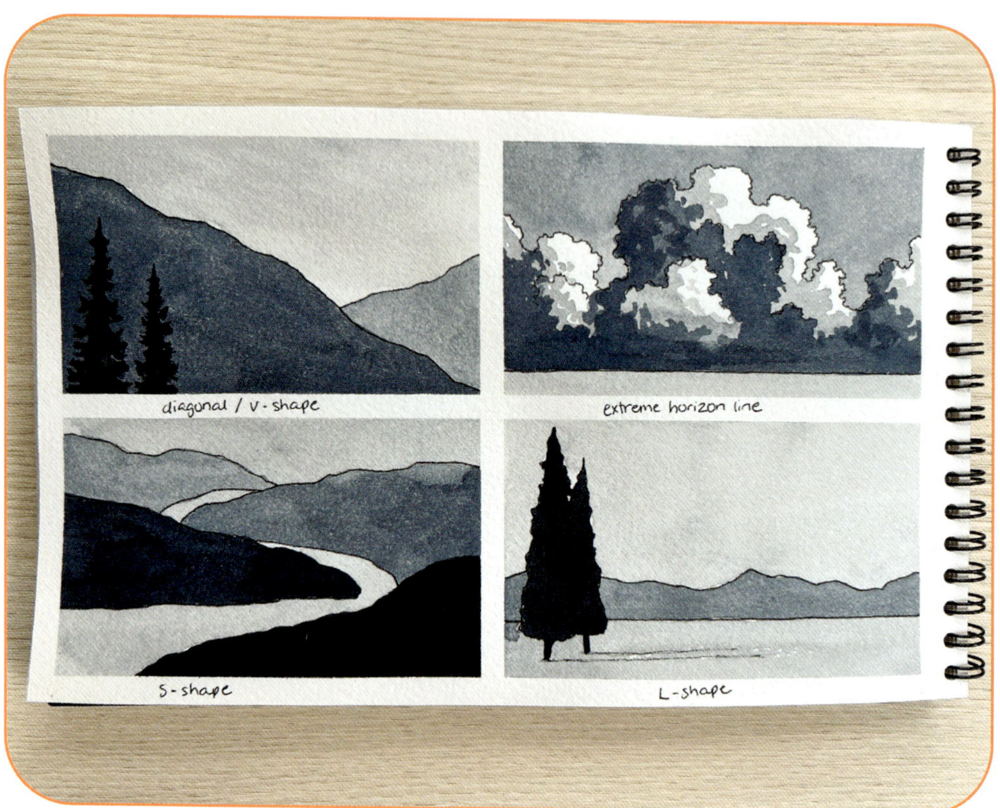

Take It Up a Notch: If you're feeling confident in your watercolor skills, use varying washes of one watercolor paint (I used Payne's Gray) to fill in your composition shapes, practicing your light source and value skills. If you're not yet feeling up to it, come back to this page after you've completed a few chapters of this book and give it a shot!

All of these composition guidelines are important to keep in mind as you take reference photos or look to start a painting. Now that you've practiced these, you'll start seeing them out and about in the world as you're taking photos. However, a reference photo doesn't have to have a perfect composition to still be useful in creating a painting—now that you know these guidelines, you can change and adjust elements in the reference photo as you bring them to your painting to create a more balanced composition!

Get Some (1-Point) Perspective

Perspective is one of those art concepts that is a bit tricky to learn at first, but once you understand the basics, you'll feel like a magician! Perspective in art is simply the technique of using a 2D medium to portray objects to look like they are in a 3D space.

If you glance around the room you're sitting in, you'll see lots of objects distorted by the angle at which you're looking at them. Maybe there's a cabinet or bookcase in the room and one side of it looks squished and narrow because it's mostly facing away from you, or maybe you have a cup sitting in front of you and the top looks like an oval rather than a circle. This is the effect of perspective—objects are distorted in some way when viewed from different angles. Our brains are very aware of this, so unless you really pay attention, you won't notice this effect in your everyday life. The problem with translating this distortion into a drawing or painting is that while your eyes are seeing the distorted shapes, your brain knows the side of the cabinet is actually perfectly rectangular, and that the top of your cup is actually a circle. What tends to happen when a beginner artist attempts

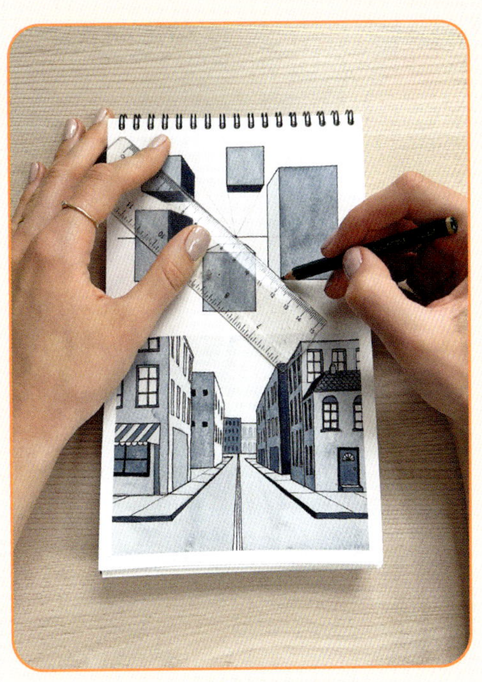

to draw 3D objects is a combination of what that person sees and what the brain knows, and the result is an oddly warped recreation of an object.

By learning a few rules of perspective, we can train ourselves to ignore our brain's tendencies to portray things as they actually are rather than how they look in that moment. We will be covering two different forms of perspective together in the next two lessons, but there is so much more to learn about perspective that I couldn't possibly fit into this book. I hope this gives you a good idea of the basic principles so that you can continue to learn and experiment with this on your own!

Before we dive in, let's understand a couple of new vocab terms:

Horizon line: the horizontal line across a scene where ground and sky meet. Sometimes it's a visible line; for example, when looking out at a body of water, there will be a clear line in the distance where the water ends and the sky begins. Sometimes there are objects blocking the horizon line from view, or there are elements of Earth extending above the horizon line like mountains or trees.

Vanishing point: a point somewhere on the horizon line to which all straight lines distorted by perspective lead.

Today's experiments will cover 1-point perspective. This is one of the simplest forms of perspective to understand and experiment with. 1-point perspective means there is one vanishing point in the composition. This occurs when all of the objects in a composition have one side facing exactly square to you.

Note in the example photos how all of the lines on the buildings (that we know in our heads to be horizontal) are distorted toward the vanishing point in the distance. Only the sides of objects facing perfectly square to us, like the bridge over the street or the side of the building in the distance, are undistorted.

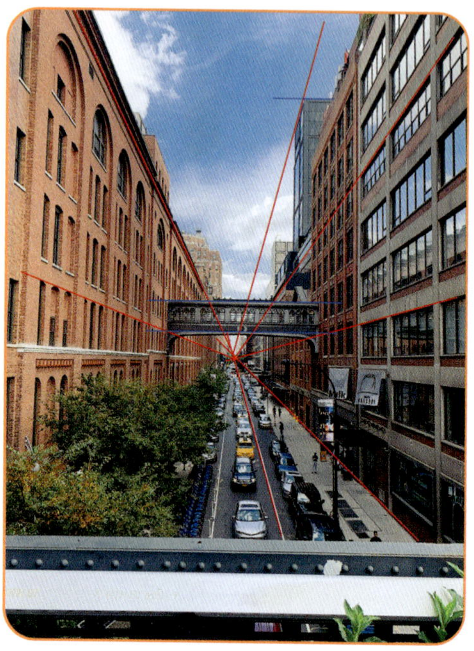

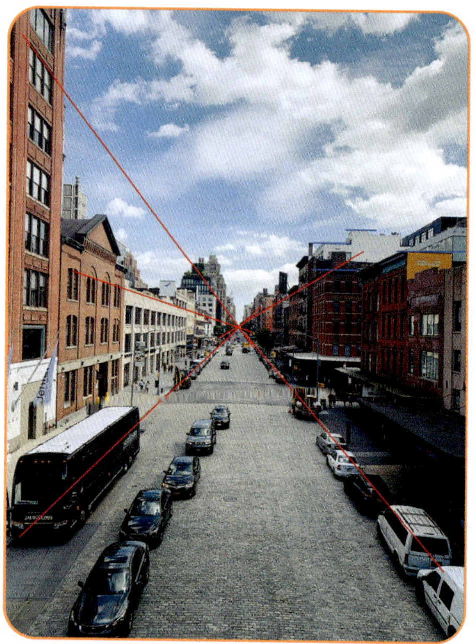

EXERCISE 1: FLOATING CUBES

To get our feet wet with this concept, we'll first create some floating blocks. For this project, you'll need:

» Watercolor paper (I used a page of my Arches sketchbook)

» Pencil

» Ruler

» Pen (ideally waterproof)

1   Start by lightly sketching a horizontal line across your paper, about halfway up the page. This is your horizon line. Then add a small dot somewhere close to the middle of the line—this is your vanishing point.

2   Sketch a few rectangles throughout your page using a ruler. They can be above the horizon line, below it or overlapping it. Just avoid putting any rectangles directly on top of the vanishing point.

3   Now use a ruler and connect the corners of the rectangles to the vanishing point. To keep it a bit cleaner, only do this for the two or three corners that are closest to the vanishing point on each rectangle—if you have to cross through the rectangle to get to the vanishing point, just skip that corner.

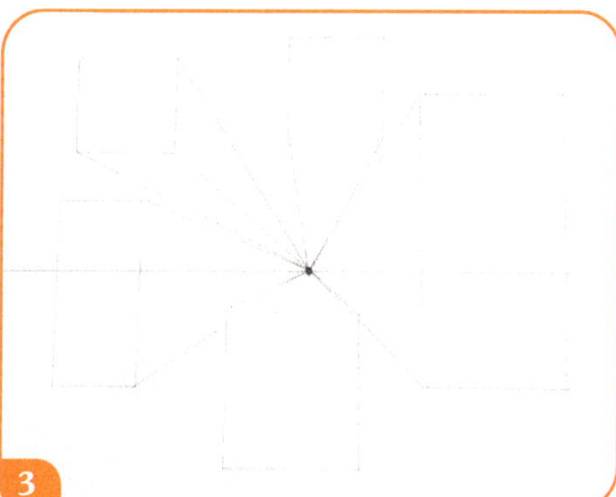

4 On each rectangle, you'll now add another vertical and/or horizontal line parallel to the original rectangle shape, connecting those lines you just drew to the vanishing point.

5 Use a pen to outline just the lines pertaining to each cube, ignoring the extra lines that go all the way to the vanishing point.

You should end up with 3D cubes floating in space. Notice how you can see the bottoms of cubes that are above the horizon line, the tops of cubes that are below the horizon line and neither the tops nor the bottoms of the cubes overlapping the horizon line. Notice also that you only see two sides of any cube directly above, below, to the right or to the left of the vanishing point, but you can see three sides of any cubes at a diagonal to the vanishing point.

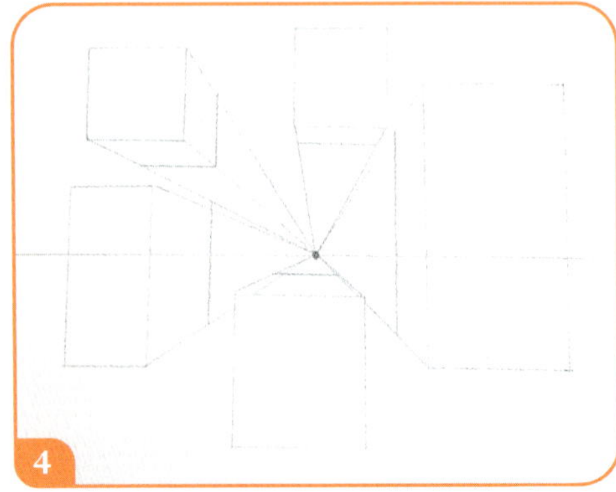

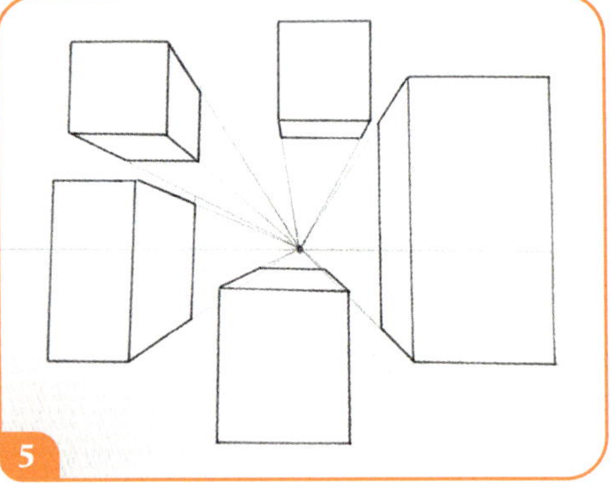

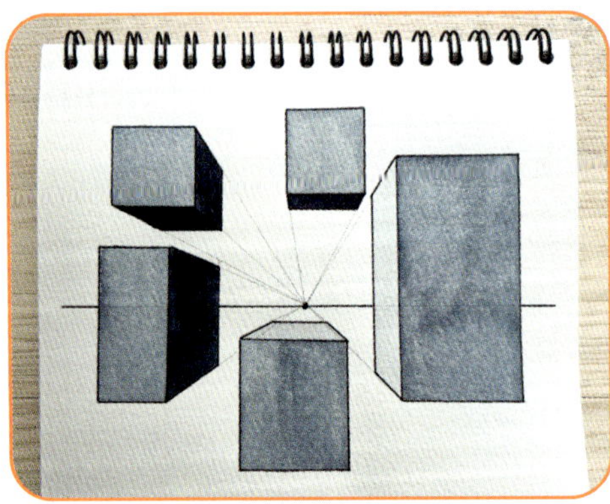

Take It Up a Notch: If you're up for an extra challenge, use one color from your watercolors to practice your lighting schemes. Decide where you want the light source to be, then add different shades of watercolor washes to each side of the cube. Sides facing your light source should get the lightest washes with the most water mixed with the paint, and sides facing away from the light source should get the darkest washes with the least water mixed in with the paint.

EXERCISE 2: CITY STREETS

Now let's put this concept to use in a more realistic exercise: creating a city block. This is a classic art class exercise I remember doing a few times throughout middle school and high school. While you most likely won't create the most realistic-looking scene (because really, how many times are all the buildings and streets perfectly facing you?), you'll start to understand how perspective works in a practical way. You may end up adding a line or a detail that suddenly looks off to you, and this is an indicator that you've made a mistake with your perspective. Pay attention to those mistakes and do your best to fix them, and you'll end up with a much better understanding of perspective! You'll need the same items from the first exercise for this one.

» Watercolor paper (I used a page of my Arches sketchbook)

» Pencil

» Ruler

» Pen (ideally waterproof)

1   Sketch in your horizon line about halfway up the paper, then add the vanishing point close to the middle of the line.

2   Start by sketching a rectangle on one side of your page, overlapping the horizon line. Then connect the corners closest to the vanishing point to the vanishing point with straight lines.

3   Add a second vertical line to the rectangle, connecting the lines you just drew to the vanishing point to form the side of your first building.

4   Add more buildings in front of and behind your original rectangle by creating more vertical lines of varying lengths and connecting the horizontal lines to the vanishing point. Remember: The sides of the buildings facing you will have perfectly horizontal lines, and the sides of the buildings facing the other side of the street are distorted to the vanishing point.

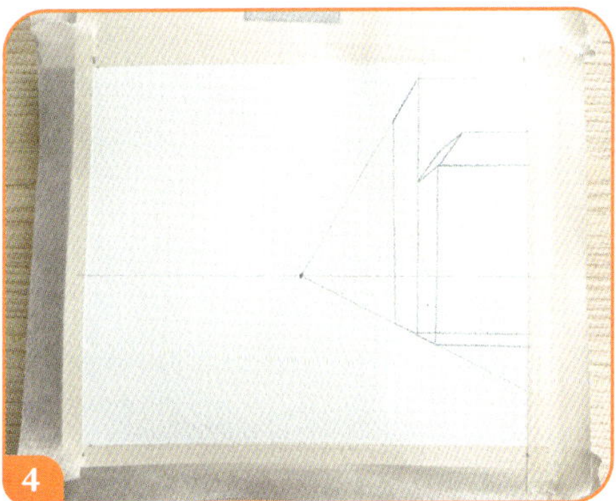

5   Repeat the same process on the other side of the paper to form the second half of the street. You can also add a sidewalk on either side by adding an extra line to the vanishing point, then a horizontal line where the sidewalk turns the corner. Add another set of lines close to the first sidewalk lines to imply a curb, and a couple of lines extending straight down from the vanishing point to create a lane line in the street.

Above the horizon line in the distance, you can add a couple small rectangles to look like distant buildings. This allows you to not have to create smaller and smaller cubes all the way to the vanishing point.

6   Start adding in as many details as you want to create a more realistic city block. Note that any windows or doors on sides of the cubes facing you will have perfectly vertical and horizontal sides. Any of these details on sides with vanishing points will only have perfectly vertical lines—the horizontal lines will point toward the vanishing point as well.

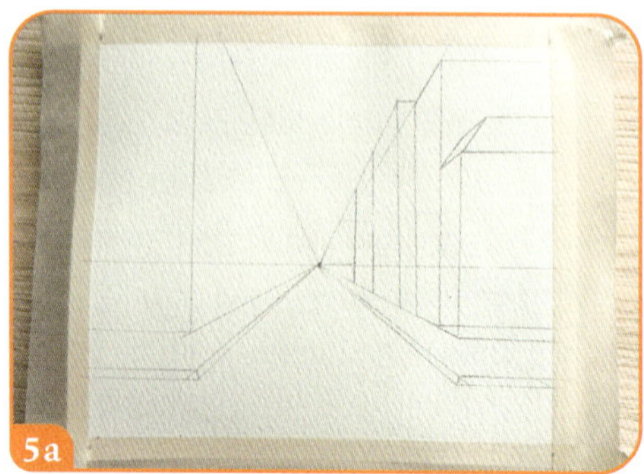

5a

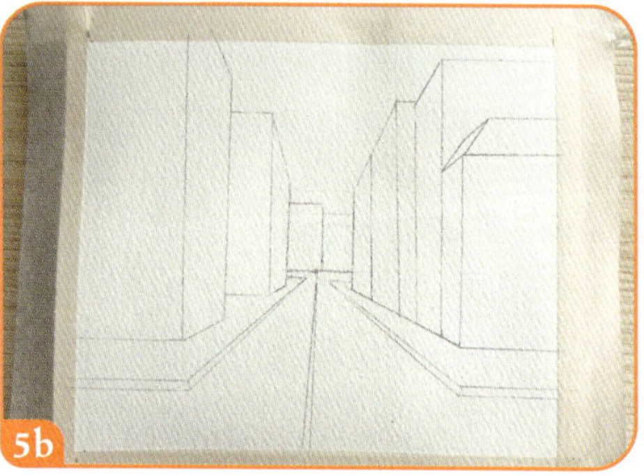

5b

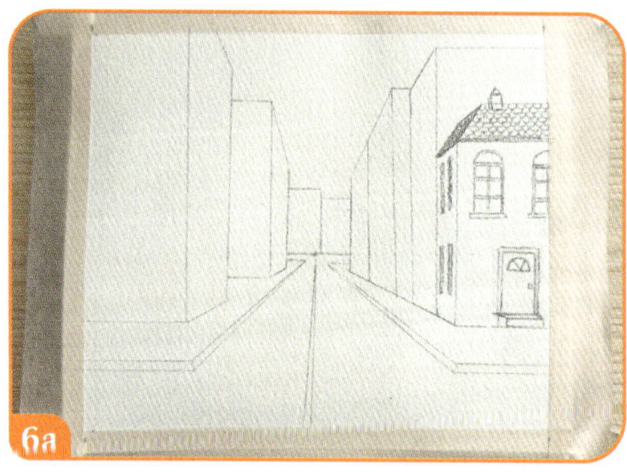

6a

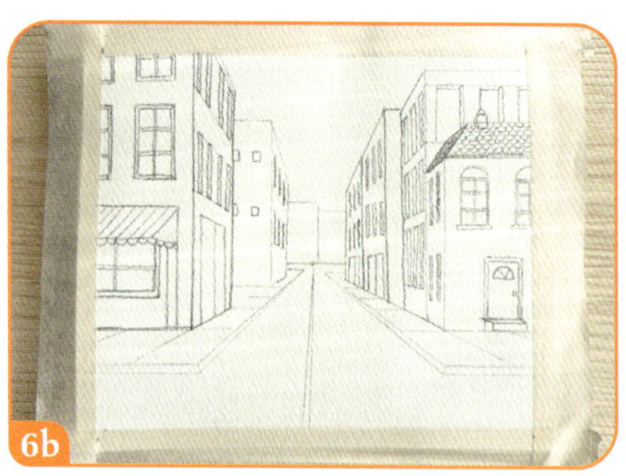

6b

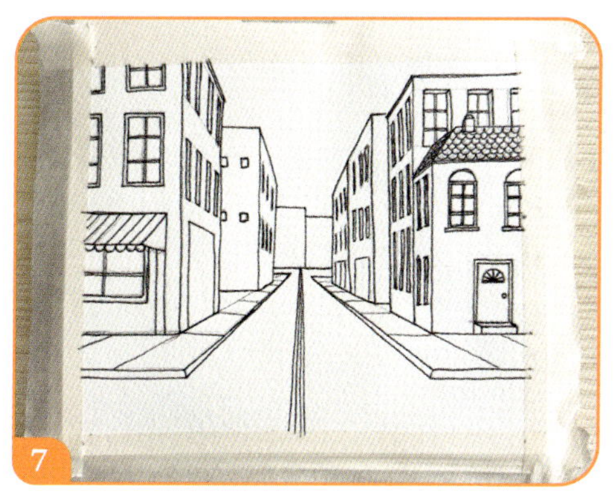

7   When you're done adding details, outline your final lines with a pen to make them stand out.

Now that you've completed your first perspective drawing, take a step back and analyze it. It doesn't have to look perfectly realistic, but are there any elements that look particularly wonky? If so, you may have misplaced a line. This is something that just takes a few tries to get right, but once you do, you'll be creating 3D objects everywhere!

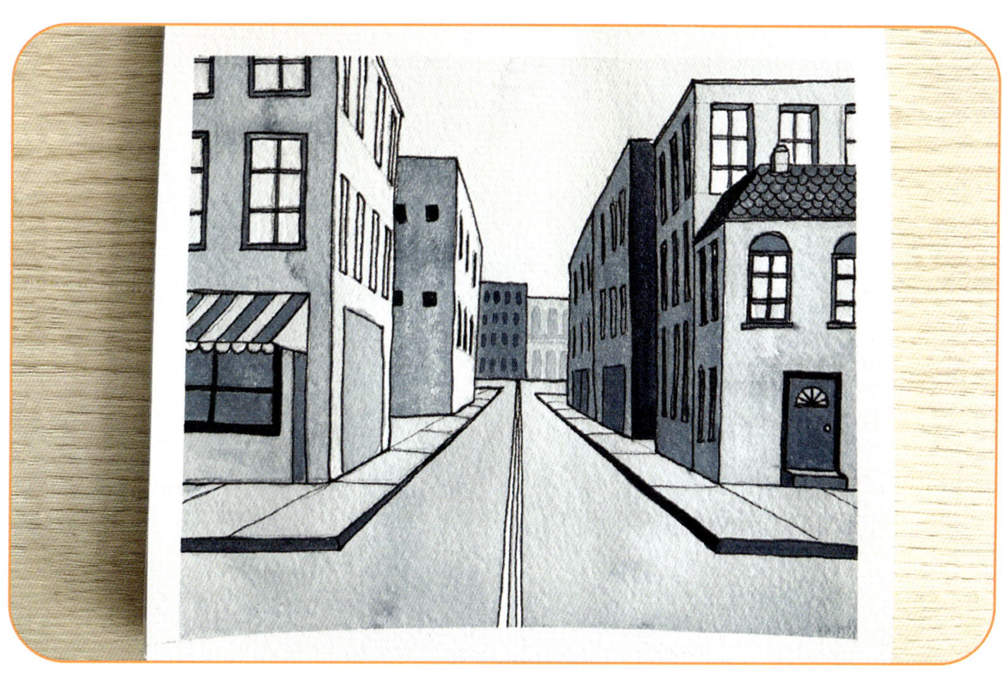

Get Some More (2-Point) Perspective

Double the vanishing points, double the fun! Today we will be practicing 2-point perspective. This kind of perspective is a bit more common in everyday life—we are often looking at objects from a bit of an angle rather than straight on like in 1-point perspective. In 2-point perspective, only vertical lines remain undistorted. Any horizontal lines we can see end up distorted to one of the two vanishing points. You can see this effect in the photo here of the 9/11 Memorial in New York City. Notice how all of the horizontal lines angle to either of the two vanishing points, which in this case are outside the frame of the photo. This is an important little tip—vanishing points can often exist outside the bounds of a composition. Let's jump right into this technique with some more floating cubes!

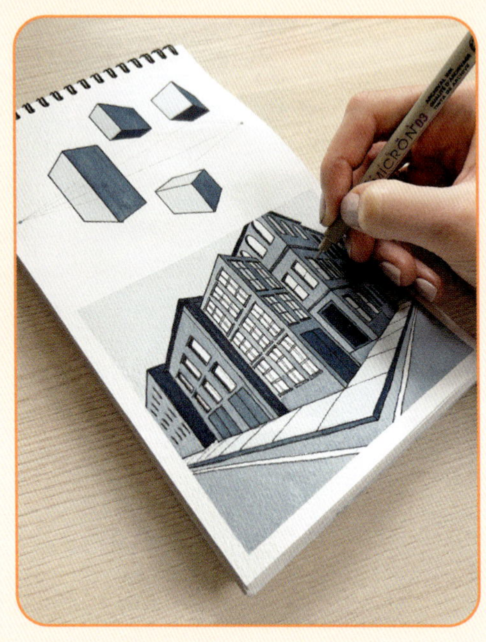

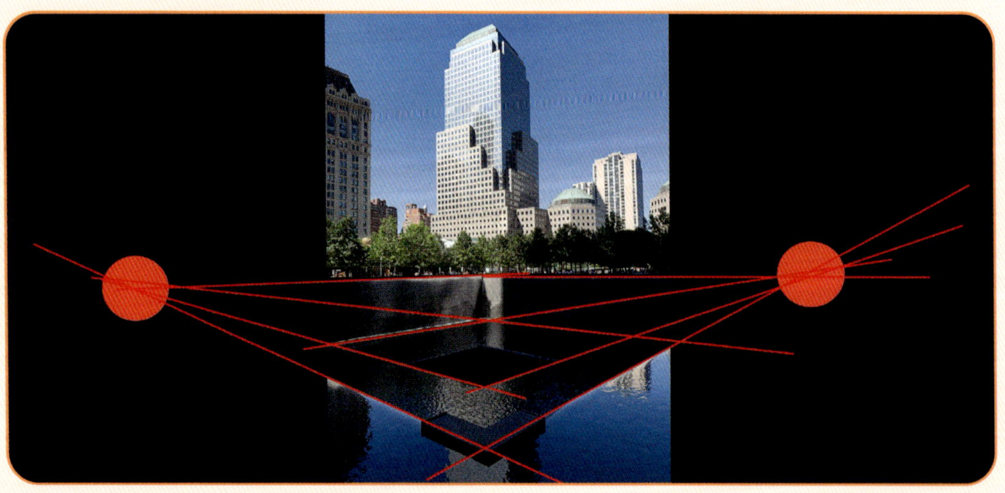

EXERCISE 1: MORE FLOATING CUBES

For this project, you'll need:

» Watercolor paper (I used a page of my Arches sketchbook)

» Ruler

» Pencil

» Pen (ideally waterproof)

1 Sketch out a horizon line about half-way up the page, then add one point on each end, close to the edges of the paper. These are your two vanishing points.

2 Next, draw a few vertical lines throughout your paper. They can be above the horizon line, below it or overlapping it.

3 Start at the top of one of your vertical lines, and connect it with a straight line to one vanishing point, then add another straight line connecting it to the other vanishing point.

4 Repeat that process with the bottom of the vertical line. You should end up with four total lines connecting to the two vanishing points.

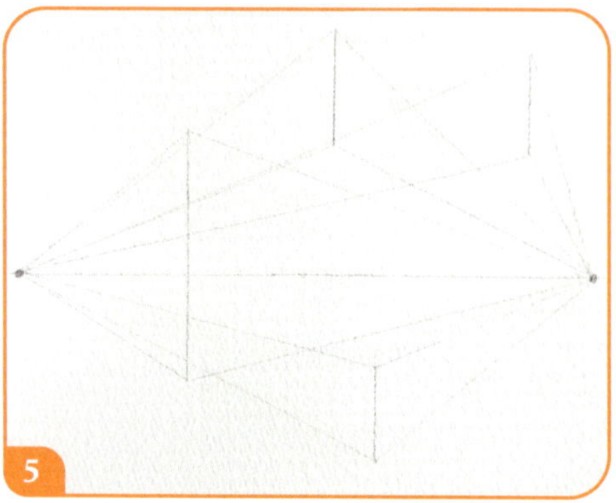

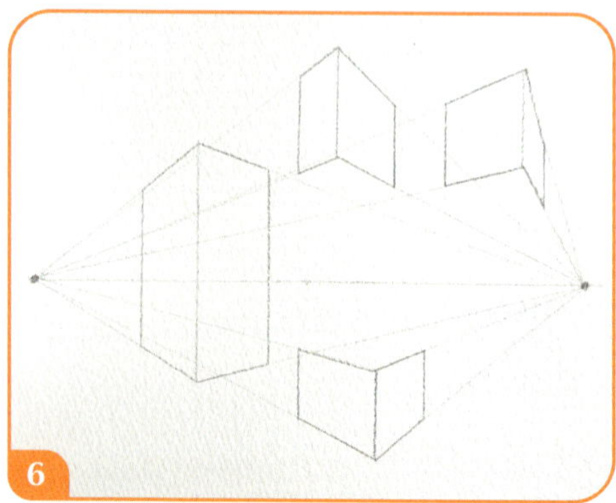

5 Repeat this process with the other vertical lines on your page.

6 Add two more vertical lines parallel to each original vertical line, connecting the two lines going to the vanishing point. You now have the sides of your cubes done.

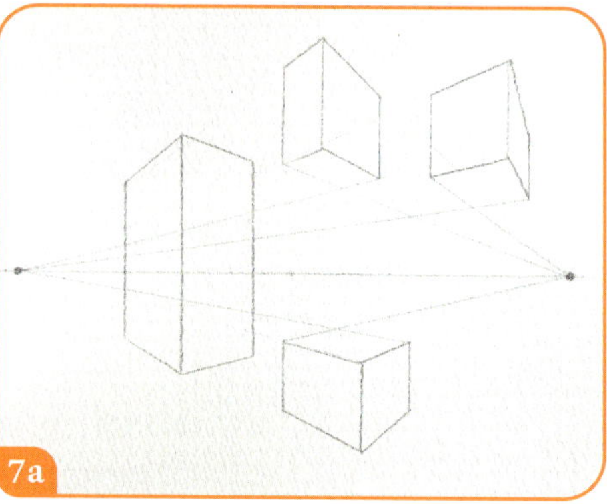

7 For any cubes above or below the horizon line, you'll be missing either the top or bottom of the cube at this point. This is the tricky part: You'll need to connect each of your new vertical lines to the vanishing point on the opposite side of the cube. For any cubes above the horizon line, you'll do this to the bottoms of the vertical lines, and for any cubes below the horizon line, you'll do this to the tops of the vertical lines. Those two new lines will cross, and that will create the third side of the cube.

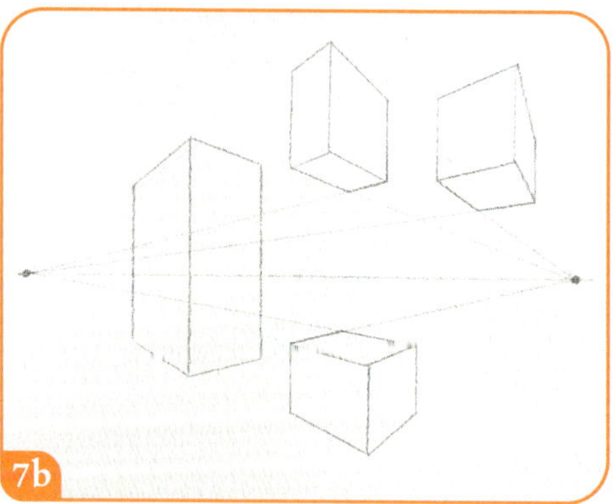

8 Outline your new cubes with a pen to define them.

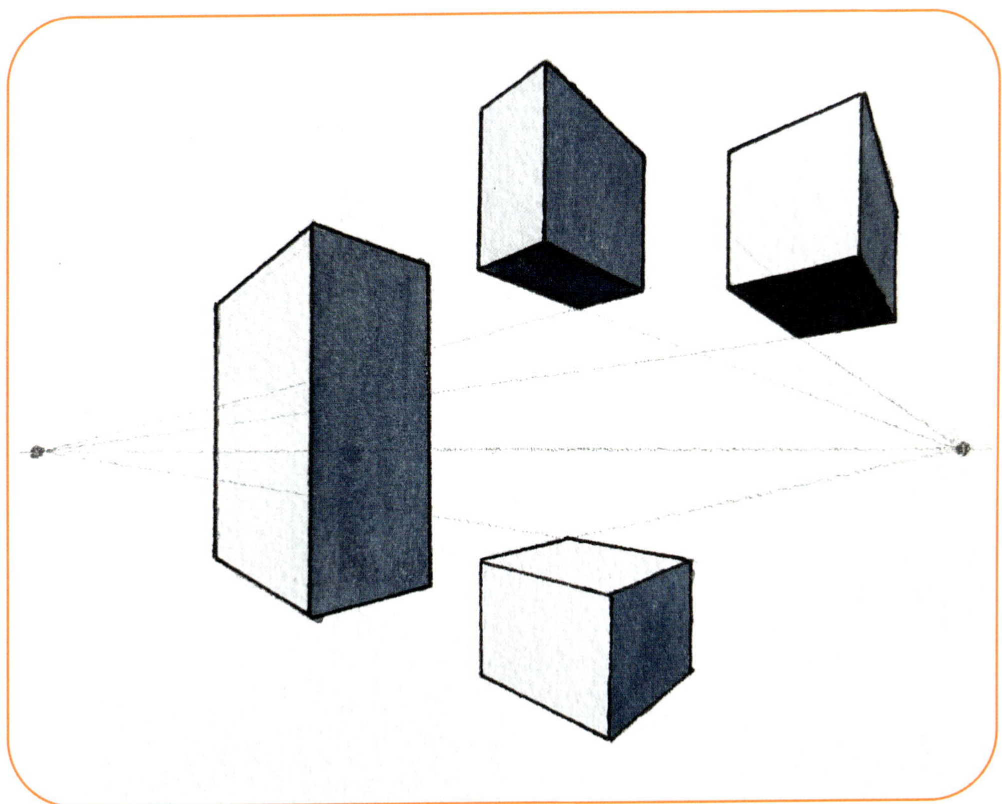

You've got your 3D cubes! Notice how, just like in 1-point perspective, the bottoms are visible on any cubes above the horizon line, and the tops are visible on any cubes below the horizon line. You don't see the top or bottom of any cubes overlapping the horizon line. Also notice how the closer a cube is to a vanishing point, the more extreme the distortion on the horizonal lines pointing to it.

EXERCISE 2: MORE CITY STREETS

Let's put this new technique to the test with another city block sketch. This time, you'll create a scene like you're standing at a corner, looking down two different streets. Use the same principles from Exercise 1—keep all vertical lines vertical, and keep all horizontal lines pointed toward a vanishing point. Again, this may not be the most realistic scene since you're making it up without a reference photo, but you'll get great practice making sure everything aligns with the perspective. You'll need the same materials as in the previous project.

» Watercolor paper (I used a page of my Arches sketchbook)

» Ruler

» Pencil

» Pen (ideally waterproof)

1   Sketch your horizon line a little less than halfway up the paper, then add your two vanishing points. If you have space around the paper area you're drawing on, you can place the vanishing points outside your drawing (you can see I placed mine on the masking tape bordering my drawing area). This can help lower the distortion and make the end product a little more realistic.

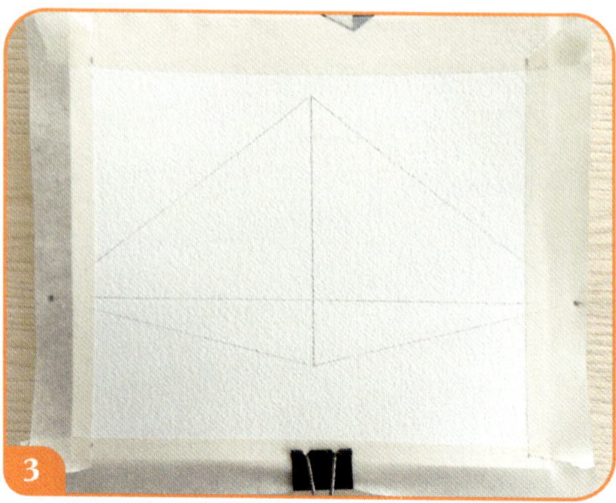

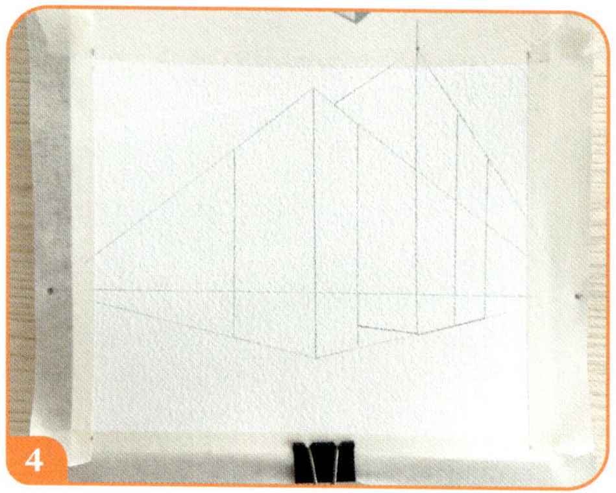

2   Place one vertical line in the middle of your paper, starting it close to the top and ending it a little below the horizon line.

3   Connect the top and bottom of this line to each of the vanishing points. This is your city block corner.

4   Add some additional cubes on either side of the corner to fill in the city block. Remember, all horizontal lines should be leading to a vanishing point!

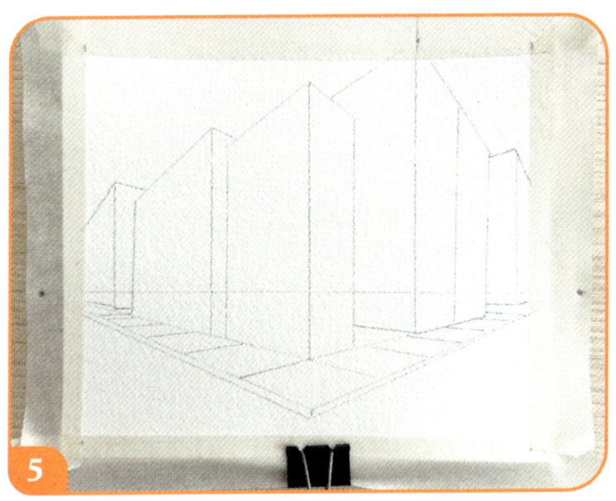

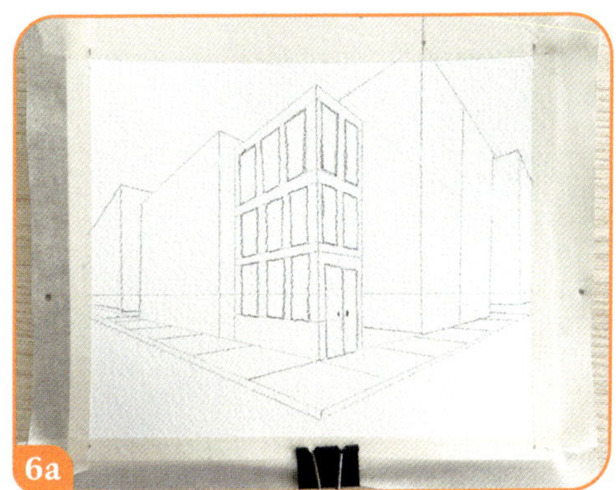

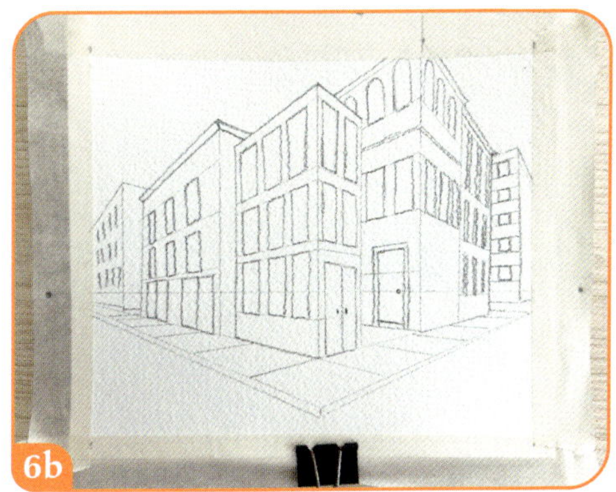

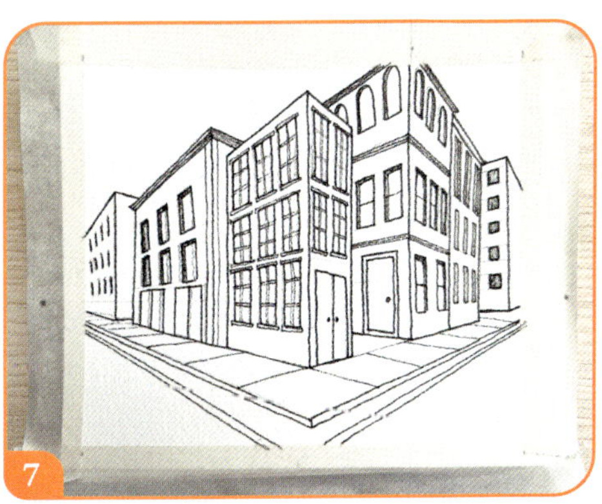

5   To make a sidewalk, mark a point a bit below the first vertical line you drew, then connect that point to each of the vanishing points. To add a curb, sketch a second set of lines close to the first set. To create the sidewalk squares, sketch lines pointing toward the opposite vanishing point. These sidewalk square lines should gradually get closer together as you get toward the edges of the page.

6   Start adding in little details like rectangular windows and doors. All vertical lines will be vertical, and all horizontal lines will point to a vanishing point.

7   Outline everything with your pen once you're happy with it!

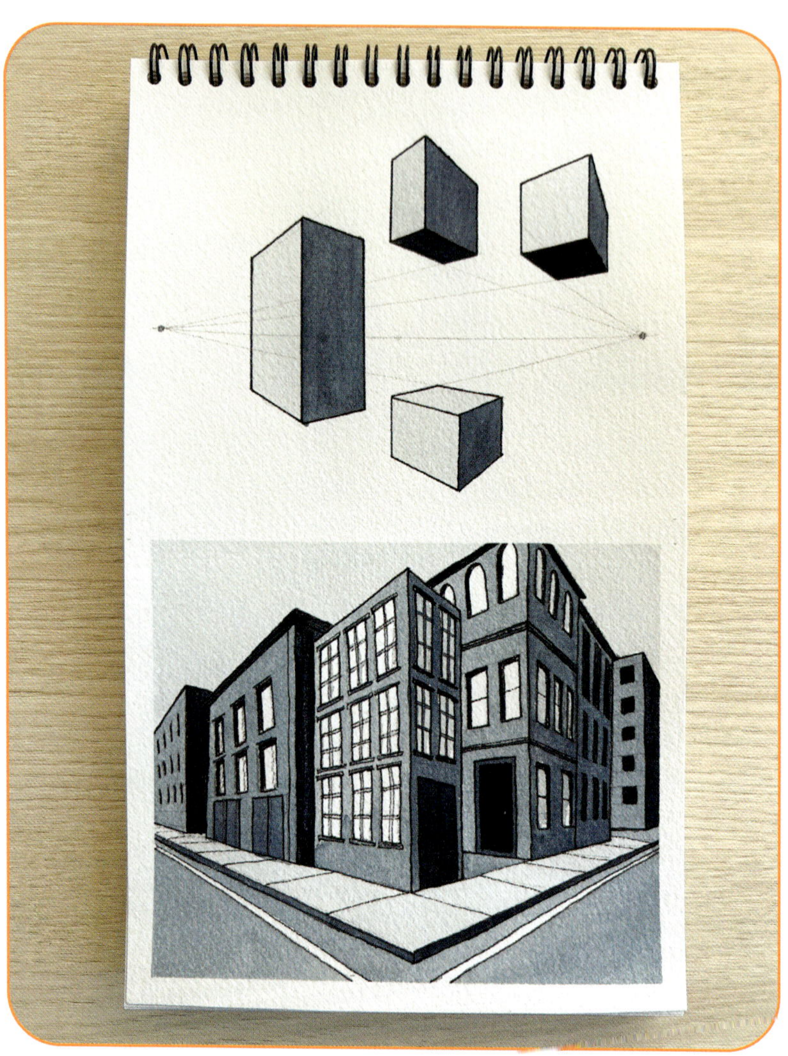

Now that you've completed your second perspective exercise, take a step back and analyze it. It doesn't have to look perfectly realistic, but are there any elements that look particularly wonky? If so, you may have misplaced a line. Again, this effect just takes practice!

Questionable Values

Value is one of the most important concepts to understand when creating art. If you can put different values in the right places, your painting will make sense regardless of the colors you choose! Let's go over a couple of vocab words that we'll use in this lesson and throughout the rest of the book:

Value: the lightness or darkness of any given color

Contrast: the total range of values in any painting

Take a look at the two photographs shown on the right. They are identical photographs, except for the contrast.

Notice how the photo on the top has a much smaller range of values, meaning the darkest areas are not that dark, and the lightest areas are not that light. This photo has a very narrow range of values, which means it has low contrast. Now let's look at the photo on the bottom—the dark areas are much darker, and the light areas look much brighter. This photo has a much wider range of values, which means it has high contrast.

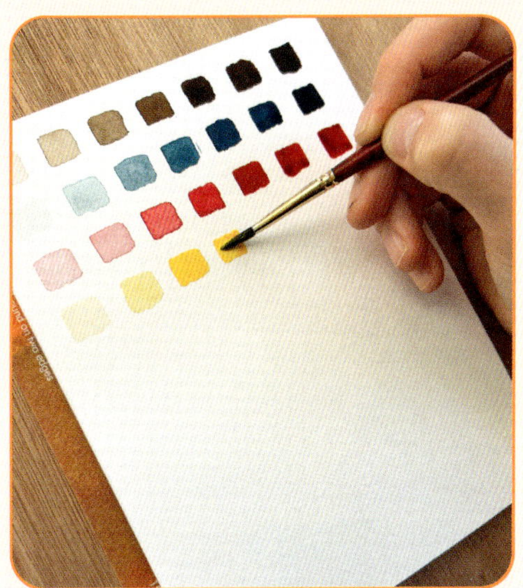

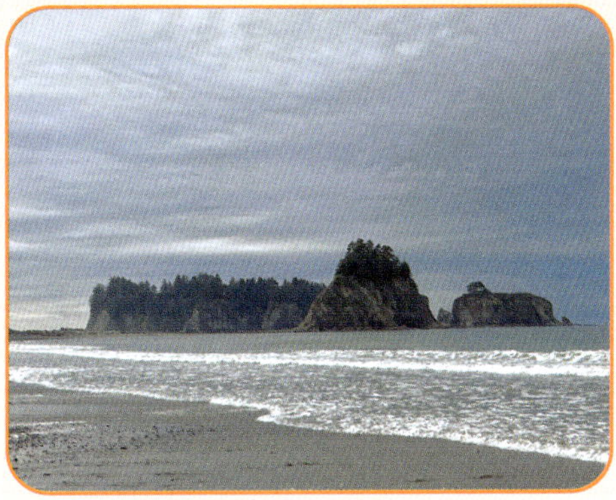

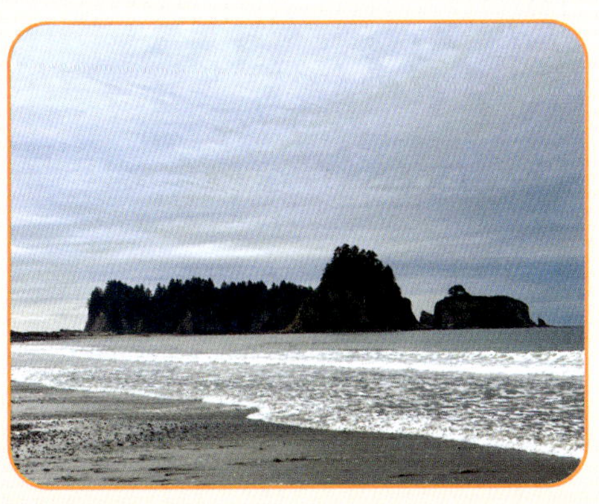

There are stylistic reasons why you might want higher or lower contrast in your paintings–low contrast is great for foggy or misty scenes, and it can often have a dreamlike quality. Higher contrast paintings are usually more visually striking, more vibrant and more compelling to your viewer. Beginner artists often have difficulty getting high contrast in their paintings–those really light and really dark colors can be scary to add, and it feels safer to stick with the mid-range values. It can also be difficult for beginners to see the true values of the different colors in a painting. In today's exercises, we're going to learn how to create different values with watercolor paint, along with an easy way to help you identify the true values of different paint colors.

EXERCISE 1: COLOR SWATCH PAIRS

To start our experiment with value, you'll need:

» Cup of water and paper towel

» Watercolor paints: 4–5 favorite colors, or colors you want to experiment more with (I used Van Dyke Brown, Aqua Green, Alizarin Crimson, Cadmium Yellow and Payne's Gray)

» Watercolor paper (I used a page of my Arches sketchbook)

» 1 medium brush (I used a 4 round)

» Phone camera

» Pen or pencil

1 Put a drop of water in your chosen colors and give them a minute to soften. Then, using only one color at a time, create a range of value swatches across your page from light to dark. I used Van Dyke Brown as my first color and started by mixing the lightest possible color I could–adding a tiny amount of pigment with a bunch of water into my mixing palette and painting my first square. Then I added a little more pigment to that mixture and painted my next square. I painted squares, but you could paint any shape for each swatch!

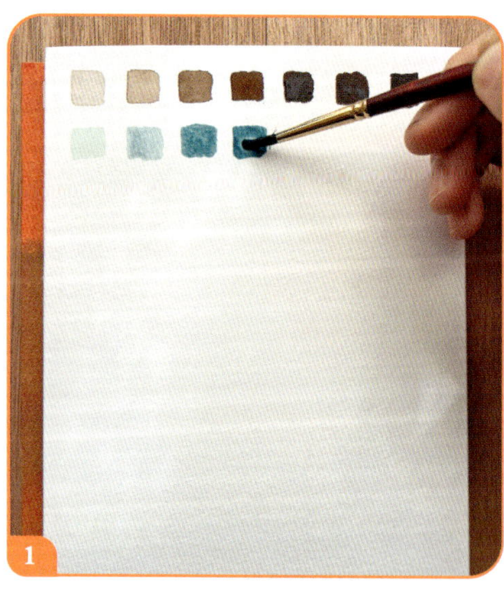

2   Create six to eight swatches per color, adding paint gradually until your last square is basically paint straight from the paint pan. Repeat this process with each color you've chosen to use.

3   Now it's time to analyze the values of each of these color swatches. With your cell phone camera, take a photo of the color swatches you've just made. On your phone, convert the photo to grayscale. Most phones have black and white filters you can use, or you can simply reduce the saturation to zero. Notice what the different color swatches look like in grayscale. See how each color creates a different range of values? Colors like yellow and red have narrow ranges of value because those pigments can't be very dark even at their most concentrated. Darker colors like brown, blue and gray have much wider ranges of value—they can be very light when mixed with a lot of water, and very dark when not mixed with water.

4   Now let's compare the values of these different swatches: Any swatches that look the same in the black and white photo have the same value. Using a pen or pencil and your black and white photo as a guide, connect color swatches with the same value.

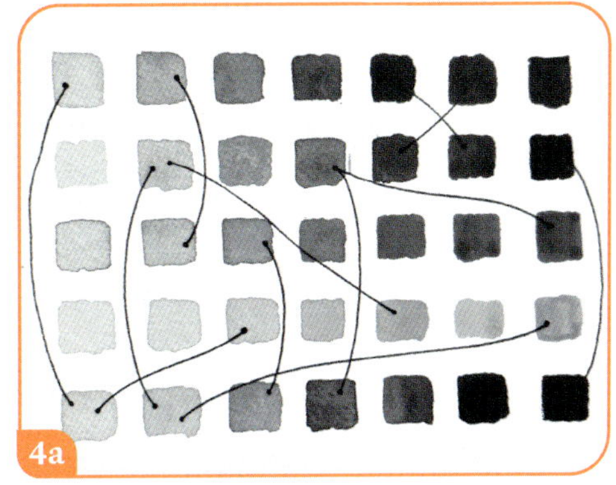

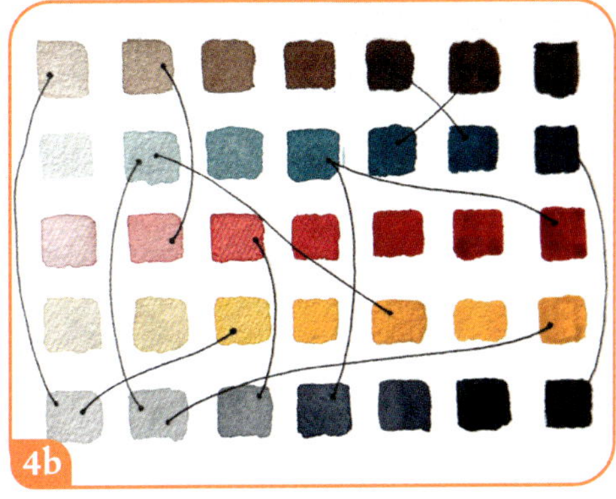

Once you've connected a few different swatches, take a look at those pairs of colors. Notice how some of the lighter colors like yellow or red have to be way more concentrated to have the same value as a watered-down darker color. Ask yourself—would you be able to match these different swatches without the help of the black and white photo? It's really difficult to do, especially as a beginner. You'll develop this skill with practice, but you can always use this grayscale photo technique in future paintings! Let's say you're creating a painting and something looks off but you can't figure out what. Take a photo of your painting and convert it to black and white, then do the same with your reference photo if you're using one and compare the two. This can help you identify any deficiencies with your values or contrast as you're working on the painting!

EXERCISE 2: MONOCHROME MOUNTAINS

Let's create a couple of super simple identical paintings to practice and compare value ranges one more time. You'll need:

» Optional: masking tape, pencil

» Cup of water and paper towel

» Watercolor paints: 1 color in the red-orange-yellow family and 1 color in the green-blue-purple family (I used Magenta and Indigo)

» Watercolor paper (I used a page of my Arches sketchbook)

» 1 medium brush (I used a 4 round)

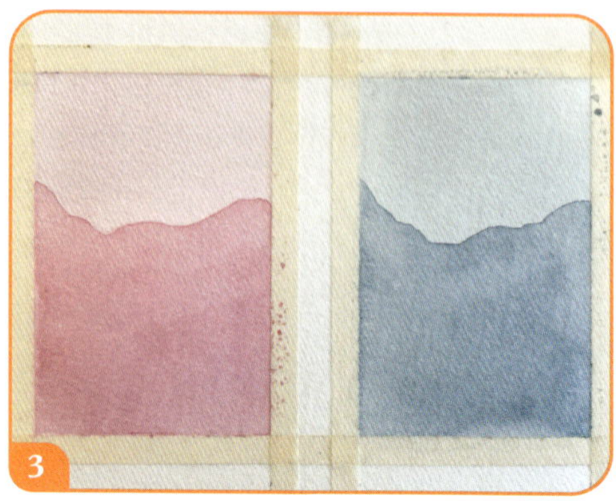

1   If you like, use masking tape to make two vertical rectangles on your paper for these paintings, or just sketch two rectangle shapes to paint into. These paintings can be as big or small as you want—I went pretty small for mine but you can do whatever feels right.

2   Start by creating a very light value with each of your colors, adding lots of water and very little pigment. Fill in one of the rectangles with one color, and fill in the other with the other color. Let it dry completely, using a hair dryer to speed up the process if you're impatient like me.

3   Add a little more pigment to each of your colors to create slightly darker values. Paint a wavy mountain range about halfway up the rectangle, then fill in the bottom half of the rectangle with paint. Let it dry completely.

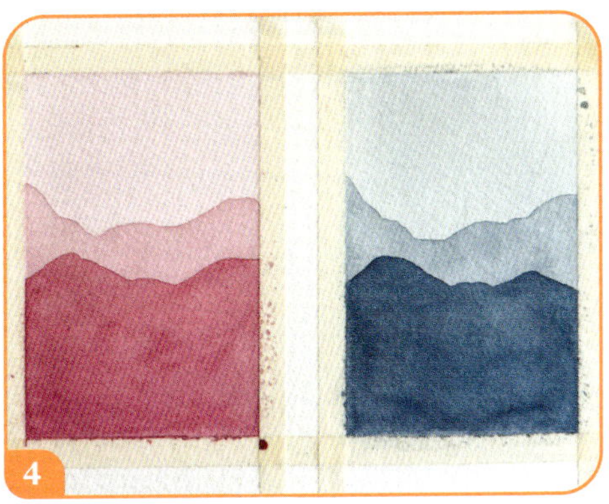

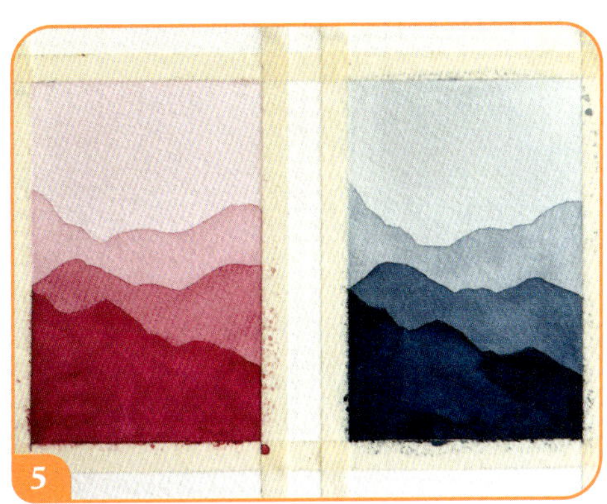

4   Add more pigment to each color and create another mountain range, this time slightly below the first one. Again, fill in the bottom of the rectangle with paint and let it dry completely.

5   Repeat this process two more times, each time adding more pigment to each mixture and making sure to dry the painting completely between layers. Your paint should be getting thicker in texture on your mixing palette, and your very last layer should be the most concentrated paint you can make with each color.

NOTE: With these layers increasing in value, we mimic an effect called atmospheric perspective: Objects that are farther away are lighter in value and lower in saturation than objects closer to you. Keeping atmospheric perspective in mind will help you create a realistic landscape, especially when there are elements (like mountain ranges) that are very far away.

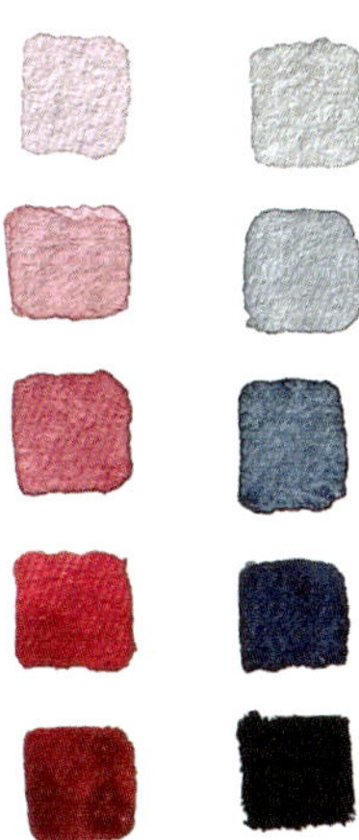

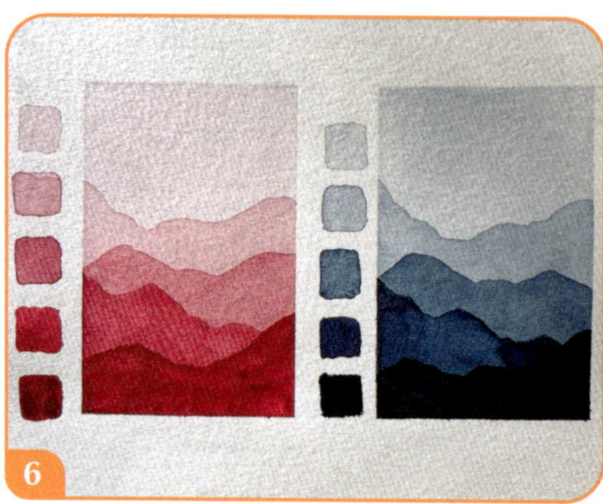

6 Once you've added your last mountain layer, take off the masking tape if you used it. Notice the difference in your paintings due to your color choices. In my example, the magenta mountain range has pretty low contrast—the last mountain layer with the most concentrated color isn't a very dark value. In comparison, the indigo mountain range has much higher contrast because I got that really dark, concentrated color in the foreground. Like I mentioned in the beginning of this lesson, neither is inherently right or wrong and there are situations when you might want a higher contrast or lower contrast painting. It is, however, important to understand value and know how to create different values with paint so that you can make educated stylistic choices when it comes to value and contrast.

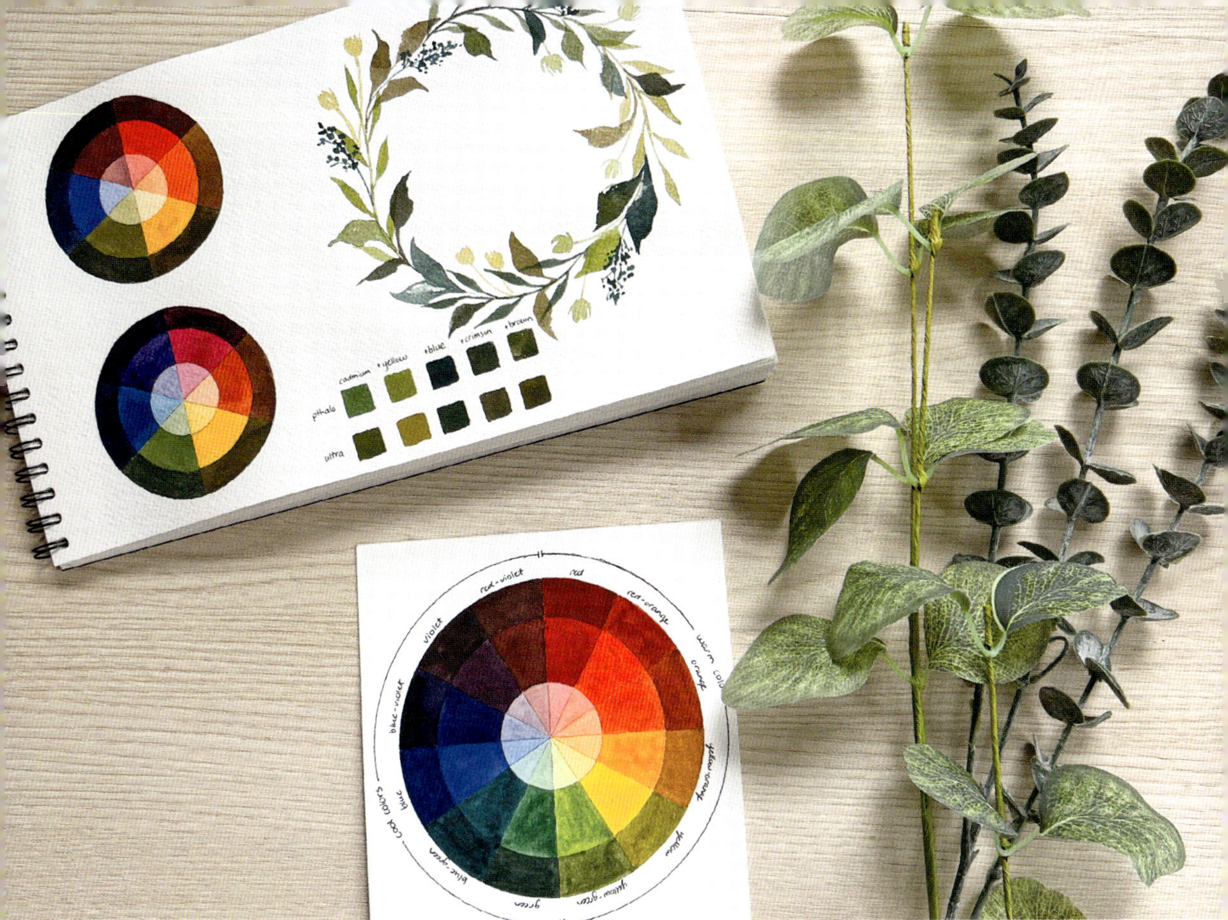

Colorful Language

In my humble opinion, our ability to see colors is one of the most magical, mystical parts of life. Not only do they make our world beautiful to look at, but colors help our brains identify objects faster and invoke certain moods or feelings. As an artist, I habitually observe color in my surroundings in much greater detail than someone who is not an artist would, and it makes me feel like I have a superpower. After you've been painting consistently for just a little while, you'll start to notice yourself doing it too!

Color theory is a term you may have heard thrown around in the areas of art, graphic design, interior design or fashion, but what actually is it? Color theory is simply the study of how different colors function together. Artists need to have a good working knowledge of color theory in order to know how to mix paint colors and to be able to put colors in the right spots to make a compelling work of art. In today's lesson, we are going to dive into the very beginnings of color theory. This rabbit hole is far too deep to be able to explore it all in one lesson, but I hope this gives you a good starting point to build off with your own research and practice!

I'll begin today's lesson by introducing you to the holy grail of color theory: the color wheel. In its purest form, the color wheel contains every color visible to the human eye. This is very hard to do (not to mention time consuming) using paint alone, but the one shown here will work just fine for our purposes. Using this color wheel, we are going to identify some new vocab terms.

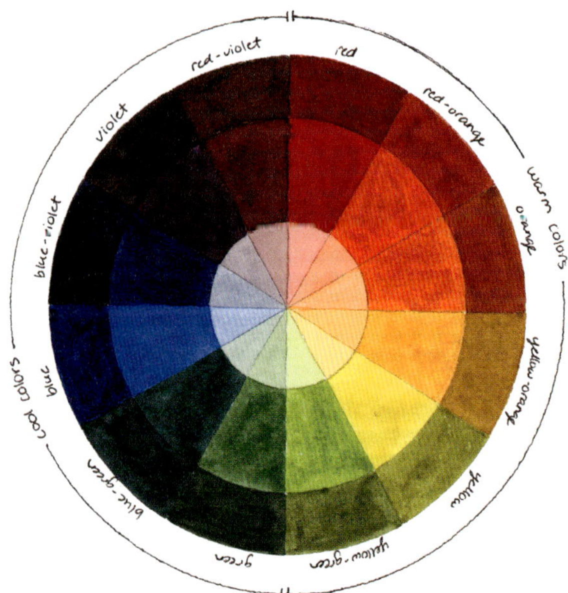

Hue: an art synonym for a specific color, like green or red or purple. You can see each hue labeled on the outside of the color wheel.

Saturation: the purity or vibrancy of a color. The middle ring on this color wheel has high saturation, while the innermost ring and outermost ring have lower saturation.

Tint: hue with white paint added (or water added in the case of watercolor). The innermost ring contains the tints for each hue in the color wheel.

Shade: hue with black paint added. The outermost ring contains the shades for each hue in the color wheel.

Primary colors: colors that can't be mixed using any other combination of colors. Traditionally the primaries are red, yellow and blue, so that's what I used in this color wheel, but more recently yellow, cyan and magenta have been used as a primary color set.

Secondary colors: the three colors created by mixing two primaries together—orange, green and purple (violet).

Tertiary colors: colors created by combining one primary and the secondary color next to it on the color wheel. They are named by hyphenating the two colors used to mix them, for example red-orange, yellow-green or blue-purple.

Complementary colors: colors exactly opposite each other on the color wheel, for example red and green, yellow and violet, and orange and blue. Complementary colors do exactly what the name suggests when placed next to one another: They complement each other. When mixing colors, adding a tiny bit of a complementary color will lower the saturation of the color you're mixing.

Analogous colors: a group of colors next to each other on the color wheel, for example yellow-green, green and blue-green. Analogous colors look harmonious when used together in a painting.

Warm colors: any colors in the red-orange-yellow half of the color wheel, with orange being the warmest color.

Cool colors: any colors in the green-blue-purple half of the color wheel, with blue being the coolest color.

> **NOTE:** Any color can be warm-toned or cool-toned based on which half of the color wheel it leans toward.

There is quite a debate in the art world about the "true" primary colors. Traditionally, red, yellow and blue have been used as the true primary colors from which all other colors are mixed. But with the invention of printers, a new group has emerged: magenta, cyan and yellow. With this new group, you'll tend to mix colors with higher saturation. Additionally, magenta and yellow can be mixed together to create a pretty convincing red hue. Since primary colors are meant to be the three colors that can't be mixed using any other combination of colors, this is a good piece of evidence that the new-school group might be the true primary color group. Some people have very strong opinions about this topic, but I personally think it's beneficial to just understand and keep both in mind when color mixing.

EXERCISE 1: THE COLOR WHEEL IS YOUR FRIEND

For our first exercise, you are going to test out the two primary color groups for yourself and use them to create your very own color wheels. You'll need:

» Pencil

» Optional: ruler, compass

» Cup of water and paper towel

(continued)

»   Watercolor paints: Cadmium Red, Cadmium Yellow, Ultramarine Blue, black of choice (or mix Ultramarine Blue and Van Dyke Brown), Magenta, Phthalo Blue

»   Watercolor paper (I used a page of my Arches sketchbook)

»   1 detail brush (I used a 2 round)

1   Start by sketching out two circles on your paper. Mine are about 2½ inches (6 cm) in diameter, but yours can be as large or small as you like.

2   Within each circle, add two more concentric circles. Then divide each circle into six wedges using straight lines. I used a ruler and a compass for this because of who I am as a person, but you can just freehand this! It doesn't need to be perfect!

3   We will be working with one circle at a time here. For your first circle, you'll need three colors: Cadmium Red, Cadmium Yellow and Ultramarine Blue. These are the three colors in the average watercolor palette that I think are closest to the traditional red/yellow/blue primary color group. Add a drop of water to each of these colors and let them soften.

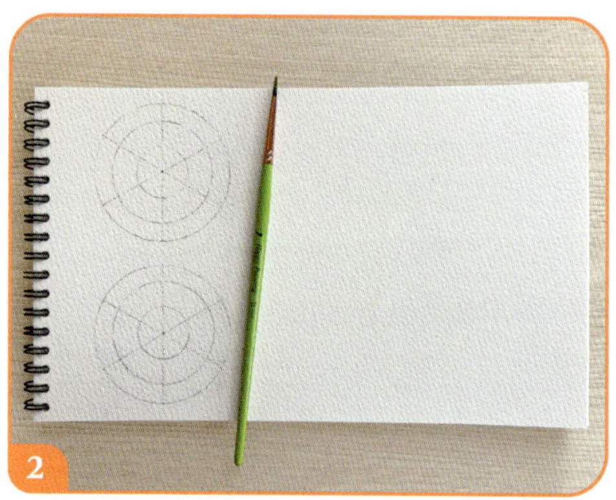

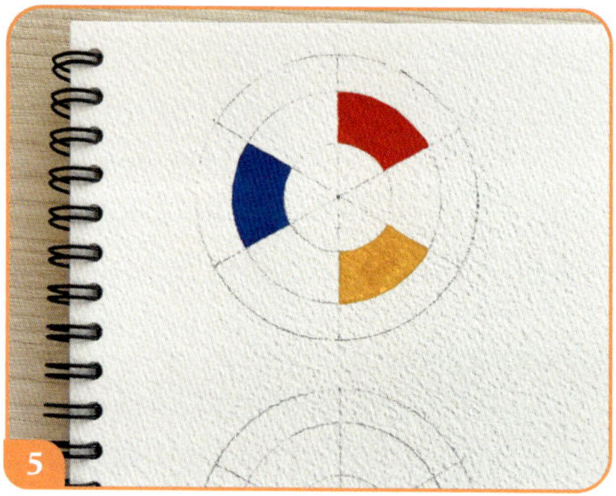

4   Once your paints have dissolved a bit, mix up a little bit of each color. Add just enough water so the paint will flow easily off your brush.

5   Find the middle ring in your first circle, and paint one of the sections red. Wash your brush, skip a section and fill in the next one with yellow. Wash your brush, skip one more section and paint the next one blue. Let it dry completely.

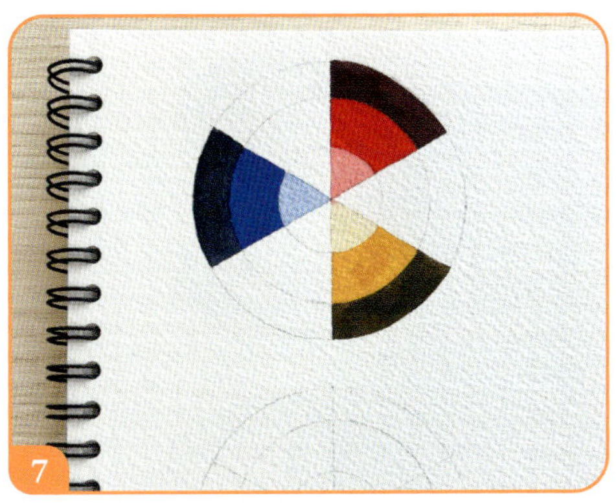

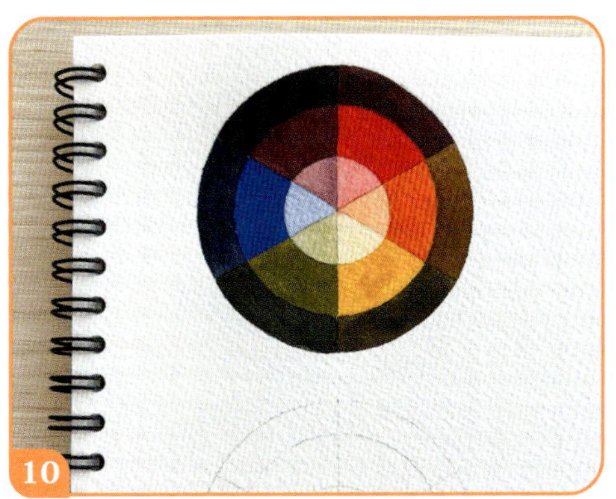

6   Now we will add the tints for these colors. Mix a generous amount of water with just a touch of Cadmium Red, then use it to fill in the innermost segment of the red wedge. Do the same thing with the Ultramarine Blue wedge and the Cadmium Yellow wedge.

7   Now, to make your shades, add a touch of black paint to a concentrated mixture of each primary color. Use these new colors to fill in the outermost ring of each appropriate wedge. Let this dry completely before moving on.

8   Combine Cadmium Yellow with a touch of Cadmium Red to create an orange color, adding just enough water to allow the paint to flow smoothly. Try to create an orange that is right in the middle between red and yellow. Fill in the section between red and yellow in the middle ring with your orange color.

9   Repeat this process for your other two secondary colors: Combine Cadmium Yellow and Ultramarine Blue to make green and fill in the section between those colors, then combine Cadmium Red and Ultramarine Blue to make purple and fill in the section between those colors. You should have the entire middle ring filled in now.

10   Finally, create the tints and shades for each of your secondary colors. Add plenty of water to each and fill in their respective spots in the innermost ring. Then add a touch of black paint to each original color and fill in the outermost ring.

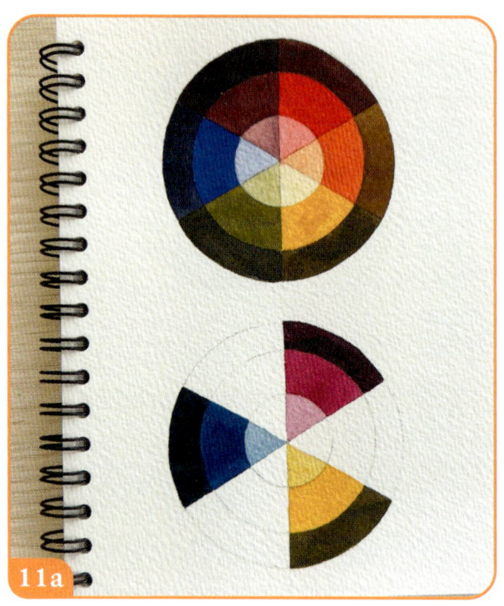

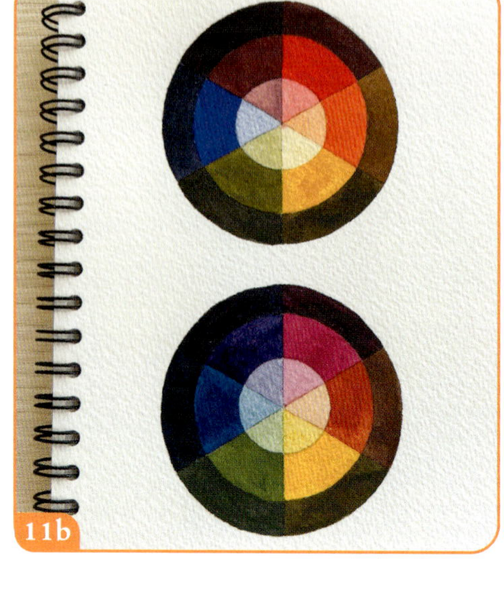

11 You've made a color wheel! Yay! Now that you know the process, you are going to do the exact same thing in your second circle using different colors: Magenta, Cadmium Yellow and Phthalo Blue. These three colors are pretty close to the cyan/yellow/magenta primary group that is more popularly used now, especially in modern printers.

Once you've painted in your second color wheel, let's compare the two. Notice the differences in the secondary colors you mixed—how do the oranges, greens and purples compare? Neither one of these primary groups is necessarily right or wrong (though some people feel very strongly one way or another), but you do end up with different secondary color mixtures.

In reality, most artists don't limit themselves to just three colors when making art. We use all of the colors in our watercolor palette in order to mix as many unique colors as possible!

EXERCISE 2: LET'S MIX IT UP

For our next exercise, we are going to test out how many different versions of one color we can create just by changing different elements. The color of the day is green, which is one of my favorites to experiment with. As you know by now, green is made by combining yellow and blue, but what happens if we change the recipe slightly? You'll end up with different shades of green, and we'll use those different shades to create a fun watercolor wreath.

For this project, you'll need:

» Cup of water and paper towel

» Watercolor paints: Cadmium Yellow, Phthalo Blue, Ultramarine Blue, Van Dyke Brown, Alizarin Crimson

» Pencil

» Watercolor paper (1 piece for your wreath painting, and 1 scrap piece for swatching)

» Optional: compass

» 1 medium brush (I used a 4 round)

1   Add a couple drops of water to each of your watercolor paint colors and give them a minute to soften. In the meantime, lightly sketch out a circle on your paper. Mine is roughly 4 inches (10 cm) in diameter, and again I used a compass because I can't help myself, but you don't have to.

2   For simplicity, let's use one yellow color (Cadmium Yellow) and two blue colors (Phthalo Blue and Ultramarine Blue) for this project. Start by mixing a true green with the Cadmium Yellow and Phthalo Blue, then mix a true green with the Cadmium Yellow and Ultramarine Blue in a separate section of your palette. Swatch both of these colors on your swatch paper.

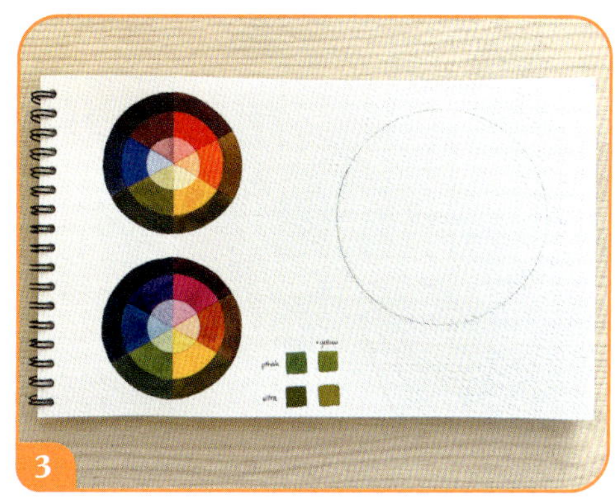

3   Now add extra Cadmium Yellow to each of these green colors you mixed and swatch them. Notice how they each lighten into more of a yellow-green color. This is an awesome way to lighten green colors while keeping them vibrant and saturated! Adding white paint or water often dilutes the color and makes it less vibrant.

4   Next, add extra blue to each of the green colors (make sure to keep track of which green was made with Ultramarine and which was made with Phthalo!) and swatch them. Notice how this darkens the green colors without causing them to lose their vibrancy, which can happen when adding black paint.

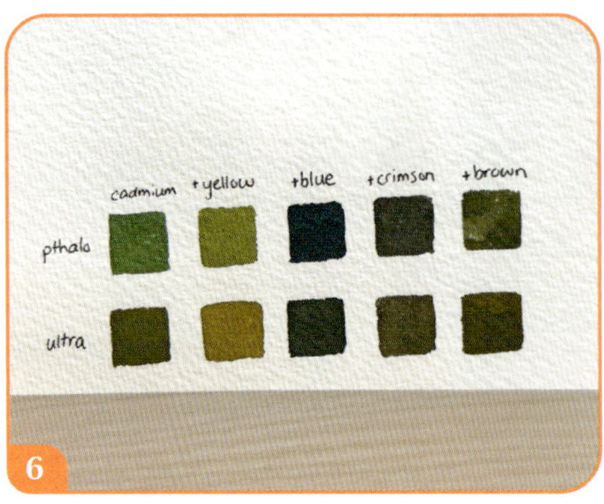

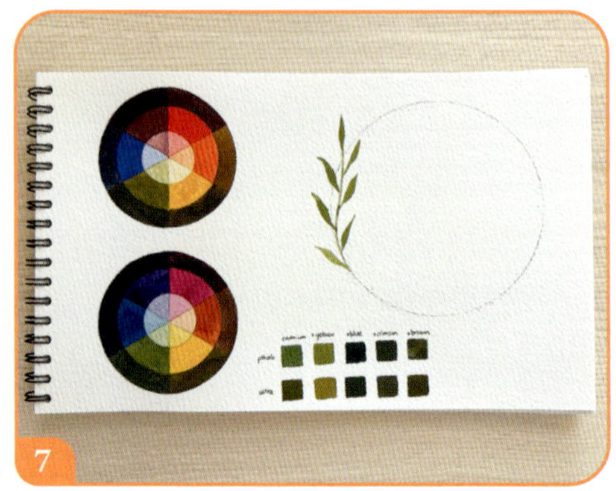

5 Add a bit more yellow to your green colors to get them back to that true green tone. Then add just a tiny touch of Alizarin Crimson (the complementary color of green) to each and swatch. Notice how this dulls down the green colors and makes them look a bit more natural?

6 Feel free to continue experimenting with making unique shades of green. You can try mixing in brown instead of red, adding water to lighten the colors or adding lots of paint to make the colors darker. Once you feel like you've explored the world of green paint, let's move on to painting our wreath!

7 Use any of the green colors you've just mixed for this wreath—it doesn't matter which one! Paint in your first vine: Start with a thin, slightly wavy line that loosely follows your sketched circle. Then use a press, drag and lift motion with your brush

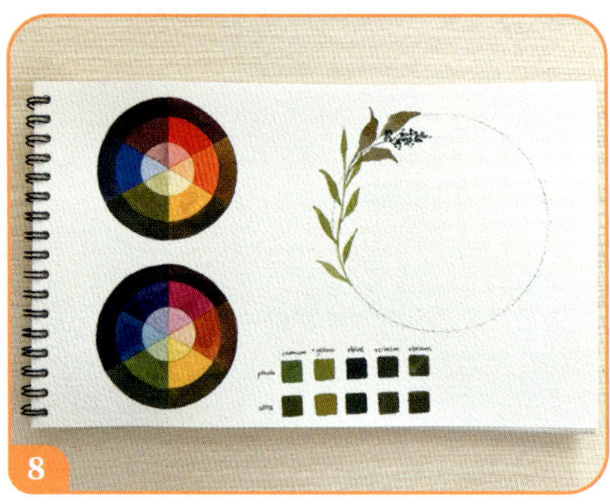

to add alternating leaves down this stem. Lifting your brush quickly, with a slight flicking motion, will give you a nice fine point to your leaves.

8 Switch to a new color and add some new leaves continuing around the circle. Change these ones up a little bit—maybe make them wider or skinnier, or wiggle your brush a little bit to give them some imperfections. You can also add some little berry branches by stippling in a few clusters of dots, then connecting them with thin lines.

9 Continue working around the circle, switching to different shades of green as you add more leaves and vines. You can also add some flower buds by painting in a feathery U-shape and connecting it to the wreath with a thin line. Once you've filled in the whole circle to your liking, you're all done!

Take a step back and make note of what went well and what you think could be improved from this lesson. Were you able to mix lots of different versions of green? Which do you like the best? How do you feel about the leaves and vines you created? If you feel like you could use some practice with brush control, you're in luck because that's what we're tackling in the next project!

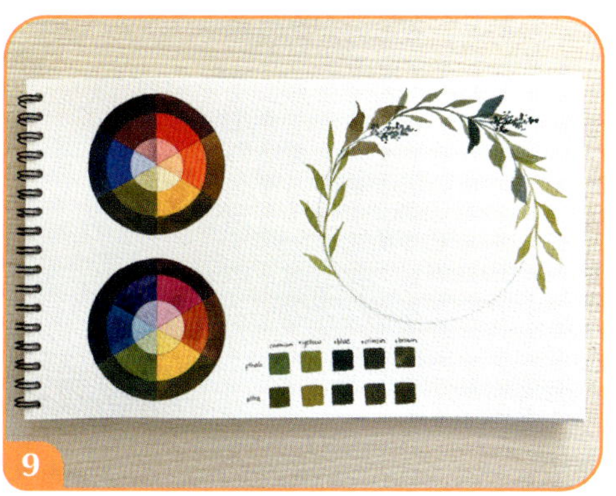

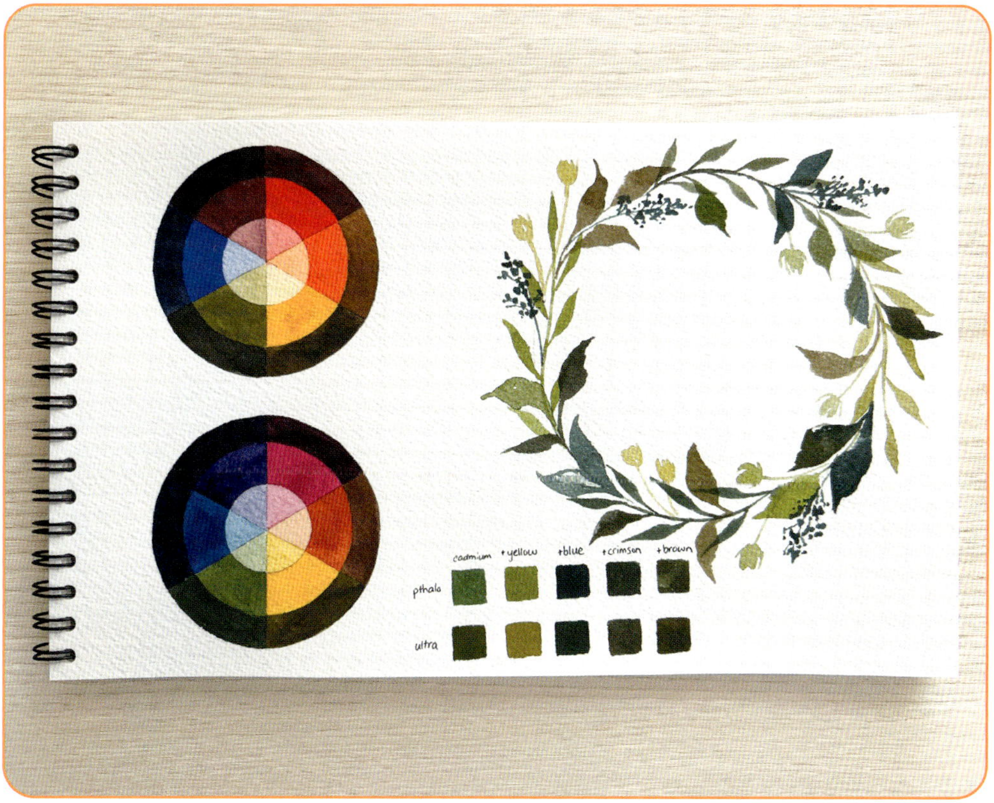

CHAPTER 2

Watercolor Essentials

How to Unravel the Mysteries of Watercolor Painting

Watercolor painting is an ancient medium, dating back thousands of years to Stone Age cave paintings. Watercolor as we know it now was developed much later around the 18th century, and since then it has captivated artists with its unique properties. It is a transparent medium, made by combining powdered pigments with a water-soluble binder, usually something called gum arabic in modern paints. When water is added to the dry paint, it activates the binder and allows the pigment to be suspended in the water. When the paint is applied to a page, it flows freely until the water evaporates, leaving behind a thin layer of pigment bound to the paper by the gum arabic. It has a mind of its own on the page, resisting your every attempt to control it and making perfectionists everywhere question their life choices. But if you push past the I-want-to-set-this-painting-on-fire stage, watercolor rewards you with a beautiful, glowing-from-within look and a movement and energy to your painting that can't be achieved with any other medium. In the following projects, we'll learn the basics of watercolor, how to use it and ways to manipulate it to get different effects.

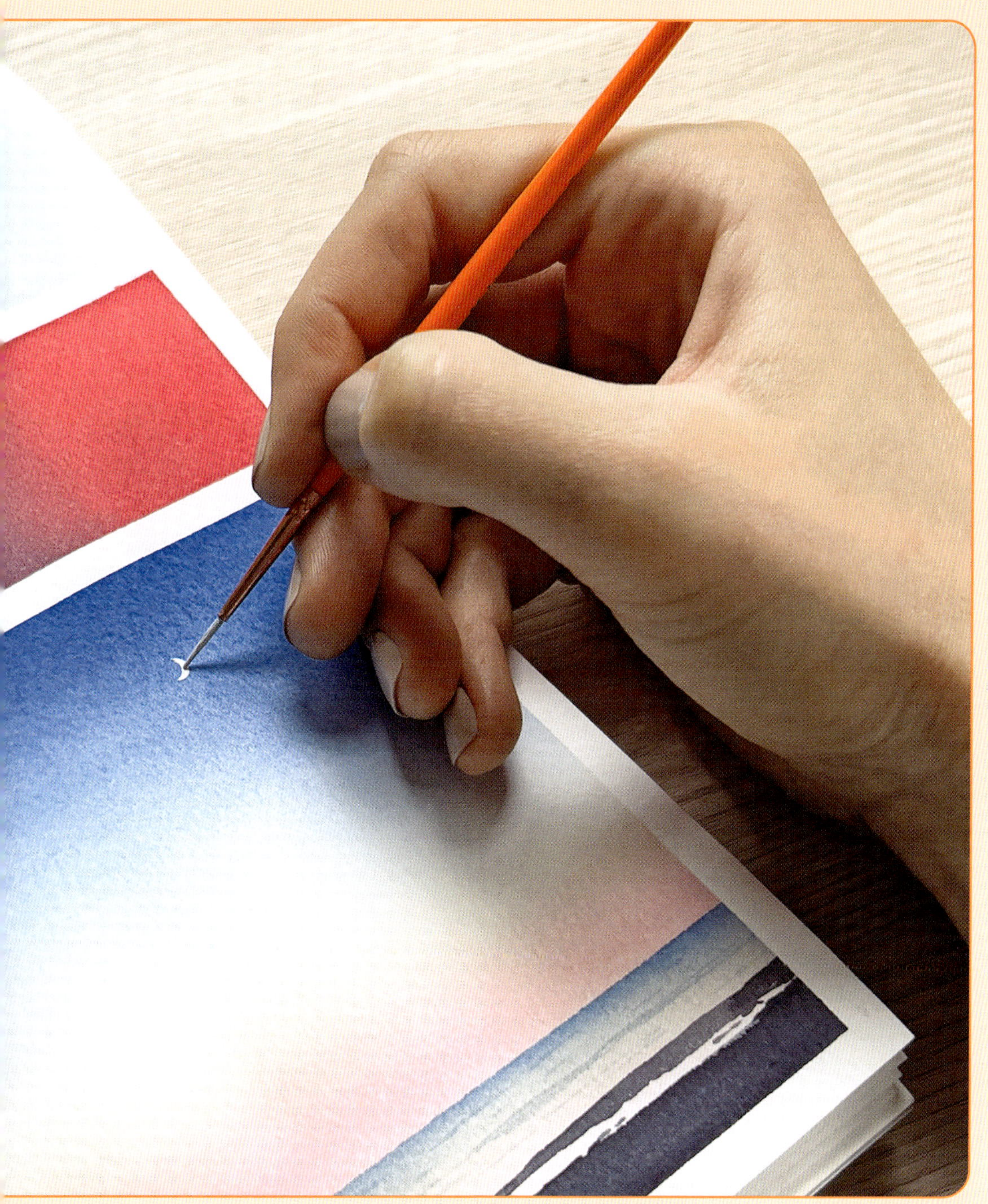

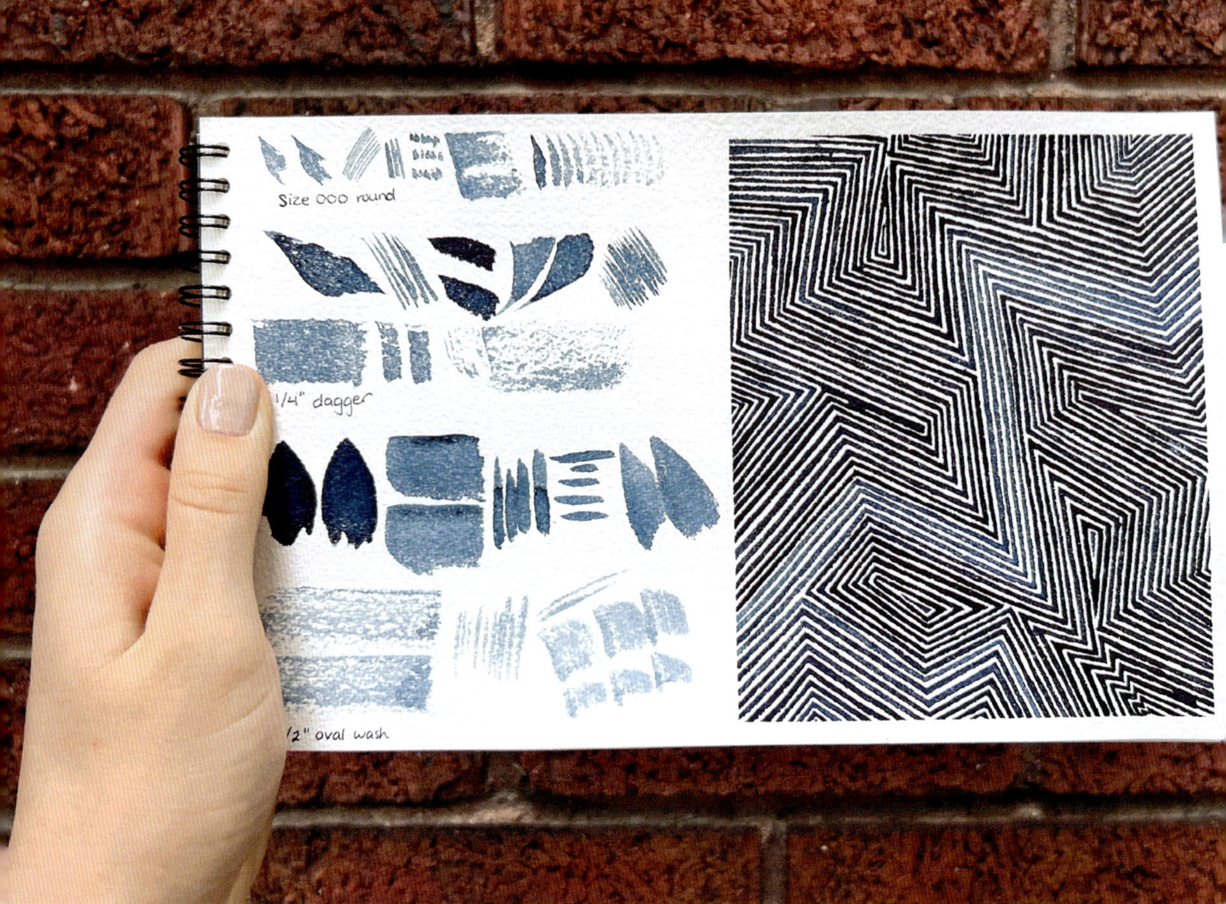

Make Your Mark

Before we can create a beautiful painting, we have to understand the materials we're working with. Mark-making is the first baby step that will start you on your journey to watercolor painting. It's also a good warm-up and a great practice to continue anytime you get new materials, and to build up the strength and muscle memory in your hand!

As you might imagine, different brushes can be used to create different marks on the page. Some brushes hold more paint than others, and there is a huge variety of shapes and sizes to choose from, so the possibilities are really endless! Round brushes are the most common and versatile in watercolor painting. Larger round brushes hold a ton of water and

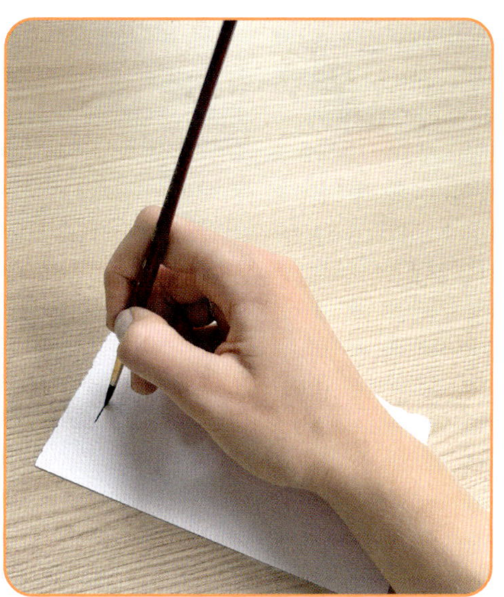

Holding your brush at a 90-degree angle can help you create dots or fine lines.

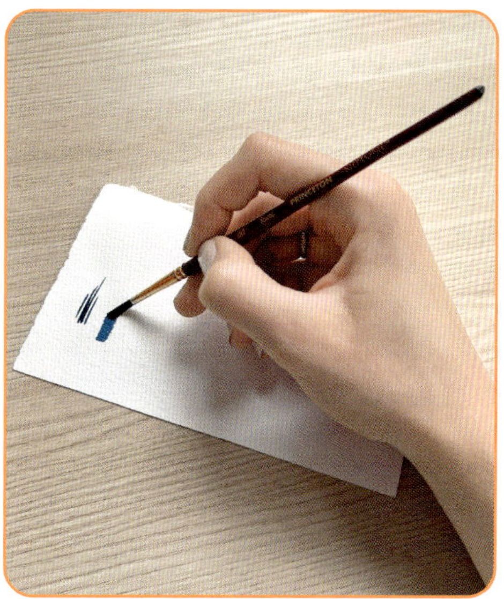

Holding your brush at a 45-degree angle (or lower) will allow you to create thicker lines or quickly cover more surface area.

paint, so they can be used to cover large areas of a painting quickly. Medium and smaller round brushes can be used to cover smaller areas, or to add details by using the sharp point. The other common type of brush is a flat wash brush. In large sizes, these brushes are also great for covering large areas of a painting with water or paint. In any size, they are great for creating geometric shapes, since the bristles are held in a flat line. There are also some other, more unique brush shapes you can experiment with: A dagger brush has a super sharp point and bristles held at a diagonal, an oval brush is shaped like a flower petal with a sharp point, and a liner or script brush is shaped like a round brush but with much longer bristles, so it can hold a lot more paint.

Each individual brush can also make tons of unique marks on the page depending on how it's used. In general, I recommend holding your brush at least one-third of the way away from the actual bristles. Holding it too close to the bristles will not allow you the freedom of movement needed to create smooth brushstrokes and should only be done when adding super fine details. If you want an even looser look to your painting, you can experiment with holding your brush farther down the barrel. You can also change the angle of your brush against the paper— hold it straight up and down to create dots or fine lines, hold it at a 45-degree angle for smooth, even brushstrokes or hold it nearly parallel to the paper to create thick brushstrokes with texture.

The last thing you can alter when using your brush is the amount of paint you load into it. When covering large areas of paper with paint, you'll want to load as much paint as possible into your brush. When creating details or defined brushstrokes, you'll want to load your brush at about 50 to 75 percent capacity. This will give you a lot more control over where exactly the paint goes, and you won't have excess paint leaking off the brush as you try to paint. To remove excess paint, you can either scrape your brush on a hard edge of your palette or you can briefly touch your loaded brush to a dry paper towel. For methods like dry brushing (page 101), you'll want to load your brush to about 10 percent, removing most of the paint with a paper towel before bringing the brush to your paper.

EXERCISE 1: DIFFERENT STROKES

For our first exercise, let's practice all of the mark-making variations we just covered.

You'll need:

» Cup of water and a paper towel

» Watercolor paint: 1 color (I used Indigo)

» 3 different brushes of your choosing (I used a 000 round, a ¼-inch [6 mm] dagger and a ½-inch [1.5 cm] oval brush)

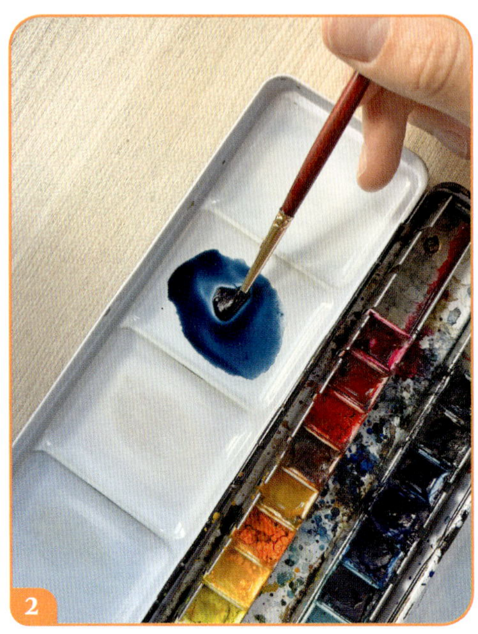

» Watercolor paper (I used a page of my Arches sketchbook)

1   Put a drop of water in your chosen color and give it a minute to soften, then mix up a puddle of paint in your palette. Be sure to add in some water so you get a mixture that flows smoothly on paper.

2   Choose your first brush and load it with paint.

3   On your paper, start making as many unique marks as you can come up with. Try stamping the brush straight down and lifting up, dragging it across the paper with light or heavy pressure, using just the tip of it or

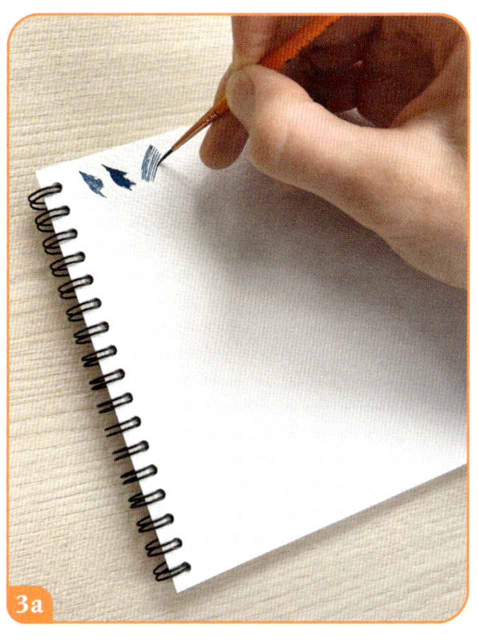

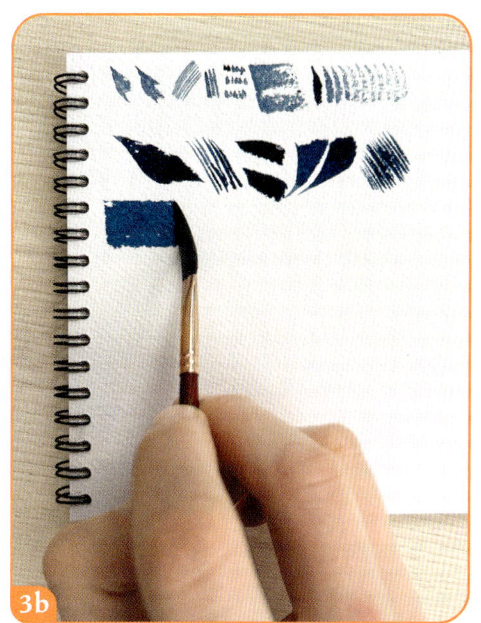

using the entire side of the brush on the paper, etc. Alter the amount of paint on the brush, the angle you hold it to the paper and how far away from the bristles you hold the brush.

4   Repeat this process with the other two brushes you selected. Be creative here and have fun!

Notice how many different marks you made with just three brushes! This is a great way to practice your brush control, develop a steady hand and get familiar with a new brush (or maybe just one you don't use very often).

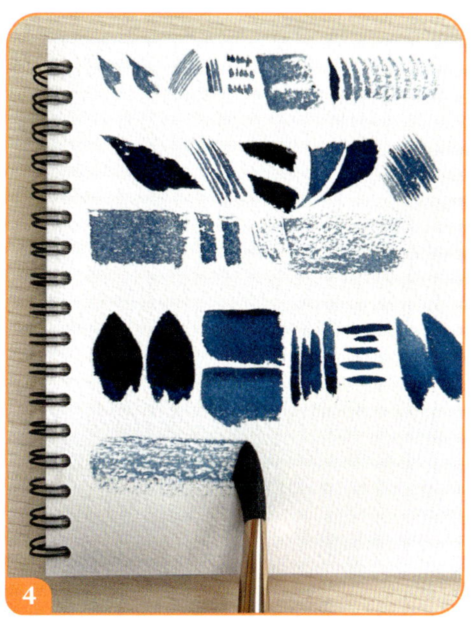

EXERCISE 2: ZENTANGLE®

Now that we're familiar with mark-making, let's get some more practice with brush control with a healthy side of patience and mindfulness. For the uninitiated, Zentangles are essentially repetitive doodles created with pens or paint, and can take many different forms. Today's exercise will consist of straight lines, but there are tons of different patterns and brushstrokes you can use to Zentangle and I'd highly encourage you to look into it more if you enjoy today's exercise.

For this exercise you'll need:

» Cup of water and a paper towel

» Watercolor paint: 1 color (I used Indigo)

» 1 brush (I used a #2 liner brush)

» Watercolor paper (I taped out a rect-angle in my Arches sketchbook)

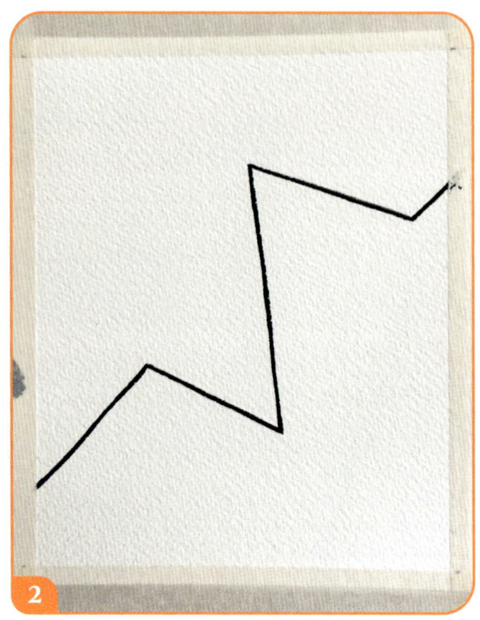

1   Put a drop of water in your chosen color and give it a minute to soften, then mix up a healthy puddle of paint in your palette. Be sure to add in enough water so you get a paint that flows smoothly on paper.

2   Load up your brush with paint, and paint a random zigzag line across your paper. Reload your brush with paint at any time as you paint the line, but try to resist the temptation to "fix" any uneven lines. Those are all part of the exercise!

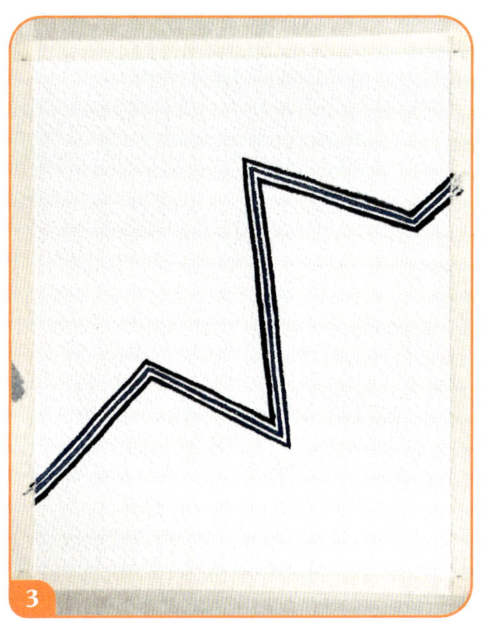

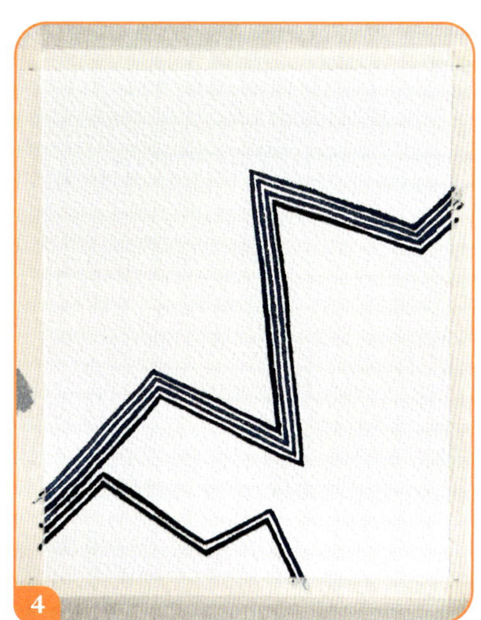

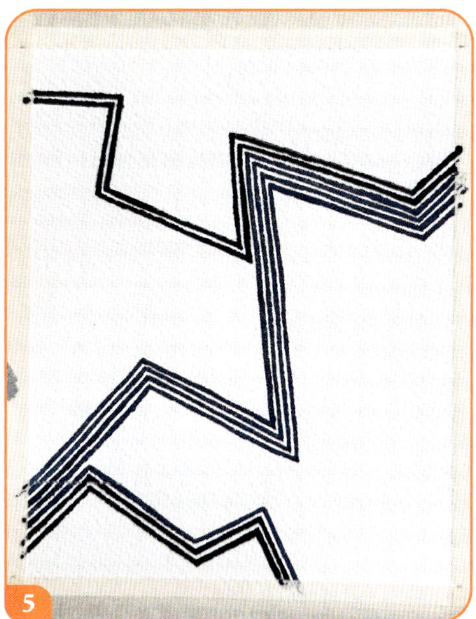

3 Follow your zigzag line with another line. Try to follow the first line as evenly as you can.

4 After adding a few lines like this, start creating some lines that branch off of your original lines. Then continue following those lines until you want to branch them off again.

5 Continue adding lines, following the previous ones, until you reach the edge of the page.

6 Sometimes you'll end up with a closed-off shape—simply line the inside of the shape with a continuous line, then repeat until the shape closes!

7 Embrace the slow but steady progress, and enjoy the mindfulness of this exercise! There's really no right or wrong way to do this, so feel free to make it your own in any way you want!

Once you've filled in your entire page with lines, you're all done! You should have a bit of an optical illusion—lines that seem to vibrate as you look at them. Reflect briefly on this exercise. Did you feel more confident in your lines as you continued to make them? How did your choice of brush affect your Zentangle? This is a great exercise to practice your brush control if you struggle with shaky hands, but it's also a lovely mindfulness exercise if you're feeling stuck artistically or emotionally!

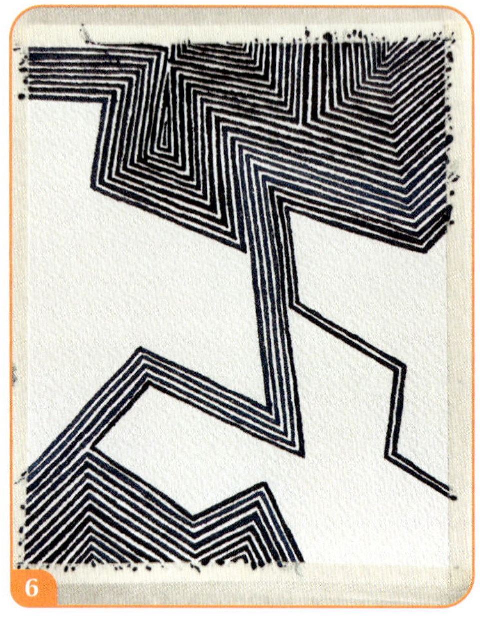

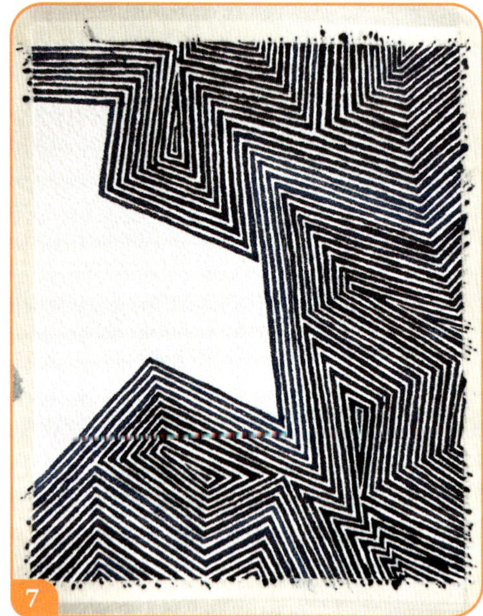

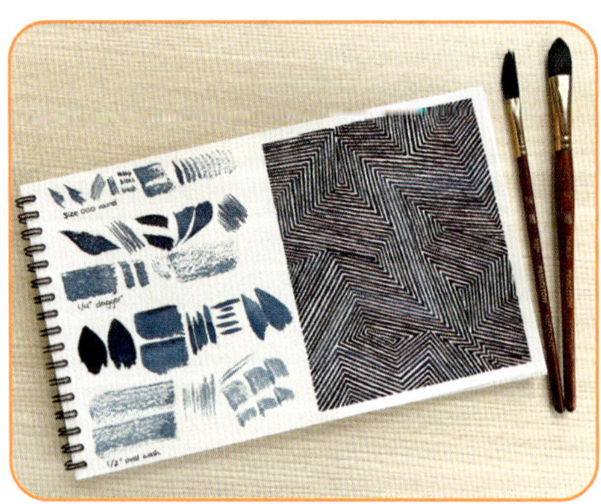

Put That Paint Down

Watercolor is a unique medium because of its reliance on water as a vehicle. Water, as you may know, often has a mind of its own and moves around in whatever space it's given. When paint pigments are suspended in that water, they are pulled around the paper with the water in seemingly random ways. Learning how to control the water and pigment on your paper, along with learning when to let go of control, is a fundamental part of watercolor. Today's lesson will focus on four different ways to apply paint to paper, along with a fun exercise that will allow you to put these new techniques into practice!

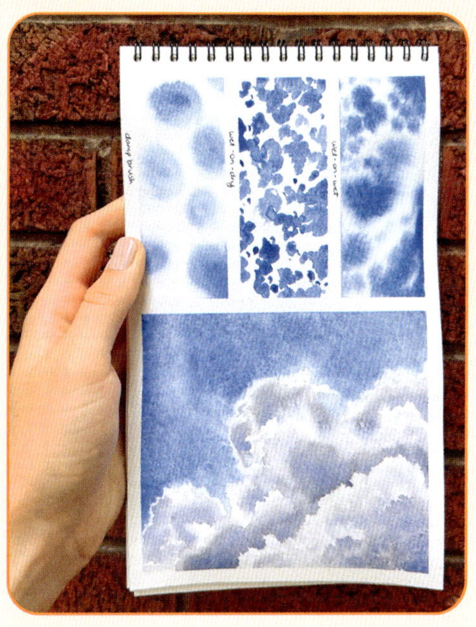

First, we'll cover the four common ways to apply watercolor to paper. These are:

Flat wash: applying a smooth, even wash of color to an area with as little texture as possible. This is a very common technique in watercolor but can be difficult to master at first.

Wet-on-wet: placing wet paint on wet paper, creating interesting textures, gradients and soft blends. Keep in mind that painting wet-on-wet also lightens the value of your paint colors because they are diluted by the water on the paper.

Wet-on-dry: placing wet paint on dry paper, giving you sharp details and defined brushstrokes. This technique allows the paint colors to remain the same consistency as they are on your mixing palette since they aren't mixing with any water on the page.

Damp brush blending: placing wet paint on dry paper, then blending the edges with a damp brush, allowing you to be more accurate with your paint placement but still get a blended, diffused edge.

EXERCISE 1: PUTTING PAINT ON PAPER

These techniques can only be mastered through practice, so let's give them a try! For this project, you'll need:

» Cup of water and paper towel

» Watercolor paint: 1 color (I used Ultramarine Blue)

» Watercolor paper (I used a page of my Arches sketchbook)

» 1 large brush, 1 medium brush (I used a 10 round and a 4 round)

» Optional: masking tape, pencil

1 Put a drop of water in your chosen color and give it a minute to soften. Meanwhile, divide your paper into four equal sections. You can use your masking tape to define each section, or just sketch four rectangles with a pencil.

2 Mix a large puddle of your chosen paint, adding some water so the paint flows easily without watering it down too much.

The Art of the Flat Wash

A good flat wash is one of the foundational skills needed to be a successful watercolor artist. While minor textures and imperfections in watercolor painting are expected, being able to put down a smooth layer of paint will really help you create beautiful paintings. When painting a flat wash, it's important that you cover the area quickly, so use a large brush and don't dillydally! Also, please resist the temptation to mess with it too much after you've put the initial layer of paint down—I promise, adding more brushstrokes will only increase the weird textures as it dries! Let's try this out.

3 Load up a large brush with the paint you mixed.

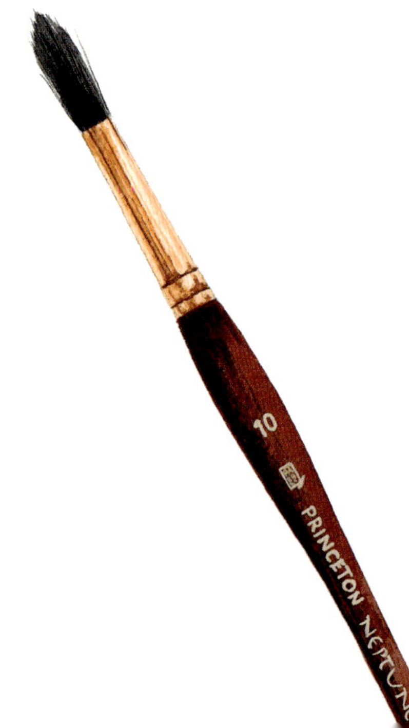

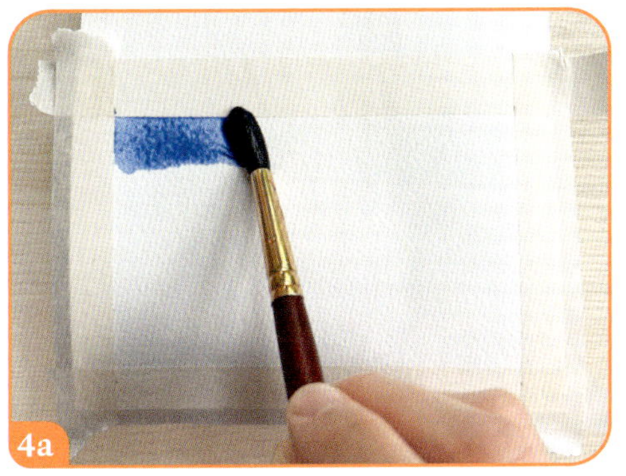

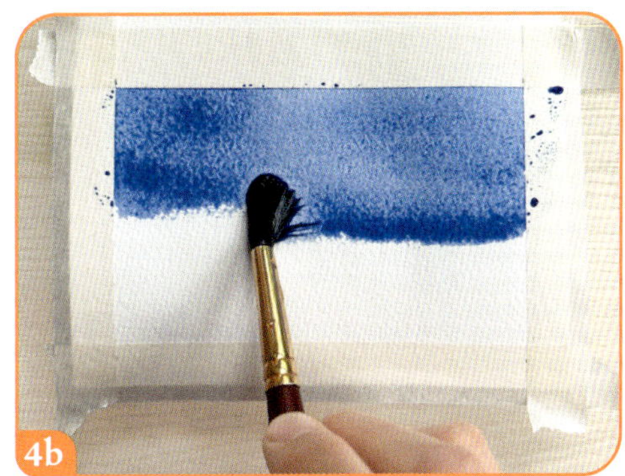

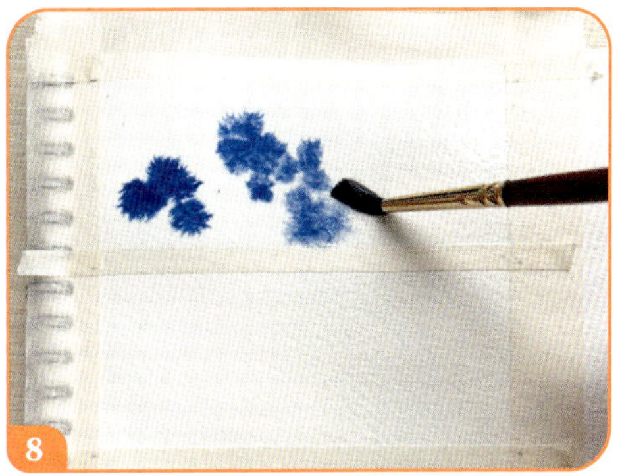

4 Using smooth horizontal or vertical brushstrokes, work back and forth to cover the paper inside one rectangle. When your brush starts to run out of paint, quickly reload it and continue working where you left off. Keep going until you've covered the entire area.

5 Once you've filled in an area, you may notice excess paint pooling at the edges and corners. Use a completely dry brush to gently touch these areas to remove the excess paint. This will help the paint dry in an even layer.

6 Keep the paper flat and let it dry all the way. You can use a hair dryer to speed up drying time, but hold it at a distance so you don't push the paint around too much.

Wet-on-Wet

7 Using a large, clean brush, cover your next rectangle in a generous layer of clean water from your cup.

8 Load some paint onto your brush (I switched to my size 4 round brush here) and drop it into random spots in this section. Let the paint spread out and flow around the page, and let it dry on its own.

Wet-on-Dry

9   Load up your brush with paint again, then move to your next section of paper. Place some random blobs of color on the dry paper. Feel free to make whatever patterns or textures you want!

Damp Brush Blending

10   Load up your brush with paint, then move to your last section of paper. Paint in a small blob of paint, then quickly clean your brush in your water cup.

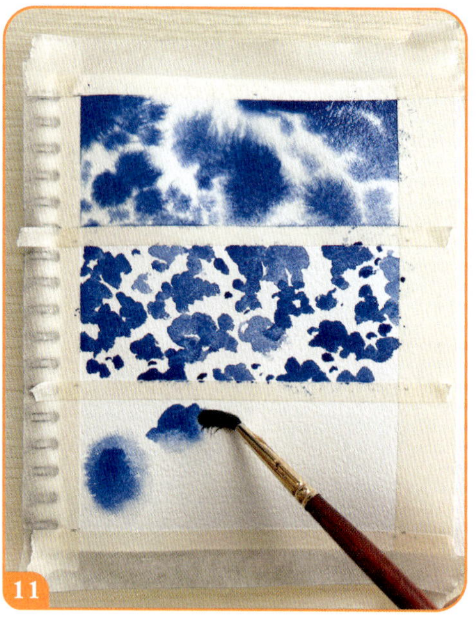

11   Dab your brush on a paper towel to remove much of the water from the brush, then drag your damp brush around the edge of the still-wet paint blob you just put down. You can do this a couple times on the same shape to get it fully blended.

12   Repeat this process as many times as you want in this section until you feel comfortable with the technique. There will be some little imperfections and that's okay! We just want to practice making those diffused edges.

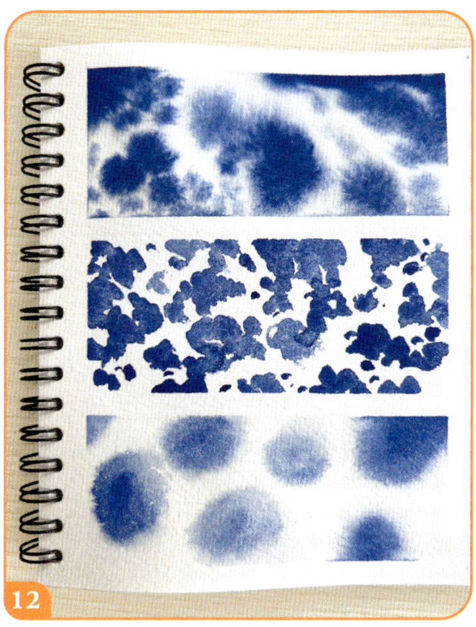

Let all four sections dry completely, then label each one with which technique you used to create it so you can reference it later!

EXERCISE 2: FLUFFY CLOUDS

Let's create a little painting study to practice these techniques! I love painting clouds with watercolor; the free-flowing paint really gives a glow and a cool sense of movement to the scene. I found a reference photo to help inspire this painting, which you can see pictured here, but this study is all about working with what the paint does on the page so don't be too worried about replicating it exactly!

For this study, you'll need:

» Cup of water and paper towel

» Watercolor paints: Ultramarine Blue, Van Dyke Brown, Alizarin Crimson

» 1 large and 1 medium brush (I used a 10 round and a 4 round)

» Watercolor paper (I taped out a 4¾ x 5½–inch area [12 x 14–cm] in my Arches sketchbook)

» Optional: masking tape

PAUSE: You'll use a lot of wet-on-wet techniques in this painting, which means you'll need to complete several steps before the paint dries. Read through all of the instructions for this project before beginning so you won't have to pause to read later!

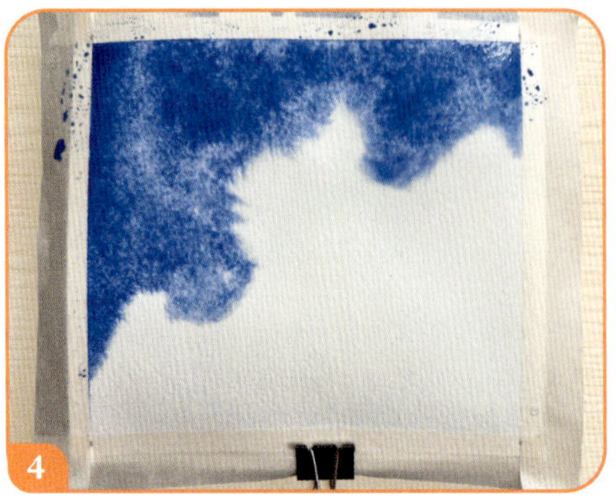

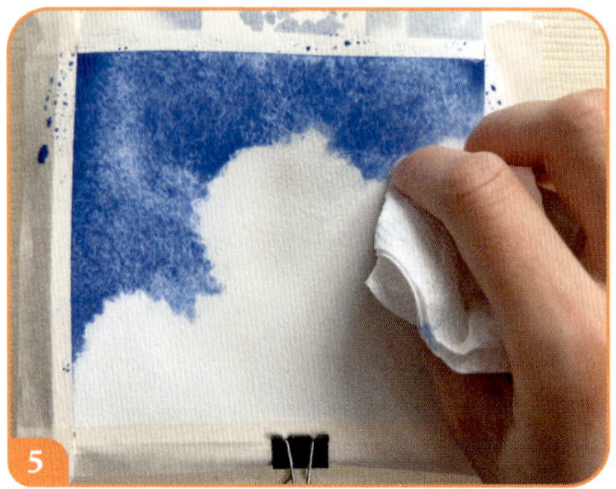

1. Put a drop of water in each color and give it a minute to soften.

2. Place two colors in your mixing area: plain Ultramarine Blue, then a gray made from a mix of Ultramarine Blue, a touch of Van Dyke Brown and a touch of Alizarin Crimson. Add a little water, but keep these paints relatively concentrated in the mixing area.

3. Using a large brush, paint a layer of clean water over your entire page.

4. Load your large brush with Ultramarine Blue and create a wiggly line across the page to develop a loose outline of some clouds, then use the same color to fill in the top half of the page above that line.

5. Scrunch up a paper towel, then press it firmly to the paper for a second or two in the spot where the white paper meets the blue paint you just put down. Work your way across the page, pressing the paper towel to lift up the pigment and water on the page to create a sharp outline of clouds.

6. Switch to a smaller brush and load it with the gray color we mixed in Step 2 (using Ultramarine Blue, a touch of Van Dyke Brown and a touch of Alizarin Crimson). Start adding shadows to the interior of the cloud. There should be some water still left on the paper in the cloud area, and you can use that for this wet-on-wet technique. In areas where the paper is dry, you can either leave the paint strokes as they are or blend with a damp brush.

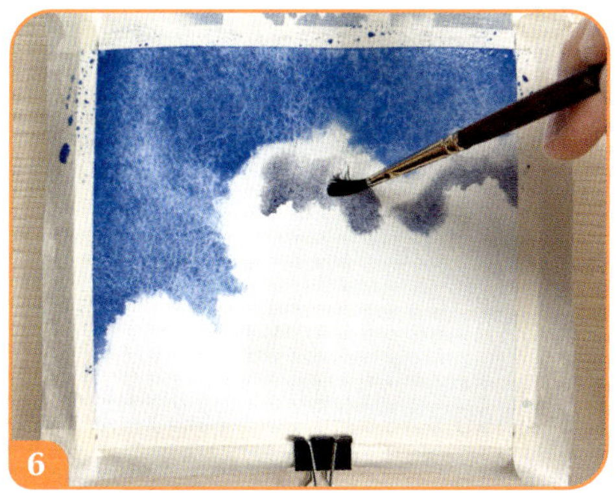

7   At any time, you can switch back to your paper towel and use it to lift some pigment from the interior of the cloud to create more cloud layers and highlights.

8   Work your way down the page in this way, using the reference photo for inspiration. You can always go back and add more gray paint to darken shadows, and you can use your paper towel to take away paint you don't want.

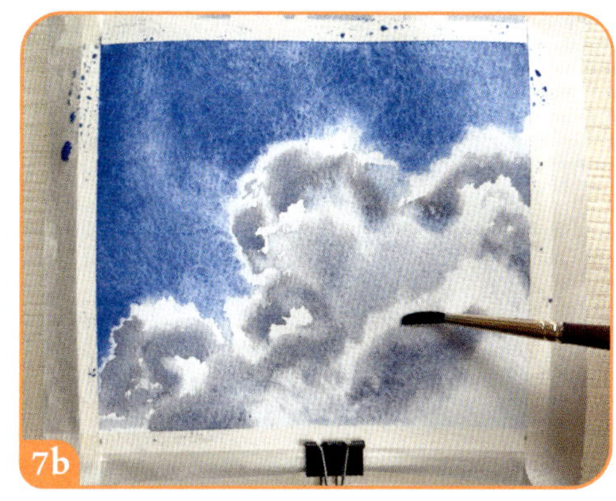

When you're happy with how your clouds look, let the painting dry completely and take off the tape! These techniques can be difficult to master, especially when you add in the time crunch of the paint drying. Wet-on-wet in particular is tough to control, so you have to learn when to try to wrangle it and when to just let it do its thing. Just like anything, the more you practice, the more automatic these techniques become and you'll be able to use them confidently in your art!

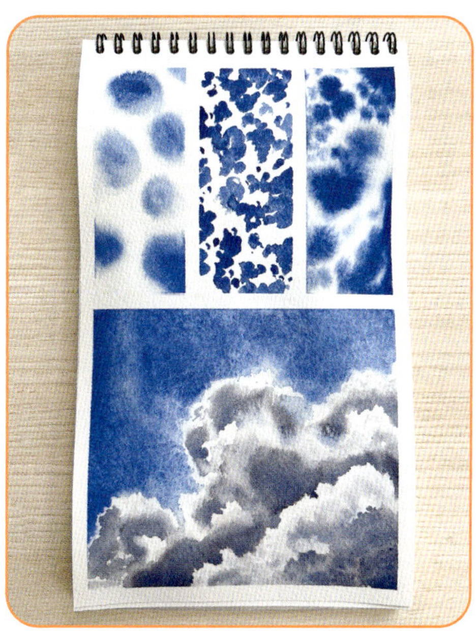

When In Doubt, Blend It Out

Another fun trick you can do with watercolor is blend seamlessly between two or more colors, or from a color to the white of the page! Watercolor takes a few minutes to dry so you have time to blend colors together, unlike when working with mediums such as acrylic paint or gouache. There is a bit of a learning curve to creating a super seamless gradient though; they can often turn out streaky, uneven or weirdly textured if you don't do it quite right. Our task today is to learn the essential tips and tricks of blending and get started on some practice!

Getting a good blend between colors really relies on a few key factors.

Quality of materials: Watercolor paper quality is the biggest determining factor in creating a seamless blend. Cheaper papers will not be able to absorb the amount of water and paint needed, and they can start to pill and crumble with more brush scrubbing. The quality of your paints and brushes will affect your gradients too, but not as much as the paper quality. This is not to say you need super expensive materials, but using paper that is 100 percent cotton and at least 140 lb (300 gsm) thickness will help a lot!

Using the correct materials: Using a large brush and making sure you've mixed enough paint to cover your paper both help a ton!

Working quickly: You have time, but not a ton of it! Gradients have to be completed while the paint is still completely wet—if parts of it start to dry and you continue messing with it, you'll end up with "blooms," which are areas where the paint dries slower than the rest of the painting and creates a darker starburst pattern. Blooms can be used intentionally to create texture, but it's important to learn how to avoid unintentionally creating them as well!

Uniform brushstrokes: Using brushstrokes that only go one direction (I like horizontal, but some people prefer vertical) helps to create a smooth, uniform blend.

One more note: Gradients can be done using either a wet-on-wet technique (adding paint to wet paper and blending) or wet-on-dry (adding the paint to dry paper and blending). Wet-on-wet gives you a little extra time because the water on the paper slows down the drying time, but it also dilutes the colors and it can be a little harder to control. Wet-on-dry dries faster, but it keeps the color strength intact and it's a little easier to control. We will be practicing the wet-on-dry version today, but I want you to know you have both options in the future and the technique itself is the same!

EXERCISE 1: GRADIENTS AND BLENDING

Now that we've gone over those four factors, let's jump into a little practice. We will be creating two different blends in this first project: one blend from a paint color to the white of the page, and one blend between two colors. You'll need:

» Cup of water and paper towel

» Watercolor paper (I used a page of my Arches sketchbook)

» Optional: masking tape, pencil

» 2 watercolor paints of choice (I used Indigo and Alizarin Crimson)

» 1 large brush (I used a 10 round)

1   Put a drop of water in each color and give it a minute to soften. In the meantime, divide your paper into two long rectangles. If you like, you can use masking tape to define the edges of each shape, or sketch out two rectangles on your paper.

2   Choose just one color for the first rectangle and mix up a concentrated puddle of paint.

3   Start at the top of your rectangle, and use horizontal brushstrokes to fill in the top quarter of the shape.

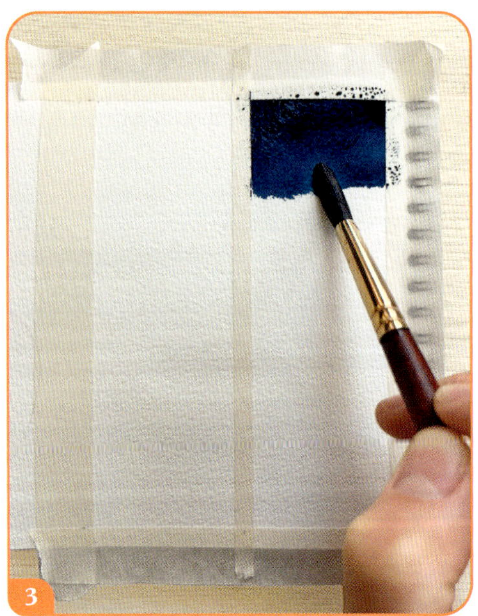

4   Quickly dunk your dirty brush in water (don't swish it) to add water to whatever paint was still on your brush. Fill in the next quarter of the shape using horizontal brushstrokes. The paint should be lighter in color now because you added water to your brush.

5   Swish your dirty brush in your cup of clean water briefly, then fill in the next quarter of the rectangle. The paint should be getting quite light now!

6   Clean your brush completely and use clear water to fill in the last quarter of the rectangle.

7   Once you've reached the bottom of the shape, quickly clean your brush and dab it on a paper towel to remove much of the water. Use your clean damp brush and horizontal strokes to blend the paint through the whole shape, starting from the light end and working your way back up!

8   You can blend the whole shape a couple times if you wish, cleaning your brush off each time and always starting from the lightest area. Once you're happy with the blend, let it dry completely.

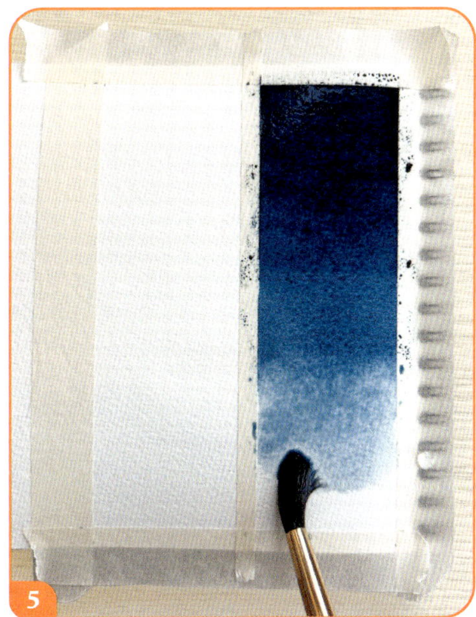

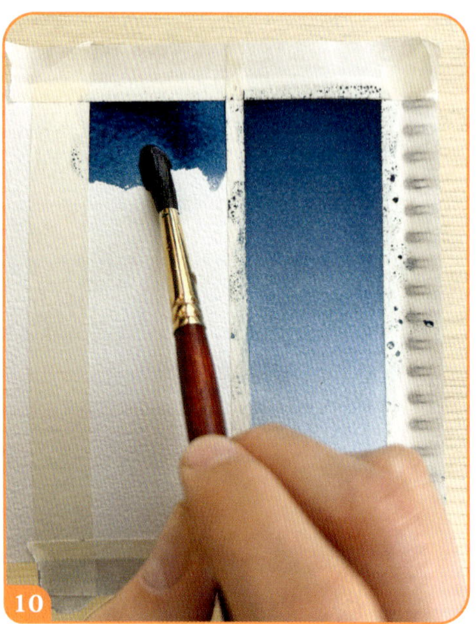

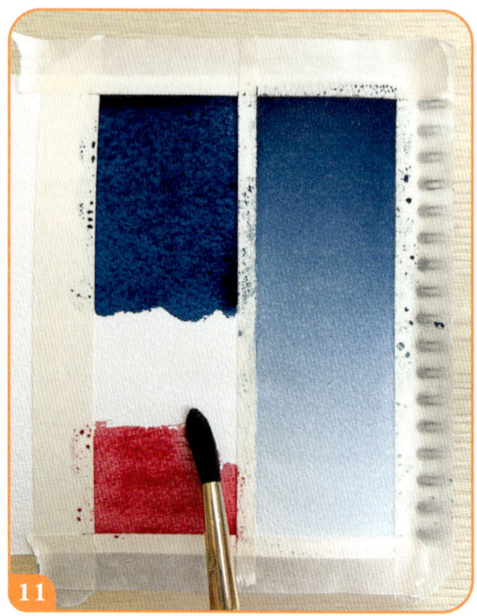

9 Now let's blend between two colors! Mix up a puddle of each of the two colors you've chosen, adding a bit of water to each so the paint flows easily.

10 Load your large brush with one color and fill in half of your second rectangle with it, using horizontal brushstrokes. Be sure to add lots of paint to the paper—it will give you extra drying time!

11 Clean your brush, then switch over to your other color and fill in the other half of the rectangle so that the two colors meet in the middle. Use horizontal brushstrokes to blend the transition.

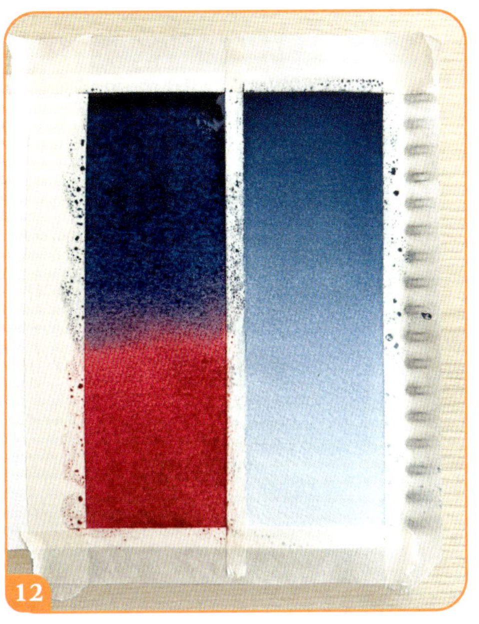

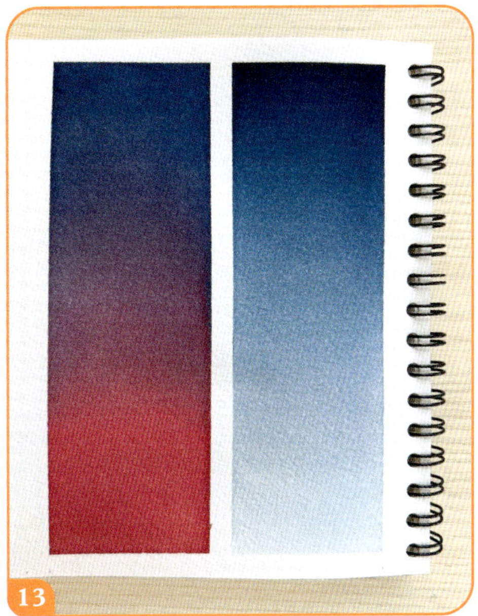

12 Use a clean damp brush to blend continuously from one end of the rectangle to the other using horizontal brushstrokes.

13 Clean the brush and repeat as needed. Let the painting dry once you are happy with it.

NOTE: I recommend starting from the end of the lighter color when doing this; I started from the Alizarin Crimson end and blended toward the Indigo! We do this because darker colors can easily overpower lighter colors. Starting from the lighter end preserves the color!

EXERCISE 2: BEACH SUNSET

Now let's apply what we've just learned to a peaceful beach sunset. I have included the reference photo above—this was a lovely sunset I got to see in South Carolina a few years ago, and it gives us a chance to put our new gradient skills to the test! For this painting, you'll need:

» Cup of water and paper towel

» Watercolor paints: Ultramarine Blue, Yellow Ochre, Alizarin Crimson

» Watercolor paper (I taped a 5 x 5½–inch area [12.5 x 14–cm] in my Arches sketchbook)

» Optional: masking tape, ruler, white gouache paint

» Pencil

» 1 large brush, 1 medium brush, 1 detail brush (I used a 10 round, a 4 round and a 0 round)

1 Put a drop of water in each of the three paint colors and give them a minute to soften. In the meantime, prep your paper and tape out the area you'd like to use for this painting with masking tape if desired.

2 With your pencil (and using a ruler if you'd like) sketch a straight line about one-fifth of the way up from the bottom of your paper. You can place a piece of masking tape right underneath this horizon line to help you get a straight line as you paint the sky.

3 Mix up your colors: a big puddle of concentrated Ultramarine Blue, a puddle of watered-down Yellow Ochre and a puddle of watered-down Alizarin Crimson.

4 Load up your large brush with Ultramarine Blue and fill in the top quarter of your page using horizontal brushstrokes.

5 Dip your brush in water (don't swish) and add a few more horizontal brushstrokes.

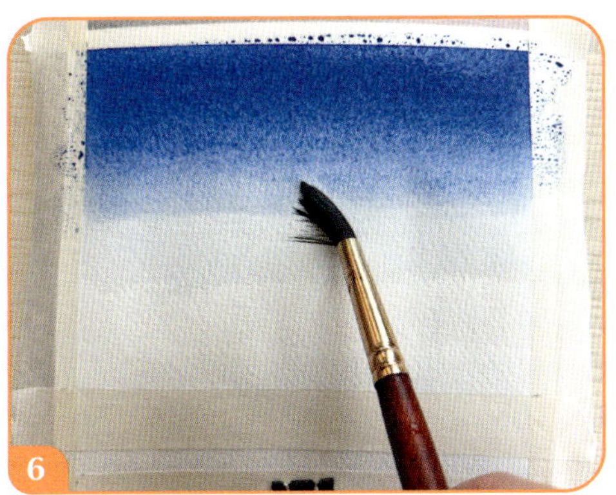

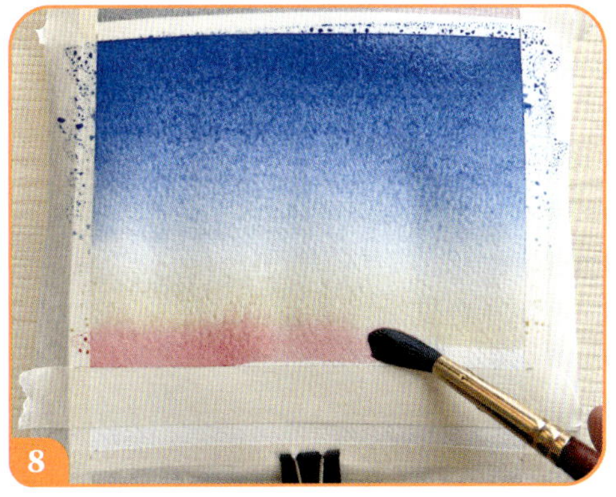

6   Clean your brush and add a few more horizontal brushstrokes with clean water. You should be about halfway down your page at this point and about two-thirds of the way through the sky section.

7   Switch to Yellow Ochre and continue adding horizontal brushstrokes, working down toward the horizon line.

8   Switch to Alizarin Crimson and fill in the rest of the sky section to the horizon line.

9   Quickly use a clean damp brush to blend these three colors together using continuous horizontal brushstrokes, starting at the horizon line and working your way to the top of the page, then let it dry completely.

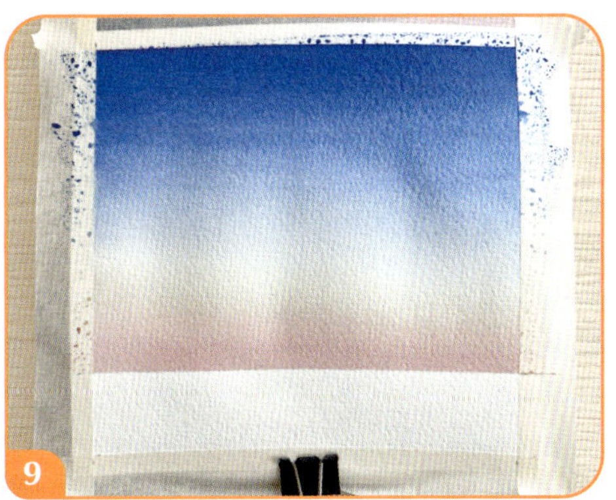

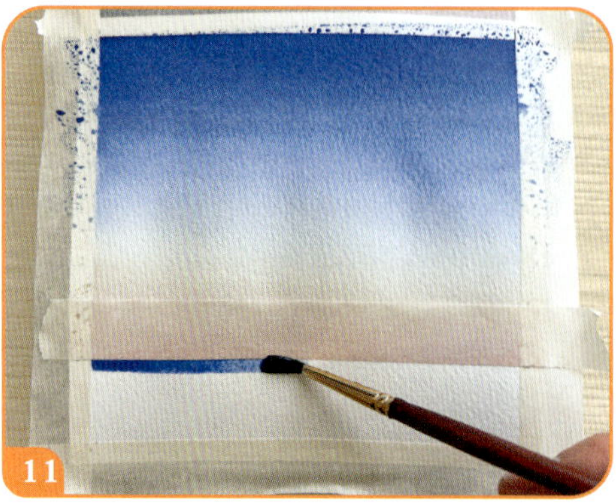

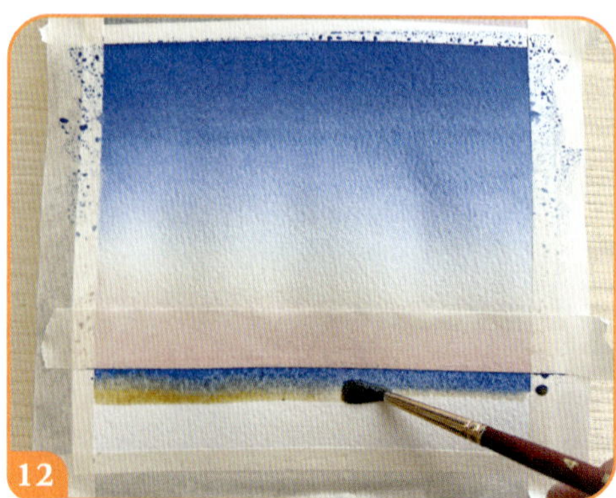

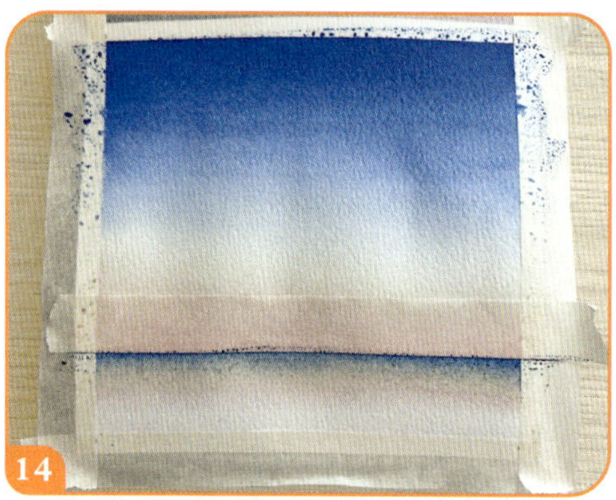

10 Optional: Place a piece of masking tape on the other side of the horizon line.

11 Switching to a smaller brush (I used my 4 round), add one narrow stripe of Ultramarine Blue at the horizon line.

12 Add a horizontal stripe of Yellow Ochre right below the Ultramarine Blue.

13 Add a little extra water to your Alizarin Crimson, then add a stripe of it underneath the Yellow Ochre. This should fill up about half of the area below the horizon line.

14 Use clean water to blend the Alizarin Crimson to the bottom of the page. Use a clean damp brush to blend this mini gradient more if needed, then let it dry completely.

15 Switch to your detail brush and some watered-down Ultramarine Blue to add a few thin horizontal dashes

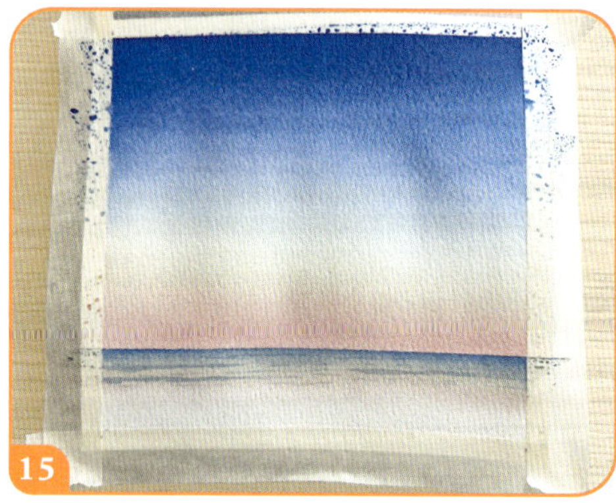

across the water section, creating a subtle wave texture. Use a light touch for most of them, then press down a little harder for a couple of them to simulate larger waves.

16 Mix all three of the colors we used in this painting together to make a purple-gray color, keeping it fairly concentrated. It may take you a minute to find the right proportions for this, so just noodle with it until you're happy.

17 Use your medium brush to paint in the sand on the beach with the purple-gray color you mixed in Step 16. Paint a line going straight across your paper about halfway down the section below the horizon line, then fill in everything below that line. You can also add some extra horizontal lines and small dashes to imitate sandbars sitting slightly out of the water.

18 Add whatever final details you want: I added a small moon in the sky using white gouache and my detail brush, but you could add a flock of birds, an airplane, a hot-air balloon or nothing at all. Whatever floats your boat! Speaking of which, you could even add a boat to your painting!

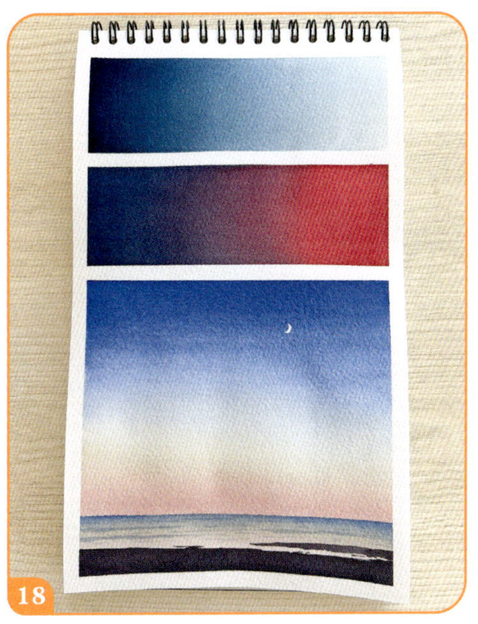

Take a step back and analyze your painting. You had the opportunity to create two different gradients in this piece. How did they turn out? Did you get a smooth blend between the colors? Take a moment to note what went well for you in this painting, along with what could be improved next time!

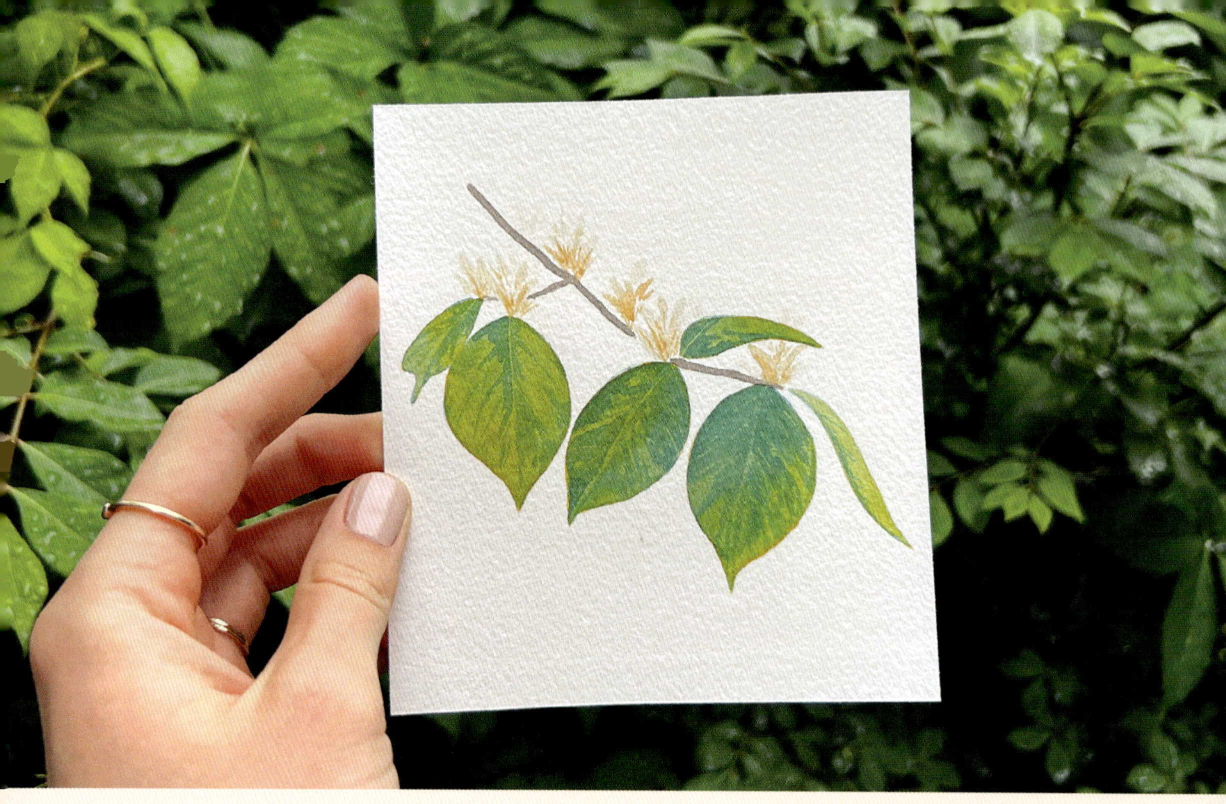

Ogres (and Paintings) Have Layers

One of the best advantages of watercolor paint is its transparency and its ability to layer with itself. Unlike opaque paints like acrylic or gouache, watercolor paints allow the white of the paper and previous layers of paint underneath to shine through. Adding multiple layers allows you to build up color depth, texture and vibrancy slowly and methodically to create a finished piece. Let's briefly discuss a few terms you'll come across in this lesson and how they relate to layering: flat wash, layer and glaze.

A **flat wash** is simply an area filled in with a single color and minimal texture. The paint can be extremely concentrated or very watered down or anything in between, and it's still a flat wash.

A **layer** can be a flat wash, but it could also be a wet-on-wet wash, a wet-on-dry detail or anything else you can think of. A layer simply refers to a single application of paint on the painting. Some areas of a painting may just have one layer; some may have many layers stacked on top of each other.

Finally, a **glaze** refers to a super thin layer of watered-down paint, applied with the intention of altering the color or tone of the layers underneath. A glaze can be applied over an entire painting, part of a painting, or can be used to add very subtle details in smaller areas of a painting.

In today's exercises, we are going to experiment with layering and glazing, then use these techniques to create a cute honeysuckle study. I highly recommend grabbing a hair dryer for these watercolor studies unless you'd like to spend an hour watching paint dry!

EXERCISE 1: LAYER UP!

For our first experiment today, we are going to practice layering a single color on top of itself to create depth and value. You'll need:

» Cup of water and paper towel

» Watercolor paint: 1 color (I used Aqua Green)

» 1 brush (I used a 4 round)

» Watercolor paper (I used a page of my Arches sketchbook)

1 Put a drop of water in your chosen color and give it a minute to soften. Then mix up a puddle of paint, adding a decent amount of water so the paint isn't super dark.

2 Paint a long rectangle across your paper. Let it dry completely.

3 Using the same paint mixture, paint over about three-quarters of the long rectangle. Let it dry completely.

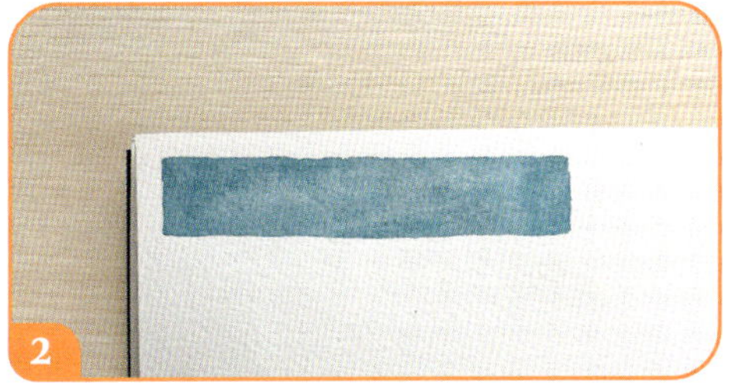

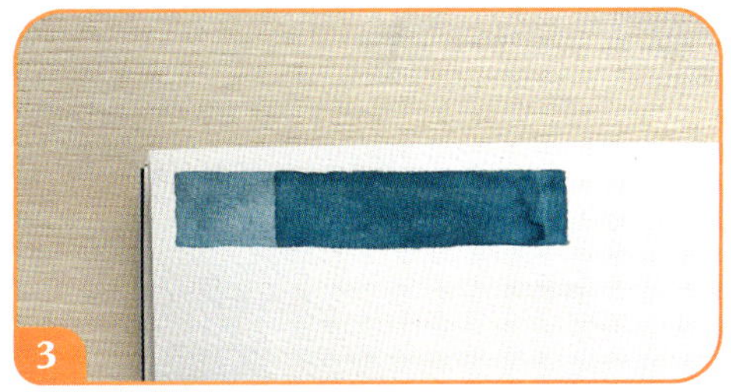

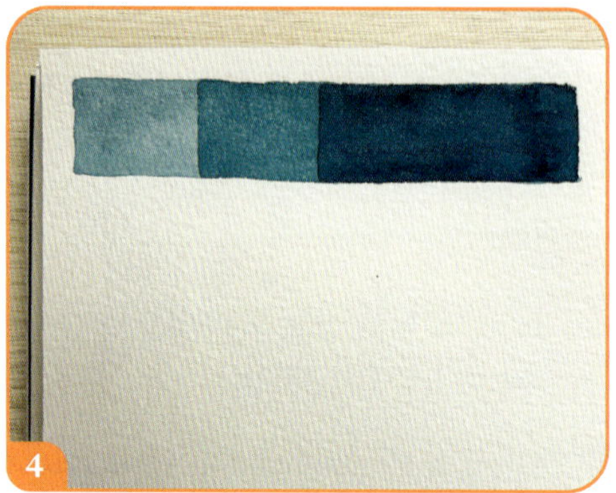

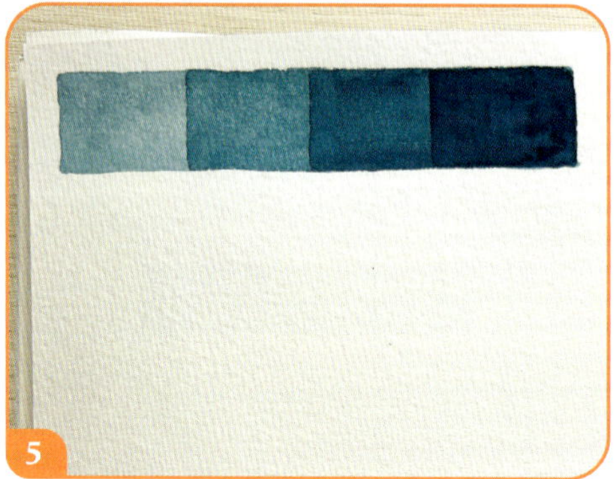

4   Again using the same paint mixture (mixing more if you need to), paint over about half of the long rectangle. Let it dry completely.

5   Finally, paint over about one-quarter of the rectangle. Let it dry completely. Notice how even though you used the same paint mixture each time, each additional layer created a darker value on the page.

For our second exercise, you'll need:

»   Cup of water and paper towel

»   Three watercolor paints: Cadmium Yellow, Magenta, Phthalo Blue

»   Pencil

»   1 brush (I used a 4 round)

»   Watercolor paper (I used a page of my Arches sketchbook)

1   Add a drop of water to each of the three colors listed above and give them a minute to soften.

2   Sketch three overlapping circles on your paper using your pencil.

3   Mix up a puddle of each of the three colors in your mixing area, again adding a decent amount of water to each.

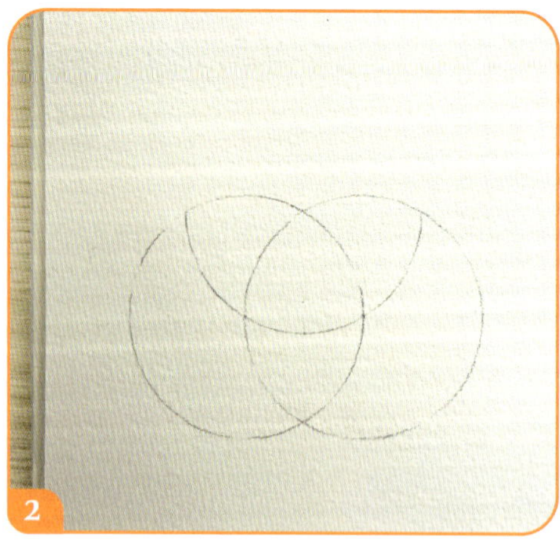

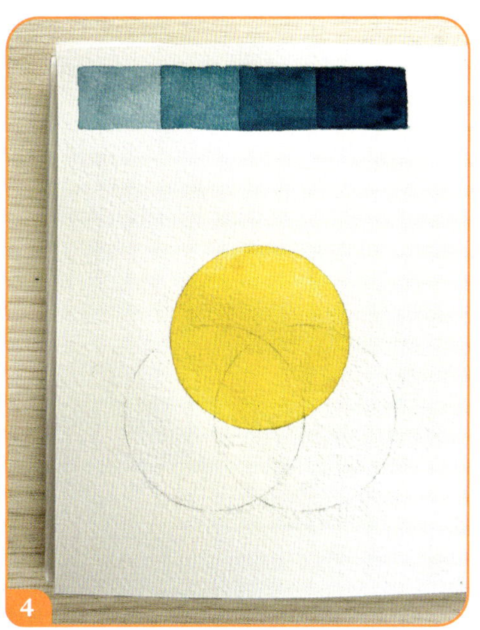

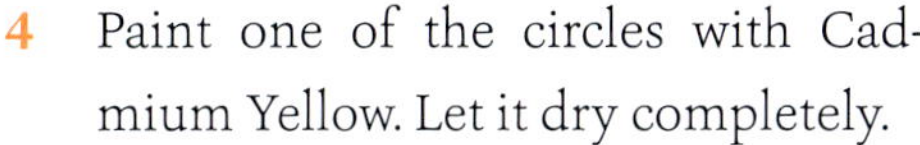

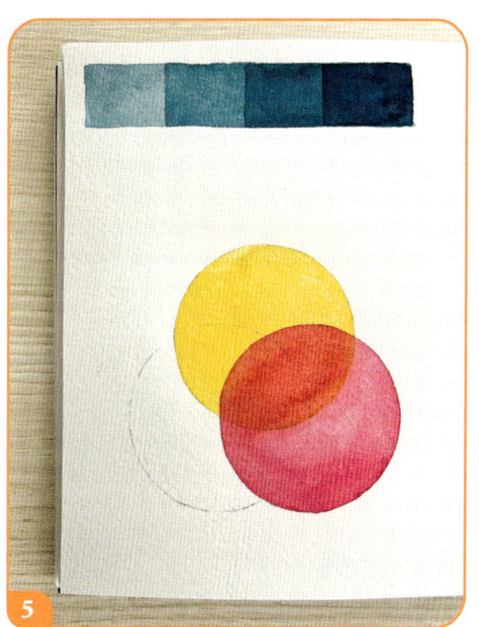

4   Paint one of the circles with Cadmium Yellow. Let it dry completely.

5   Paint the next circle with Magenta, overlapping with the yellow circle. Try not to overwork the area where the colors overlap! Let it dry completely.

6   Paint the last circle with Phthalo Blue, again not overworking any areas that overlap with the other colors. Let it dry completely.

7   Notice how you've created secondary (orange, green and purple) colors just by layering two colors on top of each other! This is a super cool effect called glazing, which can help create depth and luminosity when painting!

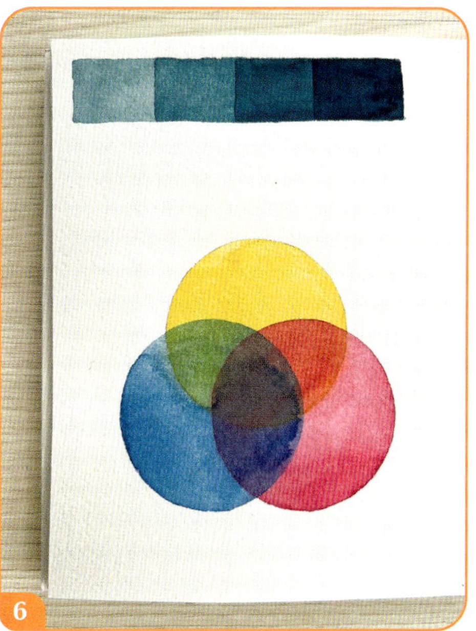

EXERCISE 3: HONEYSUCKLE

For our last layering exercise, we will be painting a little study of a branch of honeysuckle. You'll need:

» Cup of water and paper towel

» Watercolor paints: Cadmium Yellow, Phthalo Blue, Van Dyke Brown, Ultramarine Blue

» Pencil

» Watercolor paper (I used a 5 x 5½–inch [12.7 x 14-cm] piece of Arches paper)

» Watercolor brushes: 1 medium and 1 detail brush (I used a 4 round and a 2 round)

1   Put a drop of water in each of your watercolor paints and give them a minute to soften.

2   Lightly sketch out the main branch of honeysuckle using the reference photo as a guide, focusing on the five or six main leaves you see in the foreground.

3   Mix up a puddle of Cadmium Yellow, adding a bit of water but keeping a pretty strong color mixture.

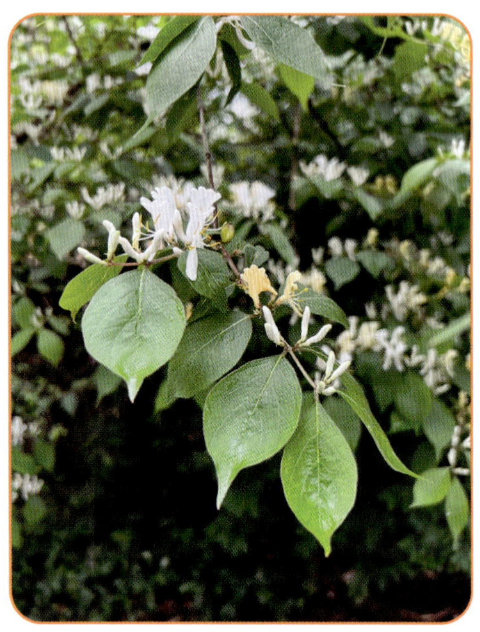

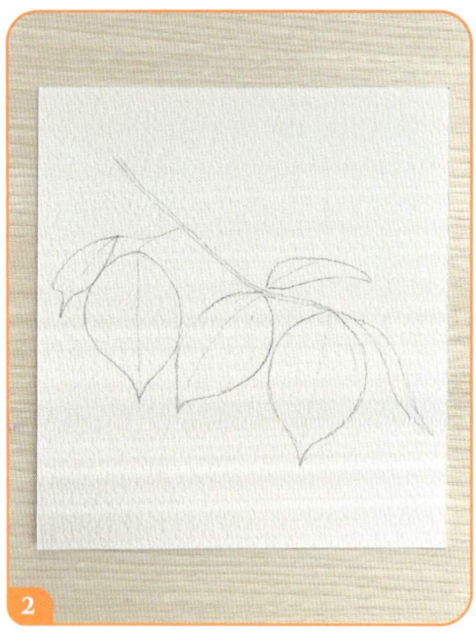

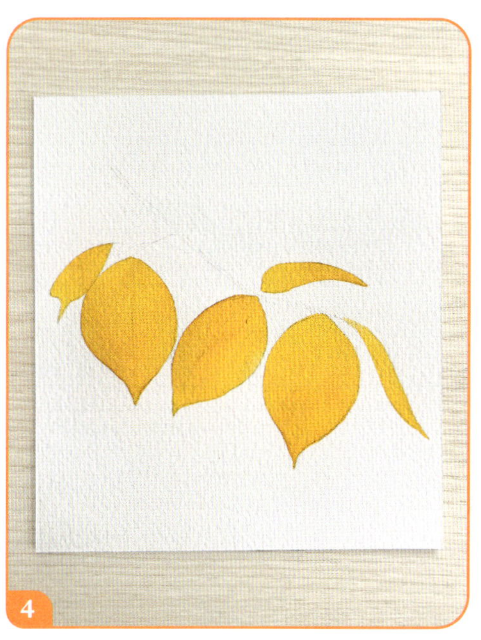

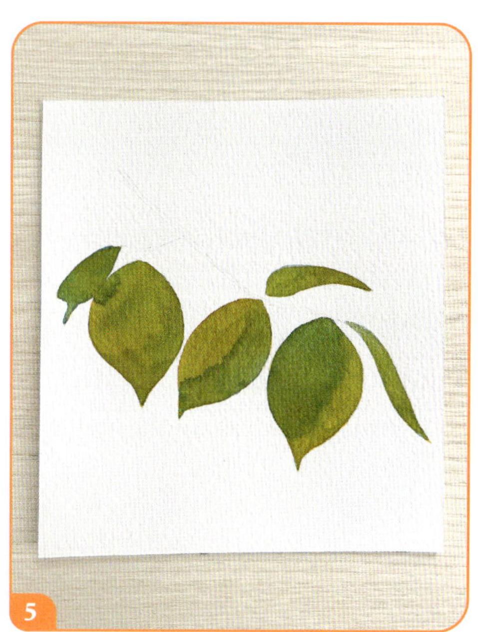

4   Use a medium brush and paint a flat wash of yellow over each leaf. Let it dry completely.

5   Mix a fairly watered-down puddle of Phthalo Blue, then use your medium brush to glaze a thin layer of blue paint over each leaf. The layering of these two colors should produce a green hue. It's important to work in thin, watered-down layers here because blue paint is so much stronger than yellow paint. Let it dry completely.

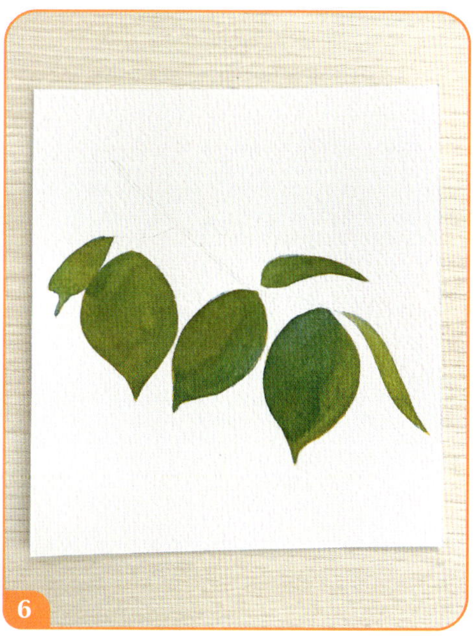

6   If you want a deeper green color, add another thin layer of Phthalo Blue paint. I did this on each leaf except the ones on the far edges. Let it dry completely.

7   Switch to a detail brush and continue using the same watered-down Phthalo Blue mixture to add some shadows and veins to each leaf. I didn't do any blending here—I just followed the general direction of the center vein and the veins branching out.

8   To add the honeysuckle, mix Cadmium Yellow with a little Van Dyke Brown and add plenty of water. Use a detail brush to add some clumps of petals that extend vertically from the branch.

9   Use a slightly stronger mixture of the previous color (add just a little more paint) and layer on a few more petals.

10 Mix a neutral brown color combining Van Dyke Brown and Ultramarine Blue, add some water and paint in a thin branch connecting the leaves and clumps of honeysuckle.

Great job! Notice how using those thin glazes to paint the leaves gives them a depth and luminosity you wouldn't get by painting them with a pre-mixed green color. Of course, you may not always want that effect, and it is time consuming, but it is a cool technique to have in your back pocket.

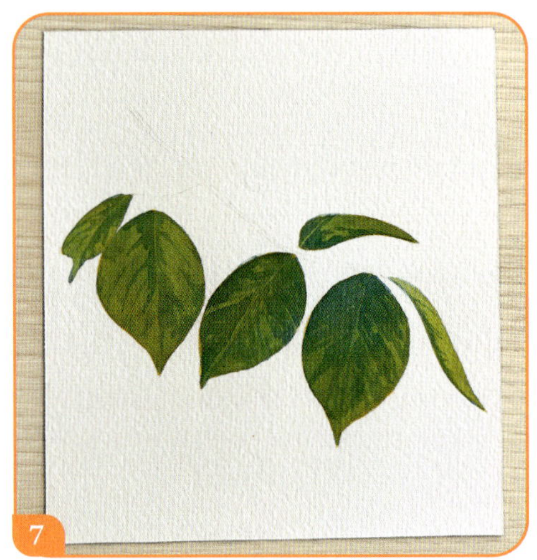

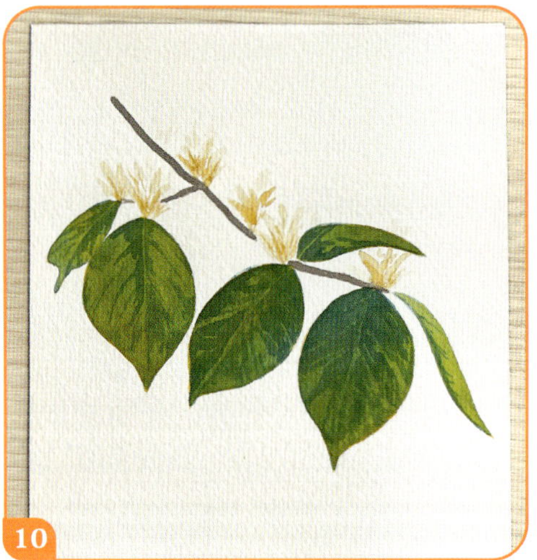

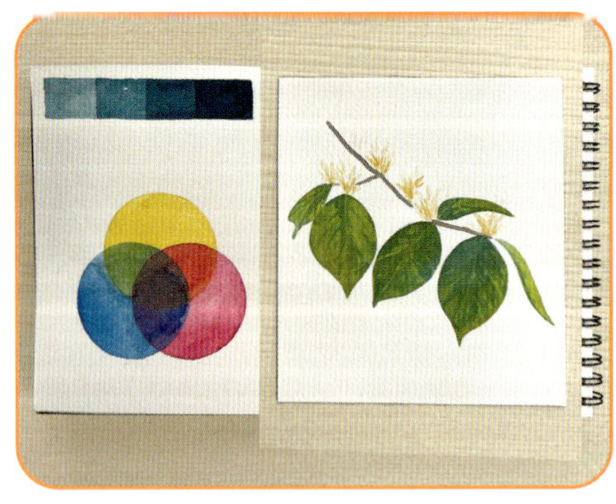

Texturize It

So far in this chapter, we've reviewed the traditional ways of using watercolor paint. But we have really only scratched the surface of everything watercolor paint is capable of. With a few household items and some slight changes in technique, there are tons of really cool textures and techniques you can add to your toolkit. Let's chat about four of my favorites before we dive in.

Dry brushing: The name is a bit of a misnomer, because your brush will still be wet, but only slightly. To create this texture, you'll remove most of the paint from your brush, then use the side of the brush to scrape paint onto your paper. The texture of watercolor paper helps grab pigment and create a rough, broken texture. I love using this technique to add texture to water scenes, grass, rock formations and a bunch more. It's super versatile, and a great way to quickly add organic texture to a painting.

Plastic wrap: Yeah, you read that right. By adding a little plastic wrap (or cling film, as some people call it) to wet paint and allowing it to dry, you can create some super interesting textures, which you can then use to inspire the rest of your painting.

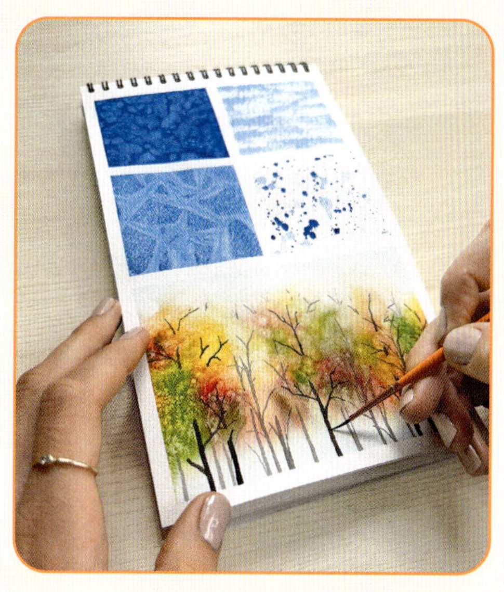

Salt: Sprinkling a little bit of salt onto wet watercolor paint is another way to add an interesting texture. Each grain of salt absorbs the water and pigment, creating a small light bloom as the paint dries. I love adding this texture when painting a cloudy sky, a forest or even a field of flowers!

Splatter: Loading the brush with paint then tapping your brush handle to flick the droplets onto the paper is not only so much fun, it's also a great way to add a loose, energetic texture to your painting. I love using this texture to paint things like moving water, snow or rain, loose flowers or trees.

In today's exercises, you'll test out these four fun watercolor textures for yourself, then use them to create a loose and expressive autumn forest!

EXERCISE 1: UNIQUE WATERCOLOR TEXTURES

Let's start with a little experiment into each of the four new textures. For this first project you'll need:

» Cup of water and paper towel

» Watercolor paint: 1 color (I used Phthalo Blue)

» Watercolor paper

» Optional: masking tape, pencil

» 1 large brush (I used a 10 round)

» Table salt

» Plastic wrap

1 Place a drop of water in the color you've chosen to use and give it a minute to soften. In the meantime, divide your paper into four sections. I used masking tape to outline the sections, but you can also just sketch four rectangles on your page and paint within those.

2 Mix up a puddle of paint in your mixing area, adding enough water so the paint flows easily.

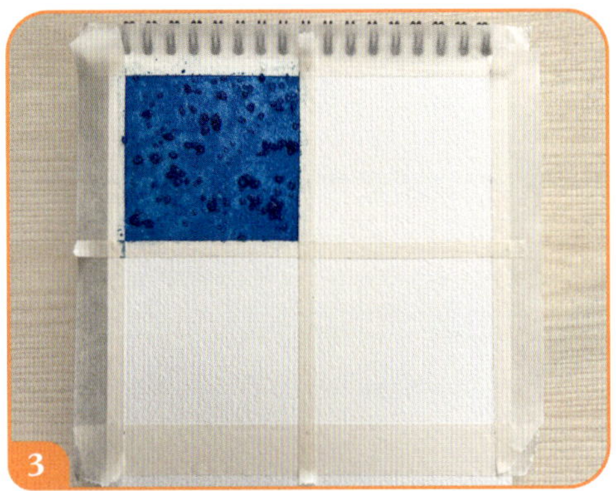

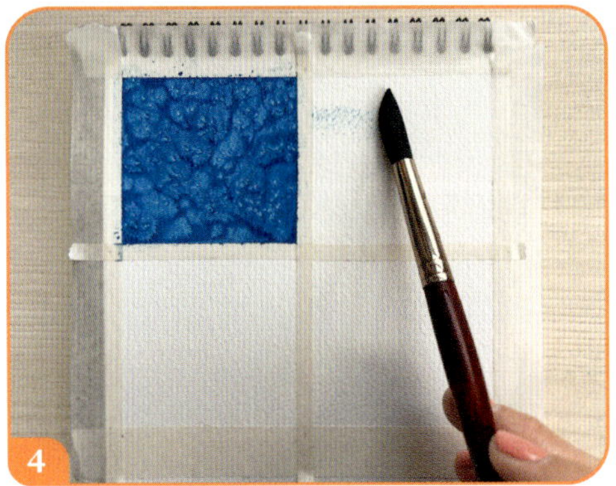

Salt

3 Fill your first section with a flat wash of paint. While the paint is still wet, sprinkle salt into the paint. Move on to Step 4 while the paint air dries.

Dry Brushing

4 Load some paint on your brush, then touch your brush to your paper towel several times to remove most of the paint. Hold your brush nearly parallel to the paper and slightly scrape the side of it along the paper to create a rough, broken texture. Let this dry before moving on.

Plastic Wrap

5   Cut a piece of plastic wrap slightly bigger than your next section of paper. Paint in a flat wash of color, then lay the plastic wrap on top of the wet paint. Scrunch the plastic wrap slightly to get even more texture. Leave it alone to dry for at least 15 to 20 minutes, ideally longer if you can wait.

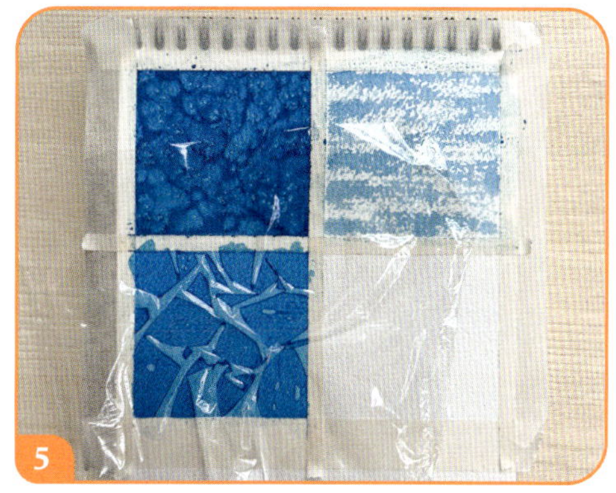

Splatter

6   Load up your brush with paint, then hold the brush a couple inches above the paper and tap it firmly with a finger. The paint should splatter down in random droplets. You can repeat this process with clean water on the brush, and the clean water droplets will interact with the still-wet paint droplets on the paper to create a multi-toned splatter effect.

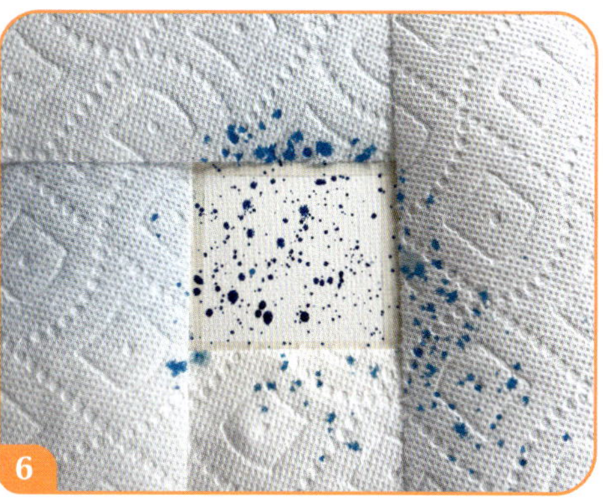

7   Once your salt section is completely dry, gently brush the salt off the page to reveal the texture.

NOTE: This technique will result in paint droplets on your hands, clothes and work surface. Lay down paper towels or scrap paper on your work surface to protect it, wear clothes you don't care about and wash your hands after painting!

NOTE: Different types of salt can interact with the paint in different ways. If you have more than one kind of salt at home, feel free to experiment to see the differences in texture.

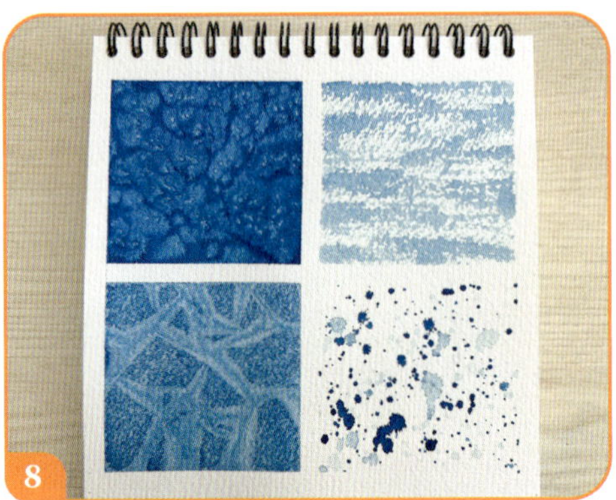

8 Once the plastic wrap section has dried for at least 15 to 20 minutes, gently peel away the plastic wrap and let the paint underneath dry all the way.

EXERCISE 2: AUTUMN FOREST

Let's put a couple of the techniques we just learned into practice with this autumn forest study. You'll need:

» Cup of water and paper towel

» Watercolor paints: Cadmium Yellow, Alizarin Crimson, Sap Green, Van Dyke Brown

» Watercolor paper (I used a 3¾ x 5½-inch [9.5 x 14-cm] section of my Arches sketchbook)

» Optional: masking tape

» 1 large brush and 1 detail brush (I used a 10 round and a 2 round)

» Table salt

1 Add a drop of water to each of your colors and give them a minute to soften. In the meantime, prepare your paper, taping the sides with masking tape if you want.

2 Mix up puddles of each of the four colors in your mixing palette, adding just a little water to keep the paint colors concentrated.

3 Cover your paper with a layer of clean water from your cup.

4 Load your brush with Cadmium Yellow and place some blobs across the page, leaving some blank space at the top and bottom. Try to create loose tree shapes here.

5   Wash your brush and switch to Alizarin Crimson and layer some blobs on top of the yellow ones.

6   Wash your brush, switch to Sap Green and repeat, adding a few dots and blobs among the other colors.

7   Feel free to go back to any of these three colors and add some paint splatter texture into this painting. The paint droplets will blend out with the wet paint and water on the paper and create a nice subtle texture. Be sure to protect any places you don't want paint droplets with paper towels.

8   While everything is still wet, sprinkle some salt throughout these blobs of color. Let the page dry completely.

NOTE: You can still use a hair dryer to speed up the drying time, but be sure to hold it high above the page so you don't blow the salt off the paper.

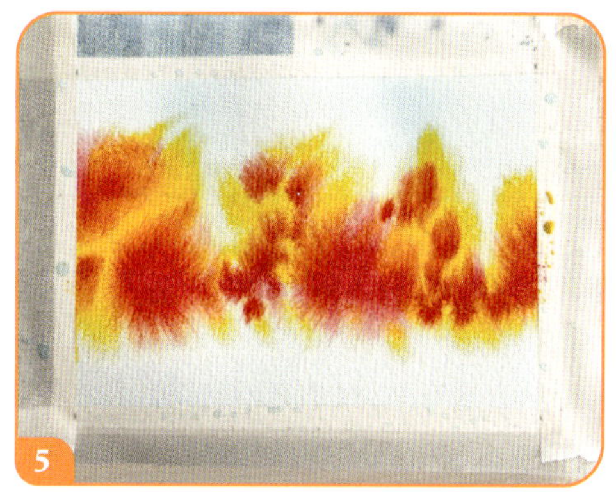

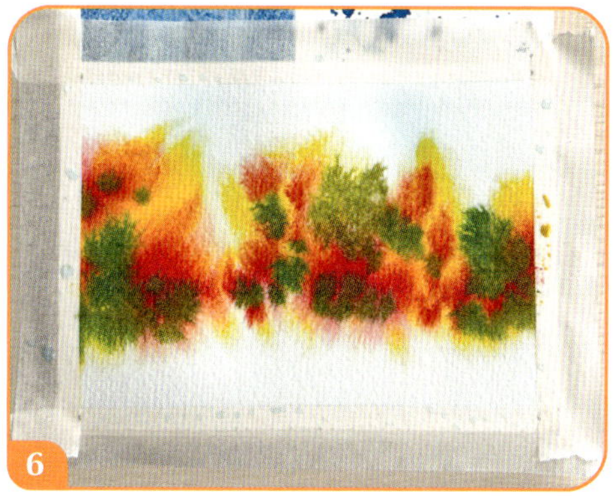

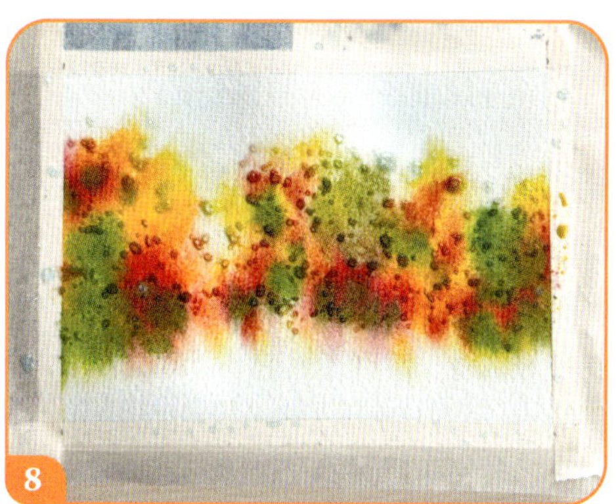

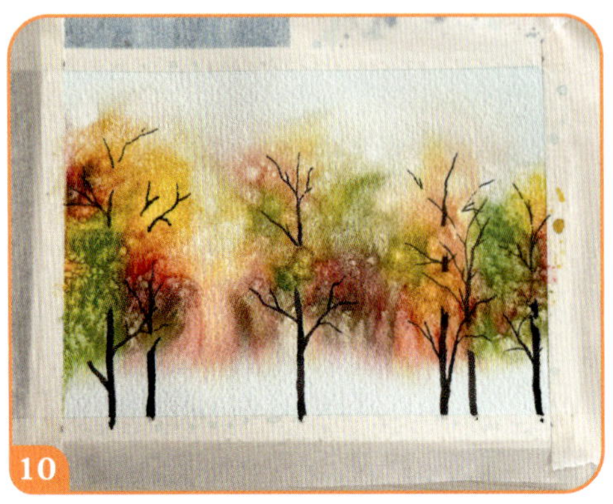

9   Once the paper is completely dry, gently scrape the salt off the page.

10   Mix up some fairly concentrated Van Dyke Brown on your mixing palette, then use your detail brush to add in a few tree trunks and branches to your painting. I like to skip painting some sections of the trunk and branches to make it look like they're hidden by foliage.

11   Water down your Van Dyke Brown to add a few more tree trunks and branches that look farther in the distance.

You've added four new textures to your watercolor toolbox! Take a moment to review both the textures from Exercise 1 and your autumn forest painting from Exercise 2. Which textures were the most successful for you? Which do you like the best? Remember, you can always refer back to this lesson and your own work in the future to refresh your memory on these four textures.

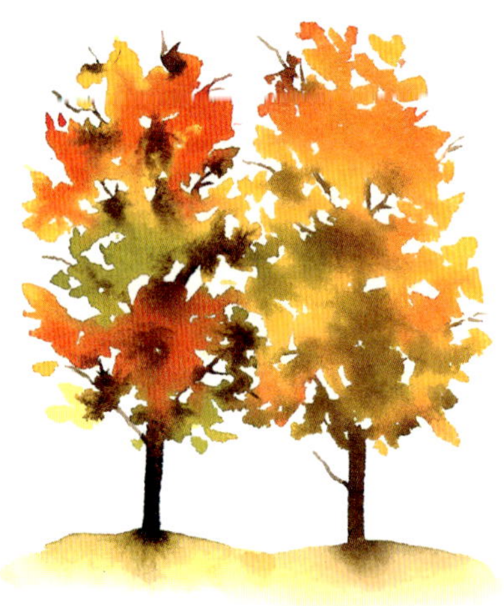

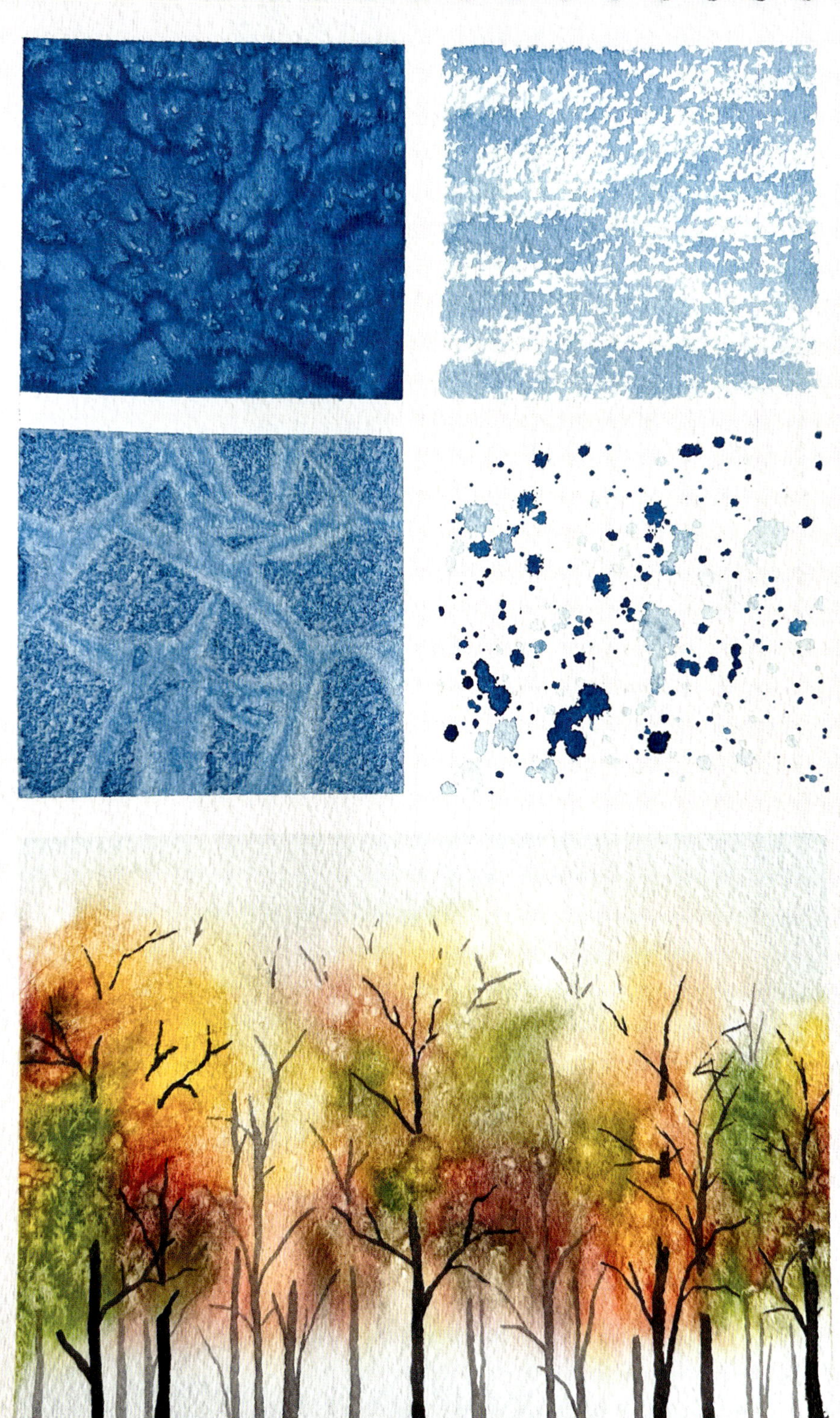

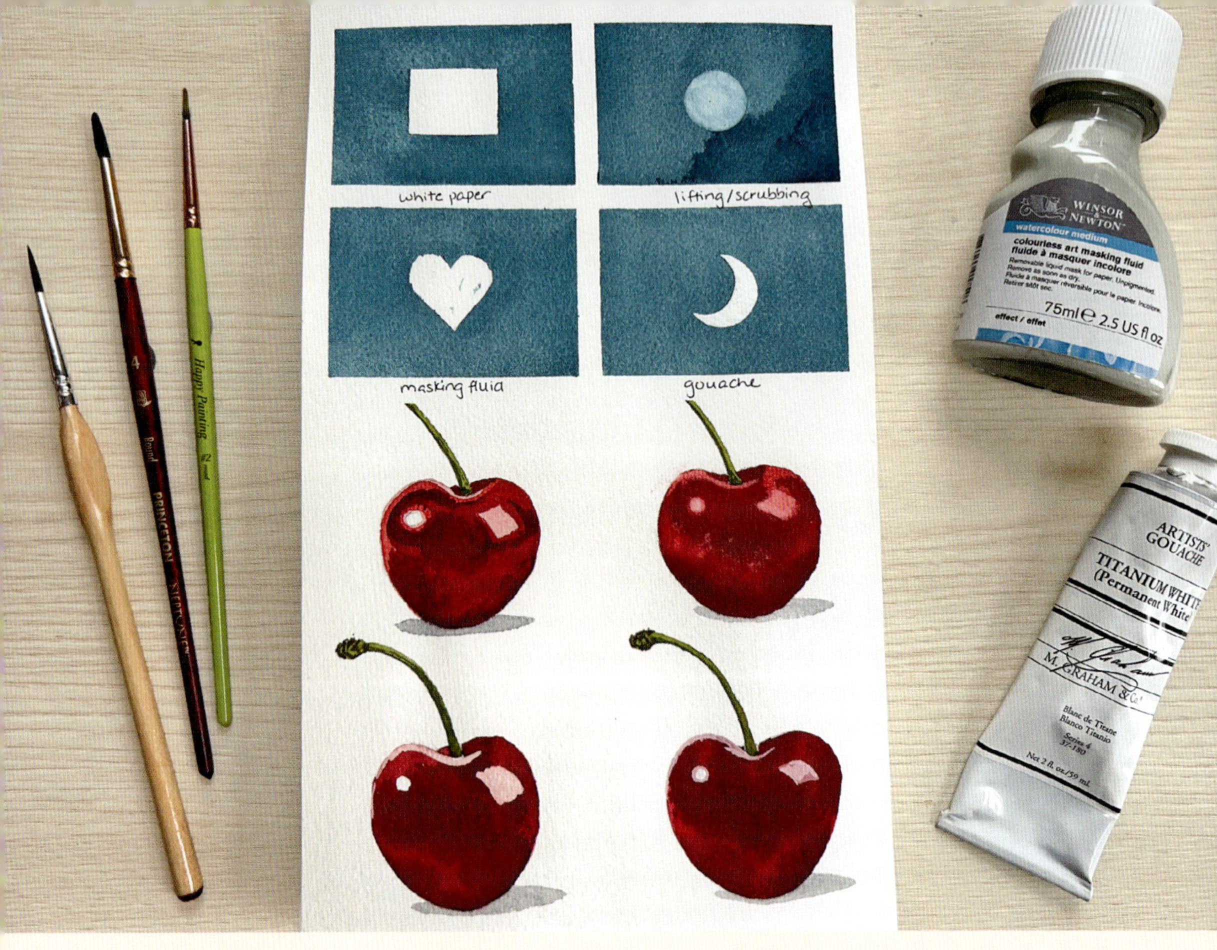

Highlight Reel

Nearly every painting requires high-lights—they are the lightest parts of the painting showing places hit by direct light, and they add a great sparkle to any object and provide good contrast with the darkest parts of a painting. Highlights in watercolor paintings can be tricky, though; watercolor is a transparent medium, which means you can't paint light paint on top of dark and expect it to show up. Traditional watercolor requires you to work from the lightest parts of your painting to the darkest, building up layers of paint to get there. Today we are going to practice four different ways to create highlights in your paintings and discuss the pros and cons of each. Note that no single one of these is better than another; it all comes down to preference for each artist.

White paper: painting around any areas you want to highlight, leaving those parts of the paper empty. This is the most "traditional" route, but can be tricky when working with lots of layers or when you want delicate, tiny highlights that are hard to paint around.

Scrubbing and lifting: a way of removing paint from the paper either while the painting is wet (lifting) or after the paint is dry (scrubbing and lifting). This technique is nice for adding highlights at the end of a painting or correcting mistakes, but it is very difficult to get the highlight back to the pure white color of the paper.

Masking fluid: a special formula of liquid latex that can be painted onto your paper. Once dry, it creates a watertight seal over the paper it's applied to, and you can paint over it as much as you want. When you want the highlight back, simply rub the masking fluid with a finger or an eraser to remove it. It's nice to not have to worry about painting around your highlights and know that the pure white paper is protected, but it requires that you know exactly where the highlights will need to be at the start of your painting. Also be aware that masking fluid can wreak havoc on the paintbrush you use to apply it. Make sure to use an inexpensive brush you don't care about, then immediately wash it with warm water and dish soap to keep it in the best shape possible!

NOTE: If you don't have masking fluid, you can create a similar effect using masking tape and an X-ACTO® knife. Cover the area with a piece of masking tape, then use the X-ACTO knife to gently cut out the shape you want. Do your best to only cut through the masking tape and not the paper underneath. Peel away the excess masking tape and you should be left with tape covering your shape. Then paint over the area as normal and remove the masking tape when you're done!

White gouache: Gouache is an opaque, water-based paint that works well with watercolor. You can use it straight out of the tube or tint it with your watercolor paint to create colored highlights. This is the least "traditional" method because it requires using another medium and sometimes the opaque gouache paint can look funky with the transparent watercolor paint, but it's very easy and convenient to use and can look really nice when used in small doses.

Now that we've discussed these four techniques, let's give them a try and you can form your own opinions. You'll need:

» Cup of water and paper towel

» Watercolor paint: 1 color (I used Aqua Green)

» Watercolor paper (I used a page of my Arches sketchbook)

» Pencil

» Optional: masking tape

» Medium watercolor brush (I used a 4 round)

» Masking fluid and a brush you don't care about of any size to apply it (you can use masking tape and an X-ACTO knife instead if you prefer)

» White gouache (I used Titanium White from M. Graham)

1. Place a drop of water into your chosen color and give it a minute to soften. In the meantime, create four rectangular sections on your paper either by sketching them with a pencil or using masking tape to mark the boundaries.

2. Lightly sketch a shape in each of the four rectangles—it can be as simple as a square in each section, or you can be more creative with your shapes.

3. Mix up a puddle of your paint color, adding enough water so the paint will flow.

White Paper

4. Choose one rectangular section to start with and simply paint the area around your sketched shape.

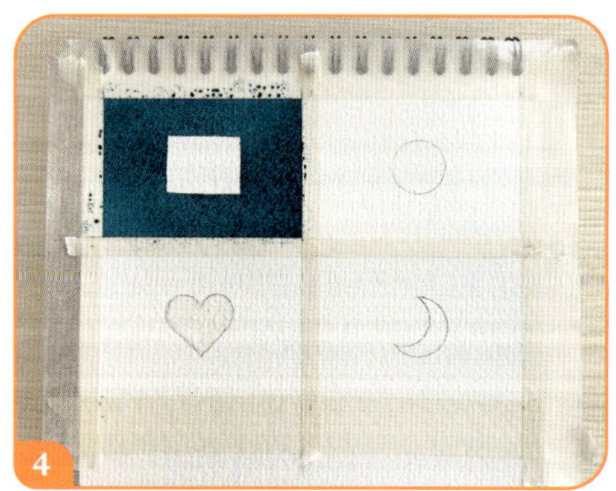

Scrubbing and Lifting

5   Move to your second rectangular section and paint the entire thing with a flat wash of paint, then let it dry completely. Use a damp brush to scrub the area within your shape for a couple seconds, then immediately dab the area with a clean paper towel to remove the paint from your paper. Repeat this process until the inside of your shape is as light as you can make it.

You can also experiment with lifting while the paint is still wet. To give this a try, put down some paint then use a completely dry brush to remove pigment where you want a lighter area. Keep your brush dry by squeezing it with a paper towel as you work, and continue lifting until the area is as light as you can get it.

Masking Fluid

6   Use a brush you don't care about to cover the shape with a thin layer of masking fluid. Let the masking fluid dry completely, then paint a flat wash over the whole rectangular section. Let the paint dry completely, then gently rub a finger or an eraser over the masked area to remove the masking fluid.

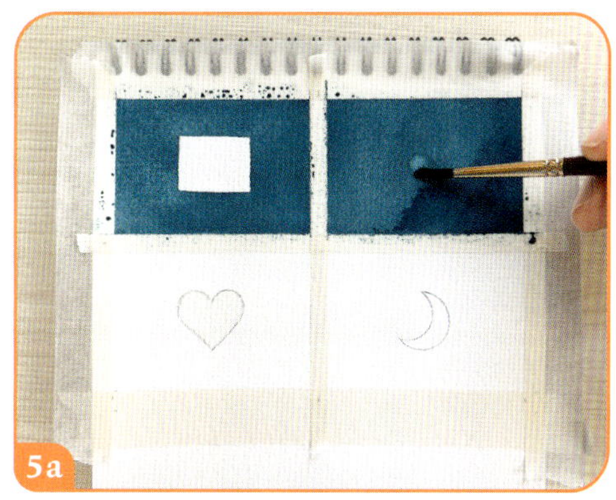

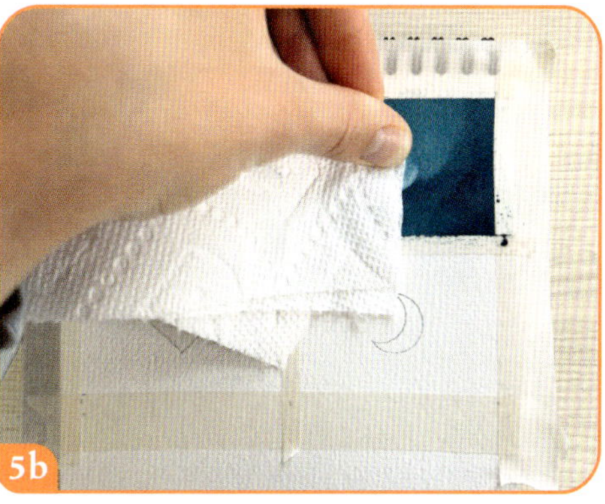

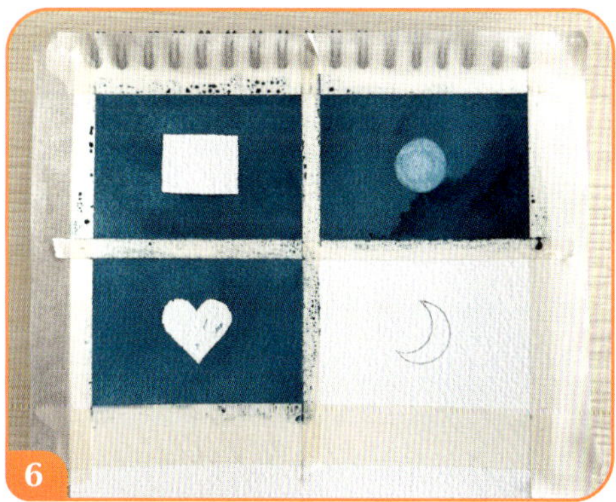

White Gouache

7   Fill in your last rectangular section with a flat wash of paint and let it dry completely. Then use white gouache to fill in the shape you sketched. Try not to overwork the paper here—sometimes gouache can reactivate the watercolor underneath if you scrub at it too much!

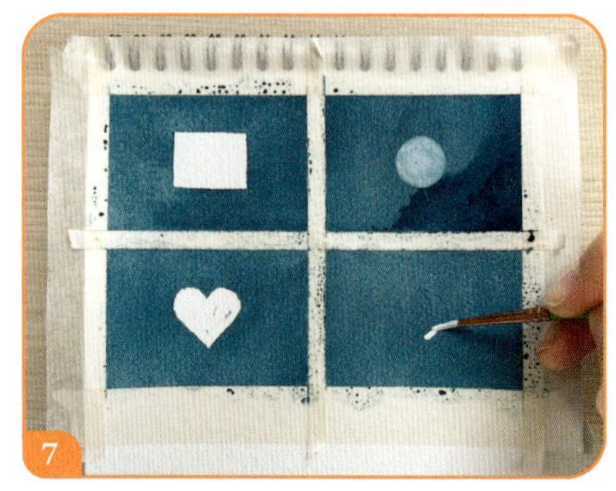

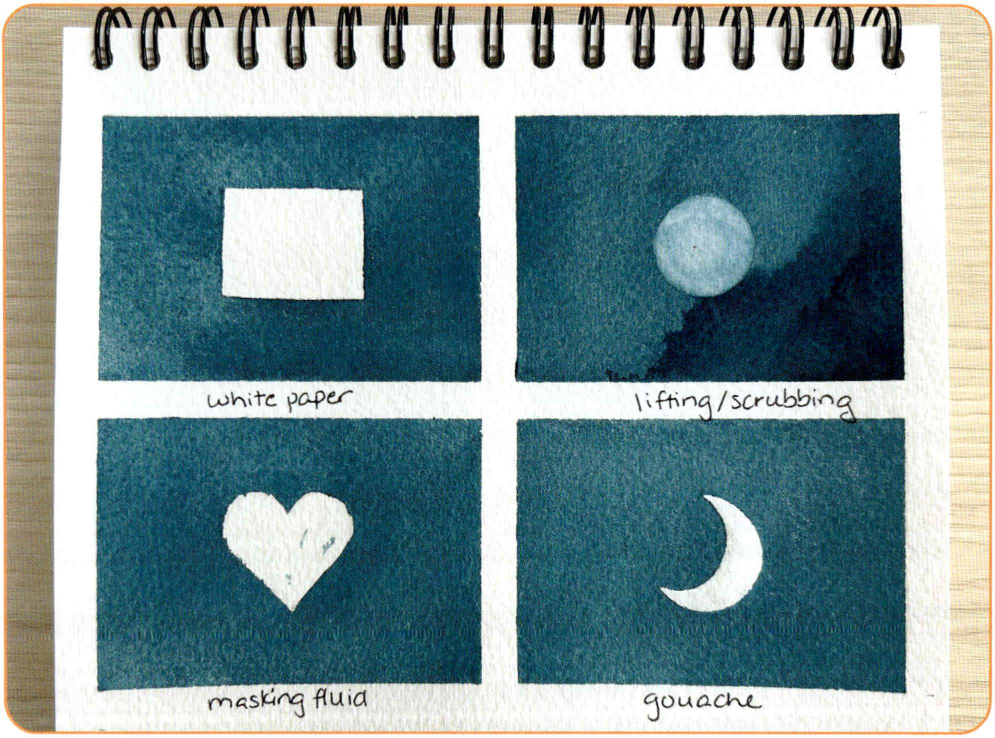

EXERCISE 2: CHERRY BOMB

Let's put all four of these highlight techniques to the test with a more realistic study! For this project, you'll need:

» Cup of water and paper towel

» Watercolor paints: Alizarin Crimson, Cadmium Red, Ultramarine Blue, Sap Green, Van Dyke Brown

» Pencil

» Optional: masking tape

» Watercolor paper

» 1 medium and 1 detail watercolor brush (I used a 4 round and a 2 round)

» Masking fluid and a brush you don't care about to apply it (you can use masking tape and an X-ACTO knife instead if you prefer)

» White gouache (I used Titanium White from M. Graham)

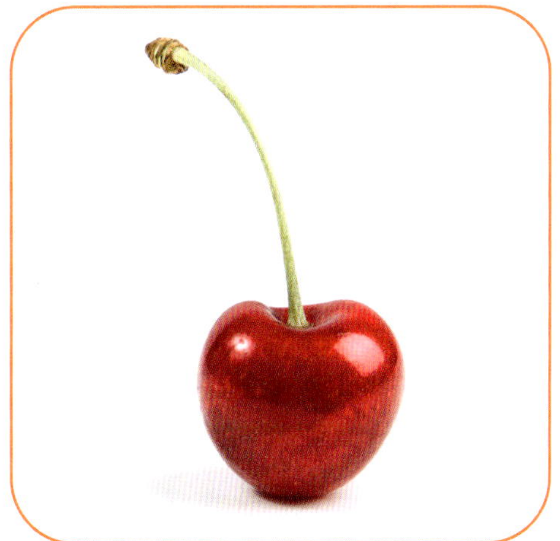

1. Add a drop of water to each of your watercolor paints and give them a minute to soften. In the meantime, sketch out four cherries on your paper using the reference photo as a guide. Be sure to lightly outline the highlights of the cherry in your sketches. You can see I included three highlight areas in my sketches on page 114: the bright white circle on the top left of the cherry, the slightly dimmer rectangular shape on the top right and the very edge of the cherry on the top left.

2. Mix up three colors for the cherries: a light red combining Alizarin Crimson and Cadmium Red plus lots of water, a bright red using the same color combo but adding less water, and a dark red combining the same colors again plus a little Ultramarine Blue.

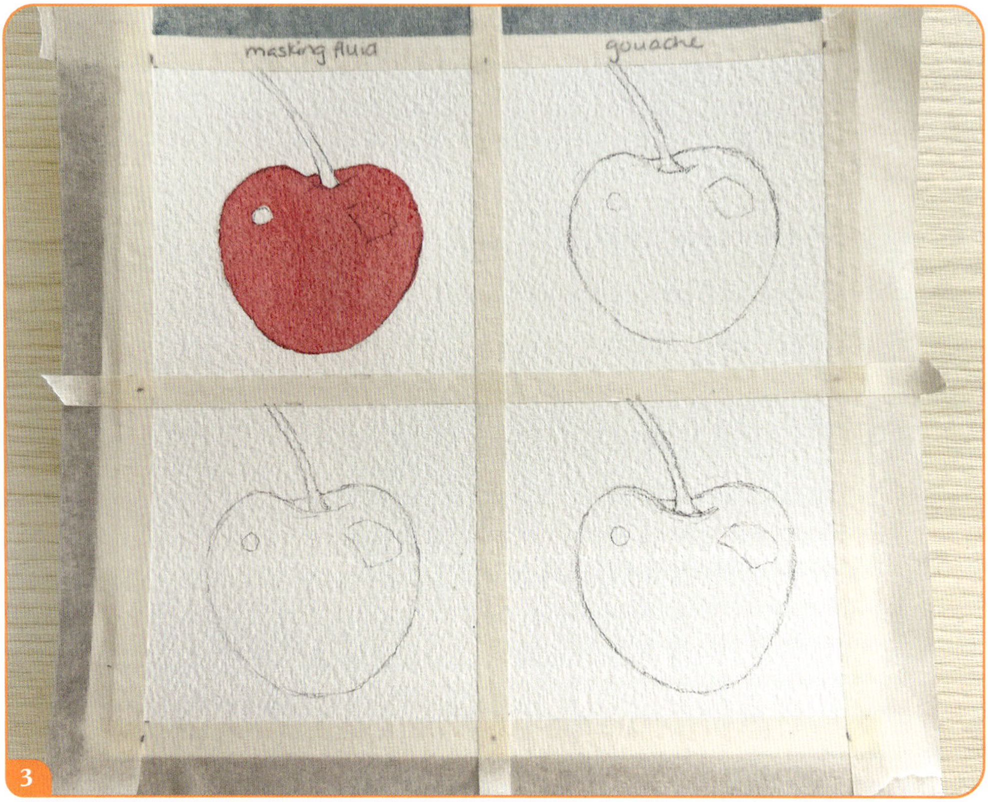

White Paper

3   For our first cherry, we will practice
    painting around the highlights. Start
    with the light red color you mixed
    and fill in the whole cherry with your
    medium brush, avoiding only the
    circular highlight on the top left of
    the cherry. Let it dry completely.

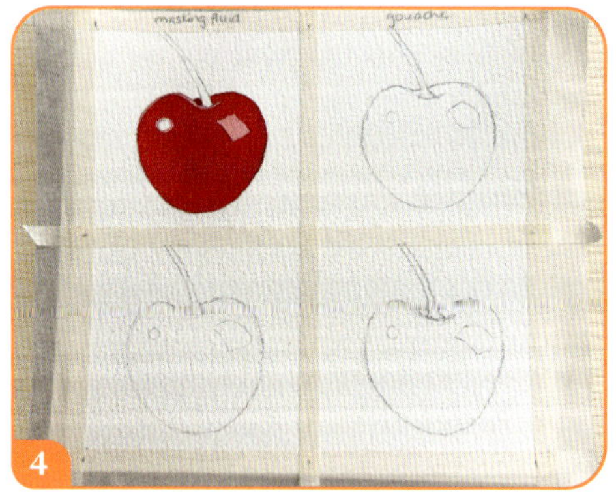

4   Switch to your bright red and add
    in another layer of paint, this time
    avoiding all three highlight shapes.

5 Switch to your dark red and add in some shadows throughout the middle and bottom of the cherry, plus the area where the stem attaches. Do this while the previous layer is still wet so the two colors blend together.

Scrubbing and Lifting

6 Moving on to our scrubbing and lifting technique, this time start with the bright red color and fill in the whole cherry shape, then quickly switch to the dark red color to add shadows and allow the two colors to mix a bit. Then let it dry completely.

7 Switch to a clean damp detail brush, scrub an area where you want a highlight for a few seconds, then press a paper towel to the area to lift the pigment. Repeat this process until your highlights are as light as you want them.

Masking Fluid

8 For the third cherry, we will practice using our masking fluid. First, paint over only the circular highlight at the top left of the cherry and let the masking fluid dry completely.

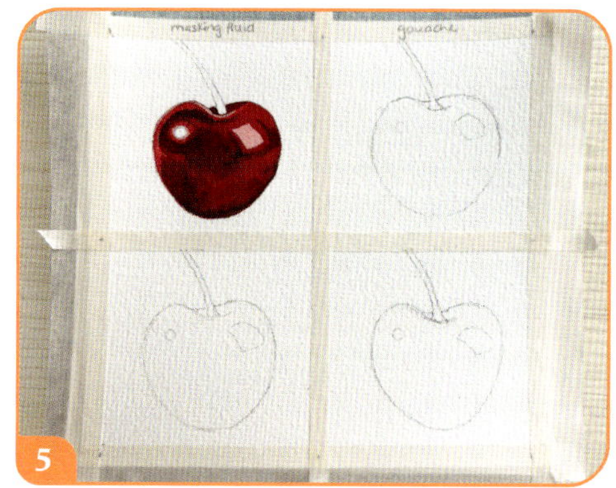

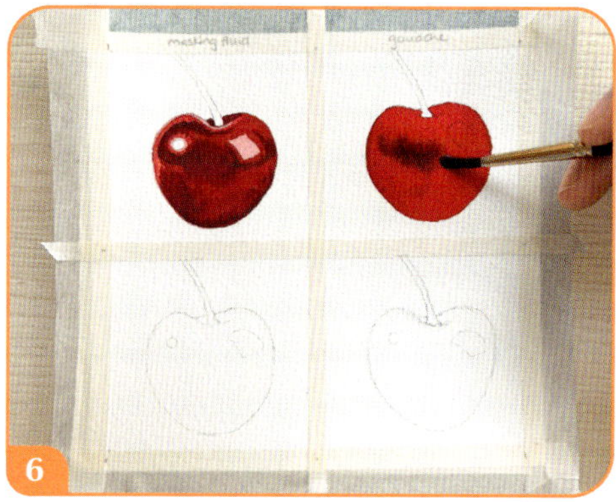

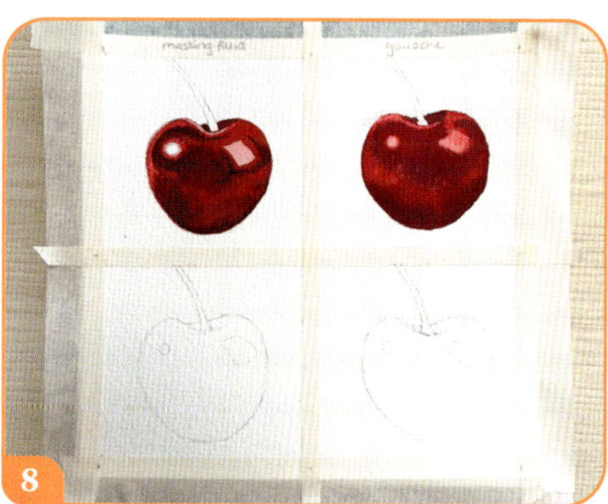

9   Paint over the whole cherry shape with the light red color using your medium brush, then let it dry completely.

10 Cover the other two highlighted areas with a layer of masking fluid and let it dry completely.

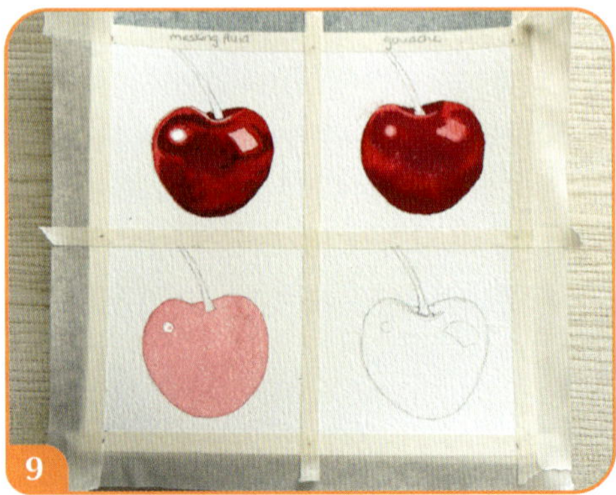

11 Use the bright red and dark red colors to fill in the entire shape in the same way you just painted the previous cherry, then let it dry completely.

12 Gently remove the masking fluid.

White Gouache

13 For the fourth cherry, we'll use gouache to add highlights. Paint the entire cherry with bright red and add in some dark red to create shadowed areas, then let it dry completely.

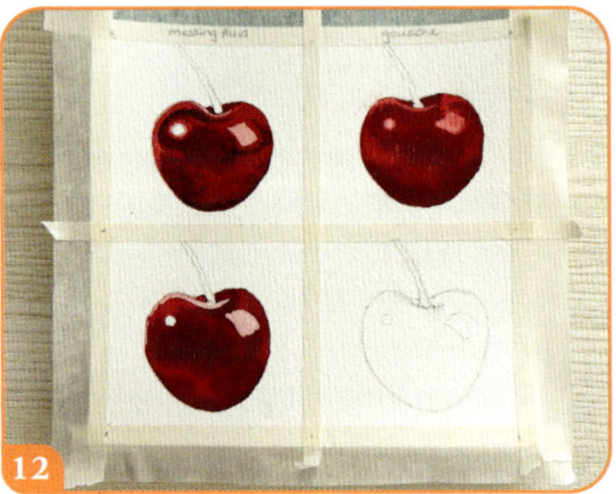

14 Use white gouache and your detail brush to add the circular highlight on the top left of the cherry, then mix a little bright red into the gouache to tint it slightly pink. Use this pink gouache to add the other two dimmer highlights to your cherry.

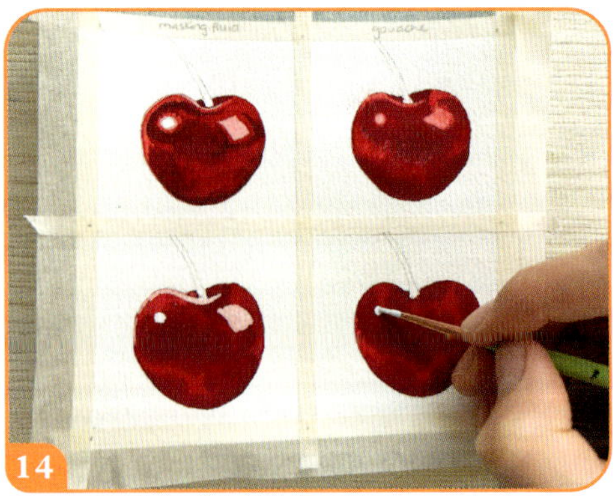

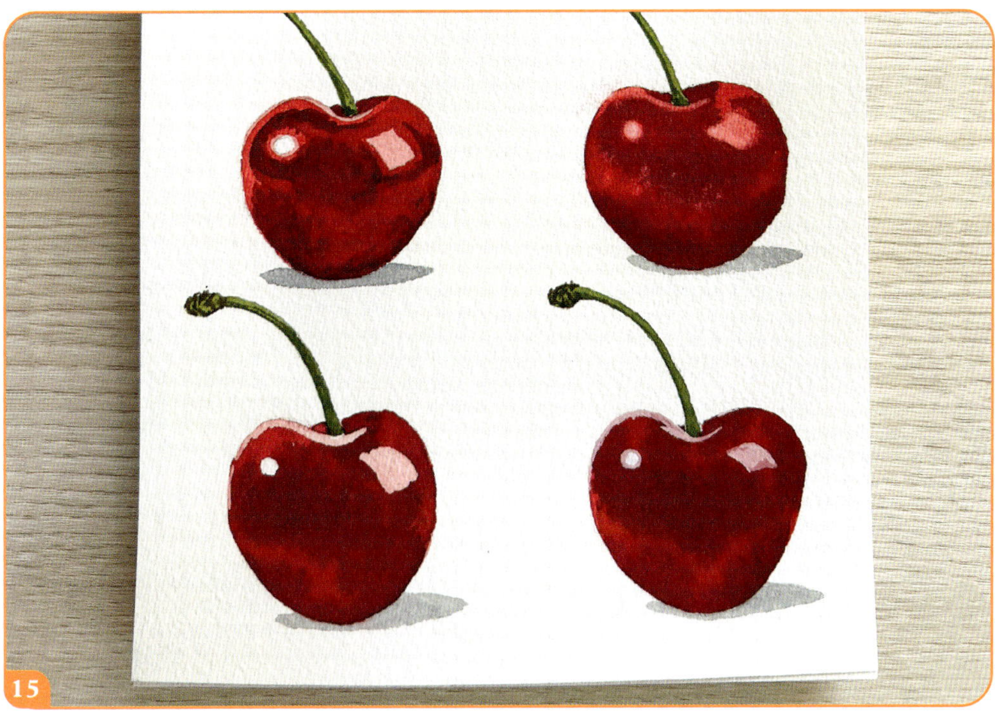

15 Mix some Sap Green, Ultramarine Blue and a little Van Dyke Brown to create a dark earthy-green color and paint in the stems of the cherries using your detail brush. You can also use a combo of Ultramarine Blue, Van Dyke Brown and plenty of water to make light gray, and add little oval-shaped cast shadows underneath each cherry!

Now that we've practiced each highlight technique a couple of times, take note of the slightly different processes used in each technique and the slightly different outcomes each one produces. Do you like the look of one over the others? Was one easier or more intuitive for you? Any of them are great to use and you can even use multiple in one painting, so just keep them in your toolkit and refer back to this lesson if you ever need a refresher!

Take It Up a Notch: Try these highlight techniques with a new subject—maybe a cluster of grapes, a marble, a glass bottle, anything that has a bit of a shine to it under direct lighting.

PART 2

Level Up

I have good news and bad news for you. The good news is that you've made it through two whole chapters and learned a ton of new art skills! I am so proud of you for making it this far!! The bad news is that even though you've completed those two chapters, you'll need to continue reviewing and perfecting those skills until they are second nature to you. There is no escape. I can, however, offer you the chance to put your new skills to the test with complete paintings. In Chapter 3, we'll create six simpler paintings using skills straight from the lessons in Part 1. Once you're comfortable creating complete paintings, Chapter 4 will take you into more advanced subject matter, where you'll have to use several techniques from earlier chapters and be comfortable making your own executive decisions. Finally, Chapter 5 will take you into some watercolor experimentation using different or unconventional materials to expand your horizons.

Throughout these chapters, I will point out the techniques from Part 1 using the note "Remember Your Fundamentals" and provide you with page references so you can easily refresh your memory. Remember, repetition and practice are the only true paths to improving your skill level, so if you feel uncomfortable with a certain technique, or if one of these lessons in Part 2 gives you trouble, I strongly encourage you to repeat it until you feel more comfortable. You'll learn something new each time and develop muscle memory that will really lock in those new skills for you. You got this! I believe in you wholeheartedly, and I am so excited for you to fill your home with some new paintings!

CHAPTER 3

Applied Techniques

Put Your New Skills to the Test

Now that you've gotten some practice using your watercolors, it's time to move on to some complete paintings. Each project in this chapter will use several of the skills you've learned in the previous two chapters, so you'll get a chance to practice them some more in a practical way. For the first three projects, you'll be painting a single subject—a butterfly, some flowers and a pumpkin. In the last three projects, you'll be creating full landscape paintings inspired by a few different subjects.

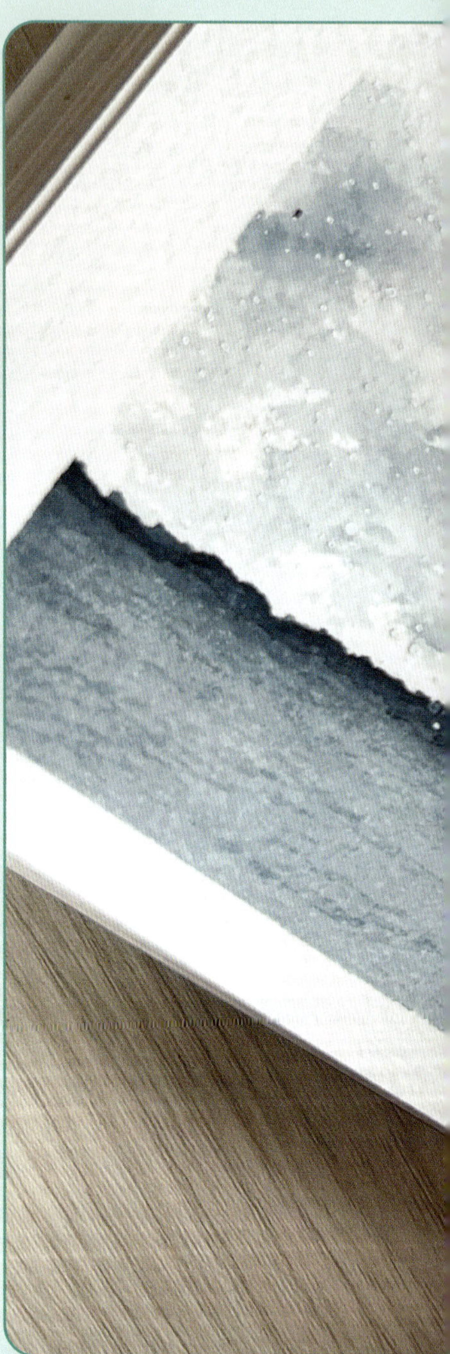

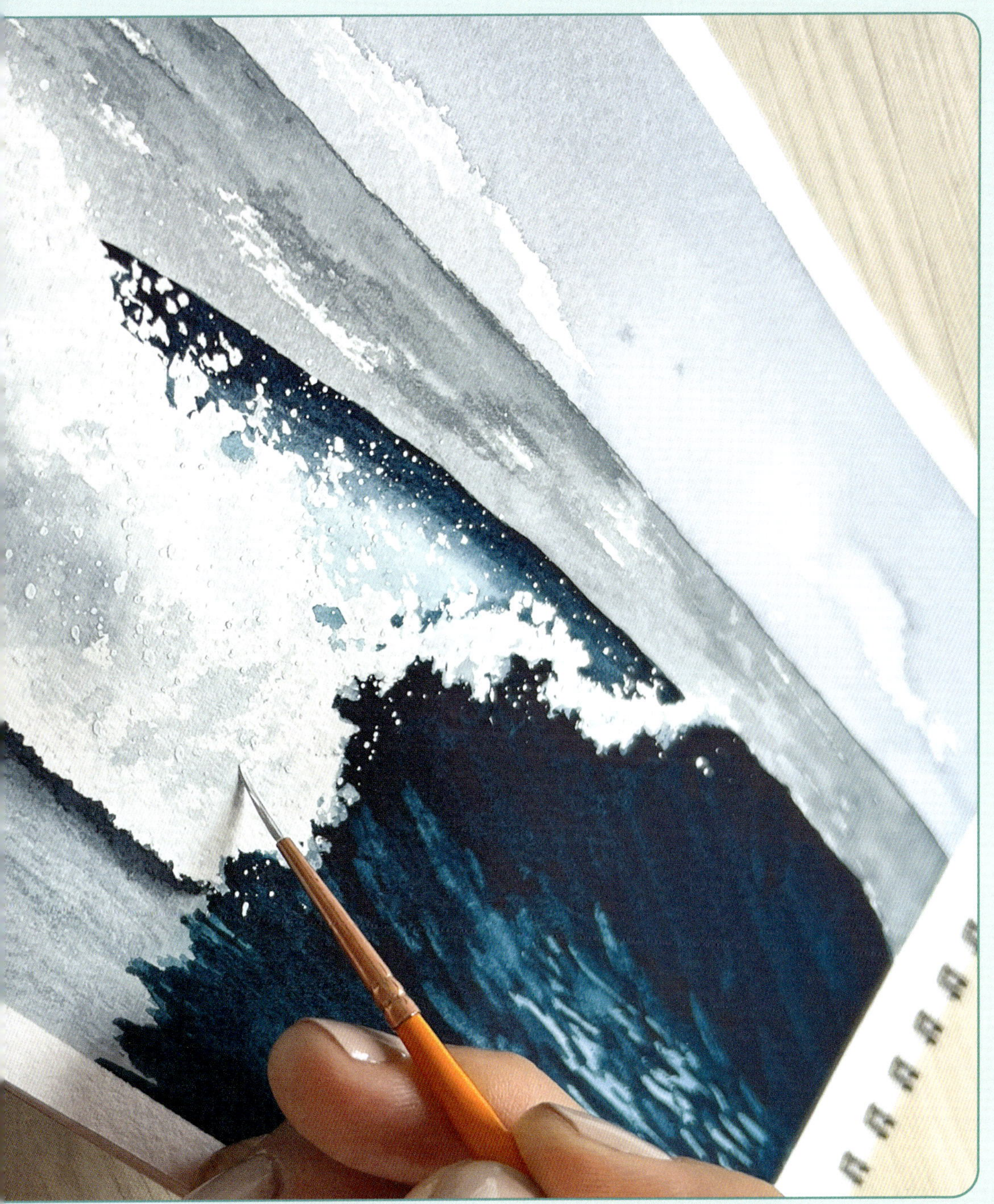

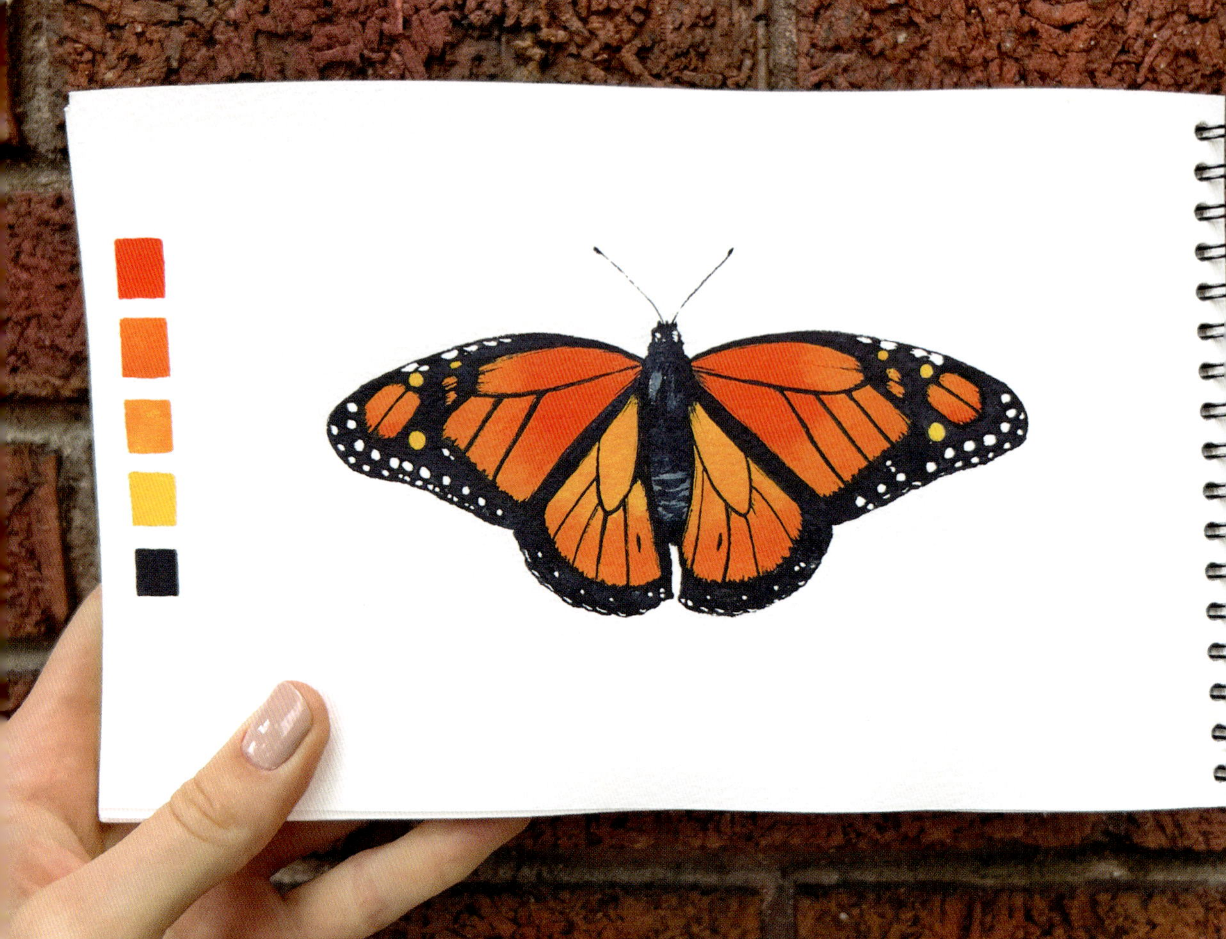

Butterfly Fly Away

Let's take a brief field trip into the world of fauna for today's lesson. I hesitated to include any lessons on animals in this book because they are often quite complex, but since butterflies are so distinctly patterned, I felt like this would be a fun introduction. You can see our reference photo of a beautiful monarch butterfly on page 123. The hardest part about this subject is the sketch—getting the correct shape and making it symmetrical could take you a while.

If you want an extra challenge, freehand your sketch. If, like me, you don't have time for all that, please feel free to trace* the general shape and pattern onto your paper (remember, all the reference photos used in this book are available online on Unsplash; the link is on page 17). When we start painting, we'll be using several of the techniques we've learned so far: gradients (page 85), flat washes (page 94), dry brushing (page 101), etc.

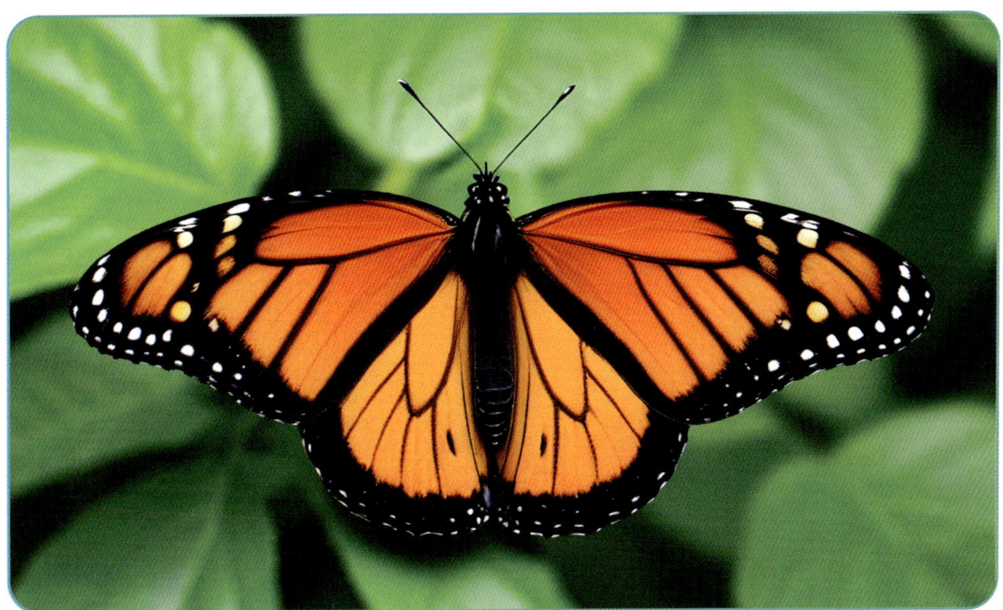

For the painting, you'll need:

» Cup of water and paper towel

» Watercolor paints: Cadmium Yellow, Cadmium Red, Payne's Gray

» Pencil

» Watercolor paper (I used a page of my Arches sketchbook)

» Optional: masking fluid and an old or inexpensive brush to apply it, masking tape or gouache

» 1 medium brush and 1 detail brush (I used a 4 round and a 2 round)

***A Quick Rant About Tracing:** Tracing a reference photo is NOT cheating, and there is nothing wrong with doing it. It saves you a ton of time that you can then spend working on your painting techniques. It is important, however, to also work on your drawing skills when you have time so that tracing doesn't become a crutch for you. There are many different ways to transfer a reference image to your paper, so feel free to research those and find the technique that works best for you.

Here's the method I personally use: I place a piece of tracing paper over my reference image and trace it with a pencil. Then I cover the back of the tracing paper with a thick layer of graphite with my pencil. Next, I place the tracing paper, with the graphite side down, onto my watercolor paper, and redraw the lines of my design using firm pressure. This forces the graphite on the back of the tracing paper onto the watercolor paper to create a traced pencil sketch.

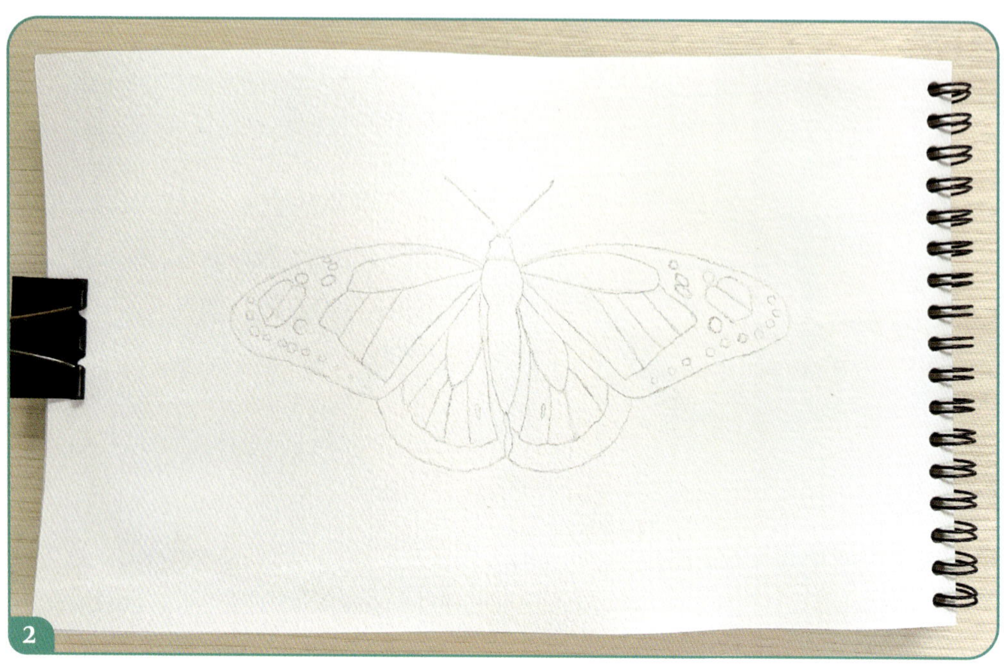

1   Add a drop of water to each of your colors and give them a minute to soften.

2   Sketch (or trace) the butterfly onto your paper, paying attention to the patterns on the wings.

3   I used masking fluid to cover the white dots I saw along the edges of the wings. You are welcome to do the same, or you can paint around those white dots, use masking tape to cover them or use gouache at the very end to paint them in. Remember, we covered four different highlight techniques (page 108), so refer back if you need a reminder!

4   Use Cadmium Yellow and Cadmium Red to mix three different oranges: a red-orange with more Cadmium Red and less Cadmium Yellow, a true orange with about equal amounts of both, and a yellow-orange with more Cadmium Yellow. Keep these colors quite saturated in your mixing palette.

Remember Your Fundamentals: Using analogous colors makes it easier to create a gradient, and they are especially pleasing to the eye. For a reminder on color interactions, return to Colorful Language (page 59).

5   We'll be creating a gradient (page 85) between colors in each of the four orange sections of the butterfly wings. Load your brush with red-orange and start with one of the top wing sections. Start at the body of the butterfly and paint about half of the section with red-orange. Immediately switch to true orange and fill in the rest of the section, allowing the paint colors to blend where they meet.

6   Repeat Step 4 on the other top wing section. Note that you don't need to color exactly in the lines right now—we'll be using a very dark color to fill in the rest of the wings later, so you can clean up the lines then!

7   Create a mini gradient using the same two colors used in Step 5 in the small rectangles on the tips of the wings, starting with true orange on top and blending into red-orange on the bottom.

8   For the bottom wing sections, create a gradient starting with yellow-orange near the body, transitioning to true orange toward the bottom of the wing.

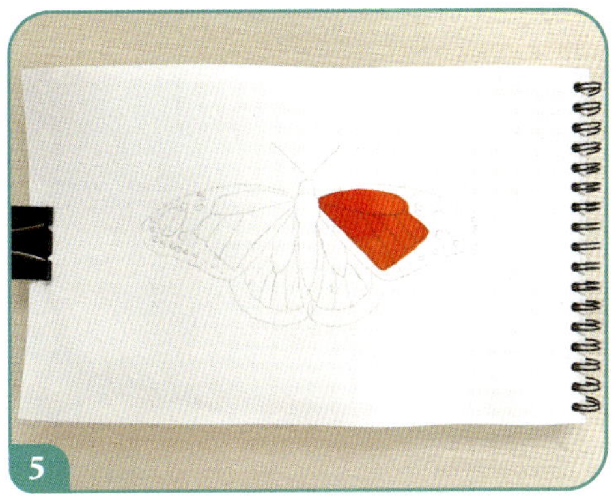

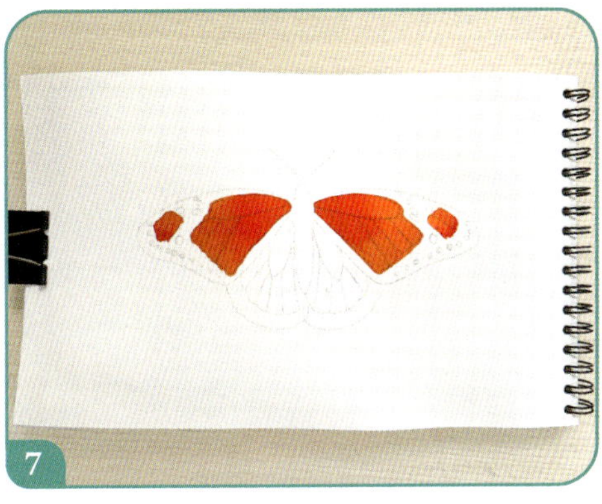

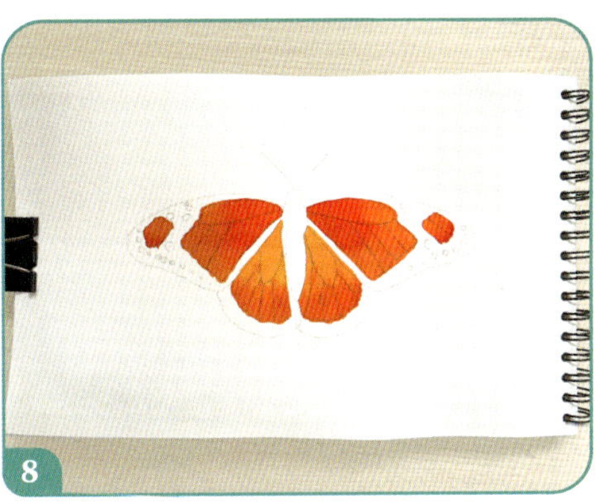

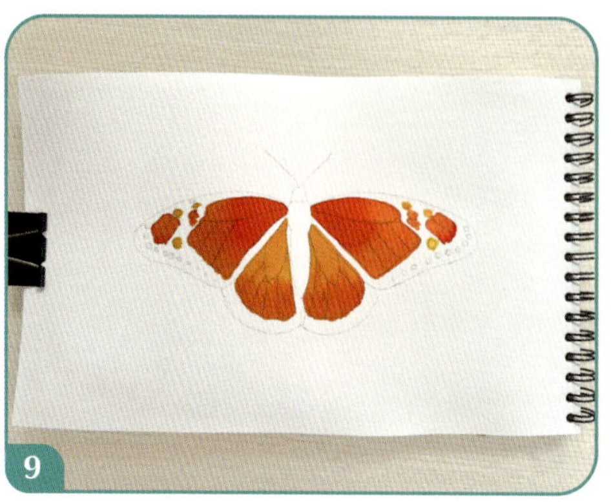

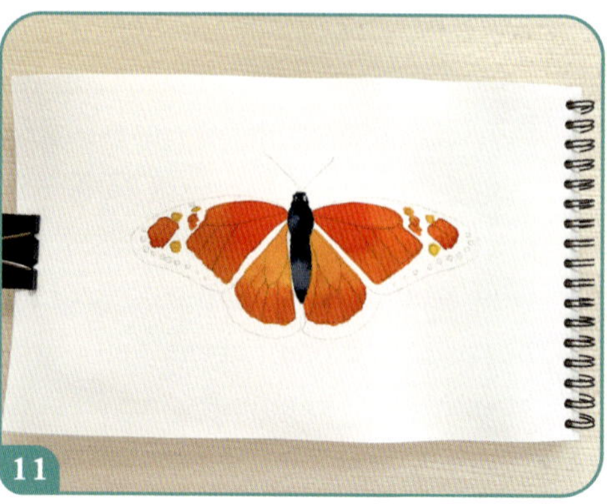

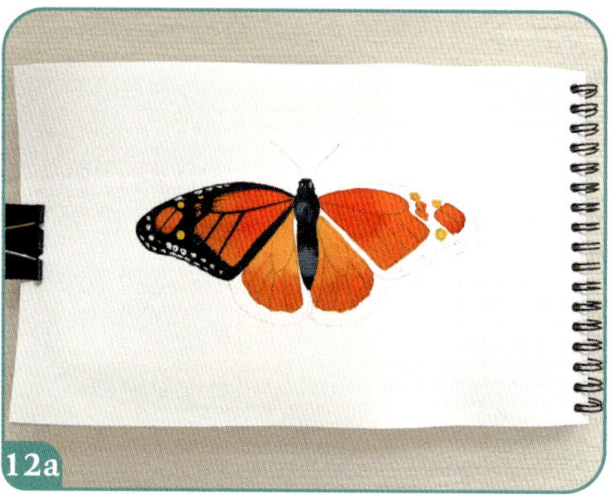

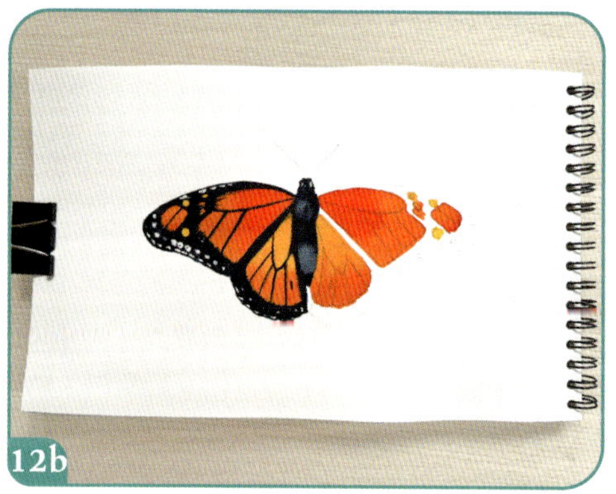

9   Use true orange and yellow-orange to fill in any of the little shapes you see at the tips of the wings, then let everything dry completely.

10   Mix up some Payne's Gray in your palette, adding only a little water to create a dark value.

11   Fill in the body of the butterfly with a flat wash, then use a completely dry brush to lift some paint to create highlights in the thickest parts of the thorax and abdomen.

12   Continue using the Payne's Gray to fill in the rest of the wings. Notice in the reference photo how there is a grainy, feathery texture around the edges of each orange shape? Use the dry-brush technique (page 101) to imitate this texture. If you didn't use masking fluid, remember to paint around the white dots you see on the edges of the wings!

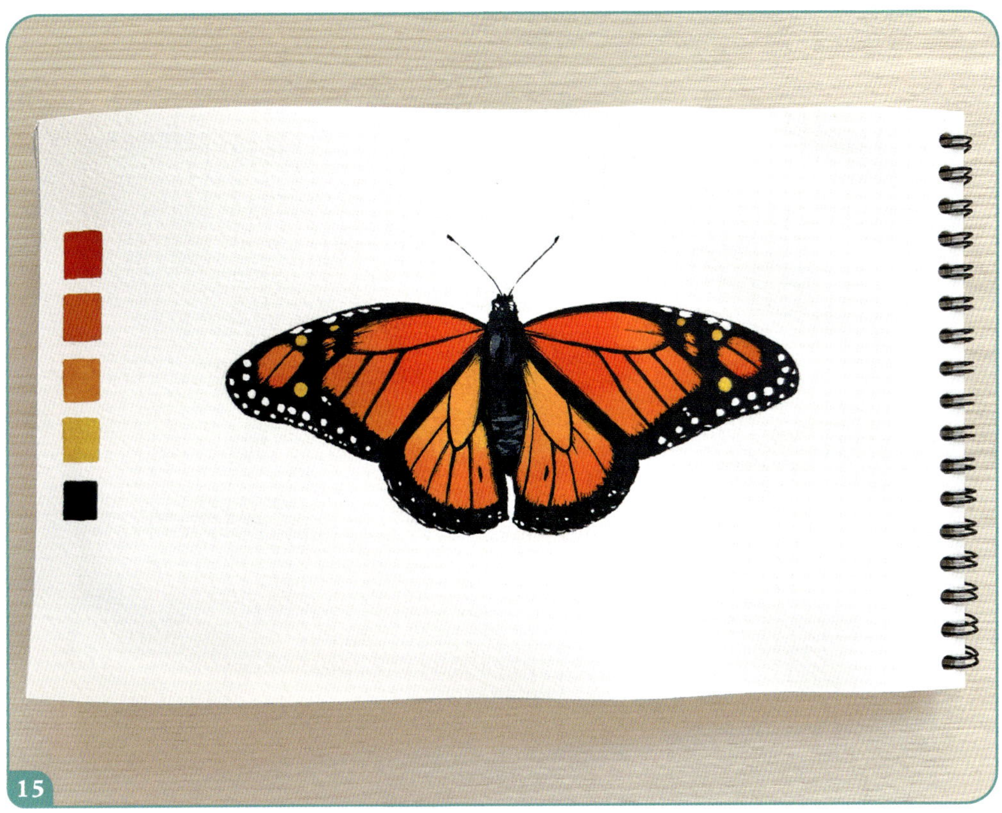

13 Use a super light touch and your detail brush to paint the antennae with Payne's Gray.

14 Add a few thick horizontal lines in the lighter part of the abdomen.

15 If you used masking fluid, rcmove it and touch up any of the shapes if necessary.

And now you have your own beautiful, vibrant butterfly! I just love recreating the patterns on these creatures; they are stunning in watercolor! Take a step back and analyze your painting. Make a note of what went well for you and what could be improved on next time!

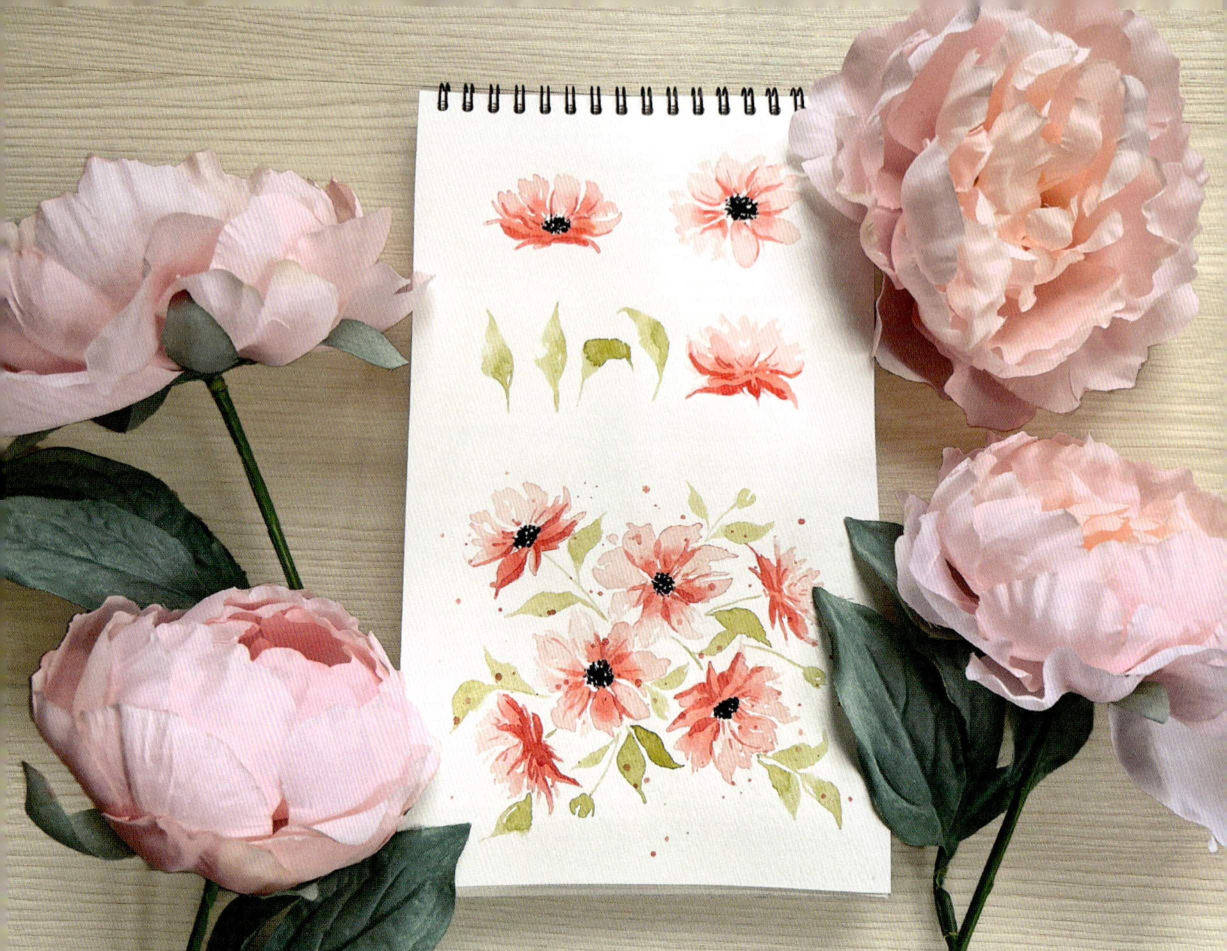

Expressive Florals

Flowers are incredibly fun and freeing to paint with watercolor—the transparency and movement of the medium really gives a special glow to the petals and leaves. There are so many different styles for painting watercolor florals, some more precise and detailed and some very loose and abstract. We'll aim for somewhere in the middle today, but just know there's a whole world of watercolor flowers out there waiting to be discovered if you find this lesson inspiring! Our flower study for today is inspired by a ranunculus field I visited with my family in Southern California. There were so many different color and shape variations, as you can see in the reference photo, so let's focus on one or two flowers today.

We'll also be experimenting with perspective in this painting, but a little differently than we did in the lessons on 1-point perspective (page 39) and 2-point perspective (page 46). As you'll notice in the reference photo, some of the flowers are perfectly facing the camera, so you see all of the petals spread out in a circle, with the center of the flower forming a smaller circle. Flowers that face slightly away from the camera form more of a domed shape, with the petals facing the camera getting foreshortened and the center of the flower turning into an oval shape. We get a side profile of flowers facing completely away, where the petals block the center of the flower from view and the petals form a semicircular domed shape. Portraying the flowers at these different angles in our painting lends realism and interest, so we'll start the lesson by painting the flowers at different angles. You'll need:

» Cup of water and paper towel

» Watercolor paint: Magenta, Yellow Ochre, Cadmium Yellow, Sap Green, Payne's Gray

» Watercolor paper (I used a page of my Arches sketchbook)

» Optional: masking tape

» 1 medium and 1 detail watercolor brush (I used a 4 round and a 2 round)

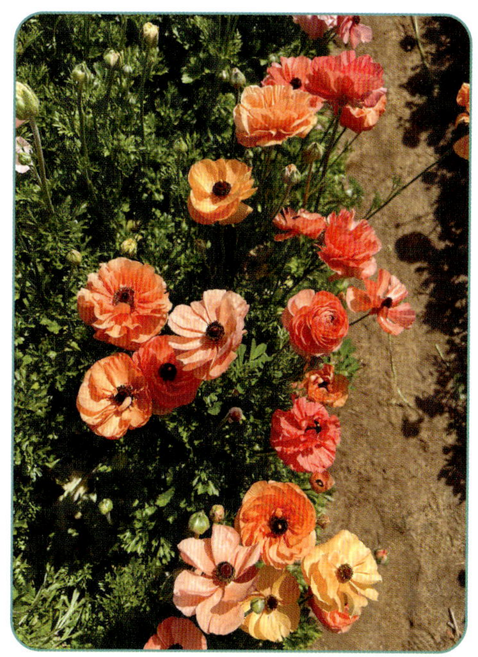

1   Add a drop of water to each of your colors and give them a minute to soften. In the meantime, prep your paper, using masking tape if you like.

2   We'll use a peach color for our flowers today, so mix up a puddle of Magenta, Yellow Ochre and Cadmium Yellow until you get a color you like, adding a small amount of water. Then take a little bit of this color mixture to a separate spot in your mixing area and add plenty of water to make a lighter version of the same color.

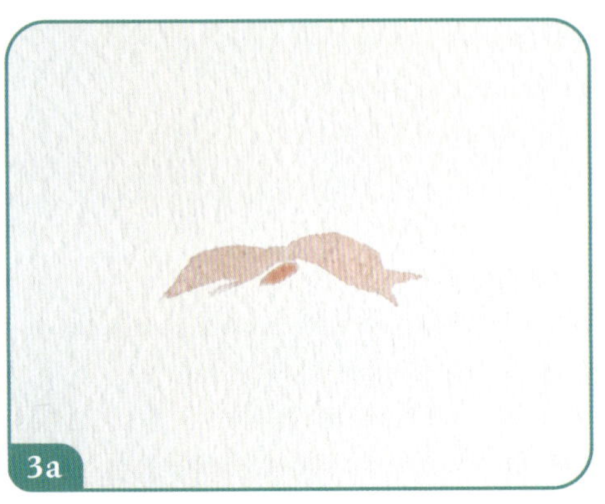

3a

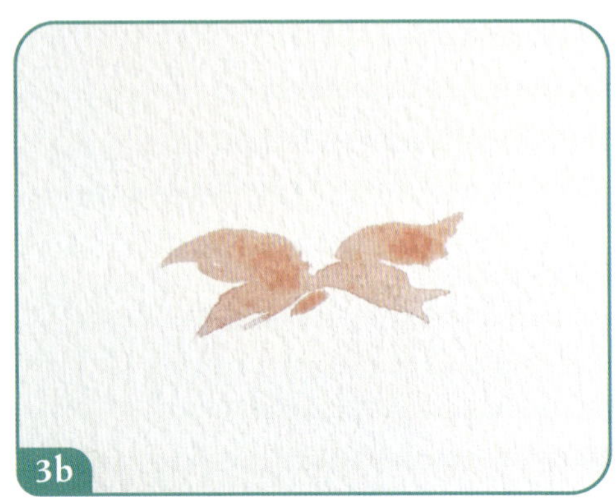

3b

3 Load your medium brush with the lighter peach color and on your paper paint in two horizontal petals facing away from each other. Then paint in a semicircle of petals on top of those two first ones. I like to use loose brushstrokes here, using a press, drag and lift motion similar to what we used for the leaves on the wreath on page 64. Try adding little wiggles and skipping some small spaces for texture.

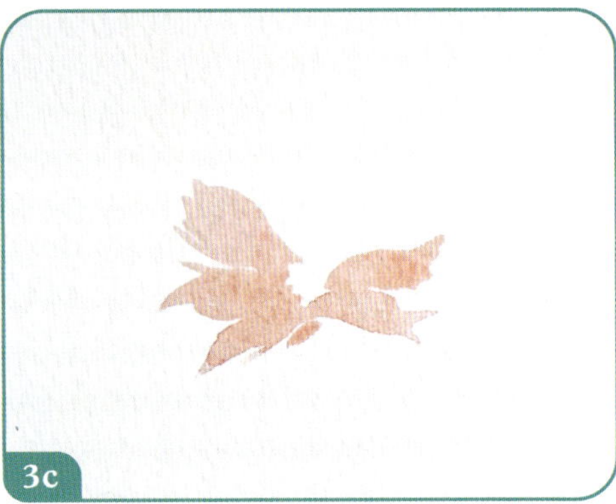

3c

3d

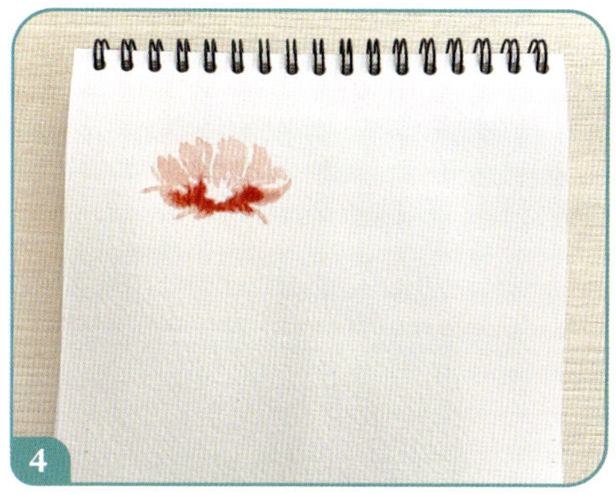

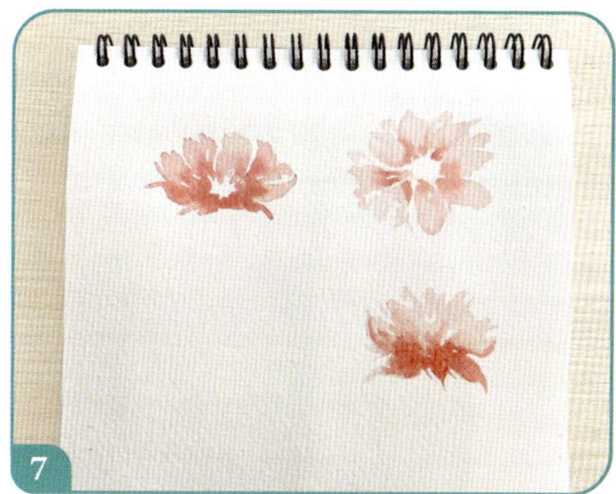

4   Before the flower dries, add a drop or two of the concentrated peach color to the bottom petals and allow the paint to spread out.

5   Now let's paint a flower facing straight up. With the light peach color, paint a small circle for the center of the flower, then add petals that radiate out from the center. Again, you can be pretty loose and messy with the petals here.

6   Add a touch of concentrated peach to the center of this flower.

7   Now practice painting a flower from the side: Add a couple downturned petals, then build up more petals on top to form the full semicircle shape of the flower. Add some concentrated peach to the base of the flower while it's still wet.

While those flowers dry, let's practice painting some leaves.

8   Mix up a light green combining Sap Green, Cadmium Yellow and just a touch of Magenta with plenty of water.

9   Use the same press, drag and lift combination to paint a leaf: Start out with a light touch to get a pointed end, press down hard as you drag the brush to get the full shape, then lift at the end to create a thin stem.

10 Practice a few straight leaves, then once you're comfortable, add a little wiggle to your brush to create some more movement and interest.

When you feel comfortable with the leaves, we'll finish up the flowers.

11 Use concentrated Payne's Gray and your detail brush to add the centers to your flowers, stippling your brush to create a bit of texture. You'll paint a circular shape for the flower facing you, and more of a flattened oval shape for the flower facing slightly up. Skip adding a center to the flower we see from the side.

12 Clean your detail brush and switch to the concentrated peach color. Add a couple of thin, defining lines to a few of the petals on each flower to add just a bit of detail.

Now that we've practiced the separate elements of this painting, it's time to put it all together in a finished painting! Move to a fresh piece of paper and tape it down if you'd like.

13 Around the center of the composition, I like to paint flowers facing toward the viewer. Add two or three, remembering to drop in that concentrated peach around the center before it dries.

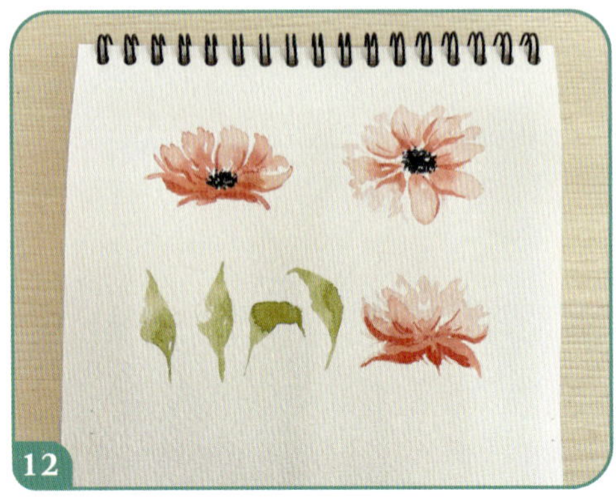

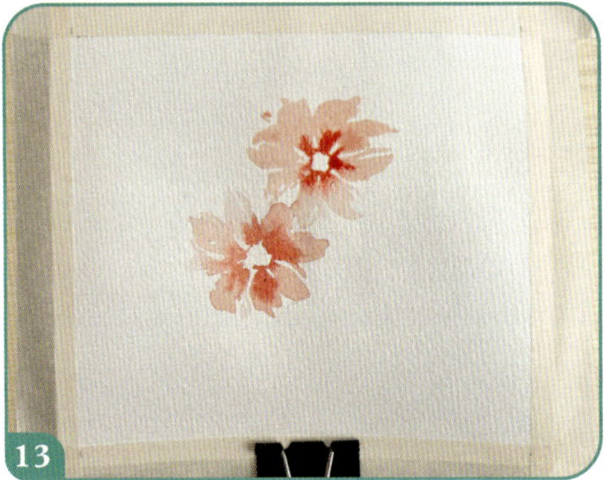

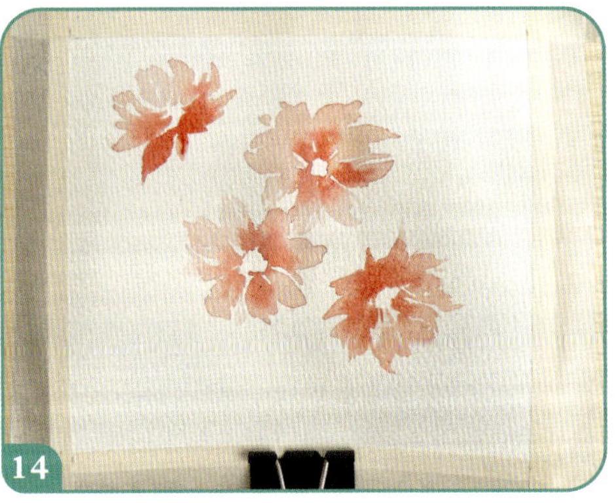

14 As you work outward, the flowers should face more and more sideways. Work your way around the page and add a few more flowers where you want them, then let them dry completely.

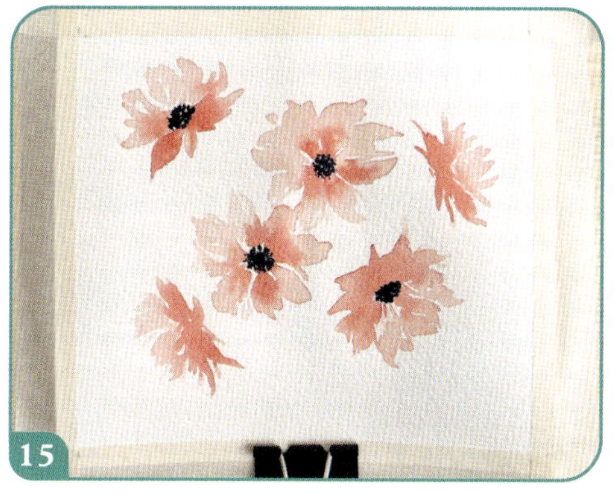

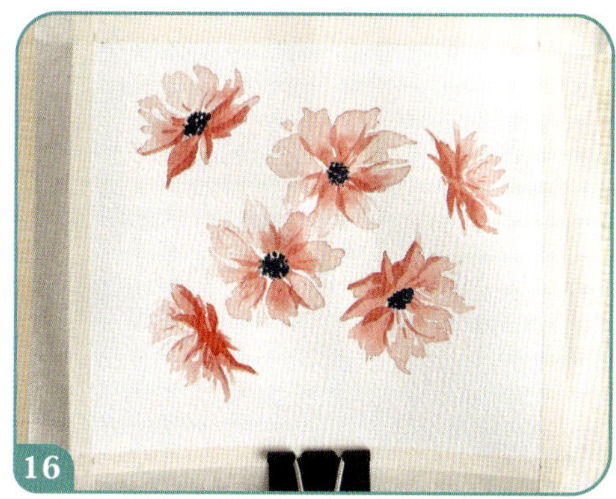

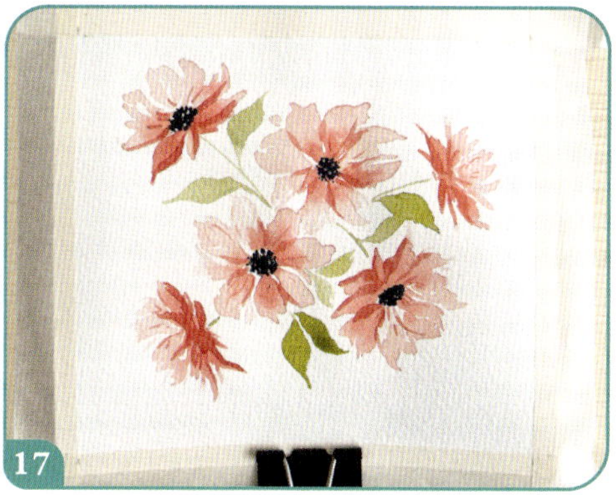

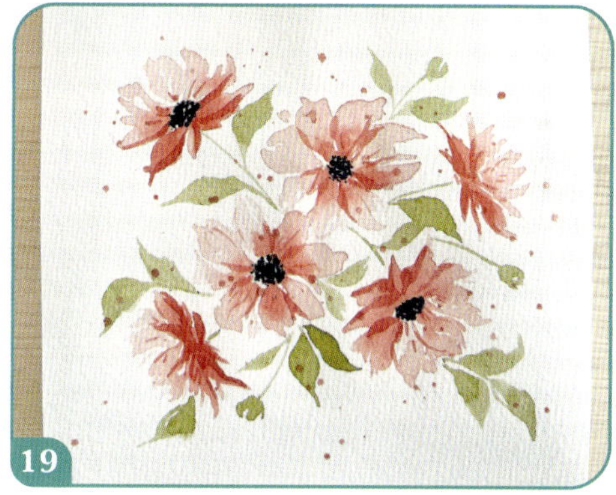

15 Add the centers of the flowers using Payne's Gray and a stippling motion with your detail brush.

16 Add the little details to the petals with the concentrated peach color, painting in thin lines and squiggles following the contours of each petal.

17 Switch to your light green color and start adding in stems using a very light touch and leaves to fill in any empty spaces and to fill out the composition.

18 Feel free to add little unopened flower buds with the same green paint by painting in a loose circle or U-shape on top of a stem.

19 Optionally, load up your brush with the watered-down peach and use the paint splatter technique (page 101) to add in some extra texture and movement.

And there you have it! Take a moment to analyze your painting—did you successfully portray the flowers from different perspectives? Does your final painting look cohesive and well-balanced? Make a note of what went well, and what could be improved next time!

Pumpkin Spice

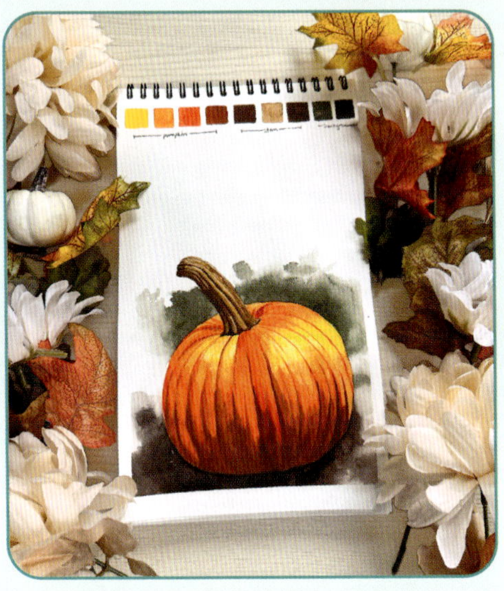

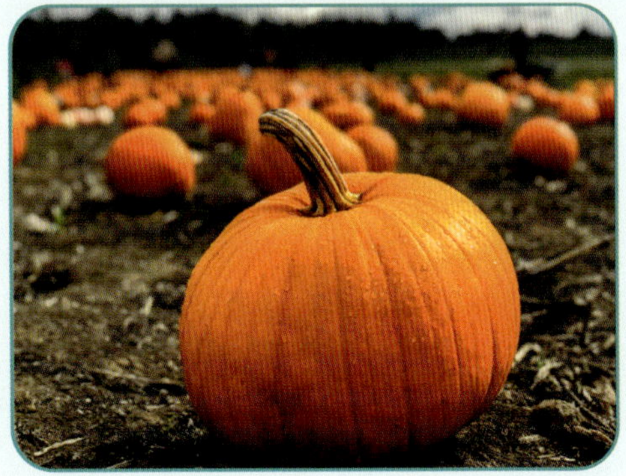

I love fall and everything that comes along with it—cooler weather, cozy sweaters, holidays, yummy food, all the classic stuff. Fall also contains fantastic painting inspiration—the vibrant colors of the changing leaves and fall harvests, the dramatic, moody rainy days, it's all so fun to paint. Today we're going to use a few of the skills we've learned so far in this book to paint a beautiful pumpkin, which I'm sure you'll enjoy no matter what time of year it is! We'll be using our light source (page 22) skills to make the pumpkin look round and three-dimensional, and we'll be using plenty of layering (page 94) and blending (page 85) with a damp brush to create the texture and depth of color we're looking for.

For this project, you'll need:

» Cup of water and paper towel

» Watercolor paints: Cadmium Yellow, Cadmium Red, Ultramarine Blue, Yellow Ochre, Van Dyke Brown, Sap Green

» Watercolor paper (I used a page of my Arches sketchbook)

» Optional: masking tape

» Pencil

» 1 large, 1 medium and 1 detail watercolor brush (I used a 12 round, a 4 round and a 2 round)

1   Add a drop of water to each of your colors and give them a minute to soften. In the meantime, set up your paper, taping it down if you'd like.

2   Sketch the general shape of the pumpkin with a pencil, using the reference photo as a guide. Be sure to add in the stem and some light indications of the ridges of the pumpkin.

3   Mix up a puddle of Cadmium Yellow plus a puddle of orange, mixed by combining Cadmium Yellow and Cadmium Red. Add a bit of water to these colors so they're not too strong.

4   Use a large brush and paint in splotches of Cadmium Yellow on the lightest parts of the pumpkin. Then quickly switch to the orange color you mixed and fill in the rest of the pumpkin, allowing the yellow and orange paints to blend on the paper. Let it dry completely.

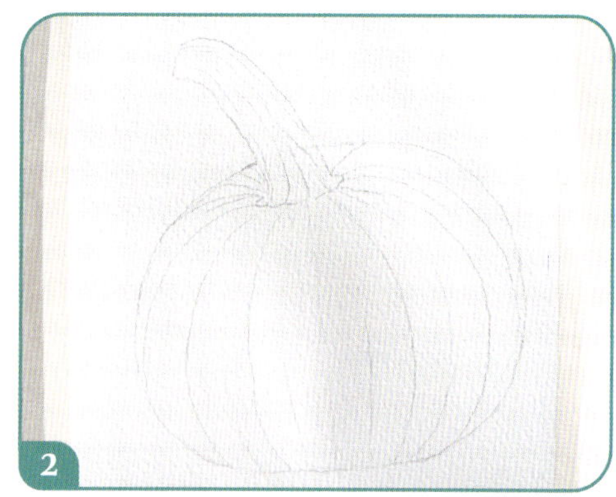

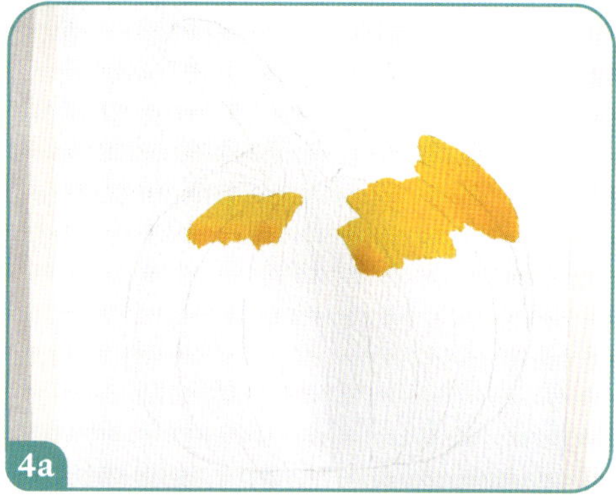

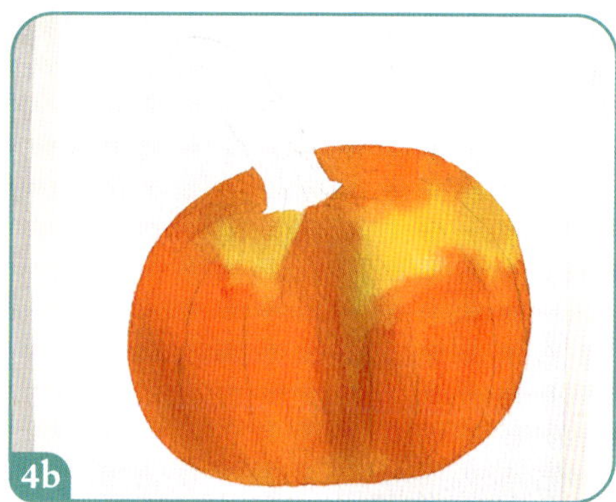

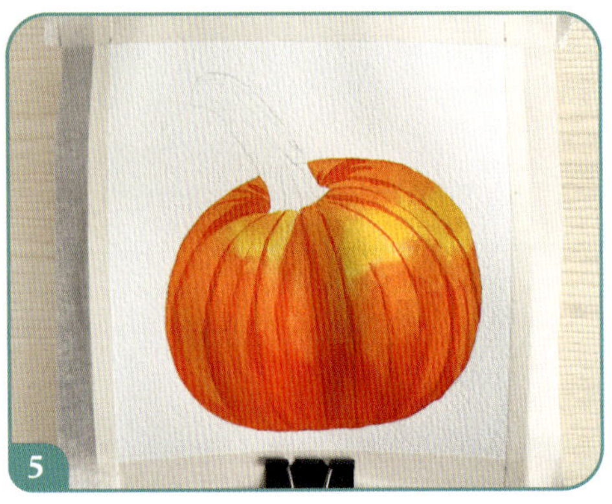

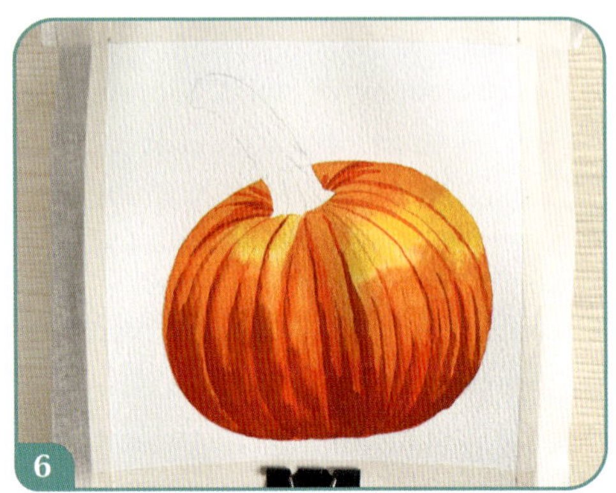

5   Mix up a red-orange color combining Cadmium Red with a little Cadmium Yellow. Use a medium brush for more control and begin adding shadow shapes to your pumpkin. On the top half, use thin lines to define the ridges of the pumpkin, but completely fill the bottom half (ish) of the pumpkin with this color to begin building up the shadows. Let it dry completely.

6   Add a touch of Ultramarine Blue to the red-orange from Step 5 to darken it a bit, and use this color to deepen the shadows in the ridges and at the bottom of the pumpkin. Use a clean damp brush to blend some of the shadow shapes into the rest of the pumpkin. Let it dry completely.

Remember Your Fundamentals: As we discussed in Ogres (and Paintings) Have Layers (page 94), each additional layer of paint darkens the value of the painted area. Layering the shadows with progressively darker colors allows you to create a smooth transition between the light and dark areas and build up the value in the core shadow of the pumpkin. Feel free to also review See the Light . . . Source (page 22) to remind yourself of the lighting principles we're using here.

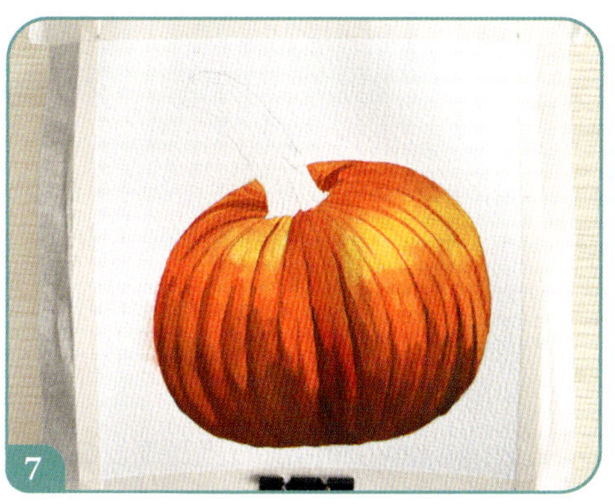

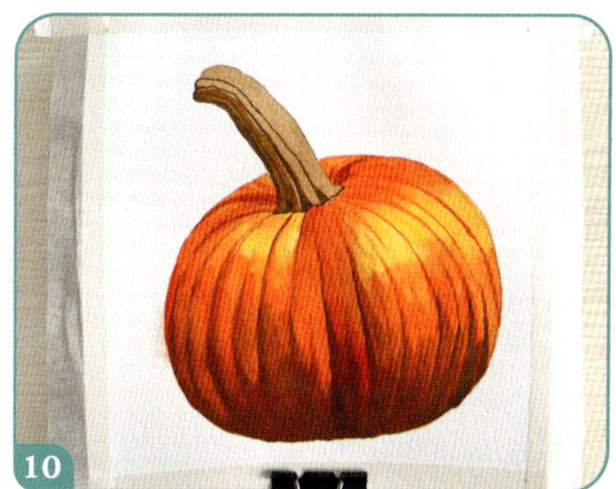

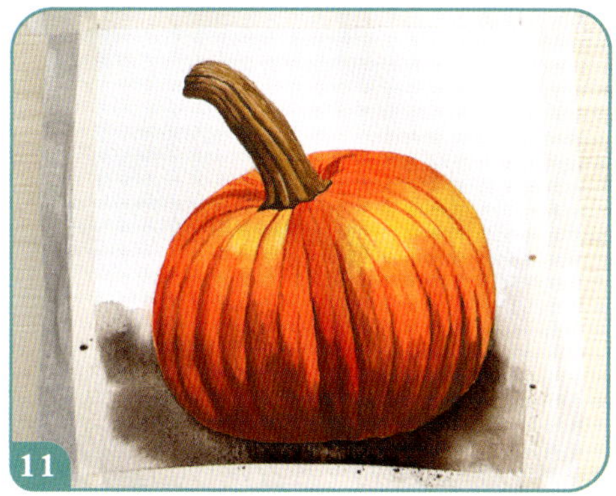

7   Add even more Ultramarine Blue to the color from Step 6 to create a dark brown shade. Create your final shadow shapes with this color, using it sparingly for only the darkest areas of the pumpkin.

8   Use a clean damp brush and any previous colors to add any additional layers you'd like to increase saturation and value. You can also use these additional layers to blend out any unwanted texture, as the addition of new paint will lightly smudge the layers underneath.

9   Mix a light brown combining Yellow Ochre and Van Dyke Brown and fill in the pumpkin stem with a flat wash.

10 Add a touch of Ultramarine Blue to the light brown from Step 9 and use a detail brush to add the ridges and textures you see on the stem, keeping in mind the light source.

11 Now it's time to add the background! Mix up a dark brown combining Van Dyke Brown and Ultramarine Blue, and a natural green color by combining Sap Green, Ultramarine Blue and Van Dyke Brown. Use a large brush to add some dark brown paint around the base of the pumpkin. While the brown paint is still wet on the page, use a clean wet brush to soften the edges and create abstract textures in the background.

12 Switch to the natural green color and paint it around the top of the pumpkin, then use a clean wet brush to blend the edges. Feel free to add some abstract, textured brushstrokes here too!

Let it dry and you're all done! How did the layering and shadow building go for you? Does the pumpkin look three-dimensional? Do the highlights and shadows make sense? Take note of what went well and what could be improved on next time.

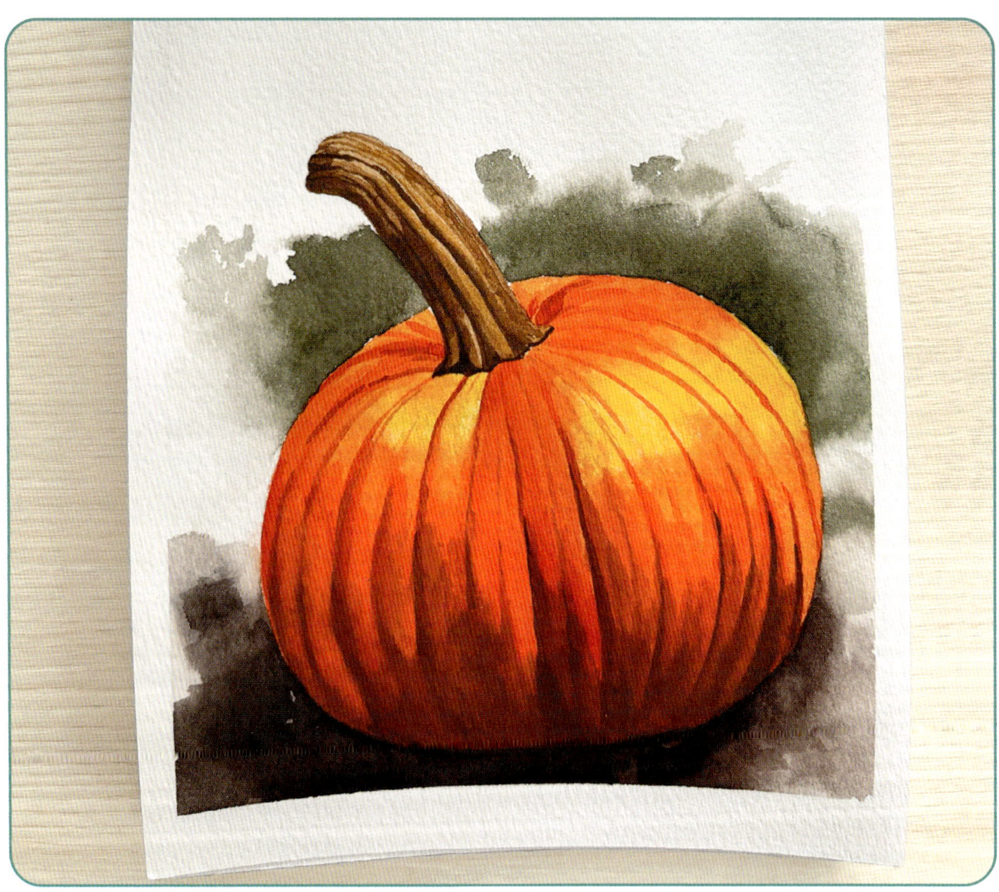

Nocturne

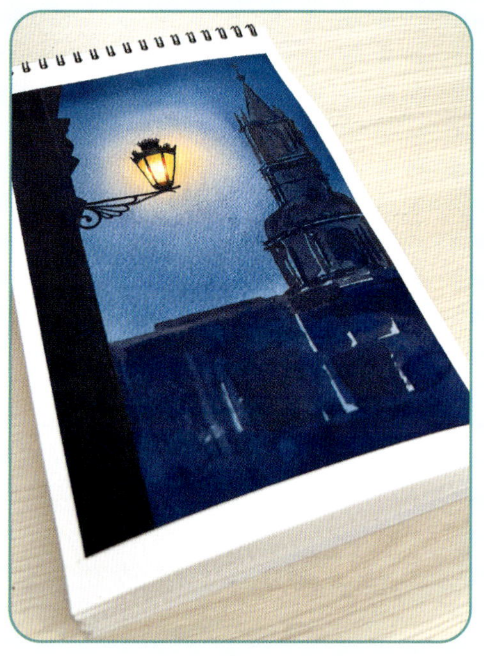

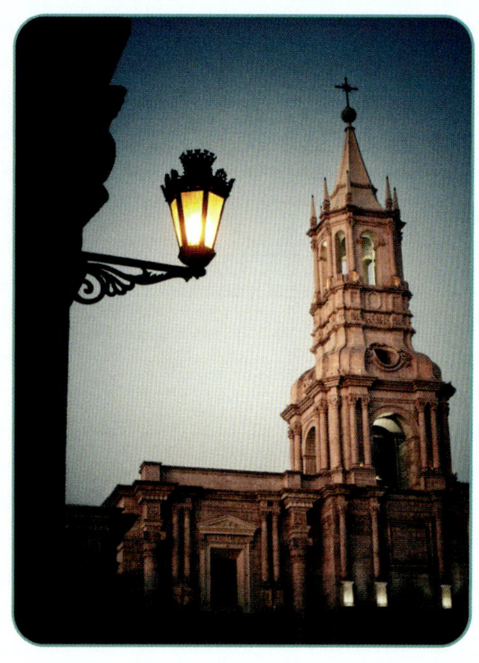

As we've discussed earlier in this book, because watercolor is a transparent medium we can really take advantage of some special effects, including making something look like it's glowing. The white of the paper is able to shine through in certain areas, and with a little knowledge of color theory, we can really enhance this effect. Today's painting will feature a glowing lamppost just before dark, with a loose, impressionistic building in the background.

Before we dive in, let's have a quick discussion about getting a proper glowing effect: Things that glow are generally warm-toned; you'll usually see yellow or orange colors around a light source and you can see them in the reference photo for this project. If we want our background for this painting to be dark blue, we'll have to find a way to smoothly transition the yellows and oranges of the lamp into the blue tones of the background. If you look back at the color wheel (page 60), you'll see orange and blue are complementary colors and there are three ways to get from one to the other.

We could go straight through the center of the color wheel and only use orange and blue, but where they mix on the page would turn brown and muddy and we don't want that for a glowing effect. We could go around clockwise from orange to yellow to green to blue, but glowing objects don't usually put off green light. This leaves us going counterclockwise: yellow to orange to red to purple to blue. It's one extra step, but having those warm reds and purples will really enhance the glowing effect as we transition to blue. Any time you're creating a color transition in a painting, it's important to think about which way around (or through) the color wheel will work best to transition between colors.

For today's project, you'll need:

» Cup of water and paper towel

» Watercolor paints: Cadmium Yellow, Yellow Ochre, Alizarin Crimson, Ultramarine Blue, Indigo, Cadmium Red, Payne's Gray

» Watercolor paper

» Optional: masking tape

» Pencil

» 1 large round, 1 large flat* and 1 detail watercolor brush (I used a 12 round, ¾-inch (2-cm) flat and a 2 round)

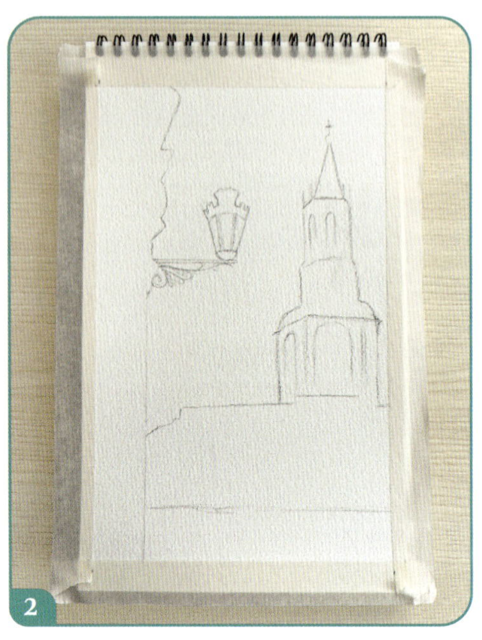

*If you don't have a flat brush, the large round brush will work just fine!

1   Add a drop of water to your paint colors and give them a minute to soften. In the meantime, set up your paper how you like, taping around the outside if desired.

2   Create your pencil sketch. Focus most of your time on the lamp as it's the focal point of the painting. The building it's attached to is a straight line with a few geometric shapes that protrude out, and the church in the background can be reduced to a few triangles and rectangles stacked on top of each other. No need to add too many details.

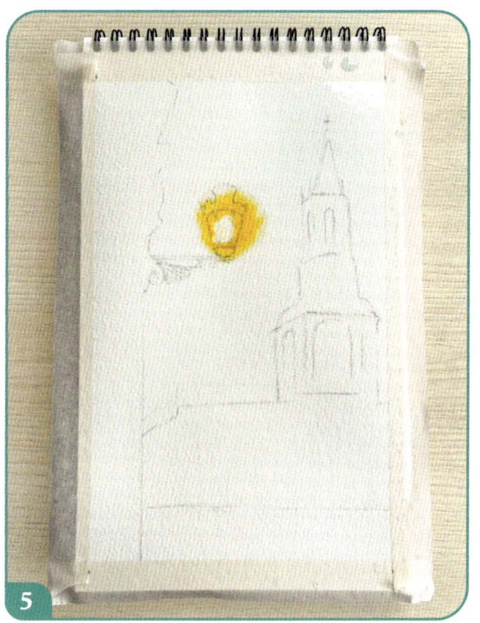

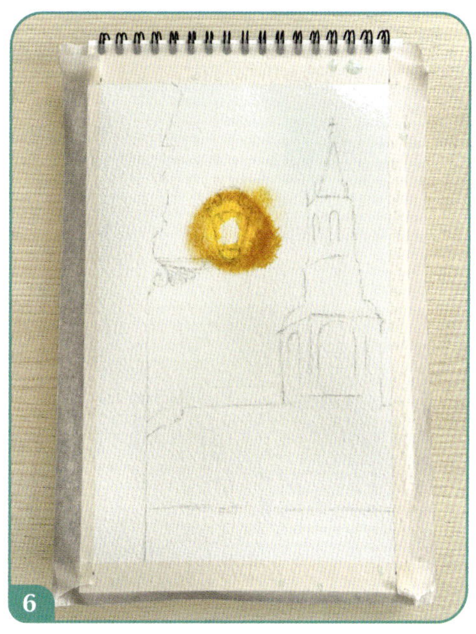

 PAUSE: The next several steps must be done in quick succession while the painting is still wet, so read through Step 9 before starting!

3   In your mixing area, prepare puddles of these colors: Cadmium Yellow, Yellow Ochre, Alizarin Crimson, Ultramarine Blue and Indigo. Keep the paints concentrated (add only a little water to each), and make sure you mix plenty of each (especially the Indigo) so you don't run out.

4   Using a large brush, paint a generous layer of clean water over the entire page.

5   Start with Cadmium Yellow and paint a small circle around the edge of the lamp. Use a paper towel to blot a highlight in the very center of the lamp.

6   Switch to Yellow Ochre and add a ring of it just outside the ring of Cadmium Yellow.

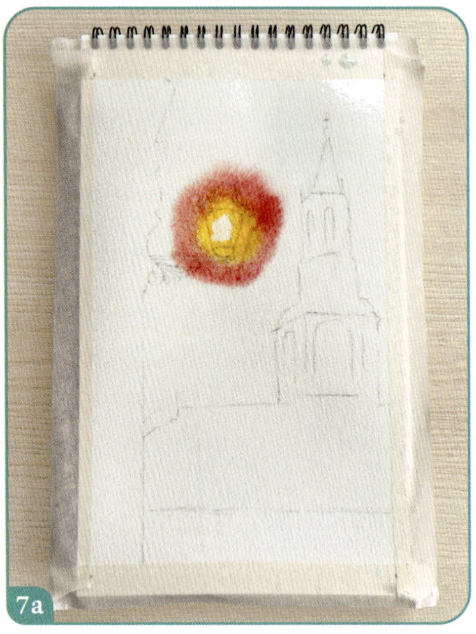

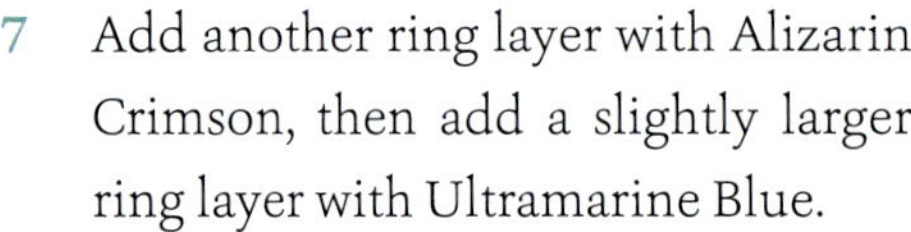

7a

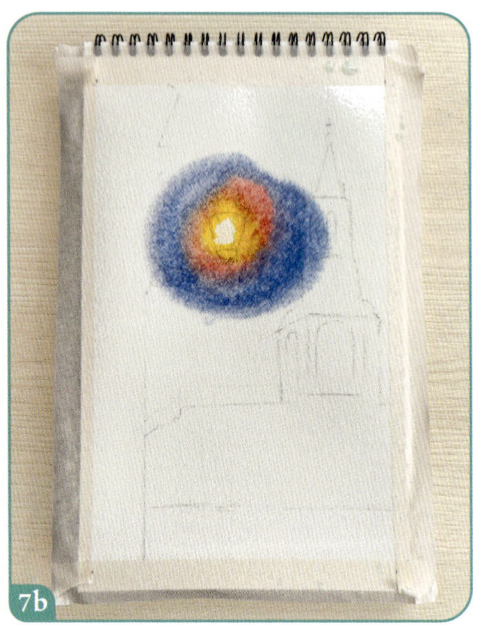

7b

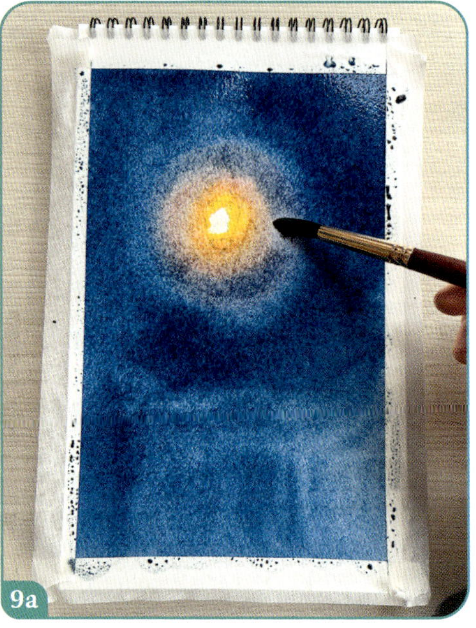

9a

7   Add another ring layer with Alizarin Crimson, then add a slightly larger ring layer with Ultramarine Blue.

8   Fill in the rest of the page with Indigo.

9   Use a clean damp brush to blend the concentric circles together and outward into the Indigo, always starting from the lamp at the center and working your way out. You can always add in some more of any color we just used if you feel you've lost it. Try and get as smooth a blend as you can, but remember that once it starts to dry you have to leave it alone! If you continue working with a wet layer after sections of it start to dry, it will dry unevenly and create blooms and unwanted texture. Let it dry completely before moving on.

Next, we'll work on painting in the church in the background. This is where I want you to put on your impressionist hat and focus on the basic shapes rather than any details.

10 First, mix up a grayish-brown color combining Yellow Ochre, Alizarin Crimson and Ultramarine Blue, adding very little water.

11 Using a flat brush if you have one (continue using a large round if not!), start to carve out the general shapes of the church in the background. You'll notice I'm not filling in these shapes completely—I'm leaving little spaces between them to act as highlights and texture.

Remember Your Fundamentals: Painting this church relies a lot on your mark-making skills. I'm using a flat brush because I know I can use the flat edge to create sharp, geometric shapes, which are perfect for a subject like this. Even if you're using a round brush on this step, you should know how to use it to create the types of marks you want. Feel free to revisit Make Your Mark (page 70) to review all of the different ways you can alter your brushstrokes, and don't be afraid to practice painting this element on a separate piece of paper if you want to test out your mark-making first!

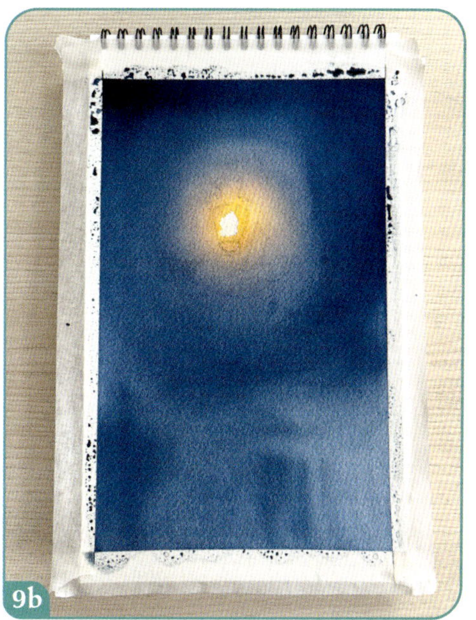

12 As you work your way to the bottom of the church, darken your color mixture by mixing in extra Ultramarine Blue. You can also use this darker color to add some basic details into the top section of the church, giving the suggestion of arches or columns.

Now that the background is completed, we can work on the real star of the show: this lamp. One super cool trick to making things look like they're glowing brightly is to paint any objects directly in front of the light with yellow and red rather than a dark color. In this case, the metal bars between the glass panels of the lamp overlap the light, so we'll use this technique when painting those.

13 In your mixing area, mix up some saturated Cadmium Yellow, Cadmium Red and Payne's Gray.

14 With your detail brush, paint the center of each of the bars supporting the lamp with yellow.

15 Quickly switch to Cadmium Red and add it to the support bars on both sides of the yellow.

16 Switch to Payne's Gray and fill in the rest of the support bar. Use a damp brush to blend all of these colors together a little bit if needed, but don't worry about getting a perfect gradient!

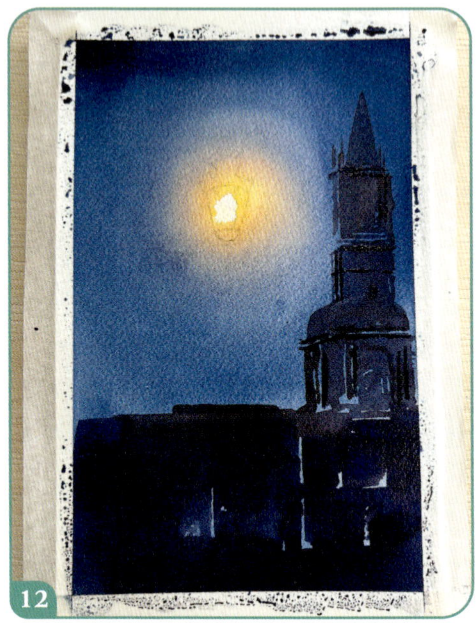

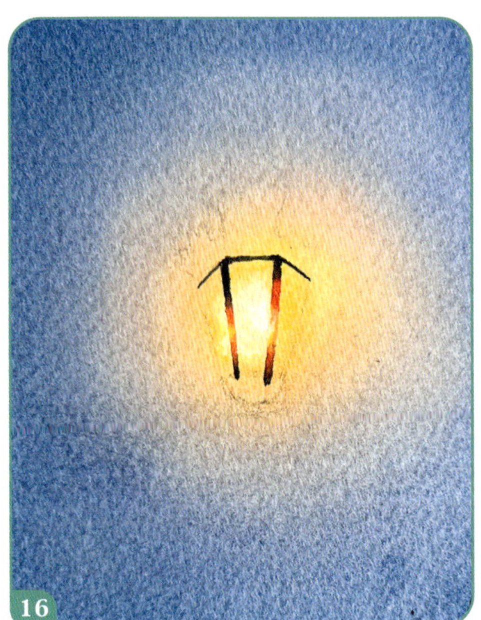

17 You can include this same effect on the base of the lamp by adding a small semicircle of yellow and red that fades into Payne's Gray.

18 Using Payne's Gray, fill in the rest of the lamp, the lamp support and the building it's attached to in the foreground.

19 Optional: Add a hint of concentrated Cadmium Yellow and/or Cadmium Orange to the outer edges of the inside of the lamp to really take the saturation up a notch!

Take off the tape and let your painting dry completely! How did this go for you? Does the lamp look like it's glowing? Take note of the things you've done well and the things you think could be improved next time!

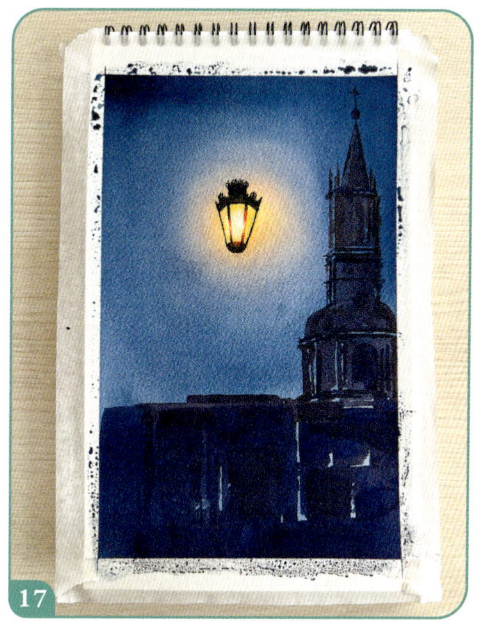

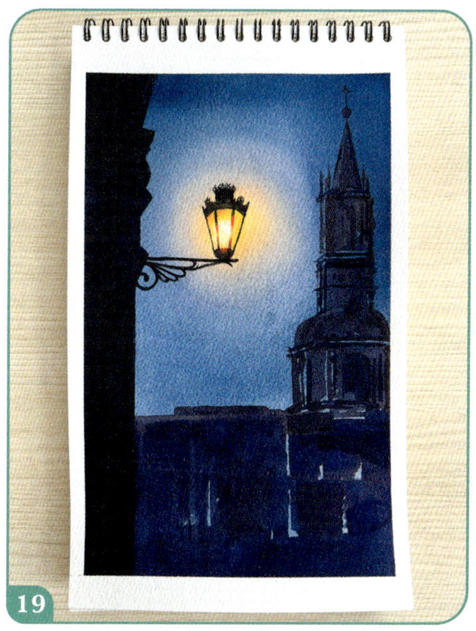

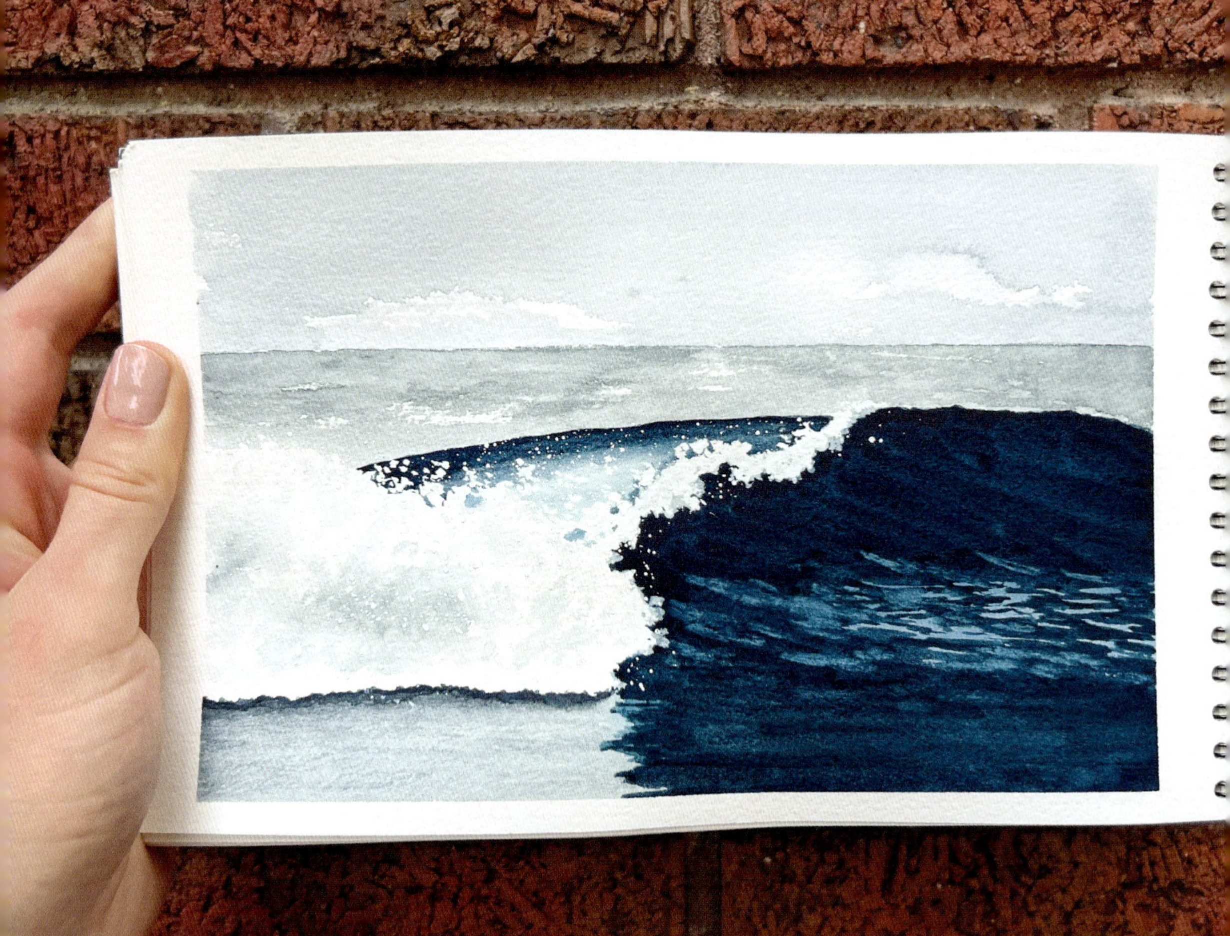

Making Waves

Ocean waves make for a really fun and dynamic painting subject. The movement of the water, the transparency and glow within the eye of the wave, and the crashing foam all have contrasting colors and textures that make for a compelling painting. This subject gives us a chance to practice combining a few different highlighting techniques (page 108) in the same painting. We will also be practicing our layering techniques (page 94) to get the saturation and depth of color you see in that deep teal water! For this project, you'll need:

»   Cup of water and paper towel

»   Watercolor paints: Payne's Gray, Ultramarine Blue, Sap Green, Turquoise, Aqua Green, Indigo, Phthalo Green

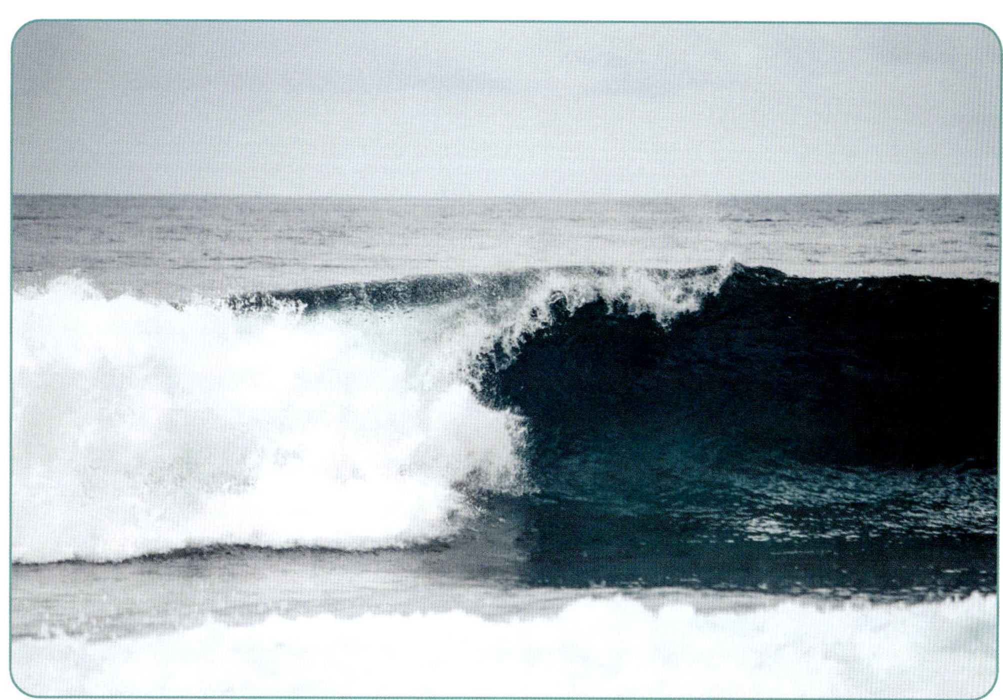

» Watercolor paper (I used a page of my Arches sketchbook)

» Optional: masking tape, white gouache

» Pencil

» 1 large, 1 medium and 1 detail water-color brush (I used a 10 round, a 4 round and a 2 round)

» Masking fluid

1 Add a drop of water to each of your colors and give them a minute to soften. In the meantime, prepare your paper as you like, taping down the edges if you want.

NOTE: If you don't have masking fluid, you can still complete this painting; you'll just need to paint around the areas you want to keep white!

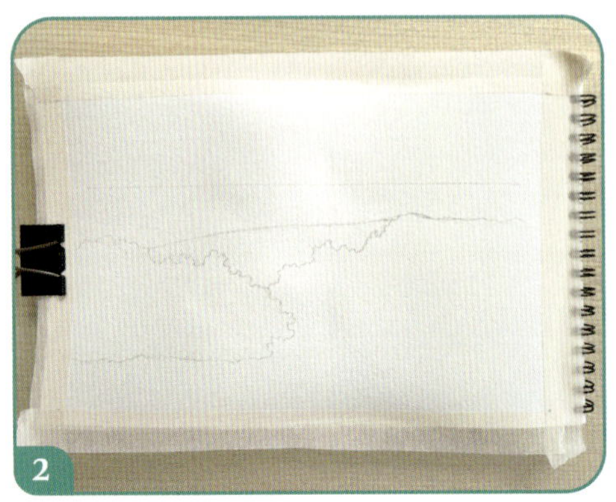

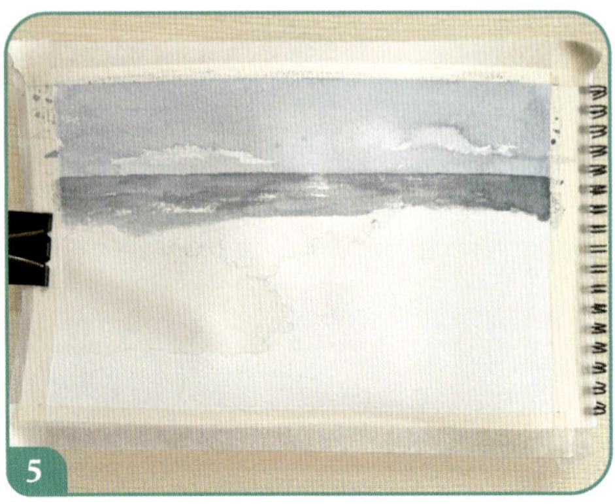

2   Create your pencil sketch. Add a horizon line about two-thirds of the way up the paper, then add in the basic shapes of the wave: Sketch in the slightly sloping top line of the wave, then sketch the water rolling over the wave and the large, cloud-like shape of the white foam. Use lots of curvy, squiggly lines for those two elements.

3   Use masking fluid to mask the entire area of white foam, plus the edges of the water curling over the wave. Try to use organic shapes and add a few random dots here and there to create droplets flying up from the wave.

4   Mix a light gray combining Payne's Gray and a touch of Ultramarine Blue plus plenty of water. Using a large brush, fill in the section above the horizon line using horizontal brush strokes. Feel free to just use a flat wash, but if you want bonus points you can add some dry brushing texture like I did to give the suggestion of clouds.

5   Add a touch of Sap Green to the light gray from Step 4 and use it to fill in the ocean section from the horizon line to the top of the wave. Continue to use your large brush horizontal brushstrokes. I encourage you to allow your brush to run out of paint on the paper to create a dry brushing texture here to give the impression of distant waves.

Remember Your Fundamentals: Dry brushing texture is super helpful when painting water. We're using it here painting the distant ocean, and we'll use it later in this project to add shadow and dimension to the foamy sections (spoiler alert!). Review the dry brushing technique in Texturize It (page 101).

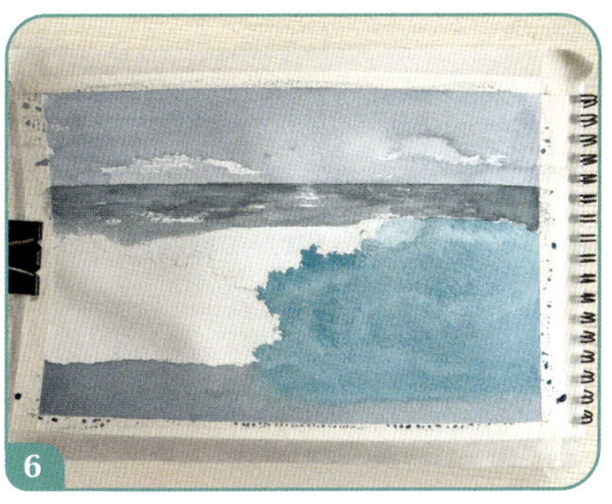

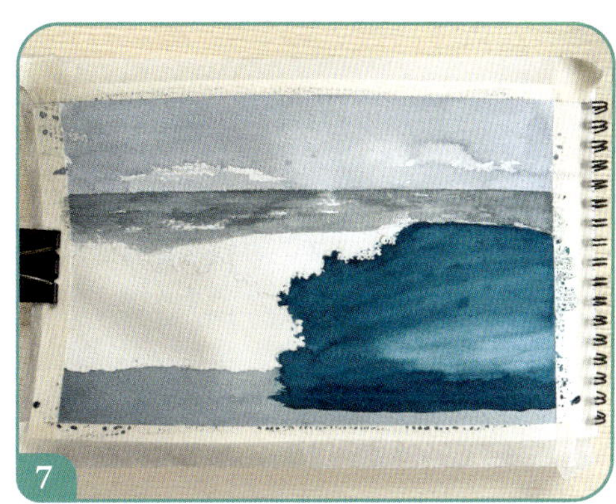

6   Mix up a puddle of watered-down Turquoise and, using a large brush, fill in only the section inside the wave and down to the bottom of the page, leaving the space directly below the foamy section blank. While this is still wet, add some of the ocean-gray paint from Step 5 underneath the foamy shape, allowing it to blend with the turquoise paint. Let it dry completely.

7   Mix up some Aqua Green in your palette and use it to darken the wave area. Keep the area at the base of the wave lighter by painting around it, then use a clean damp brush to blend the harsh lines. Use horizontal brushstrokes to create a wiggly line at the boundary between the teal color of the wave and the light gray ocean color in the reflection of the foamy section.

NOTE: You'll notice in the progress photo here that I did not paint the turquoise color all the way to the bottom of the page, and instead brought the ocean-gray color along the bottom of the whole painting. I ended up changing my mind on this later; you can see in Step 8 how the dark teal color of the wave extends all the way to the bottom of the painting. This is a case of do as I say, not as I do!

8   Mix a concentrated dark teal color combining Indigo and Phthalo Green and very little water. Use this color to darken the wave to its final color, again leaving the area below the foamy section alone. Leave a few lighter spots showing through around the base of the wave, and use a clean dry brush to remove extra pigment for more light spots in that area if desired. Try to use brushstrokes that generally follow the direction of the water—horizontal below the wave and diagonal to the left within the wave.

9   With a medium brush and your Turquoise color, paint in a small triangle shape in the area where the water is curling over the wave.

10 Immediately add in the dark teal color from Step 8 to fill in the top of the curling wave above the turquoise triangle and use a clean damp brush to blend.

11 Let it dry completely and remove the masking fluid.

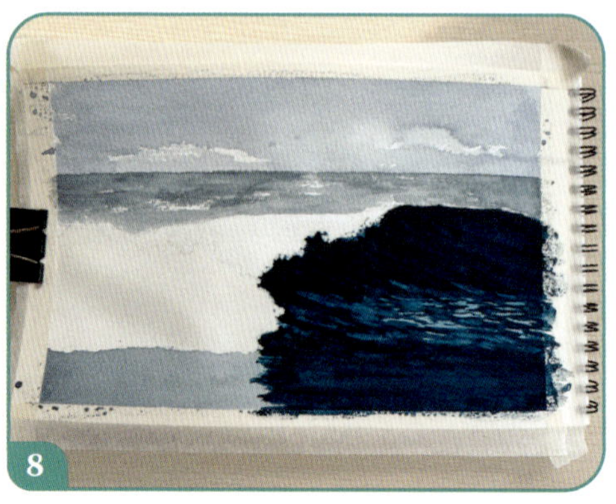

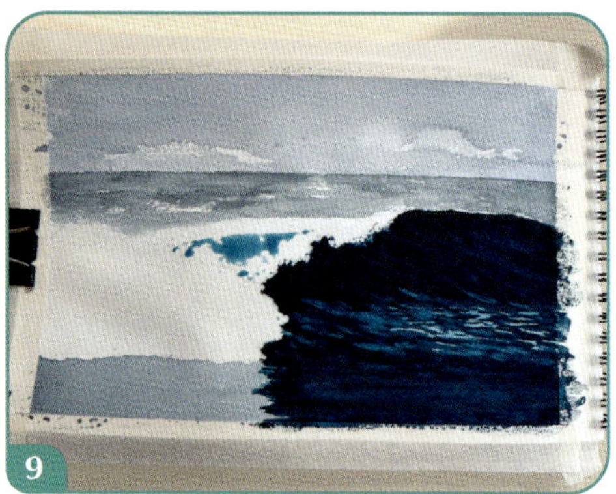

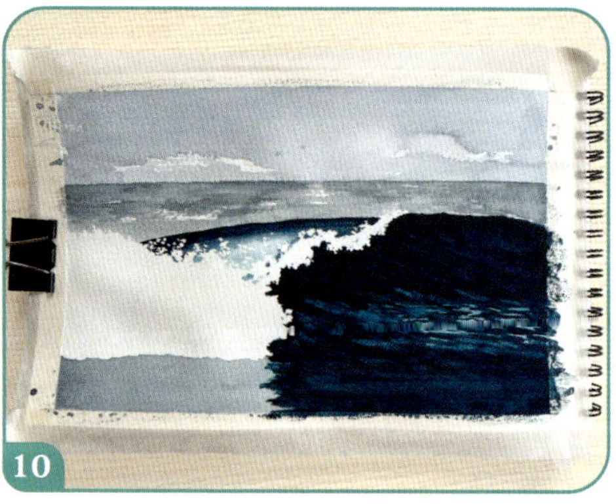

12 Use the ocean-gray color from Step 5 and a detail brush to add some shadows to the foamy section. Use the side of the brush and a rough dry brushing texture to imitate the shadows in the foam, blending with a clean damp brush to soften it when desired.

13 Continue using the ocean-gray color to add some little shadows to the foam on the water curling over the wave.

14 Make your ocean-gray color slightly darker by adding more paint to it and use it to add a shadow underneath the bottom edge of the foamy section.

15 Optional (but so worth it): Slightly water down some white gouache and splatter it over the foamy section of the wave. Use paper towels to protect the rest of your painting and your workspace, and add as much paint splatter as you want!

Once you're happy with these final details, you're all done! Take off the tape and analyze your work—do you feel like your highlights were successful? Do you have a sense of movement in your painting? Take note of what went well and what you could improve on next time.

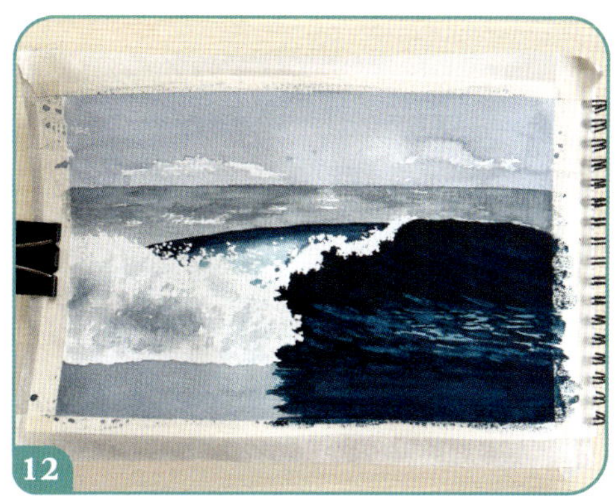

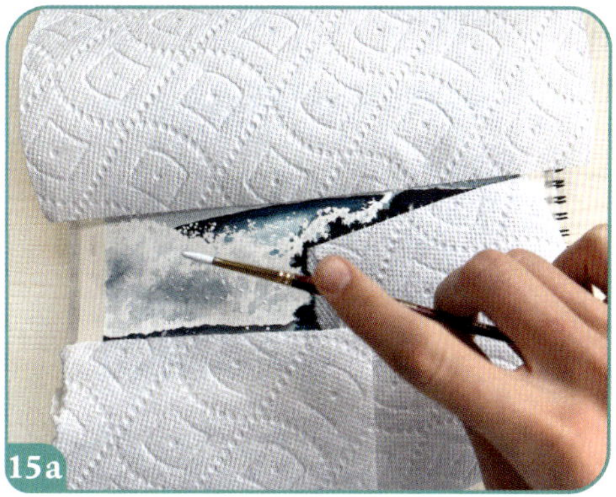

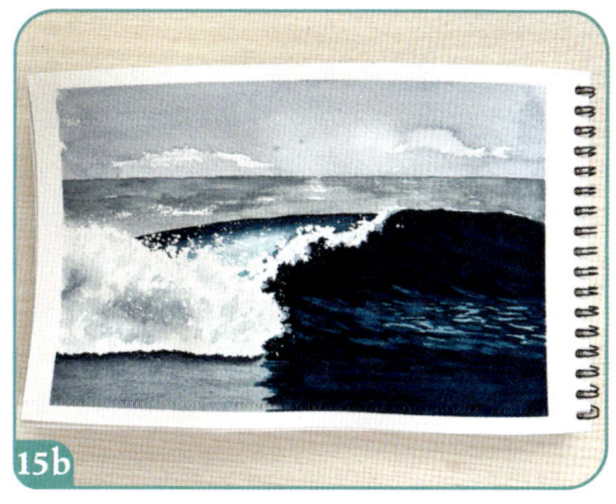

Limited Palette

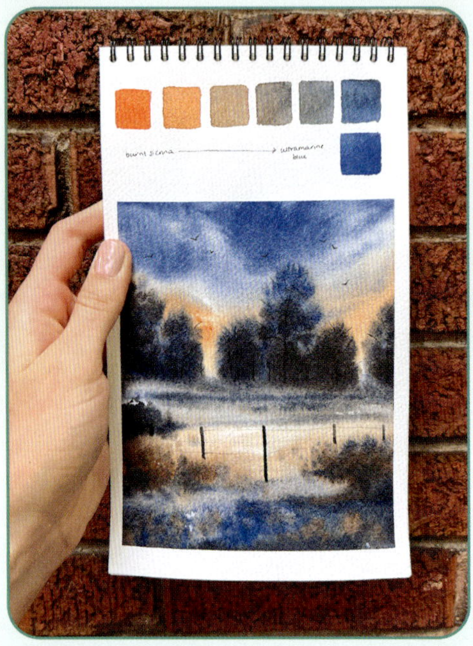

While you may have a bunch of different colors available to you in your watercolor set, you don't always need to use them all. Sometimes limiting yourself to one color to create a monochromatic painting helps you practice getting correct values. Limiting your palette to only two or three colors gives you a few more color options, but not that many. This forces you to get creative with your color mixtures, use what you have available and rely on value and contrast (page 53) to create a compelling painting. Today we will be experimenting with my favorite two-color palette—Burnt Sienna and Ultramarine Blue—and adding in the extra challenge of painting the majority of the painting in a wet-on-wet style, which gives the painting a blurry, almost dream-like quality. For this painting, you'll need:

» Cup of water and paper towel

» Watercolor paints: Burnt Sienna, Ultramarine Blue

» Watercolor paper (I used a page of my Arches sketchbook)

» Optional: masking tape

» Pencil

» 1 large and 1 detail watercolor brush (I used a 10 round and a 2 round)

When working with a limited color palette, it's important to figure out the range of colors we have available to us before we start.

1   Add a drop of water to the two colors and give them a minute to soften. Then mix up a small puddle of Burnt Sienna and paint a small square on your paper.

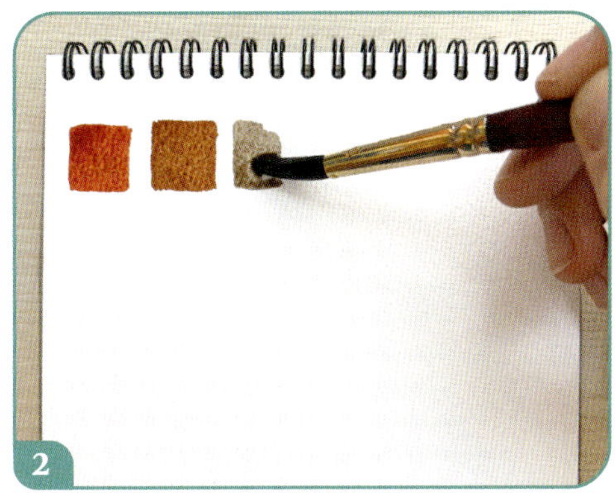

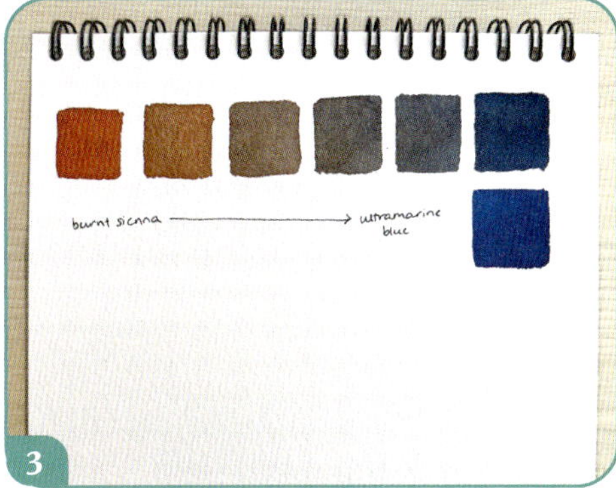

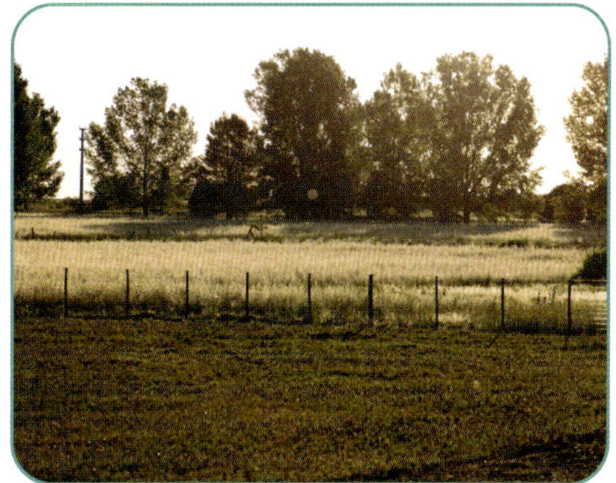

2   Add a little bit of Ultramarine Blue to the Burnt Sienna and paint another square using this new color.

3   Continue adding Ultramarine Blue to this color mixture and painting squares until you end with pure Ultramarine Blue.

Now you can see the range of colors you have available for this painting when the two colors are mixed together in different proportions. I love this color combination because it results in a beautiful range of warm browns and cool grays, plus the vibrancy of the pure Burnt Sienna and Ultramarine Blue on their own.

Remember Your Fundamentals: When picking colors for a limited palette painting, I prefer picking complementary colors (colors opposite each other on the color wheel) because they look good together, and give you a good range of muted colors when the two are mixed together in different proportions. You can always review color theory by revisiting Colorful Language (page 59).

Now let's get started on the painting. I'm taking light inspiration from the reference photo you see above for the composition, but since we're using colors you don't see in this painting and a wet-on-wet technique, we'll allow lots of room for improvising.

4   Tape down your paper if you want and sketch in a horizon line about halfway up the paper.

5   Prep a few colors in your mixing palette—pure Burnt Sienna, pure Ultramarine Blue and a couple combinations of the two colors using different ratios. Add very little water to keep the paints as concentrated as possible!

6   Cover the entire paper with a generous layer of water using a large brush.

7   Paint in some sweeping horizontal brushstrokes of Burnt Sienna just above the horizon line.

8   Switch to Ultramarine Blue and add sweeping horizontal strokes to the top of the paper, gently blending with the Burnt Sienna already there.

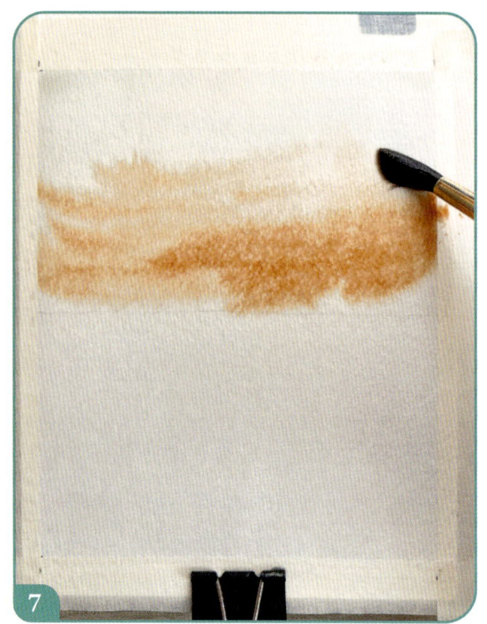

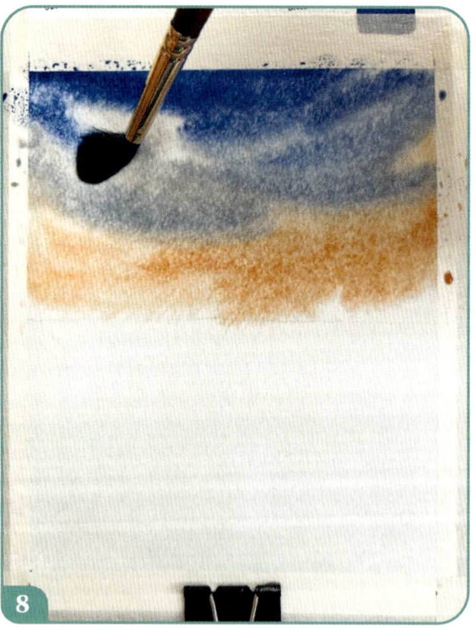

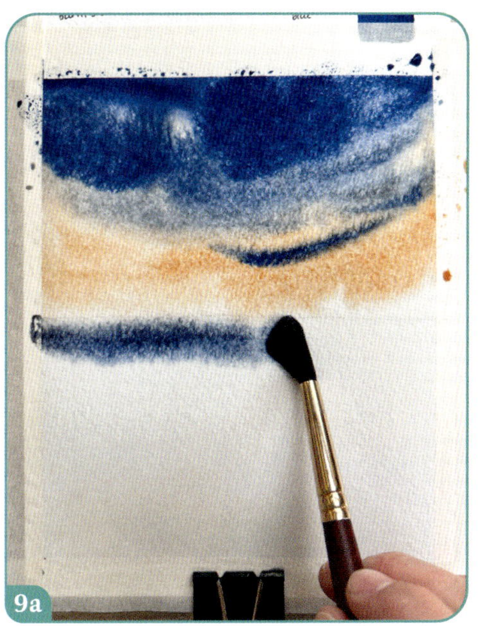

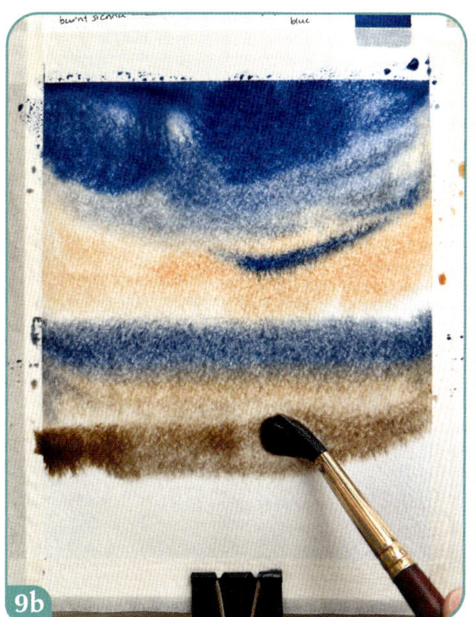

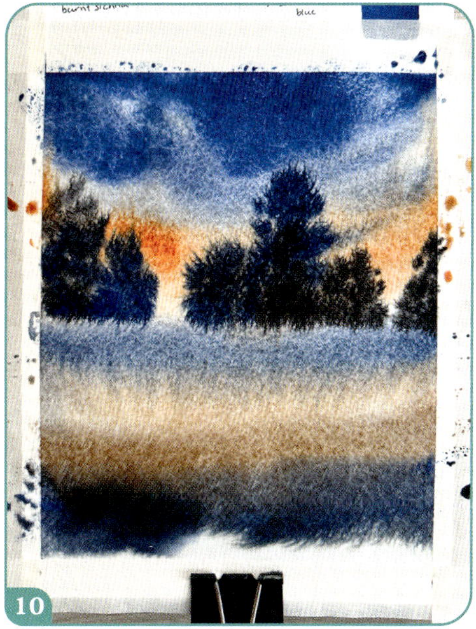

9   Next, start working on the land below the horizon line. Use horizontal strokes to add stripes of a few different color mixtures, working your way down. I used darker colors at the horizon line and at the bottom of the page, and lighter colors favoring Burnt Sienna in between.

10   With a very concentrated gray color, use a dotting motion to develop some tree shapes at the horizon line. Since you're painting on wet paper, the paint should spread out into a very organic, treelike shape without too much work on your part.

11 Add some random horizontal lines and clumps of dots to create texture in the land area, using different shades of concentrated paint mixtures.

NOTE: Because your paper is saturated with water, it will lighten any paint colors you place on it. As you continue to work with the wet-on-wet technique, you can keep layering different shades of concentrated paint in any areas you want extra dark, like the trees for example.

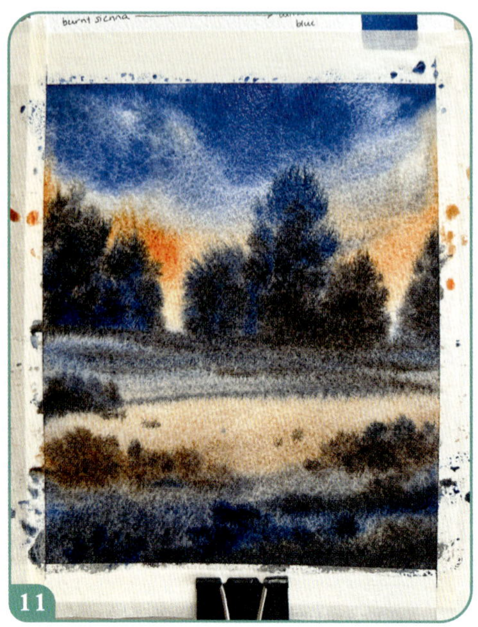

12 Dry off your large brush completely and use it to lift paint anywhere you want a highlight. Some good spots are right in the center of the land section and in the sky.

13 You can continue layering and adding detail while the painting is still wet, but once it starts to dry, leave it alone and let it dry all the way.

14 Lastly, we'll add a couple little details to bring the painting to life. Using a dark gray shade and a detail brush, add some fence posts, strategically placing them behind some of the foliage in the field. Use a watered-down gray color and a super light touch to paint the wires between the fence posts.

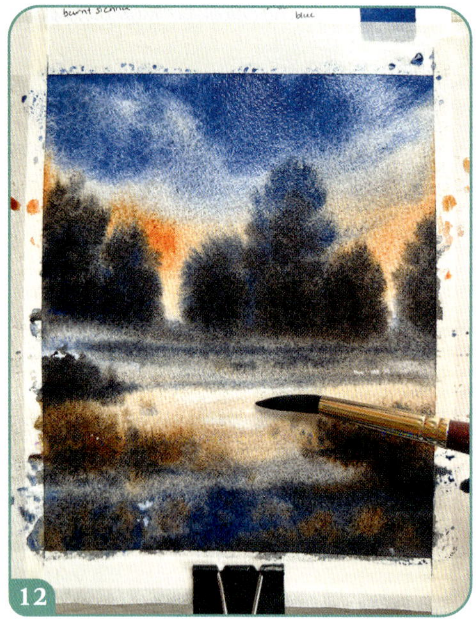

15 Switching back to a more concentrated gray or neutral brown color, add the suggestion of tree trunks and branches on the trees in the distance.

16 Add a few V-shapes in the sky to create a small flock of birds flying over the scene.

You've completed your limited palette painting! Take a step back from your painting and analyze it–did you develop a good range of values in your painting? Make a note of what went well and what could be improved next time. This challenge is SO beneficial for your watercolor practice, so I'd encourage you to try it again in the future. Pick one warm color and one cool color, choose a subject and see what you can make happen!

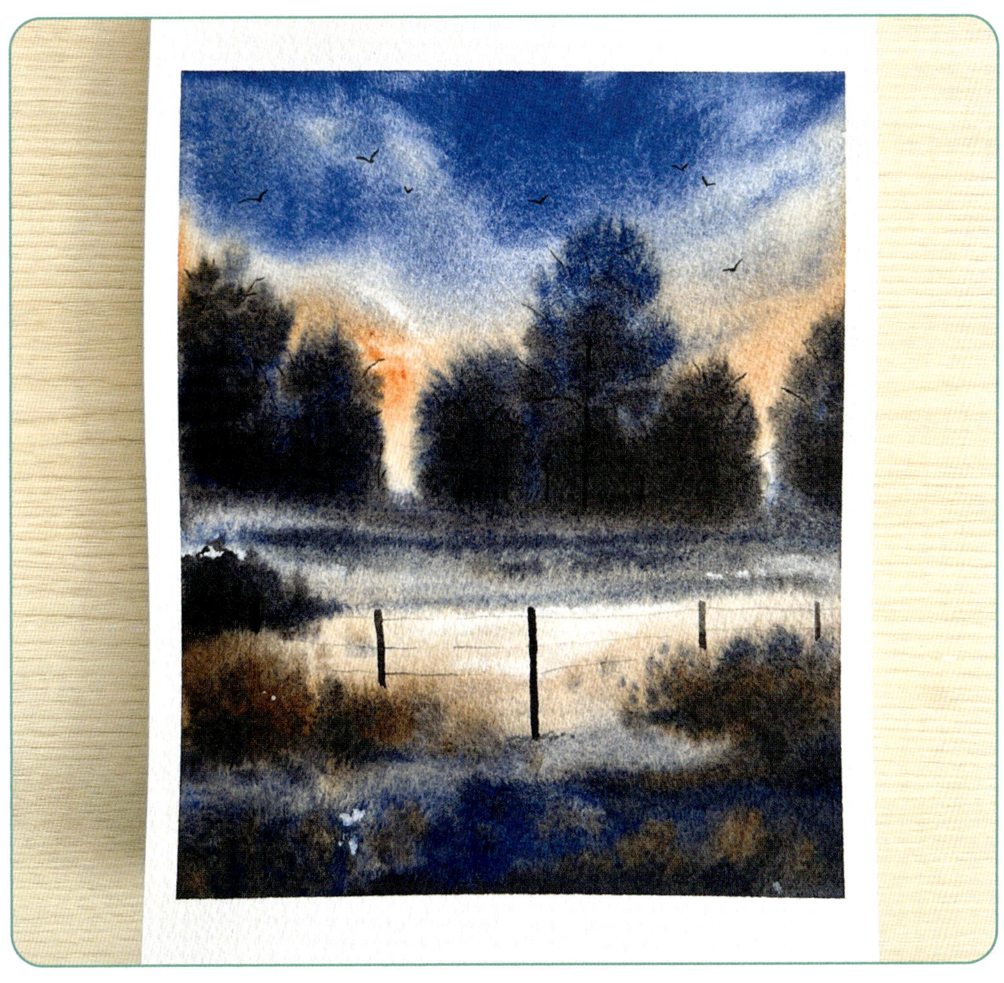

CHAPTER 4

Advanced Subjects

Expand Your Watercolor Knowledge with These Captivating Subjects

In this next chapter, we'll tackle some more complicated subjects together. You've worked your way through over half of this book at this point, so your watercolor muscles are looking huge! As I've said before, you'll continue to use the basics we learned in Chapters 1 and 2, so if there's ever a technique you're struggling with, just flip back to those sections and review. This chapter covers landscape subjects like water, sunlight and snow, plus some observational paintings of everyday objects to hone our realism skills. Enjoy getting outside your comfort zone!

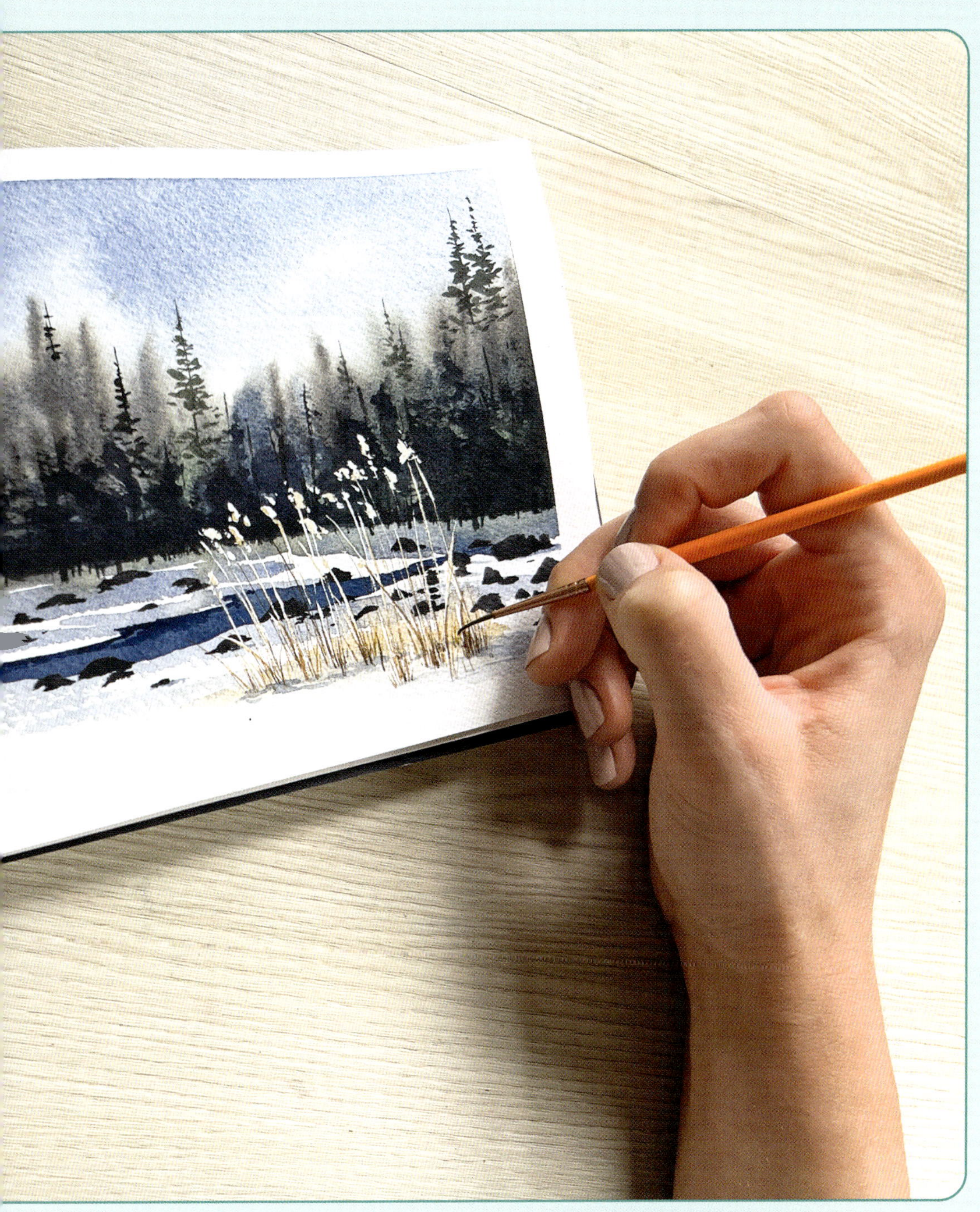

Upon Further Reflection

As we move further into more complex painting subjects, it seems fitting to talk about painting scenes with water elements. Water is one of my favorite subjects to paint in any medium because it's a challenge—an illusion that only works if you use the correct colors and brushstrokes. In our lesson today, we'll focus on water reflections specifically, but we'll explore different water subjects later in this book.

There's a science to water reflections—objects above the water will reflect in a mirror image onto the water below, but are often distorted by any movement in the water. To get our feet wet, we're going to tackle a sunset scene with a simple water reflection. The reference photo you see here is from Florence, Italy, with a gorgeous sunset over the peaceful Arno River.

For this project, you'll need:

» Cup of water and paper towel

» Watercolor paints: Alizarin Crimson, Cadmium Yellow, Indigo, Yellow Ochre, Ultramarine Blue

» Watercolor paper (I used a page of my Arches sketchbook)

» Optional: masking tape

» Pencil

» Masking fluid and a brush to apply it with

» 1 large, 1 medium and 1 detail watercolor brush (I used a 12 round, a 4 round and a 2 round)

1   Add a drop of water to each of your colors and give them a minute to soften. In the meantime, set up your paper, taping it down if you'd like.

2   Sketch out the basic shapes of this scene, starting with a horizon line around the middle of the paper, then adding the outlines of the trees and buildings. I added a little extra detail to the buildings, which you are welcome to do too, but you can also keep them simple silhouettes if you'd prefer. Sketch in a mirror image outline of the buildings in the bottom half of the paper, and sketch in the lights on the buildings and their reflections in the water.

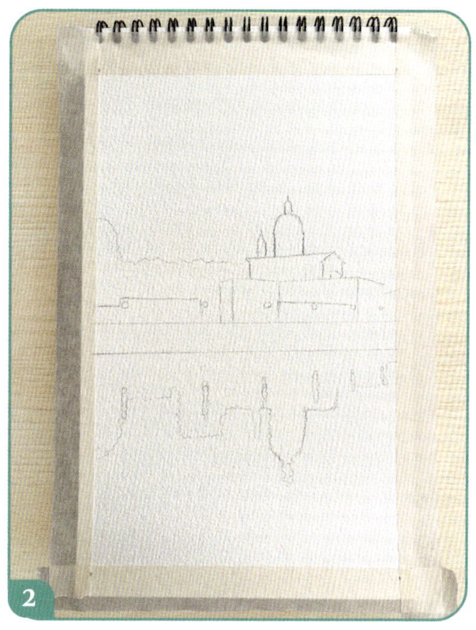

3   Use masking fluid to cover the lights and light reflections. If you'd like to use a different highlighting technique like gouache, lifting or just painting around those highlights, you are welcome to do that instead.

Remember Your Fundamentals: We covered four different highlight options in Highlight Reel (page 108). If you need to review any of the highlight techniques, make sure to check back there first!

4 Mix up big puddles of the following three colors for the sky gradient: Alizarin Crimson, Cadmium Yellow and a dark blue-purple color combining Indigo and Alizarin Crimson.

5 Using a large brush and working quickly, paint a semicircle of Cadmium Yellow at the right side of the horizon line. Quickly switch to Alizarin Crimson and build up the semicircle into the sky, then use the dark blue-purple mixture to fill in the rest of the sky section. Use a clean damp brush to blend the colors together into a smooth gradient, always starting in the yellow section and blending outward into the blue-purple color to prevent muddying the yellow color. Then let it dry completely.

Remember Your Fundamentals: Gradients strike again! You can always review on page 85.

6 Repeat Step 5 on the bottom half of the page, creating a mirror image of the gradient in the sky, then let it dry completely. I like to turn my paper around 180 degrees when painting the reflection because it makes for a more comfortable painting motion.

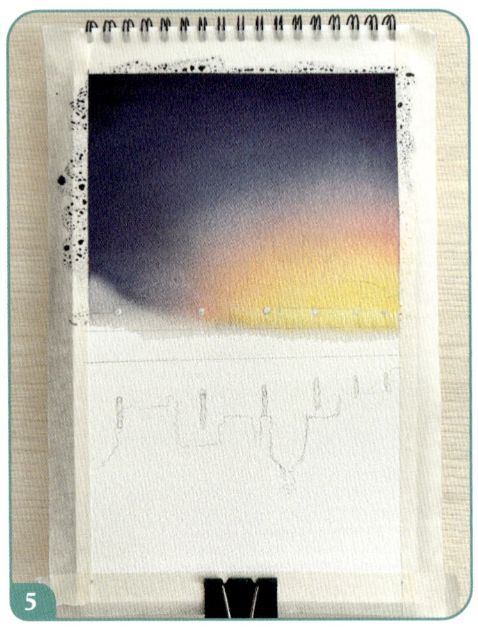

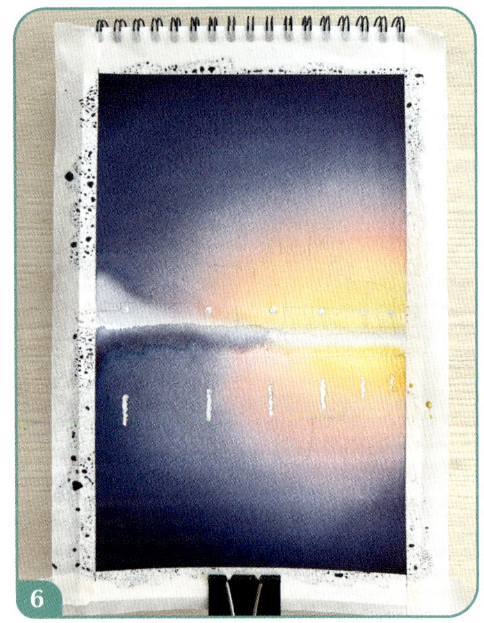

7   Mix a dark brown color combining Yellow Ochre, Alizarin Crimson and Ultramarine Blue, adding very little water. Add more Yellow Ochre to this mixture to lean it more toward a brown tone.

8   Use a medium brush and fill in the slightly lighter building shapes in the upper half of the painting with a flat wash.

9   Add more Ultramarine Blue and Alizarin Crimson to your brown color mixture to darken it and use it to fill in the rest of the building and tree silhouettes on the top half of the paper.

10 Use the same dark color and a medium brush to add a couple little hints of windows, doorways and building textures, but nothing too detailed.

11 Continue using the dark color to fill in the entire reflection in the water section.

NOTE: The edges of each object in the reflection are not smooth; they are blurred by tiny, mostly horizontal lines created by the ripples in the water. Use a very light touch to paint horizontal lines around the edges of each object in the reflection, and feel free to switch to your detail brush when doing this for more control.

12 Remove the masking fluid from the highlight areas. Use a little watered-down Yellow Ochre and a detail brush to blend the edges of the lights on the buildings into the surrounding dark paint. Outline the highlight reflections in the water with the same Yellow Ochre, but no need to blend.

13 Add any final details: Refine the ripples in the reflection, add another layer of paint to the buildings or reflection to deepen the color, etc.

Once you're happy, take off the tape and admire your work! Painting water reflections successfully can really feel like a magic trick when the illusion comes together. Make sure to analyze your painting and take note of what went well and what could be improved on for next time!

Trompe l'Oeil

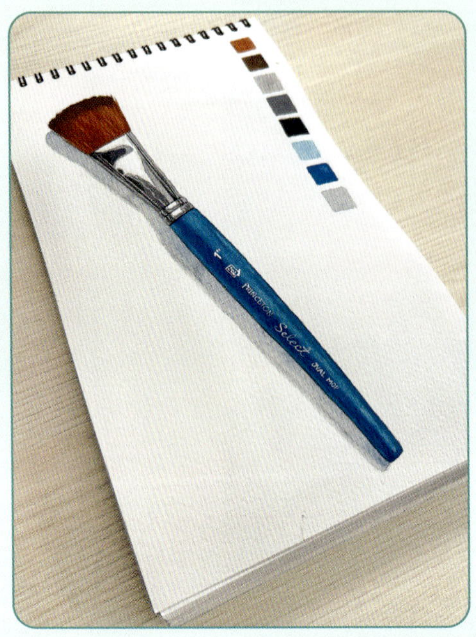

Not knowing what to paint is the constant thorn in the side of many artists. The blank page is intimidating and inspiration can be hard to come by. When this happens, one trick is to simply paint the objects within your reach. They might look ordinary, but when you truly observe and recreate an object with paint, you notice all of the minute color tones, shadows and textures, and it can really help you build up your realism skills. This style is called "trompe l'oeil," which is a French art term meaning "trick the eye," and involves painting small, everyday objects life-sized and as realistically as possible to give the illusion that the object is actually sitting there on your paper. Our subject today is something you will all have if you've been working your way through this book with me: a paintbrush! I chose a brush for myself, and I encourage you to choose one of your own brushes for this project rather than copying mine. I'll walk you through the steps I took to paint my brush for you to use as a guide, but this is your chance to use your observation skills and what you've learned so far to paint a subject independently! Be brave, my fledglings!

For this painting, you'll need:

» Cup of water and paper towel

» Watercolor paints: colors to match your paintbrush (I used Burnt Sienna, Ultramarine Blue, Van Dyke Brown and Turquoise)

» Watercolor paper (I used a page of my Arches sketchbook)

» Optional: masking tape

» Pencil

» Your brush of choice to use as the painting subject

» 1 medium and 1 detail watercolor brush (I used a 4 round and a 2 round)

» White gouache

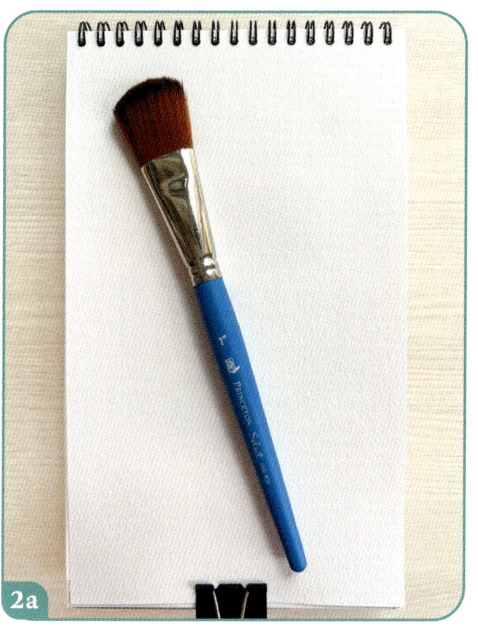

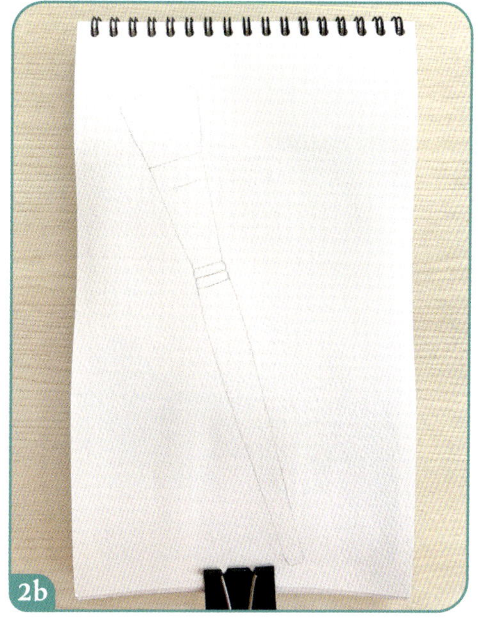

1   Add a drop of water to each of your colors and give them a minute to soften. In the meantime, prep your paper how you like it, taping the edges down if desired.

2   Sketch the shape of your paintbrush freehand, or if you want to be efficient like me, just plop that brush down on the paper and trace around the outside with your pencil. As you work, keep the paintbrush you're painting either on the paper next to your sketch or just off to the side so that you can constantly observe it from life.

3   I started with the bristles, which are a light auburn color with a darker brown at the ends. I mixed up both colors combining Burnt Sienna and Ultramarine Blue, using more Burnt Sienna for the auburn color and more Ultramarine Blue for the darker brown color. I put down a flat wash of the auburn color throughout the entire bristle shape, then immediately dropped in the darker brown color at the end of the bristle shape and let the colors gently blend.

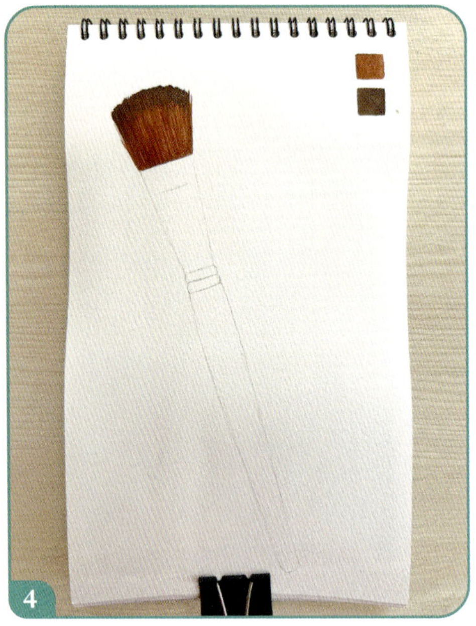

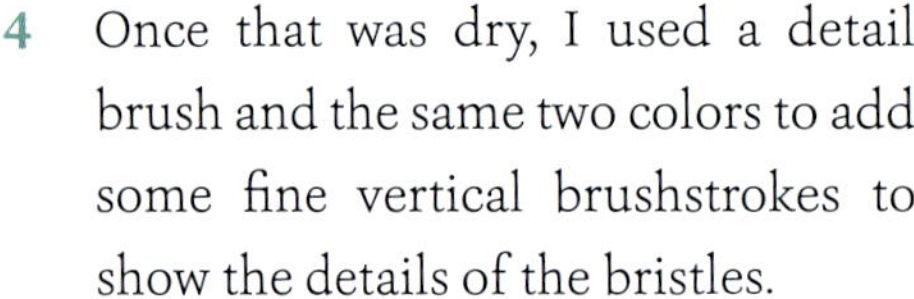

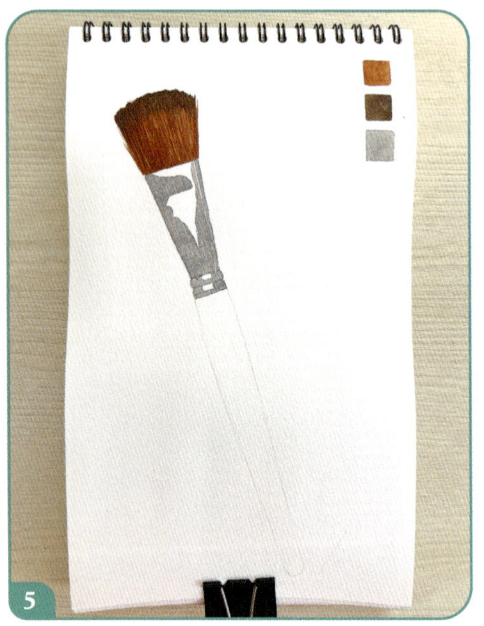

4   Once that was dry, I used a detail brush and the same two colors to add some fine vertical brushstrokes to show the details of the bristles.

5   For the metal piece that connects the bristles to the handle, I carefully observed the light and shadow patterns reflecting off of it. Then I mixed a light gray by combining Van Dyke Brown, Ultramarine Blue and plenty of water and used that to paint everything but the lightest spots in this section.

6   I darkened the gray color by adding more pigment to it and added a few squiggly shapes and lines within the shaded section to create more detail.

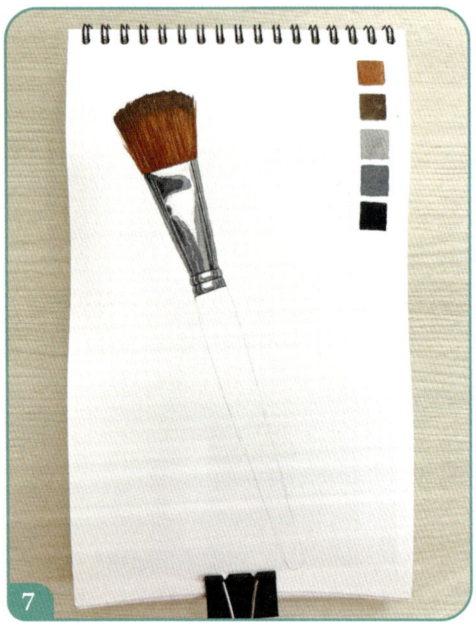

7   I mixed up a very dark gray and added just a couple dots and shapes where I saw the darkest colors in the metal handle.

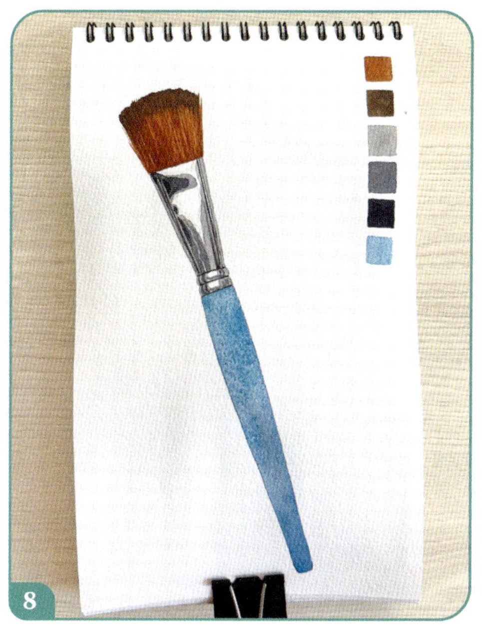

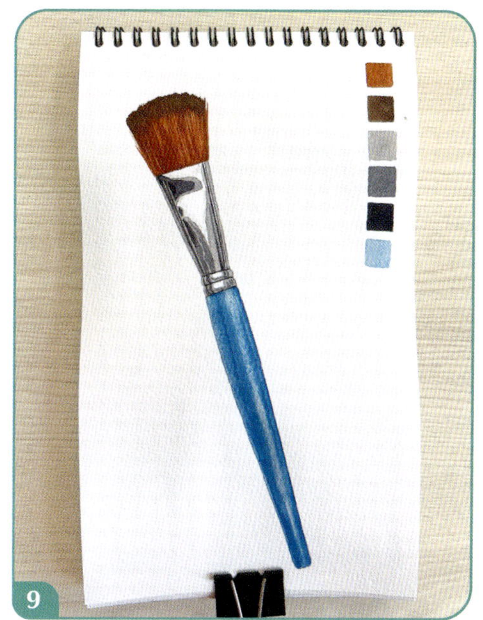

8   To paint the handle of the brush, I combined Turquoise and Ultramarine Blue to match the color and added plenty of water. I started with a flat wash over the whole shape and let it dry.

9   With a slightly more concentrated version of this same color, I started building in my shadow and highlight areas, using a clean damp brush to blend out any harsh lines.

10 I created a darker version of this color by adding more Ultramarine Blue and used that to create my darkest core shadow on the handle, blending the edges of the shadow shape with a damp brush.

Remember Your Fundamentals: The most important factor in getting a realistic optical illusion is nailing the lighting scheme. We covered this in our very first chapter See the Light . . . Source (page 22). I encourage you to truly observe how the light in your environment is bouncing off your paintbrush—are you painting in natural light or local light? Is the light strong, producing extreme highlights and shadows? Or is it diffused, producing less contrast? How is the light affecting the colors of the brush? Use thin layers of paint to slowly build up the shadows until they match what you're observing!

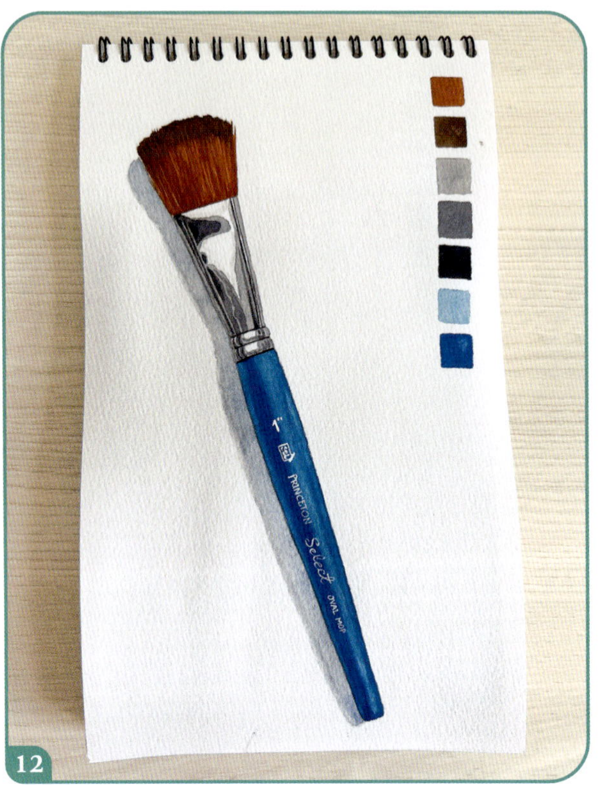

11 I used white gouache and a tiny 0 round detail brush to carefully copy the white lettering on my brush.

12 Finally, I went back to the light gray I used in Step 5 and added a cast shadow to the brush, copying the shape and size of the cast shadow I saw in real life. I blended the edge of the shadow with a clean damp brush to soften it.

When you're done, you should have a relatively realistic recreation of the paintbrush you chose. The illusion often works best when seen in peripheral vision or at first glance, so step away from your painting or put it to the side and glance back at it after a few minutes to see if you got a successful illusion. Whether you did or not, this project can really help you build up those observation skills along with your color mixing skills. Make sure you take note of what went well and what could be improved on for next time. If you'd like to take it up a notch, choose a different, maybe slightly more complex object from your home and attempt to recreate it in watercolor! Maybe a food item, a piece of jewelry or an action figure—the possibilities are endless!

Let the Sunlight In

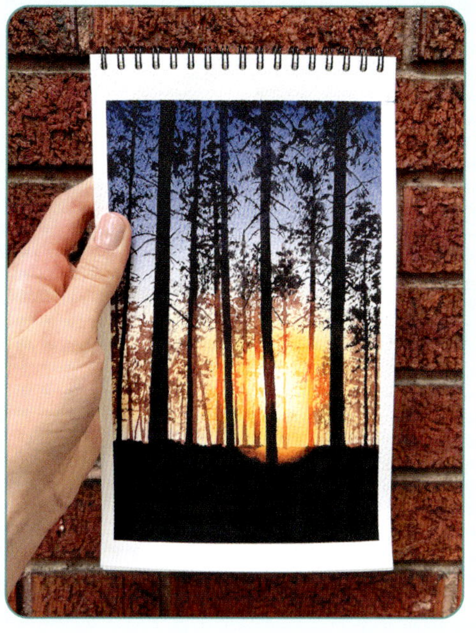

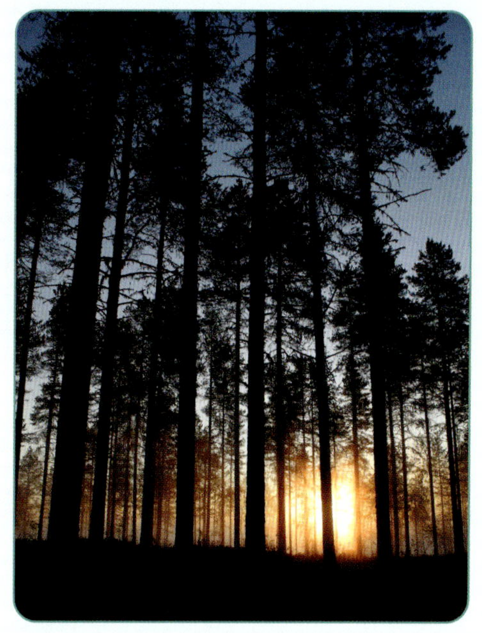

We had a little bit of practice painting glowing objects in Nocturne (page 139), and today I want to lead you through a landscape painting that will give you more experience with those principles. I found a beautiful reference photo of warm sunlight shining through a dark forest at sunrise. You'll get lots of practice painting realistic trees throughout this painting, but the main thing I want you to take away from this piece is observing and painting sunlight.

For this project, you'll need:

» Cup of water and paper towel

» Watercolor paints: Cadmium Yellow, Yellow Ochre, Ultramarine Blue, Alizarin Crimson, Cadmium Red, Payne's Gray, Van Dyke Brown

» Watercolor paper (I used a page of my Arches sketchbook)

» Optional: masking tape

» 1 large, 1 medium and 1 detail watercolor brush (I used a 12 round, a 4 round and a 2 round)

» Pencil

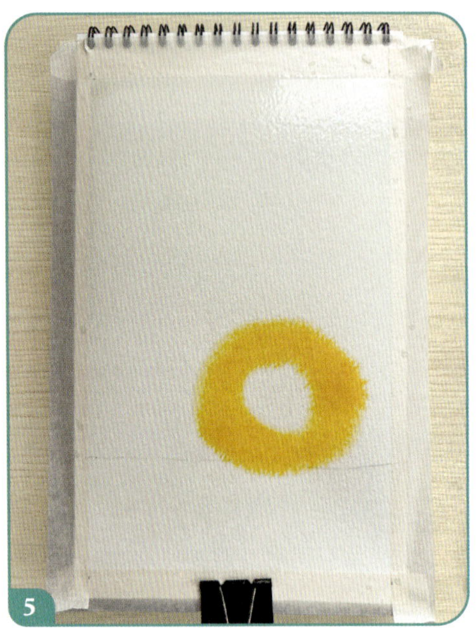

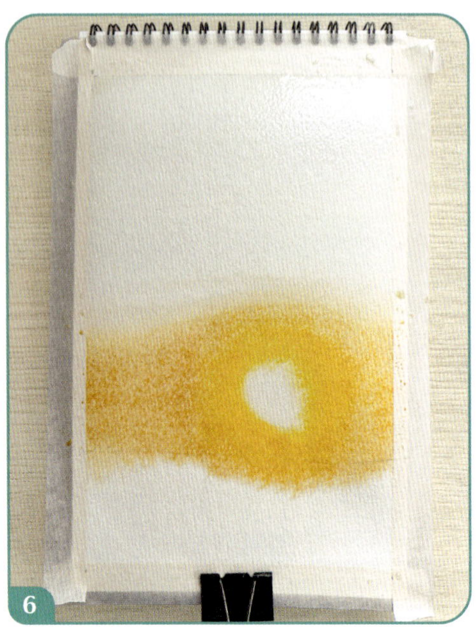

1   Add a drop of water to each of your colors and give them a minute to soften. In the meantime, prep your paper how you like it, taping the edges down if desired.

2   Mix up puddles of Cadmium Yellow, Yellow Ochre and a dark blue combining Ultramarine Blue and a little Alizarin Crimson. Keep the colors concentrated on your mixing palette, only adding a little water.

3   Sketch a loose horizon line about one-quarter of the way up the paper.

4   Use a large brush to cover your paper with a thick layer of water.

5   Load your brush with Cadmium Yellow and paint in a circle just above the horizon line and slightly to the right of center. Make sure to leave some white paper showing in the middle of the circle.

6   Clean your brush and switch to Yellow Ochre. Paint around the circle of Cadmium Yellow and out to the sides of the paper. Blend the top edge into the white of the paper with a clean damp brush.

7   Working from the top, paint in the dark blue color. Keep the most concentrated color at the top of the page, then allow the color to lighten as it mixes with the water on the paper as you work your way down.

8   Use a clean damp brush to blend the transition between colors. Let it dry completely.

9   Mix up the following colors to paint the trees:

»   Yellow: Cadmium Yellow

»   Orange: Cadmium Red and Yellow Ochre

»   Light Brown: Yellow Ochre, Alizarin Crimson and a touch of Ultramarine Blue

»   Black: Payne's Gray and a touch of Van Dyke Brown (you can also just use black if you have it on your palette)

In Steps 10 through 18, you'll paint the trees in two layers—the lighter, sunlit trees in the distance first, then the darker trees in the foreground. Take a close look at the sun in the reference photo. Notice how any tree trunks or foliage directly in front of the brightest part of the sun are bright yellow in color? As you move away from the sun, the trees turn red, then light brown, then black. Try to imitate this pattern with your paint.

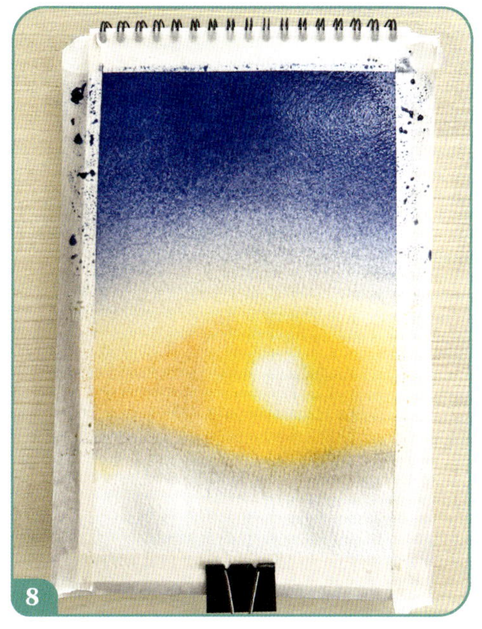

Remember Your Fundamentals: We can create high contrast in this painting (and further enhance the glowing effect) by keeping in mind the value range of the colors we use. Using lighter, saturated yellows and reds for the distant trees, then transitioning to black paint for the foreground trees will create a huge value range and high contrast, which make a compelling painting. If you need to review the importance of value and contrast, flip back to page 53.

10 Using your detail brush with Cadmium Yellow, paint the start of a thin tree trunk through the white sun spot on your paper.

11 Quickly switch to the orange color you mixed in Step 9 and add it to the tree trunk on either side of the Cadmium Yellow. The colors should blend together if you do this quickly enough, but if not, you can use a damp brush to blend.

12 Switch to the light brown color you mixed in Step 9 and continue the tree trunk on either end, bringing the bottom to the horizon line. As you work your way up the tree, start adding some loose foliage and branches. I like to scrape the side of my detail brush on the paper to get a rough, dry-brush texture. I find it works perfectly for these types of trees.

13 Finish painting the top of the tree with the black color you mixed in Step 9. The top of the tree should be about a third of the way from the top of the page.

14 Paint in the first layer of trees this way, working your way across the horizon line. Make sure to make the trees different heights and sizes for variety.

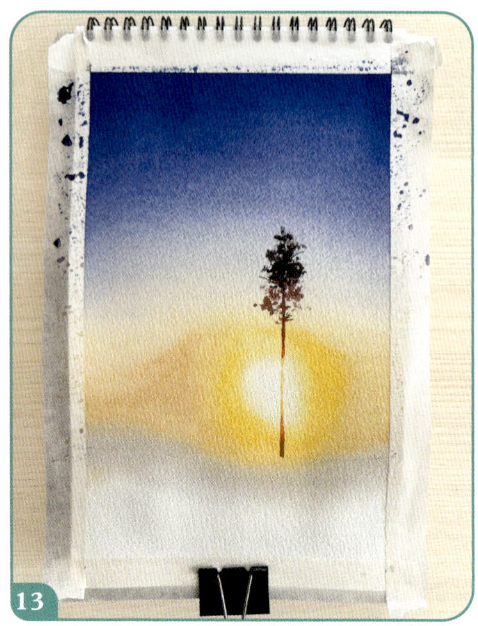

For color, follow these general rules of thumb:

» Anytime the background is white, use Cadmium Yellow to paint the trees.

» Anytime the background is Cadmium Yellow, use orange to paint the trees.

» Anytime the background is Yellow Ochre or a transition color, use light brown to paint the trees.

» Anytime the background is blue, use black to paint the trees.

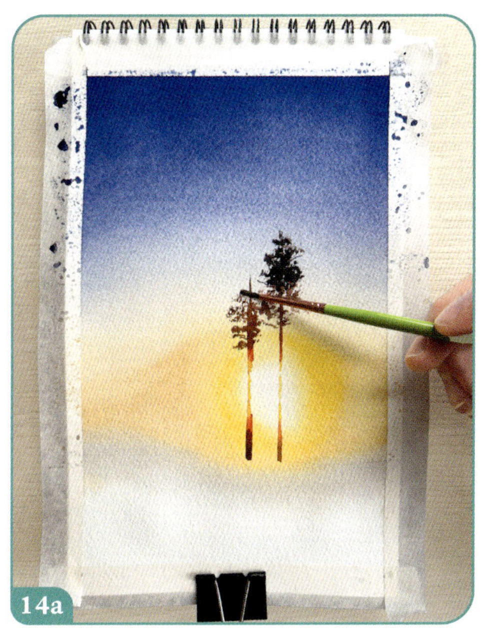

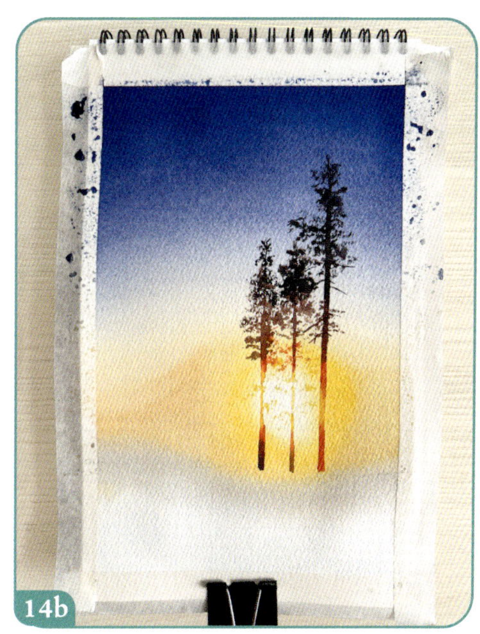

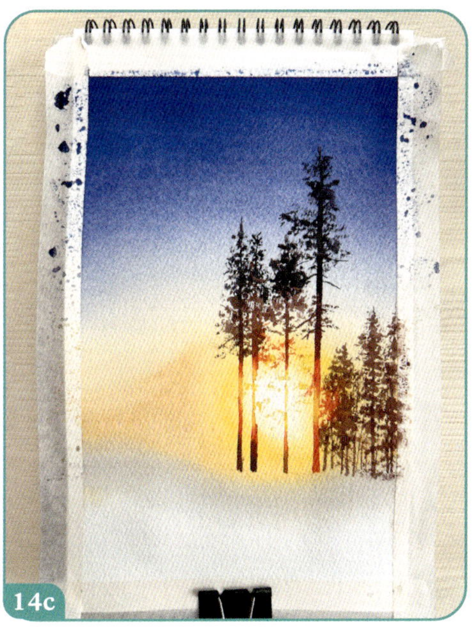

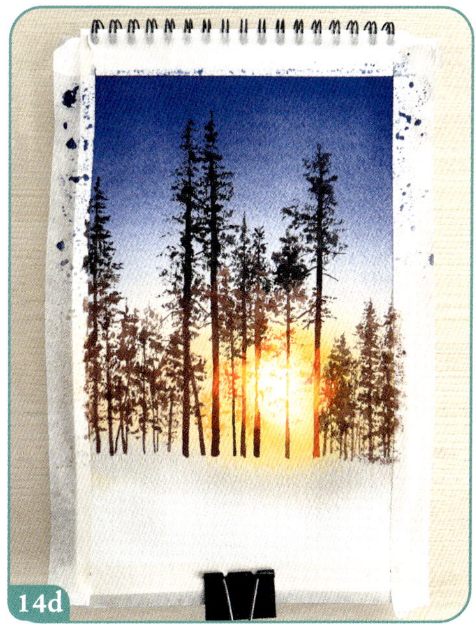

15 Paint in the first layer of the ground using the same colors we've been using. Paint a small line of Cadmium Yellow at the horizon line just below the sun, then a small semicircle of orange, then fill in the rest of the ground with light brown. Let it dry completely.

16 Leaving the small semicircle of yellow and orange alone, paint over the rest of the ground with black.

17 Start painting in a few foreground trees using just black paint. Note that these trees are much thicker and extend all the way off the paper, so you won't see as much of the foliage. Add plenty of crooked branches and some foliage using that same dry brushing texture.

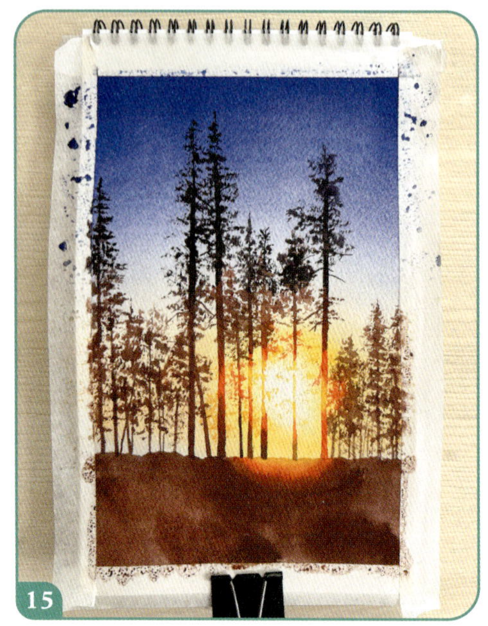

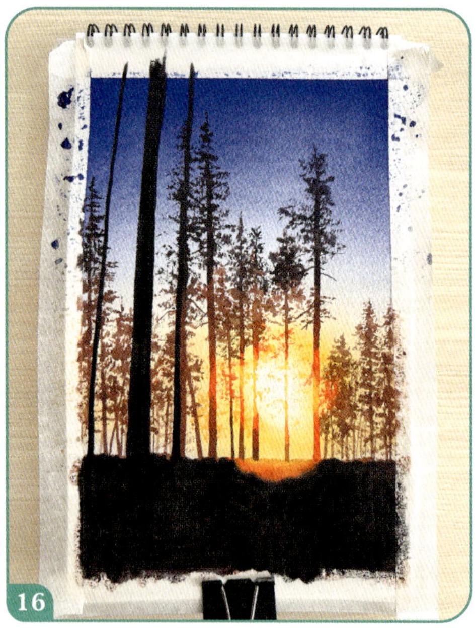

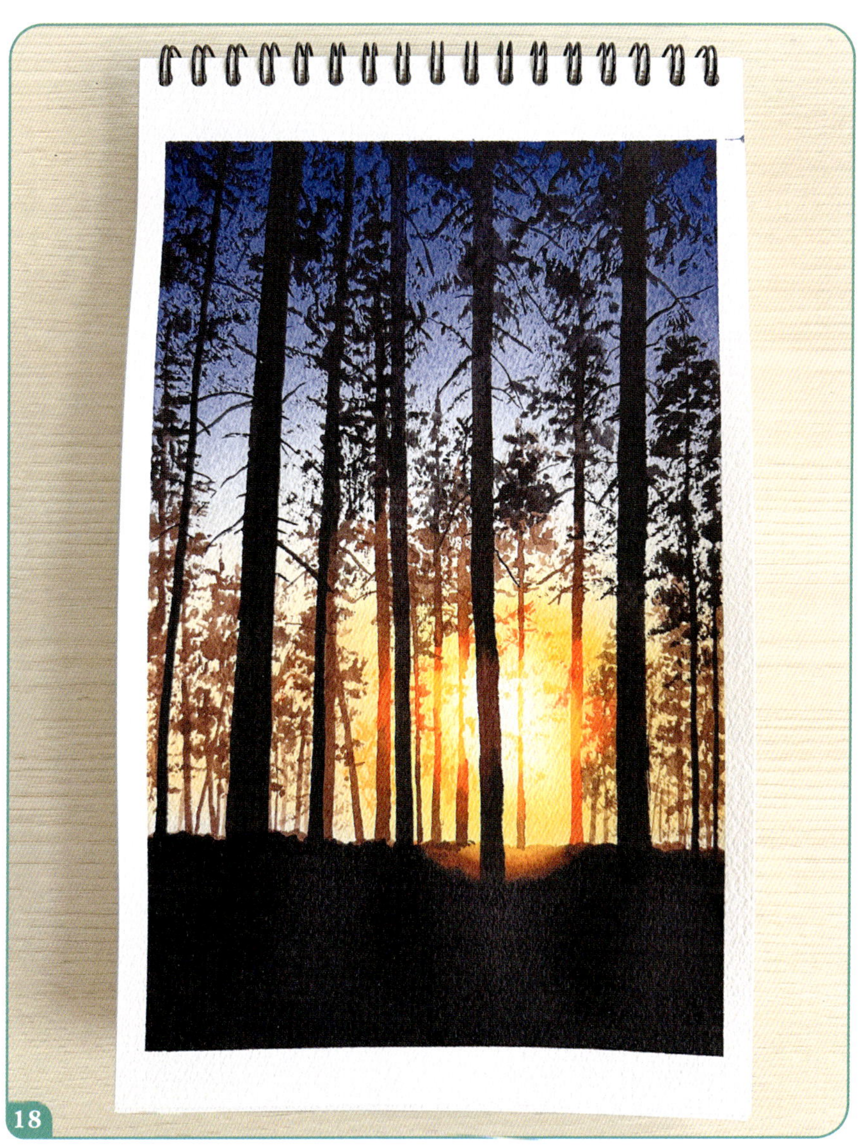

18 When painting a foreground tree over the sun spot, use the light brown from Step 9 to paint the section of trunk overlapping the sun. This will add just a hint of glow to this foreground tree.

When you're happy with the trees, you're all done! Take off the tape, step back and analyze your painting. Did you get a realistic glowing effect around the sun? How did your trees turn out? Make a note of what you did well and what could be improved next time.

Wash and Fold

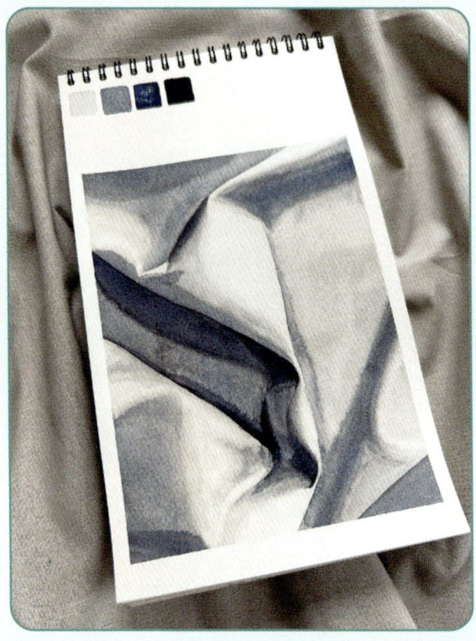

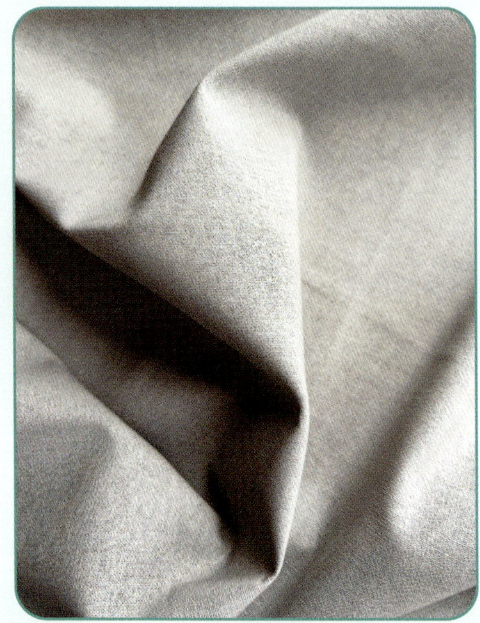

When it comes to painting subjects, there's not much that will help you practice form and value quite like fabric. The folds create different planes that catch the light or sit in shadow, and closely observing and recreating them will help you immensely with other subject matter. For today's painting, I *artfully* scrunched a spare piece of fabric on my desk and took a reference photo, which you can see pictured here. You'll mainly use your light source (page 22) and value (page 53) skills to paint this piece, along with your layering (page 94) and blending

(page 85) skills, so make sure to review those chapters if you need to. To paint this fabric, you'll need:

» Cup of water and paper towel

» Watercolor paints: Ultramarine Blue, Van Dyke Brown

» Watercolor paper (I used a page of my Arches sketchbook)

» Optional: masking tape

» Pencil

» 1 large and 1 medium brush (I used a 12 round and a 4 round)

1   Add a drop of water to each of your colors and give them a minute to soften. In the meantime, prep your paper how you like it, taping the edges down if desired.

2   Sketch the major shapes created by the fabric. Feel free to do a little shading with your pencil to keep track of where those dark shadows are.

3   Mix together Ultramarine Blue and Van Dyke Brown to make a neutral gray color, and add plenty of water to make a very light gray tone. Use a big brush to cover your entire page with this color and let it dry completely.

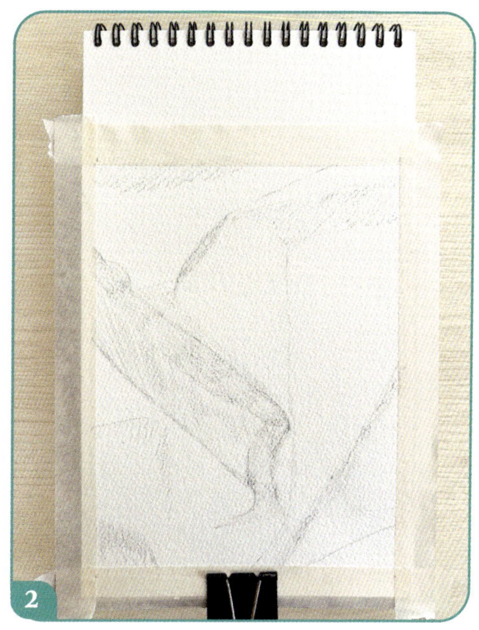

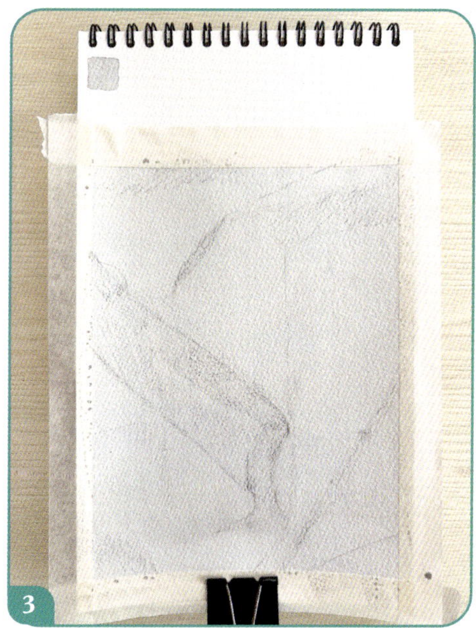

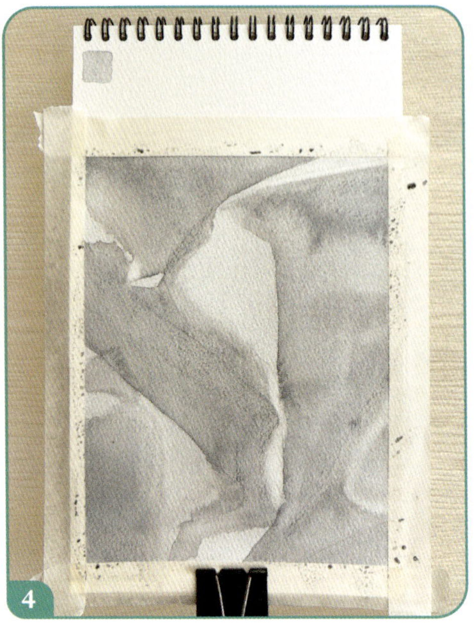

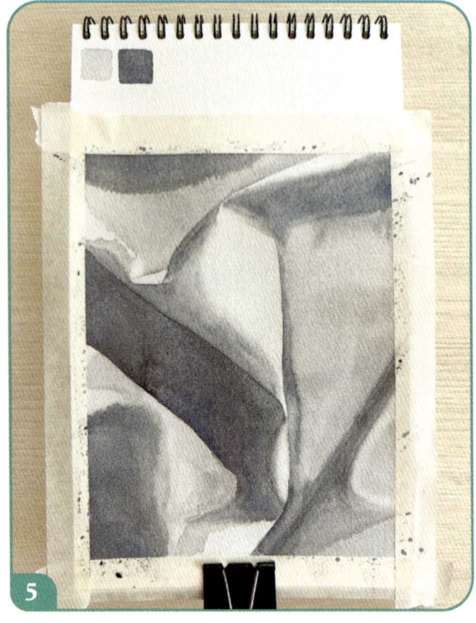

4   Add just a touch of each color to your working puddle of paint to darken it slightly. With this new color, continue to use your big brush and paint everywhere except the lightest parts of the fabric. Work in sections, and use a clean damp brush to blend the edges of your brushstrokes while the paint is still wet to get rid of harsh lines. This will help give you the soft look of fabric!

5   Add more Ultramarine Blue and Van Dyke Brown to your gray color mixture to darken it even more. Now we are starting to define the shadow shapes, so fill in anywhere you see an actual shadow in the reference photo, switching to your medium brush if you need more control. Again, work in sections and blend harsh lines with a clean damp brush. This layering technique allows you to build up the value of the shadows slowly, working from light to dark until you're happy with the contrast in the painting.

Remember Your Fundamentals: Layering is a great way to slowly build up darker areas of your painting, so you don't have to commit to your darkest color right away. It also helps to build up depth and dimension! You can review the principles of layering and glazing on page 94.

6   Mix up your darkest gray, still adding just a bit of water so the dark areas aren't too dark, and paint in the darkest shadow shapes you see. You can continue to work in layers here and build up to those dark areas.

7   With a clean damp brush, use a scrubbing and lifting technique (page 109) to clean up any highlights that got lost, or get rid of any unwanted textures.

Take off the tape, step back and analyze your painting! Did you get a realistic fabric look? Did you get enough contrast in your painting? Make a note of what went well and what could be improved on next time.

Take It Up a Notch: Try this on your own and grab something from your closet with an interesting fabric or pattern. Scrunch it up, make sure you have a strong light source and either paint it from life or take a photo and paint it from the photo!

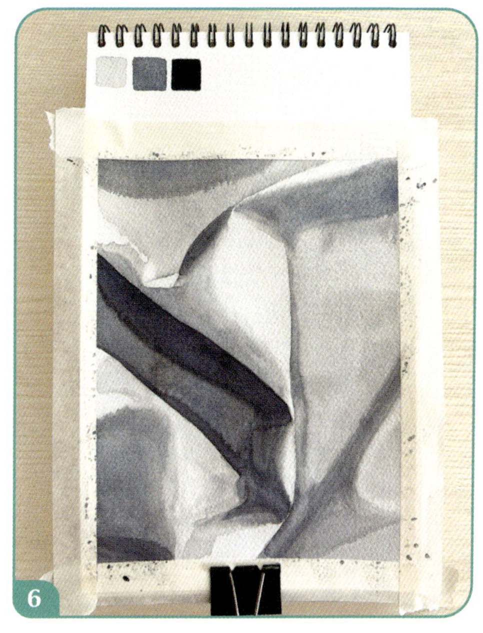

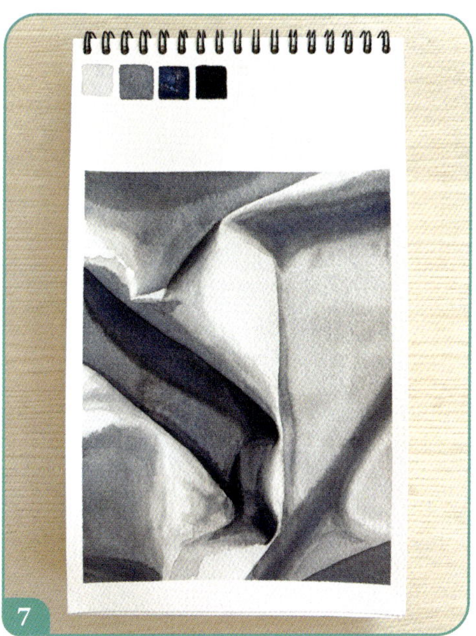

Not All That Glitters

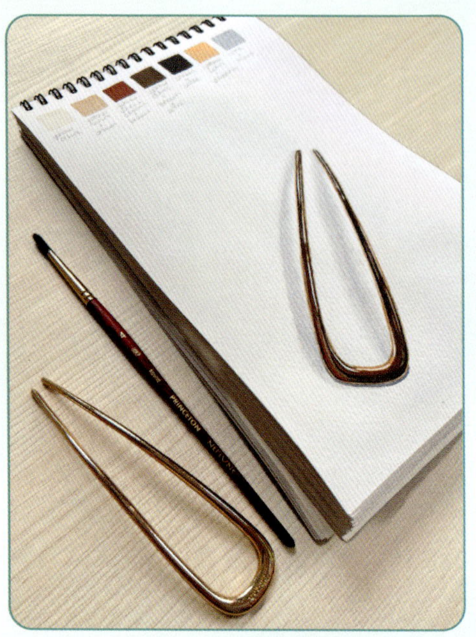 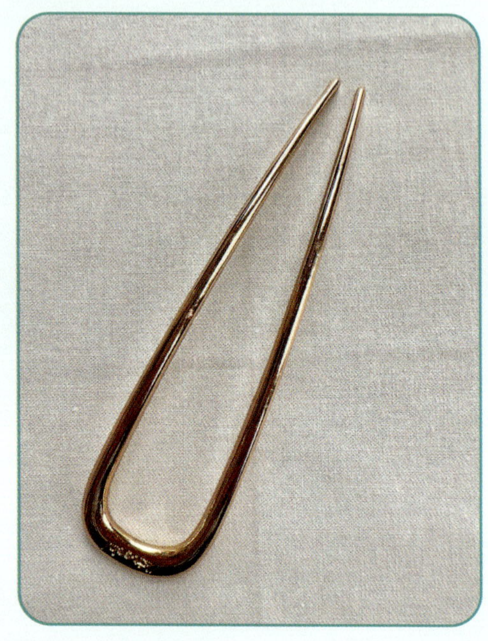

Metal objects can be tricky to capture in a painting. In your head, you think you know what gold or silver looks like—but since those metals are reflective, most of what you're seeing in a metal object are the distorted reflections of the surrounding environment. Today we are going to experiment with painting a gold hairpin in the trompe l'oeil style (page 166) to get a feel for painting a metal object. Take a really close look at the reference photo and notice all the different colors and patterns that come together in this gold hairpin. In order to successfully recreate this subject in a painting, we'll need to pay extra close attention to the actual shapes and colors we see, rather than what we think we see. For this painting, you'll need:

» Cup of water and paper towel

» Watercolor paints: Yellow Ochre, Van Dyke Brown, Alizarin Crimson, Ultramarine Blue

» Watercolor paper (I used a page of my Arches sketchbook)

» Optional: masking tape

» Pencil

» 1 medium and 1 detail brush (I used a 4 round and a 2 round)

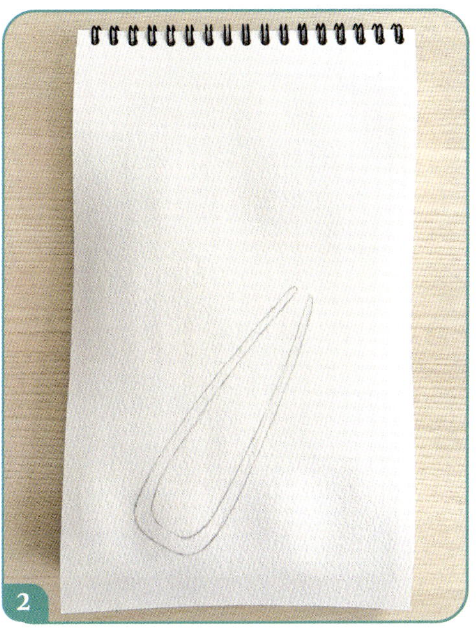

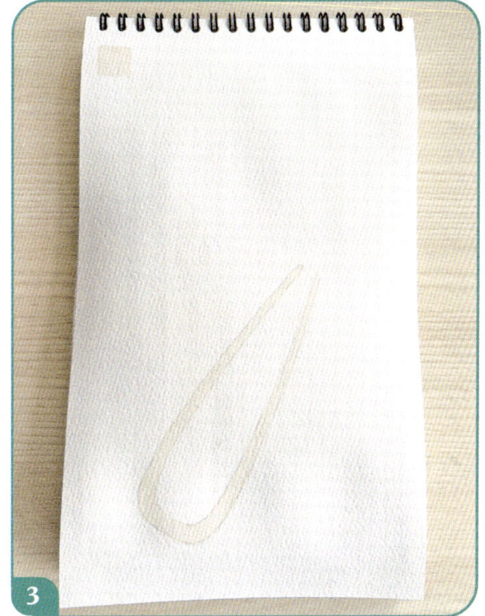

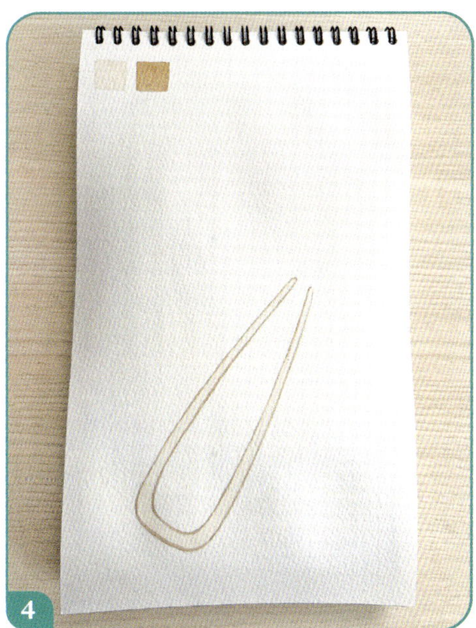

1   Add a drop of water to each of your colors and give them a minute to soften. In the meantime, prep your paper how you like it, taping the edges down if desired.

2   Lightly sketch the shape of the hairpin using the reference photo pictured on the previous page.

3   Mix a very light wash of Yellow Ochre, adding plenty of water, and fill in the entire hairpin shape with your medium brush. Let it dry completely.

4   Mix a slightly darker golden color, combining Yellow Ochre, a touch of Van Dyke Brown and some water. Use this color and your detail brush to outline the hairpin shape.

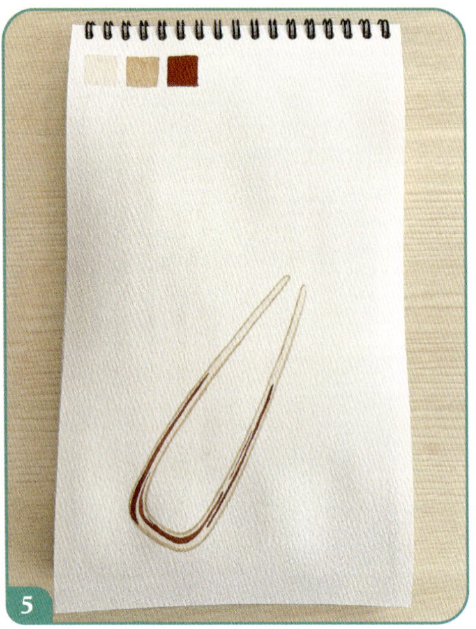

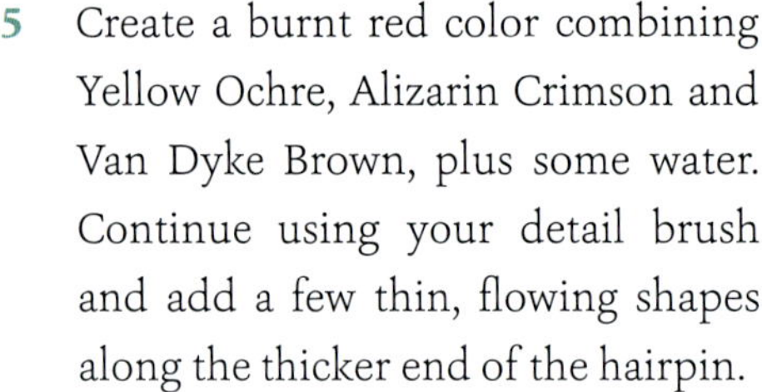

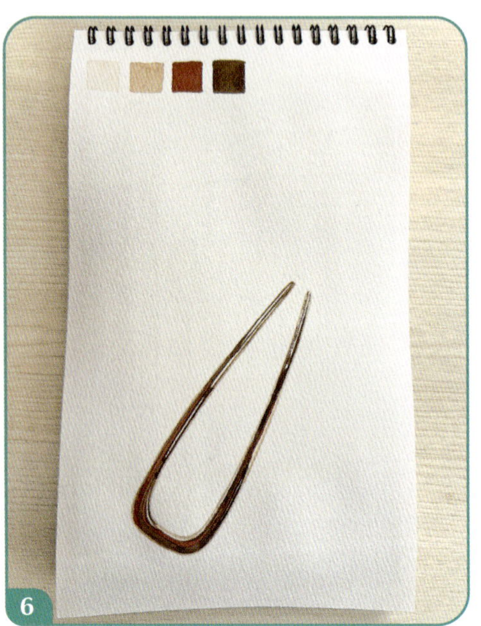

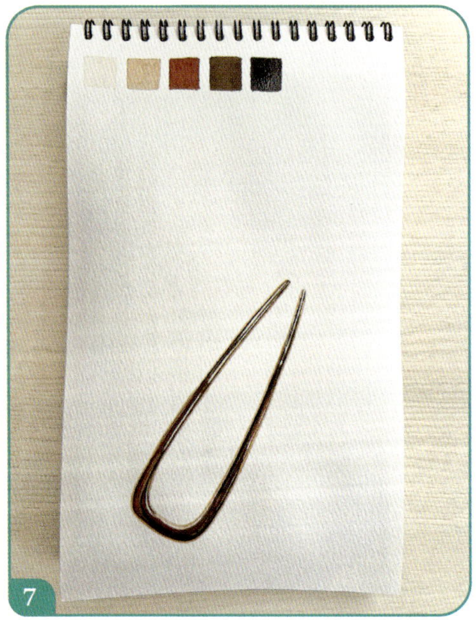

5   Create a burnt red color combining Yellow Ochre, Alizarin Crimson and Van Dyke Brown, plus some water. Continue using your detail brush and add a few thin, flowing shapes along the thicker end of the hairpin.

6   Working toward the darker colors now, mix a brown color by combining Yellow Ochre, Van Dyke Brown and a touch of Ultramarine Blue. Take note of where the highlights are on the hairpin, and use this color to fill in any areas that are not highlights.

7   Mix your darkest color, a dark brown, by combining Van Dyke Brown and Ultramarine Blue. Use this color sparingly to add the darkest lines and shapes you see in the hairpin.

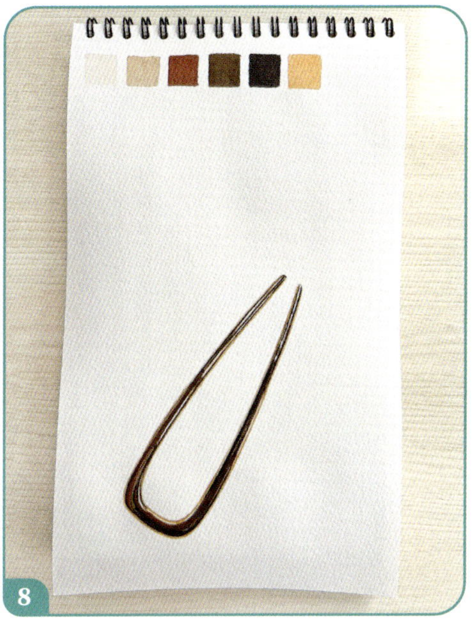

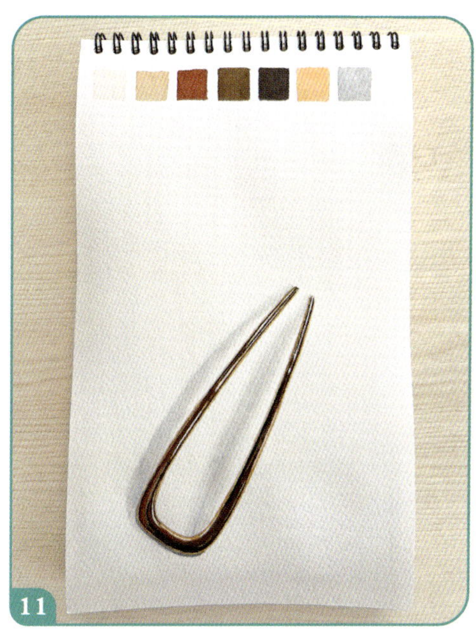

8   For the last details, mix a classic gold color combining Yellow Ochre and a touch of Alizarin Crimson. Use this color to enhance the gold tones in the hairpin, particularly around the outside edges.

9   Take a look at your work so far and make any adjustments needed, going back to a previous color if necessary to add more detail or depth of color.

Remember Your Fundamentals:

To increase the realism, you can use the scrubbing and lifting technique (page 109) to reintroduce any highlights you may have lost, lighten areas that got too dark or blend the transitions between colors.

10   When you're happy with how the hairpin looks, mix a light gray, combining Ultramarine Blue and Van Dyke Brown plus plenty of water. Use this color and a medium brush to add the cast shadow, blending the edges of the shadow shape while the paint is still wet to diffuse them. Let it dry completely.

11   Use a detail brush and the same gray paint to add a little extra shadow at the base of the hairpin.

Take a step back and assess your painting. Did you get a convincing illusion of gold? Take note of what went well for you and what could be improved next time!

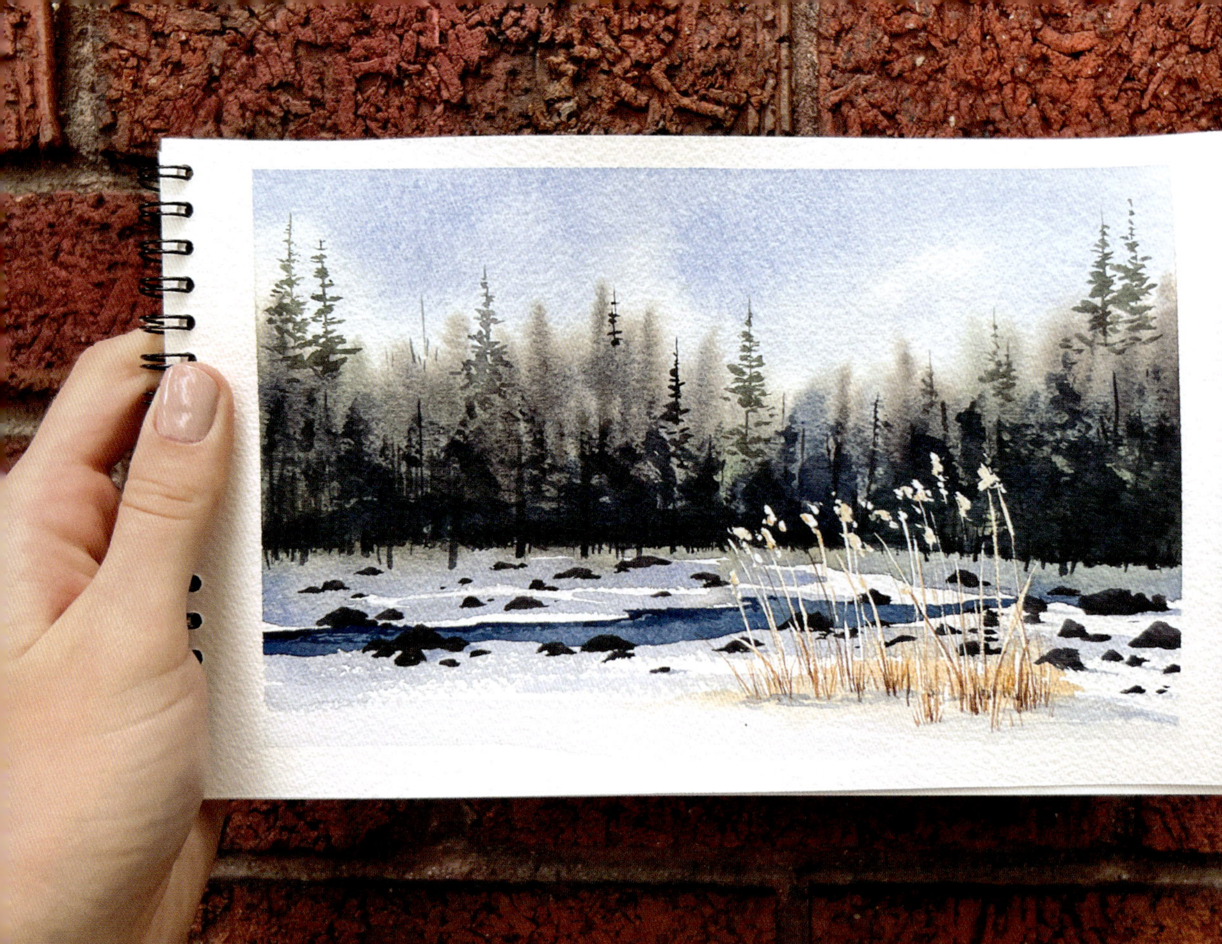

Spring Thaw

Snow is one of those subjects that can be tricky to capture with watercolor—it's pure white, so what color are you supposed to use to paint it? While it can be tricky at first, snow is a subject that actually gives you a lot of freedom to experiment with color. I prefer to use the colors of the surrounding landscape, plus a warm-toned blue-violet color to create shadows. Today we'll be tackling the beautiful winter landscape you see pictured here, capturing the dense forest of trees, the snowy ground and the river running through it. The most compelling part of this reference photo (in my opinion) and the element I want to make sure you incorporate is the contrast between the dark forest in the background and the warm, sunlit grasses peeking through the snow. This combo gives you a high value range (page 53), and the warm orange and yellow tones of the grass look great

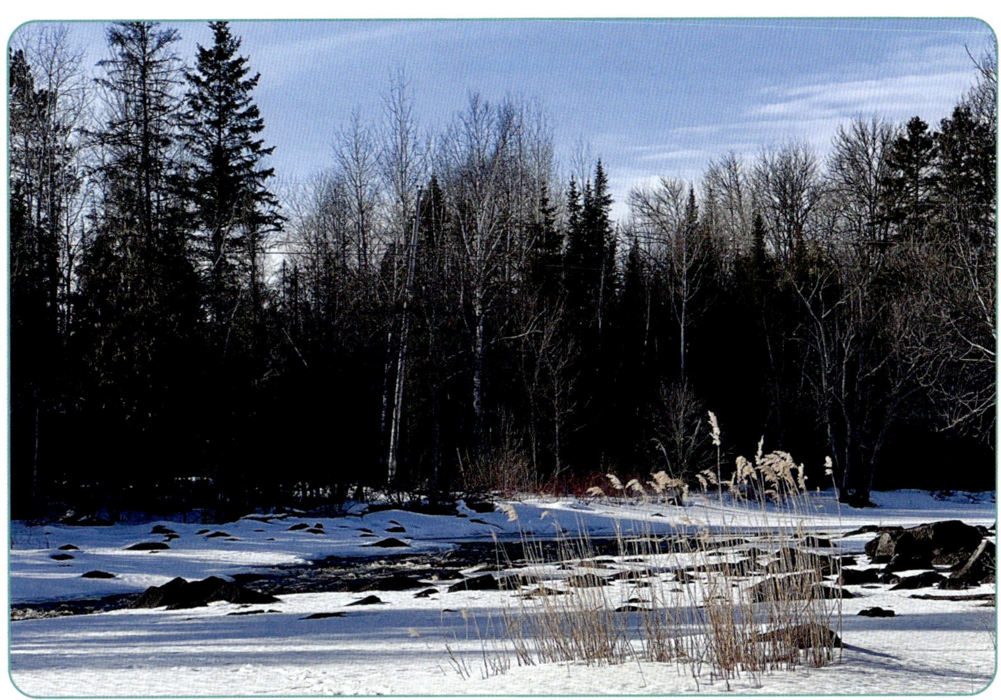

next to the complementary tones of the purple snow shadows and blue hues in the forest (color theory, page 59). Buckle up for this one; we're gonna have some fun! You'll need:

» Cup of water and paper towel

» Watercolor paints: Ultramarine Blue, Sap Green, Van Dyke Brown, Alizarin Crimson, Yellow Ochre, Payne's Gray

» Watercolor paper (I used a page of my Arches sketchbook)

» Optional: masking tape

» Pencil

» Masking fluid and a brush to apply it with

» 1 large, 1 medium and 1 detail brush (I used a 10 round, a 4 round and a 2 round)

1 Add a drop of water to each of your colors and give them a minute to soften. In the meantime, prep your paper how you like it, taping the edges down if desired.

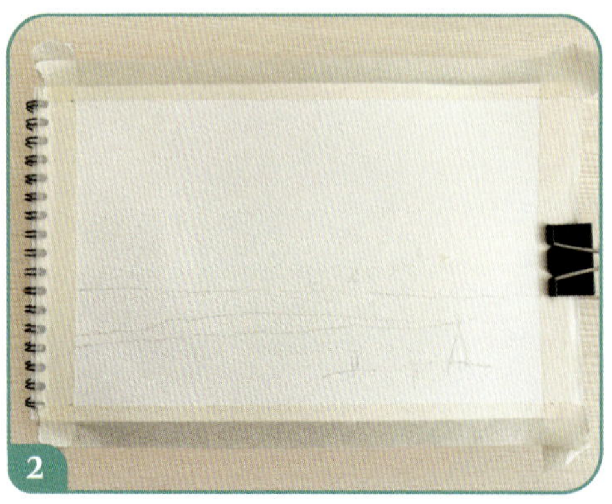

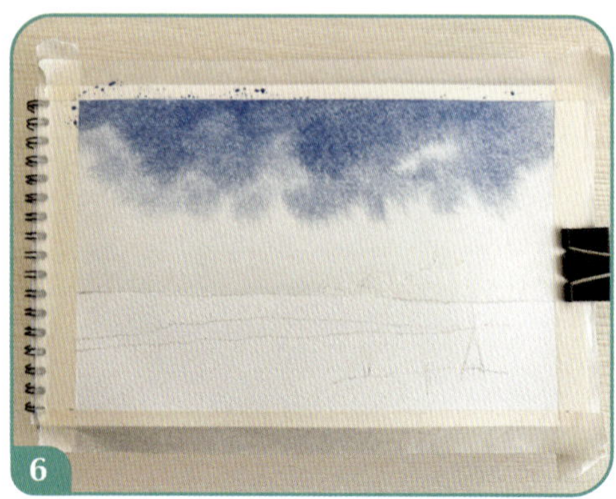

2 Sketch the basics of the landscape: the horizon line, the river, the mound of snow where the grass is and a few lines to indicate the clumps of grass.

3 Use masking fluid to mask the fluffy tops of the grass, plus some thin lines to mask the stems. Make sure the masking fluid is completely dry before moving on.

4 On your palette, prep three colors: Ultramarine Blue, Sap Green and neutral brown combining Van Dyke Brown and Ultramarine Blue. Keep these colors concentrated in your palette.

5 Using a large brush, cover the paper above the horizon line with a layer of water.

6 Load your brush with Ultramarine Blue and paint in some sweeping brushstrokes in the top half of the sky section.

7   Switch to Sap Green and, starting at the horizon line, dot in some loose tree shapes.

8   Switch to the neutral brown color you mixed in Step 4 and continue adding tree shapes, using dotting motions or vertical lines. You can add more Ultramarine Blue or more Van Dyke Brown to your paint mixture to add some color variation as you paint.

9   Before the painting dries completely, mix two more colors: combine Ultramarine Blue with a touch of Alizarin Crimson and some water to make the snow shadow color, and some plain Yellow Ochre with water for the grass.

10   Use your large brush and long sweeping motions (be brave) to sweep the snow shadow color over the bottom half of the landscape. Make sure to leave some white spaces, and allow your brush to run out of paint on the paper to get some extra texture. This color will likely blend with the still-wet top half of the landscape, and that's fine!

11   Before the snow shadow color dries, sweep a little yellow ochre over the grass section. It will probably look a little messy at this point and that's okay! Let it dry completely.

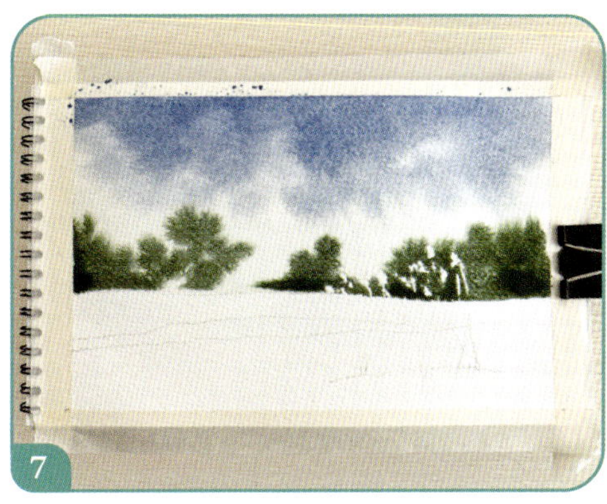

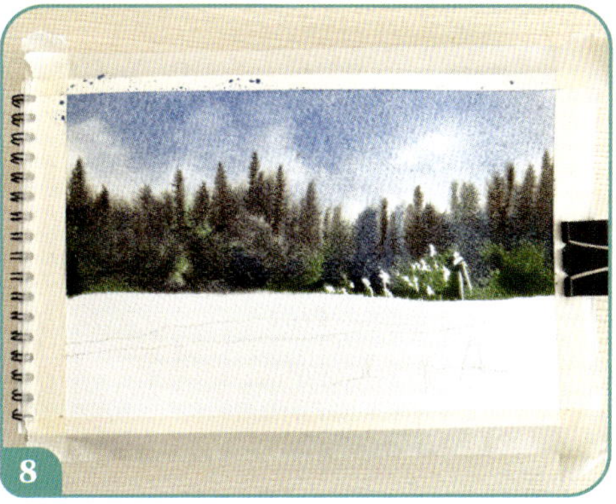

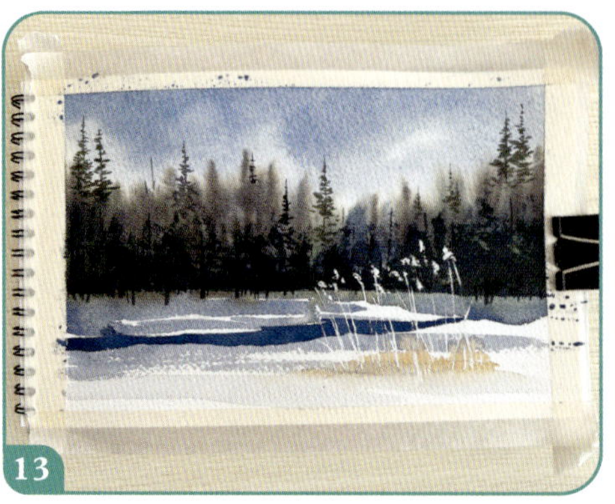

13

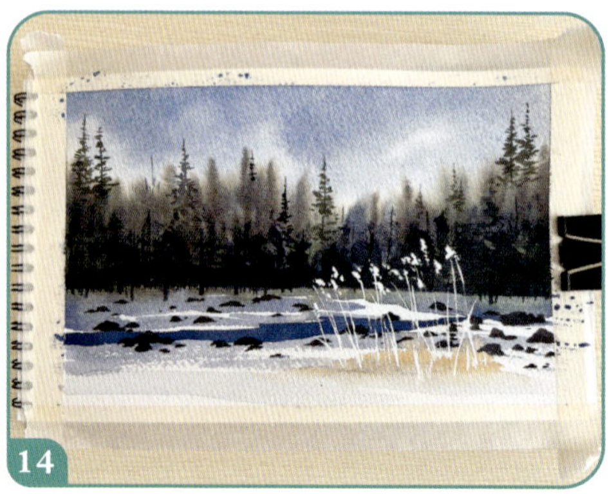

14

12 Mix a dark blue color combining Ultramarine Blue and Payne's Gray. With your medium brush, use this color to carve out the river shape through the snow.

13 Go back to the same colors from Step 4 (Ultramarine Blue, Sap Green and neutral brown) and layer in some depth to the forest. Use your medium and/or detail brush to add some trees peeking out the top of the tree line, and layer in plenty of trees at the horizon line to darken that part of the forest. You can also add a few tree trunks extending just below the horizon line.

14 Use a dark neutral brown (a mix of Van Dyke Brown and Ultramarine Blue) and a detail brush to add lots of lumpy rocks in the snow on either side of the river.

15 Remove the masking fluid from the grass and mix up some Yellow Ochre on your palette, plus a darker golden-brown combining Yellow Ochre and Van Dyke Brown.

16 Use your detail brush to add some color to the grass, using the Yellow Ochre for the tops of the grasses and stems, then adding in shadows and depth to the bottoms of the stems with the darker brown color.

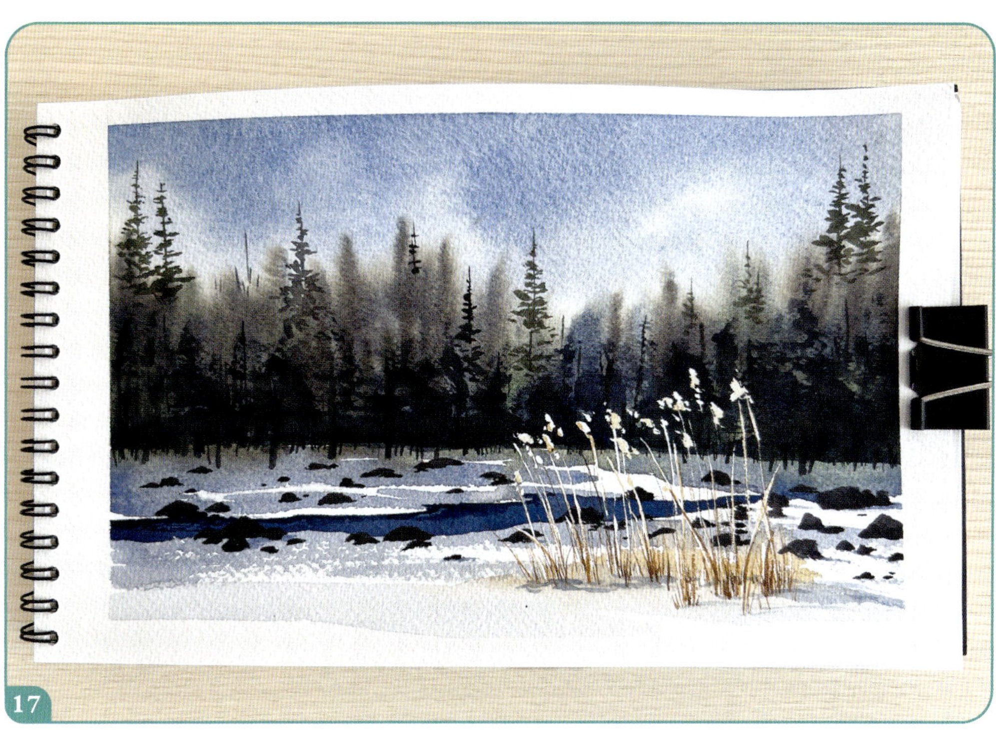

17 Finally, use the snow shadow color from Step 9 (Ultramarine Blue with a touch of Alizarin Crimson and some water) and a detail brush to add some small cast shadows around the base of the grass and any rocks that need a shadow.

All done! That was complicated, so great job tackling it with me! Take a step back and analyze your painting–did you get a convincing illusion of snow? Make note of what went well and what could be improved next time!

Take It Up a Notch: Next time you want to give a snowy landscape a go, try experimenting with different techniques to portray snow falling. You could add salt to the background layers for extra texture, and you could use gouache paint splatters as a final detail to create snowflakes falling!

CHAPTER 5

Experimentation

Unique and Fun Ways to Play with Watercolor

We're getting close to the end of our time together, so it's time for me to get on my soapbox one last time. I often hear people ask "Can I do this?" or "Am I allowed to do that?" with watercolor and with art in general. I'll let you in on a little secret—there are absolutely no rules about what you do with your own art materials in your own home. In fact, I highly encourage you to use your supplies in all the wrong ways (safely, of course) because how else will we discover new techniques and styles? All of the techniques in this chapter exist simply because an artist or creative somewhere just gave something new a try. Let those intrusive thoughts guide you and see what happens! Having a playful and experimental mindset when it comes to art can really help release you from the shackles of perfectionism, and you might discover a whole new style that you love along the way!

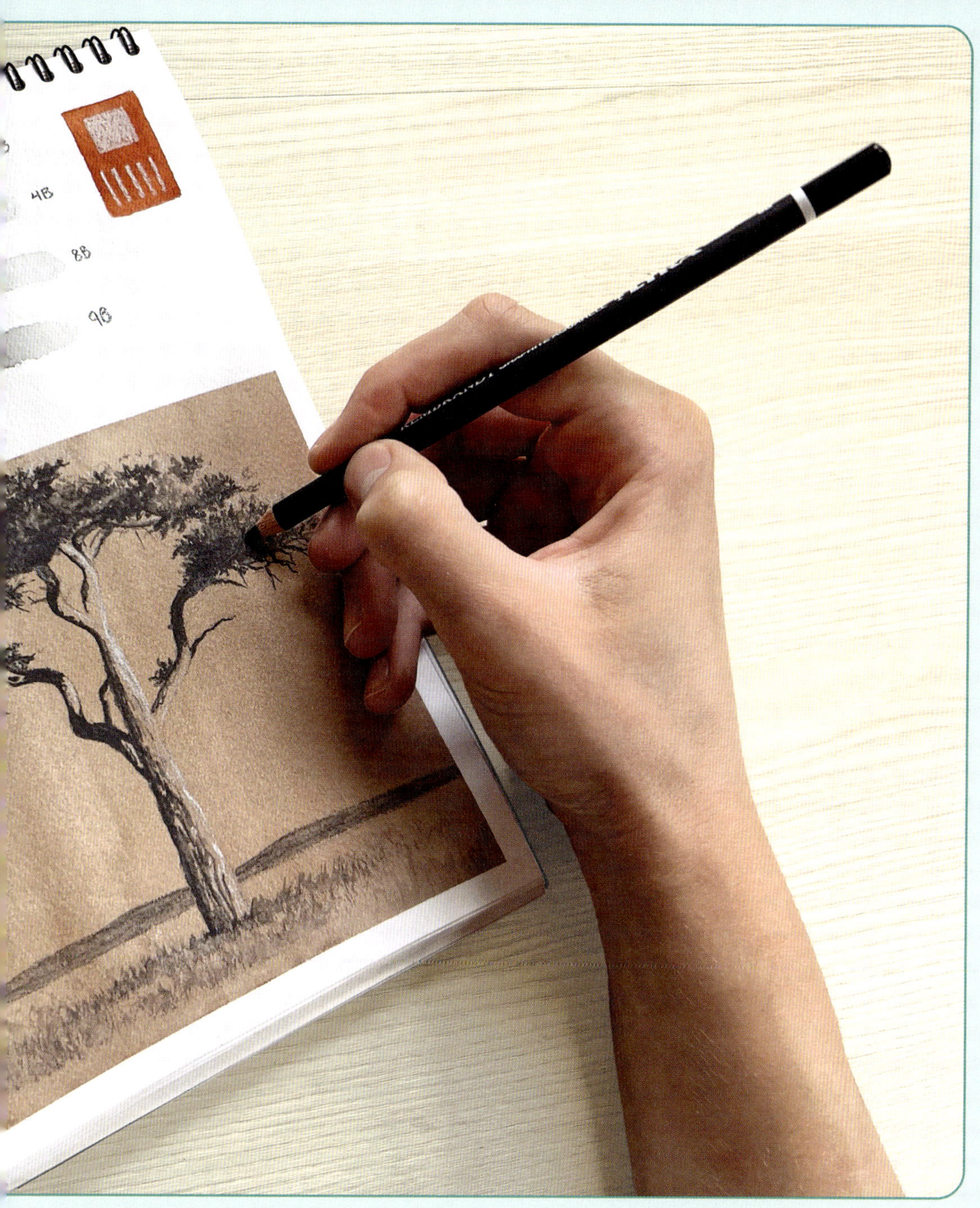

4B
8B
9B

Nature's Mosaic

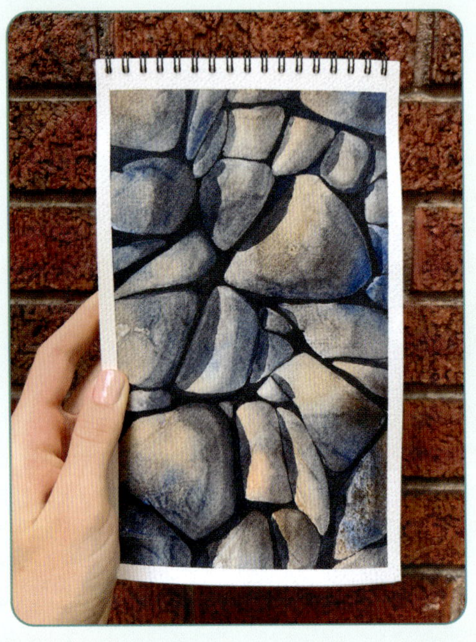 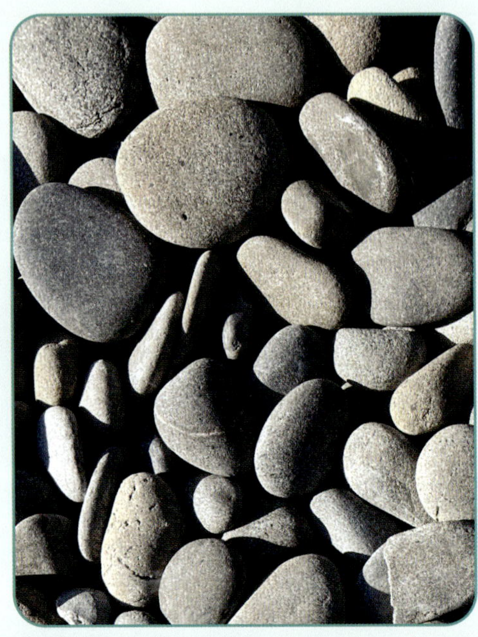

I grew up taking trips to the rocky beaches of western Washington—I loved collecting sea glass and balancing on the driftwood and playing tag with the waves. Sifting through the rocks of these beaches is an adventure too; at first glance they all look gray and dull, but when you get closer, you'll see some amazing red, yellow, green and blue-gray colors, especially when the sun is shining. The reference photo you see here is from Ruby Beach— the beach was covered in these smooth gray rocks that actually have yellow and orange tones where the sun hits them and purple and blue tones in the shadows. To create a painting inspired by this reference photo, we are going to use a few of the techniques we've talked about in this book so far: wet-on-wet paint application (page 77), paint splatter and plastic wrap texture (page 101), blending with a damp brush (page 77) and working with a consistent light source (page 22). Let's make a rockin' painting!

For this project you'll need:

» Cup of water and paper towel

» Watercolor paints: Yellow Ochre, Burnt Sienna, Ultramarine Blue, Van Dyke Brown

» Watercolor paper (I used a full page of my Arches sketchbook)

» Optional: masking tape

» 1 large and 1 medium brush (I used a 12 round and a 4 round)

» Plastic wrap—get a piece slightly bigger than the size of your paper

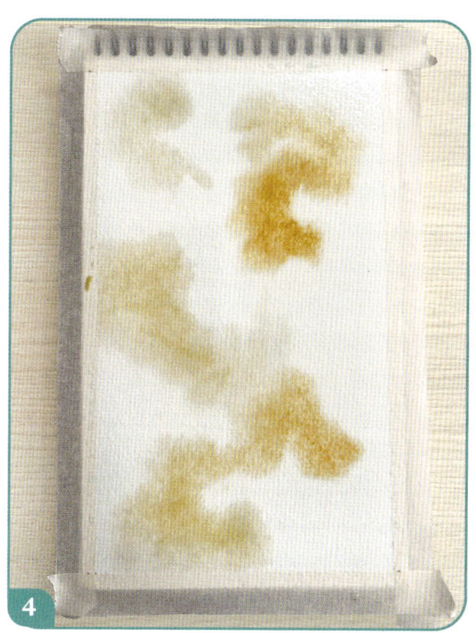

1   Add a drop of water to each of the four paint colors and give them a minute to soften. In the meantime, set up your paper how you like, taping it around the outside if desired.

2   Mix up puddles of each of your four colors in your mixing area, keeping the paint fairly concentrated.

3   Cover your entire paper with a generous layer of clean water with your large brush.

4   Add random splotches of Yellow Ochre to your paper.

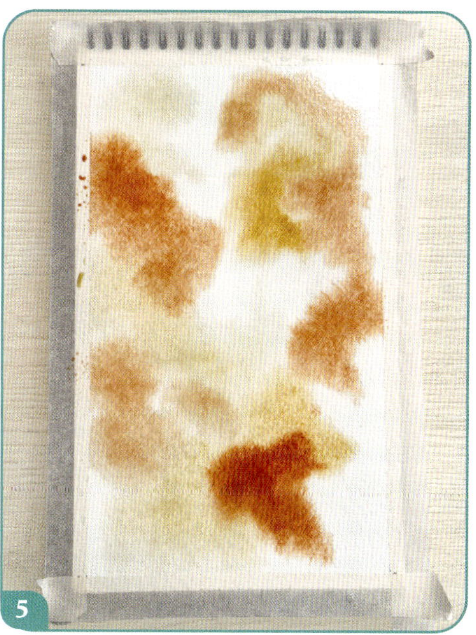

5   Quickly switch to Burnt Sienna and add more random splotches.

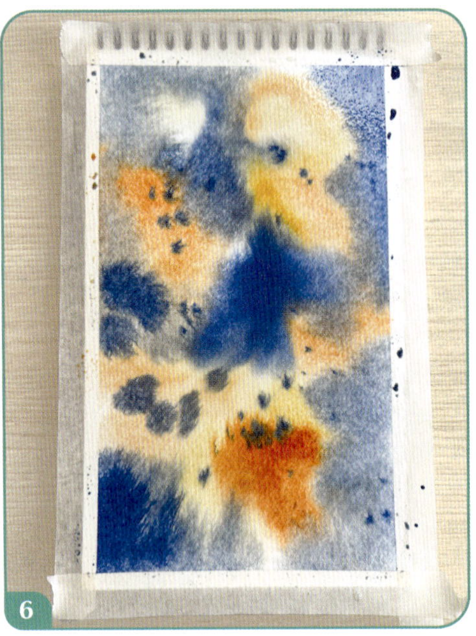

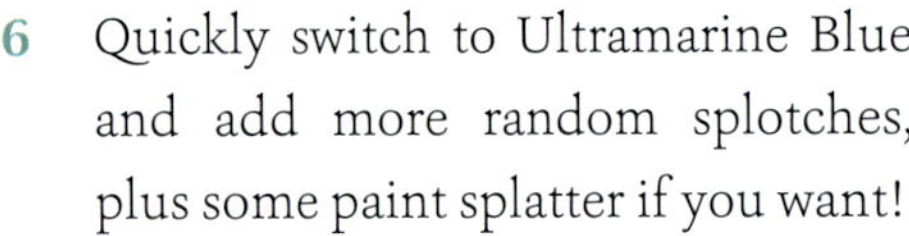

6

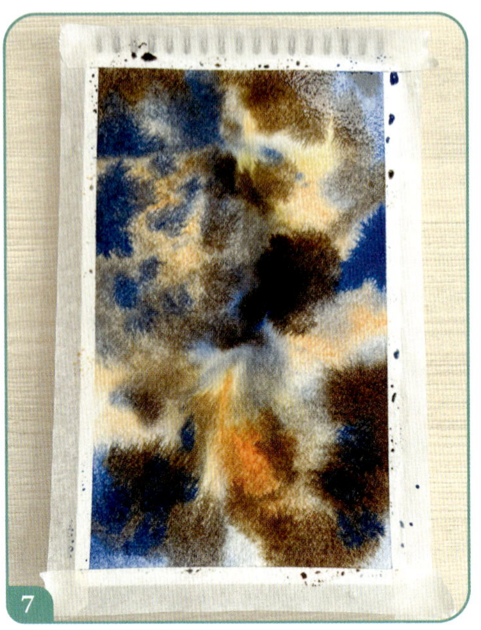

7

6   Quickly switch to Ultramarine Blue and add more random splotches, plus some paint splatter if you want!

7   Quickly switch to Van Dyke Brown and fill in any areas not already filled in, plus more paint splatter if you want!

8   Place your plastic wrap over the wet paint and scrunch it a little to create large geometric shapes. Let the painting air dry for at least 20 minutes, ideally longer if you have the time.

Remember Your Fundamentals: We covered this plastic wrap texture technique back on page 101, if you need a review!

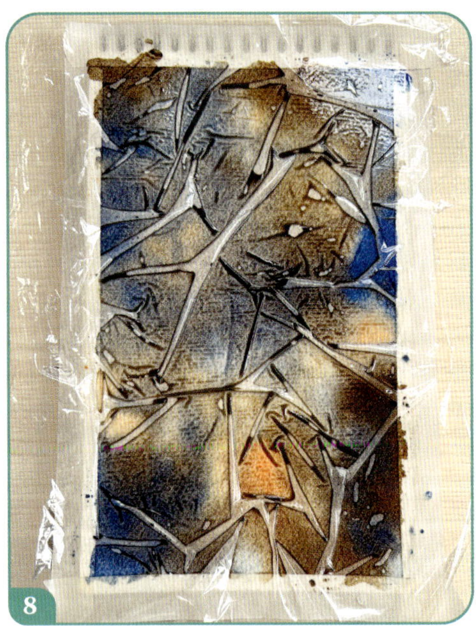

8

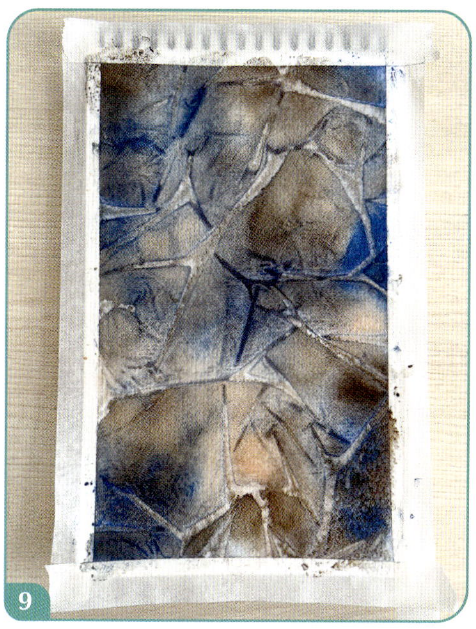

9

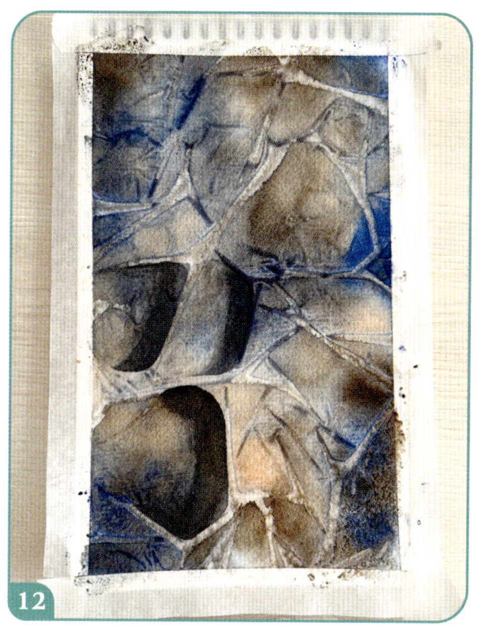

12

9   Carefully remove the plastic wrap and let the paper dry completely before moving on. You should now have some interesting shapes and textures throughout your paper.

10   Switch to your medium brush and mix up a cool gray color combining Ultramarine Blue, a little Van Dyke Brown and water.

11   Pick which direction your light source (page 22) is coming from. The light is coming from the left in the reference photo, so I made all my shadows on the right side of each rock. Pick out a rock shape on your paper and add a thick stripe of gray paint on the left side.

12   Quickly clean your brush and dab off excess water on a paper towel, and use your clean damp brush to blend the edge of this gray paint stripe into the rest of the rock shape.

13 Repeat this process for each rock shape you see. They may be different shapes and sizes, but make sure the shadow is always on the same side of each rock. I also like to use this shadow to round out the corners of the rock shapes so they aren't so pointy.

14 Next, let's add some cast shadows. Since the light is coming from the left, each rock will cast a shadow on the rock to its right. Use a slightly more concentrated version of the same gray paint from Step 10 to add an irregular crescent shape on any rock that might have a cast shadow. You don't have to add one to every rock—some are too far apart for the shadow to reach and some might be too flat to cast a long shadow. Use your imagination here!

15 Now mix up a darker gray color, using the same color combination of Ultramarine Blue and Van Dyke Brown and adding much less water. Use this color to fill in the spaces between the rocks.

16 Now that you've filled in the darkest shadows between the rocks, you may notice some of the lighter shadows on the rocks look too light. You are always welcome to continue to layer more shadows on the rocks with the lighter gray paint until they look correct to you.

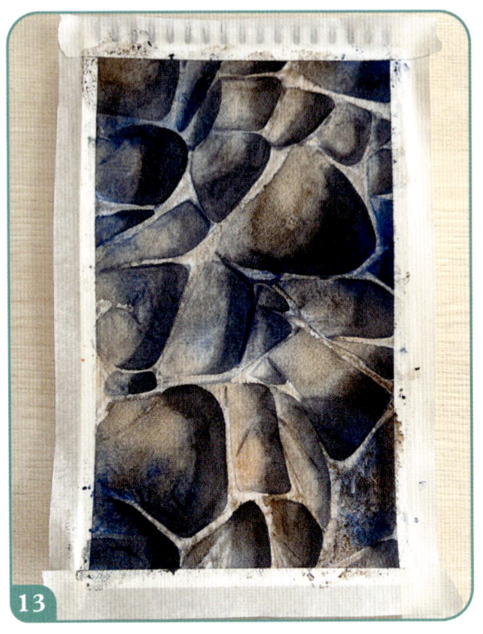

13

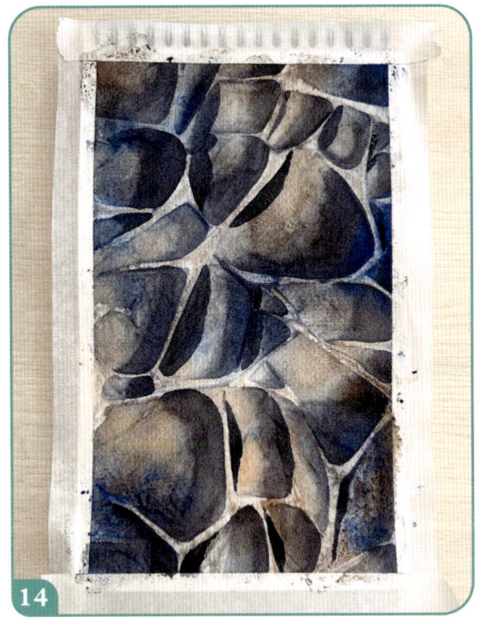

14

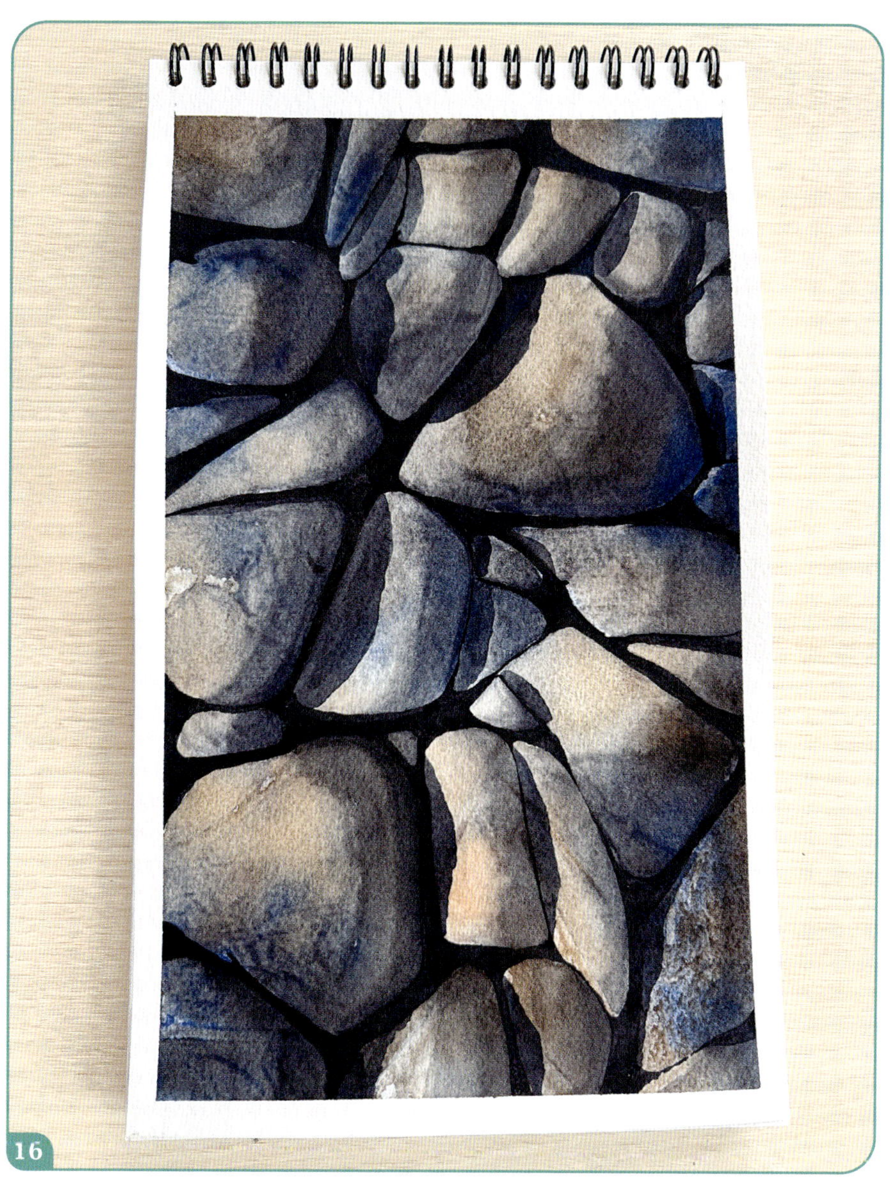

16

Once you're happy with the details, take off the tape if you used it and you're all done! Take a step back and analyze your painting—were you able to produce a convincing lighting scheme with highlights, core shadows and cast shadows in the correct places? Did the plastic wrap texture help you create organic rock shapes and patterns? Take note of what went well for you and what could be improved on next time!

Ink and Wash

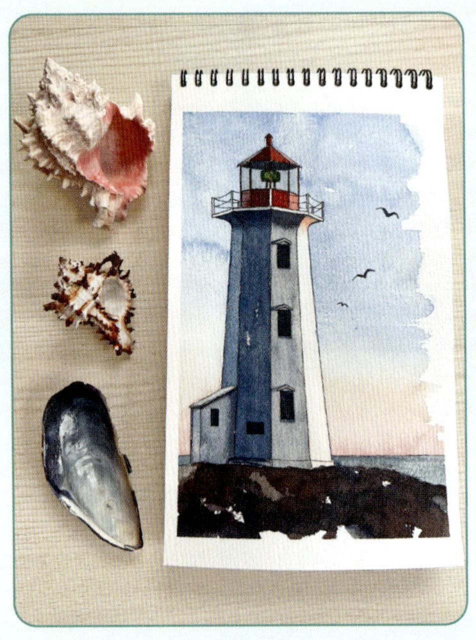

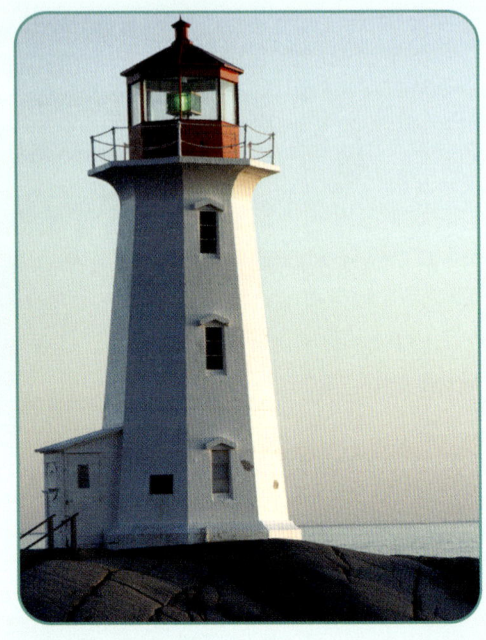

One of my favorite mixed media combos is pen drawing plus watercolor, also called ink and wash. It creates a loose and fun illustrative style common in genres like urban sketching and fashion design, and the addition of pen marks can add a ton of detail and movement to the overall watercolor painting. For this painting, we'll be drawing the lighthouse you see in the reference photo here with a pen, then using simple watercolor washes to bring it to life, using our gradient skills (page 85), flat washes (page 77) and layering (page 94). You'll be able to use your 2-point perspective skills (page 46) when sketching the lighthouse—notice how the

horizontal lines at the top sections angle down and away. For this project, you'll need:

» Cup of water and paper towel

» Watercolor paints: Yellow Ochre, Alizarin Crimson, Ultramarine Blue, Van Dyke Brown, Phthalo Green

» Watercolor paper (I used a page of my Arches sketchbook)

» Optional: masking tape, ruler

» Pencil

» Waterproof ink pen (I used a Micron pen, size 0.3)

» 1 large, 1 medium and 1 detail water-color brush (I used a 10 round, a 4 round and a 2 round)

1 Add a drop of water to each of your colors and give them a minute to soften. In the meantime, prepare your paper, taping it down at the edges if desired.

2 Use a pencil to sketch in the basic shape of the lighthouse. The base can be simplified into a tapering column with four facets, and the red top is a shorter column shape also with four facets and a triangular roof. Add the windows and the guard poles on top, but don't get bogged down by too many details. In the background, add in the horizon line and the rough outline of the rocks the lighthouse stands on. I used a ruler to get straight lines, but free handing it will give you a looser and more expressive feel.

3 When you're happy with your pencil sketch, outline the whole thing with your waterproof pen. Feel free to add extra lines for added detail and texture, or a little bit of crosshatching (crisscrossing lines packed closely together) to add some shading.

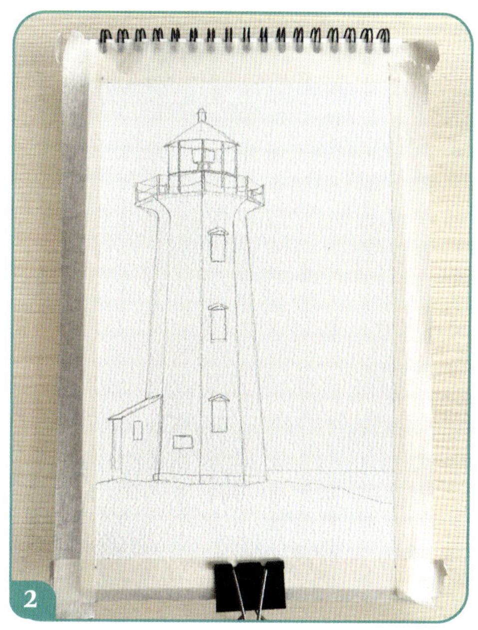

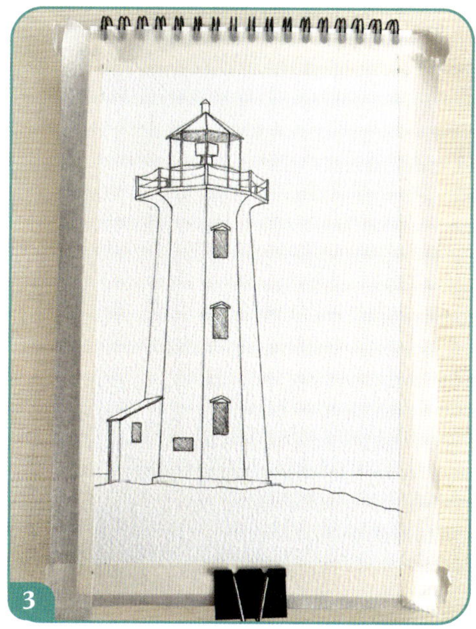

4   Let's start painting the lighthouse. Notice in the reference photo how each facet has a different tone since the light is coming from the right side. To paint the far right side of the lighthouse, mix Yellow Ochre and a touch of Alizarin Crimson and add a ton of water to create a super light color. Paint a flat wash over the far right lighthouse section, then let it dry completely.

5   Moving left, the next section can be painted with a neutral gray, combining Ultramarine Blue and Van Dyke Brown in about equal proportions. Be sure to add some water, then add a flat wash over the second-from-right section. Let it dry completely.

6   The next section is the darkest in tone and a bluer gray, so to your neutral gray from Step 5, add more Ultramarine Blue and just a touch more Van Dyke Brown. Use this color to paint the third section and the long side of the little shack at the base of the lighthouse. Let it dry completely.

7   The last, left-most section is slightly lighter and bluer from the reflected light. Add more Ultramarine Blue and water to the color from Step 6 and paint in this final section plus the roof and the short side of the little shack. Let it dry completely.

8   Paint the top of the lighthouse by mixing up a rusty red color, combining Alizarin Crimson with a little Yellow Ochre and a little Van Dyke Brown. Use a watered-down version of this color for the right-most section, more concentrated mixtures for the second and third sections, then a slightly lighter mixture for the left-most section.

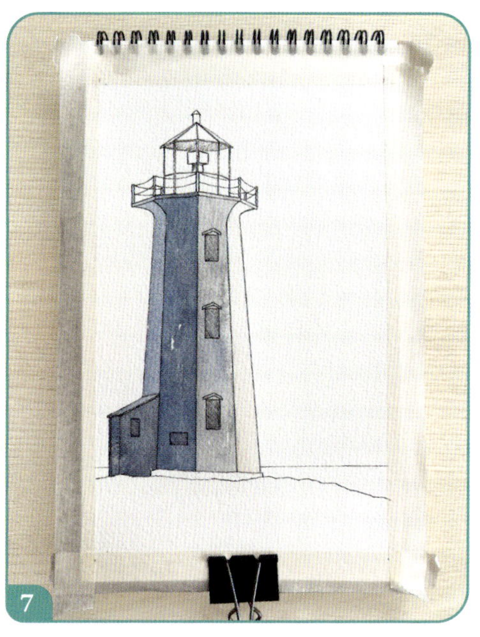

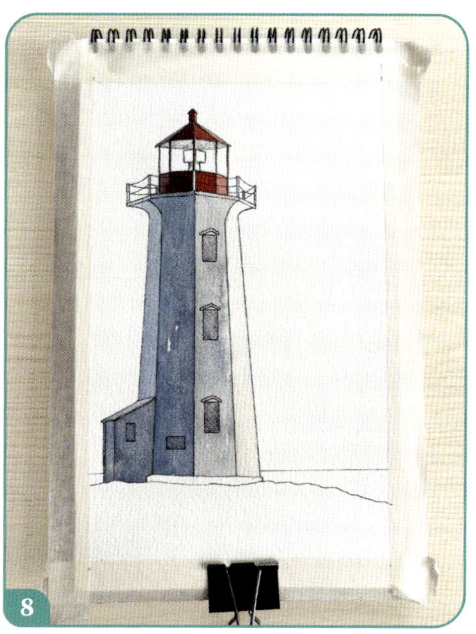

9   Add shadows to the overhang at the top of the lighthouse. Combine Ultramarine Blue and Van Dyke Brown to make a gray color and use that as the shadow on the left three sections of the lighthouse. Simply paint in the shadow shape in each section, then use a clean damp brush to smoothly blend the shadow color into the base color of the lighthouse. For the right-most section, use a more concentrated mixture of Yellow Ochre and a touch of Alizarin Crimson for the shadow.

10 Use the same dark gray color from Step 9 to fill in the windows.

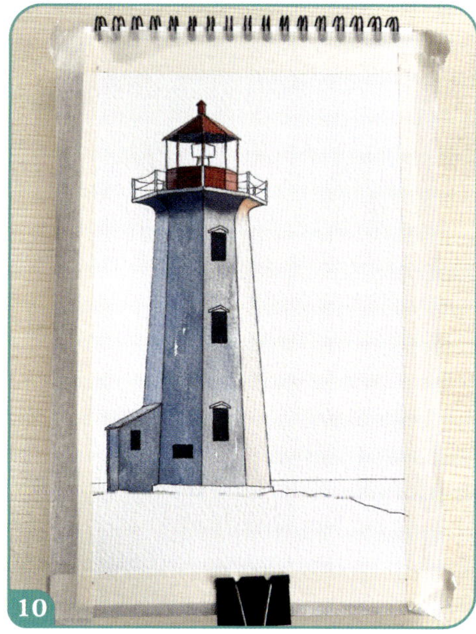

11 To paint the background, mix up puddles of watered-down Alizarin Crimson, Yellow Ochre and Ultramarine Blue. Create a gradient in the sky starting with Alizarin Crimson at the horizon line, blending that into Yellow Ochre and filling in the rest of the sky with Ultramarine Blue.

12 Fill in the ocean section with a mixture of Ultramarine Blue and a touch of both Van Dyke Brown and Yellow Ochre.

13 Mix up a dark brown color combining Van Dyke Brown and a little Ultramarine Blue and fill in the rocks at the base of the lighthouse. Feel free to add a few different tones of brown here by changing the ratio of Van Dyke Brown to Ultramarine Blue in your mixing palette as you work.

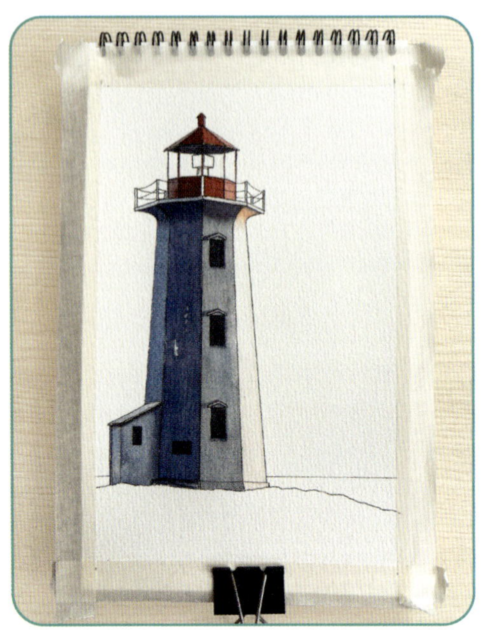

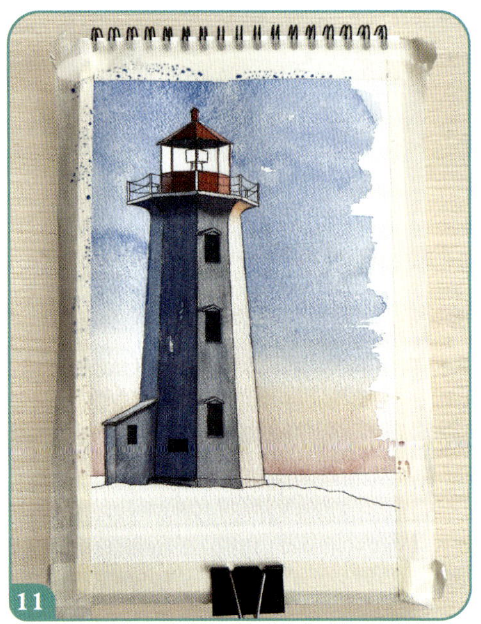

11

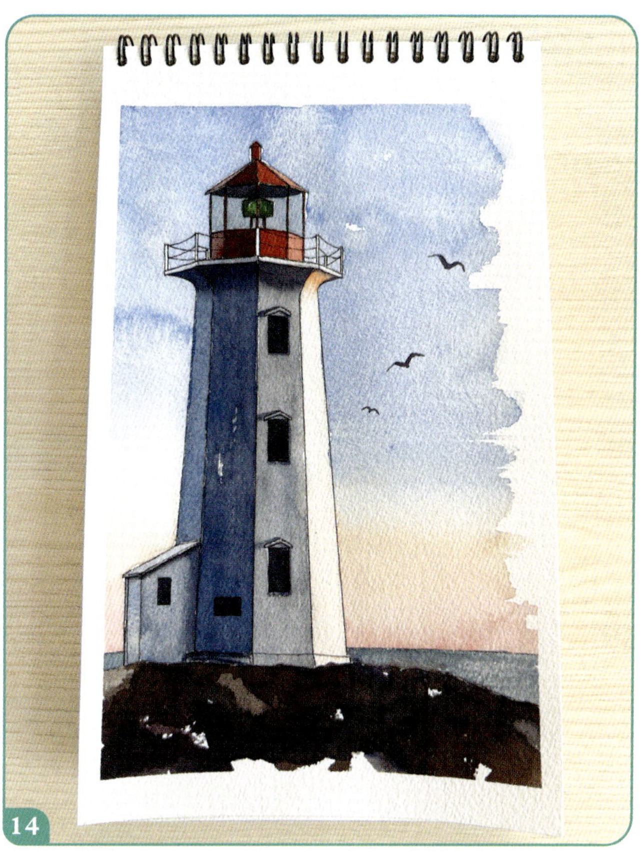

14 Add the final details: Use Phthalo Green to fill in the light inside the lighthouse, use a detail brush and the blue-gray color from Step 6 to add some shadows to the windows, and use the dark gray color from Step 9 to paint some seagulls in the sky. To paint the seagulls, simply paint a wide, upside-down "W" shape. Use heavier pressure in the middle of the W and lighter pressure on the ends. Make them slightly different sizes to show some are closer and some are farther away.

Take off the tape if you used it and admire your work! Take a step back and analyze your painting–do you feel like you were able to successfully combine the two mediums to create a cohesive painting? How does the feeling of this painting differ from the look of an all-watercolor painting? If you had to do it again, would you add more details with your pen or less? Make note of what elements of your painting were successful, and what could be improved on next time.

Watercolor Graphite

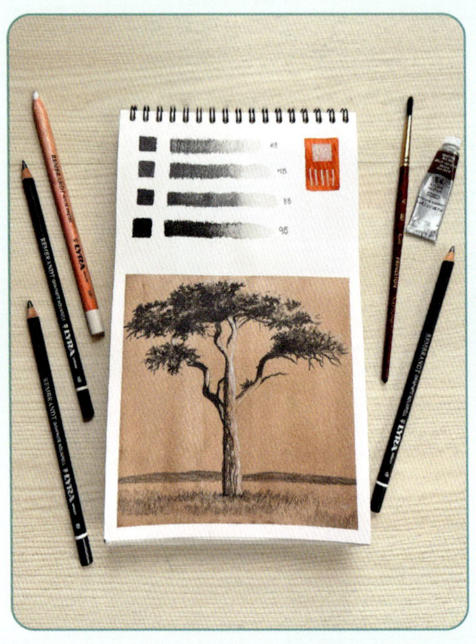

My local art store offered a virtual class on watercolor graphite back in 2023 and on a whim, I decided to sign up for it. I'd tried watercolor graphite once or twice in grade school, but hadn't worked with it since then. I took the class and found I really enjoyed the combination of sketching and watercolor, especially on toned paper using a chalk pencil for highlights. I've played around with this medium a few times since then, and I'm excited to introduce it to you all today! For those of you who have never encountered it before, watercolor graphite is a regular-looking pencil with specially made graphite that can be activated by water. This means you can sketch with it and erase it like you can with a normal pencil, but you can also use a wet brush to activate the graphite and create beautiful watercolor effects. It's a great way to practice value studies or test out a painting idea before committing to a full painting, and because it's just a pencil, it's really easy to take traveling with you. So let's give it a try together! For this project, you'll need:

» Watercolor paper (I used a page of my Arches sketchbook)

» At least 1 watercolor graphite pencil (I have an HB, 4B, 8B and 9B, but you can totally do this with just one pencil! I'd suggest an 8B!)

» Cup of water and paper towel

» 1 detail watercolor brush (I used a 2 round)

» Watercolor paints: Burnt Sienna and/ or Van Dyke Brown

» White chalk pastel pencil

» Optional: masking tape, fixative spray

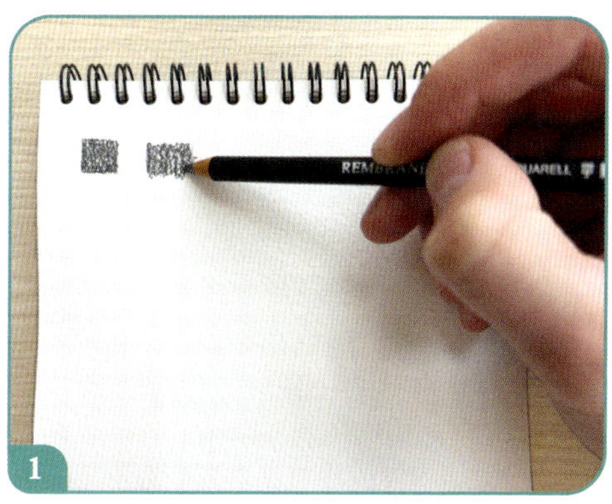

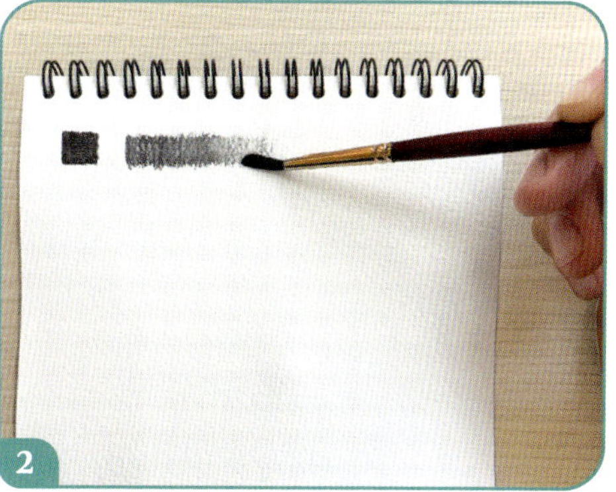

1   Sketch a square on your paper and fill it in thoroughly with your watercolor graphite pencil. Then sketch a long rectangle and create a gradient, using heavy pressure to fill in the left side of the rectangle and lightening the pressure as you move to the right.

2   Use a damp brush of any size to activate the watercolor graphite on the page. Fill in the square, then pass over the gradient from left to right.

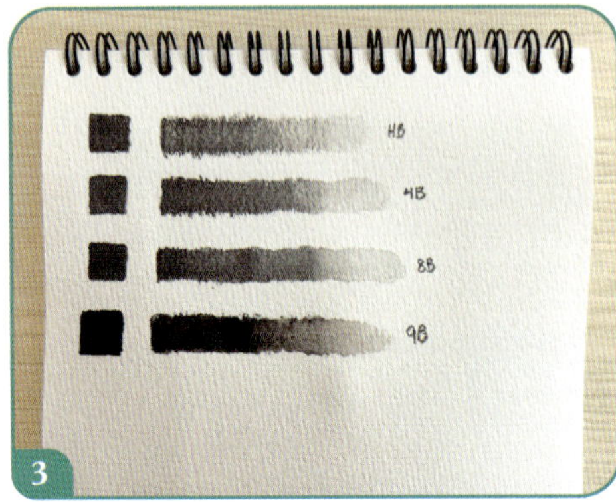

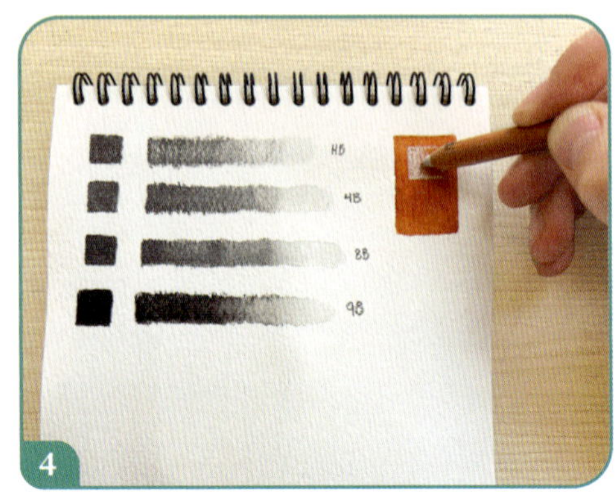

3   Repeat this process for each water-color graphite pencil you have if you have more than one.

4   To test the white chalk pencil, paint a small square of watered-down paint of any color (I used Burnt Sienna) in your swatch area and let it dry completely. Make a few marks over the watercolor paint with the white chalk pencil. Chalk pencils are not water soluble, so the marks will stay as-is!

5   If you'd like to test out anything else with these pencils before we try a real painting, feel free to do so! You could try dipping the pencils into water and sketching with them, you could try painting with just the graphite picked up by your paintbrush or you could sketch onto a wet paper surface—be creative and curious!

Now that we are familiar with the water-color graphite/chalk pastel combo, let's try it out on a painting of this beautiful acacia tree!

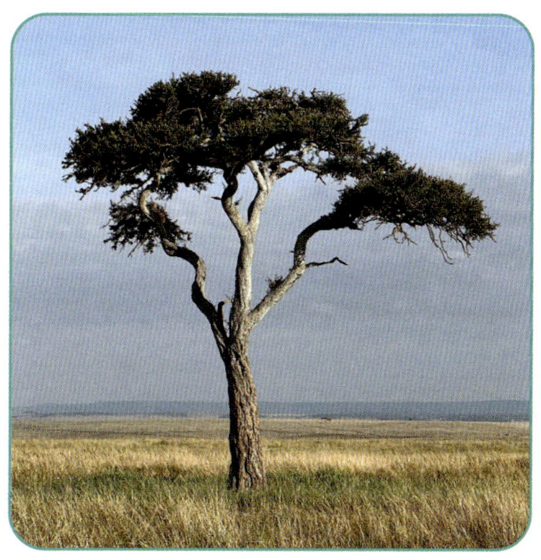

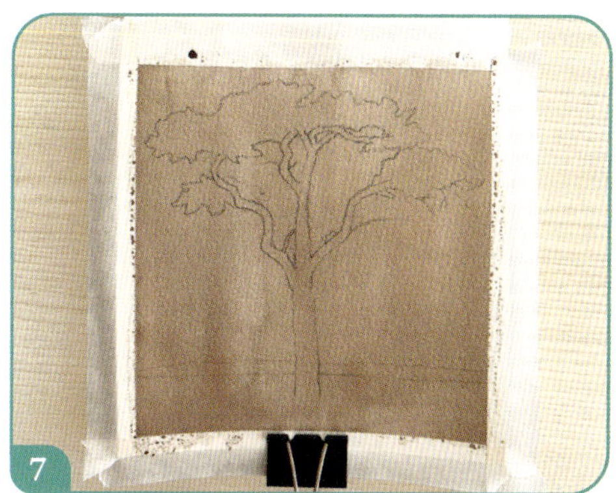

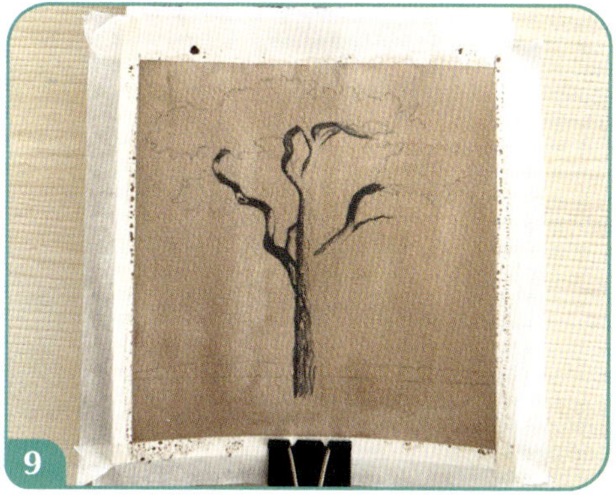

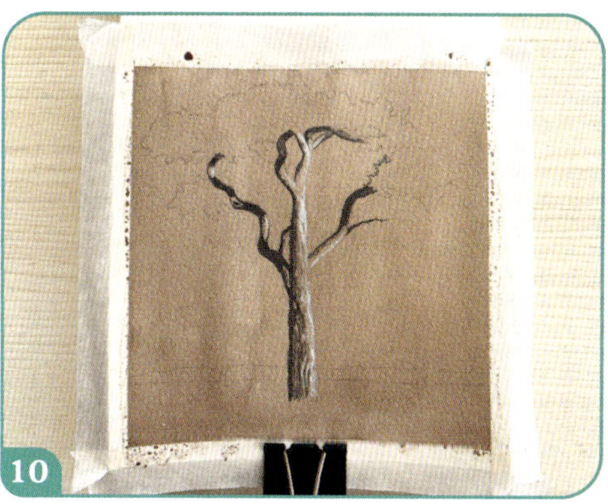

6   Tape down the edges of your paper if you'd like, then fill in your paper area with a light to medium wash of a neutral color like Van Dyke Brown or Burnt Sienna. Let it dry completely.

7   Use your watercolor graphite pencil to lightly sketch the shape of the tree. Add in the trunk and curvy branches, then outline the major sections of foliage at the top of the tree.

8   Start shading in the darkest parts of the trunk and branches, focusing on where the light is coming from in the reference photo and avoiding the lightest areas. Add some vertical lines and dots to the trunk for bark texture.

9   Use a clean damp detail brush to activate the watercolor graphite and use it to lightly blend the details on the trunk and branches.

10   Use your chalk pastel to add highlights in the lightest parts of the tree trunk and branches.

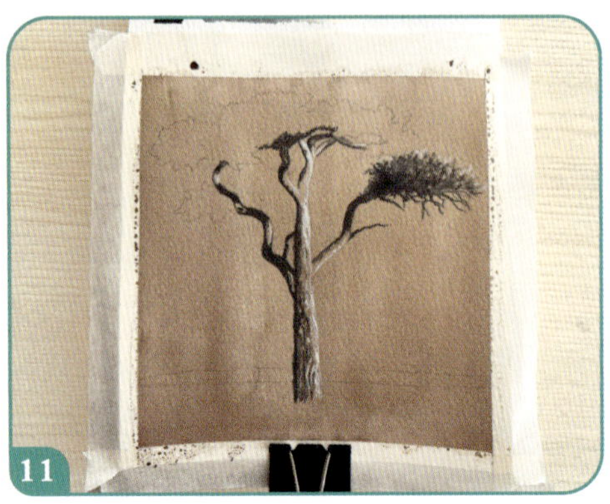

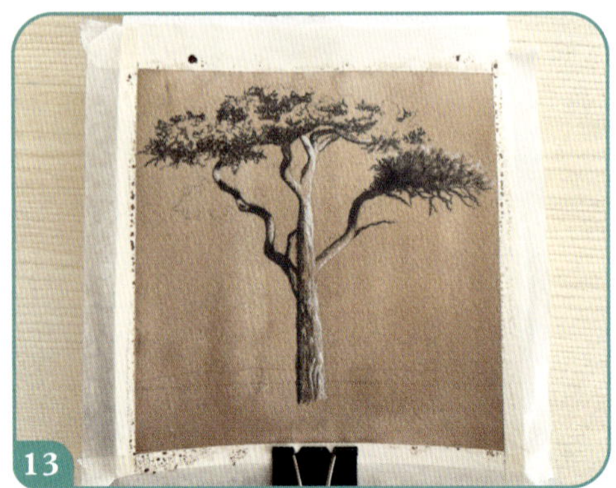

11 Using a scribbling motion to add texture, fill in the sections of foliage at the top of the tree, again staying aware of the lightest and darkest parts of each shape.

Remember Your Fundamentals: Keep in mind that these pencils (just like your paintbrushes in Make Your Mark [page 70]) can be used differently to create a wide range of textures. Experiment to create a unique texture for the bark of the tree, another unique texture for the leaves of the tree, and another texture for the grass and background.

12 Activate the graphite with your clean damp brush and smooth out the pencil marks.

13 Add some highlights to the outside of each foliage section with the white chalk pencil using the same scribbling motion.

14 Using a light touch with your watercolor graphite pencil, fill in the hills in the distance and add some subtle grass texture. Blend with your damp brush, and add subtle highlights with the white chalk pencil to the grass if desired.

15 Optional: Spray your work with a layer of workable fixative to lock it in.

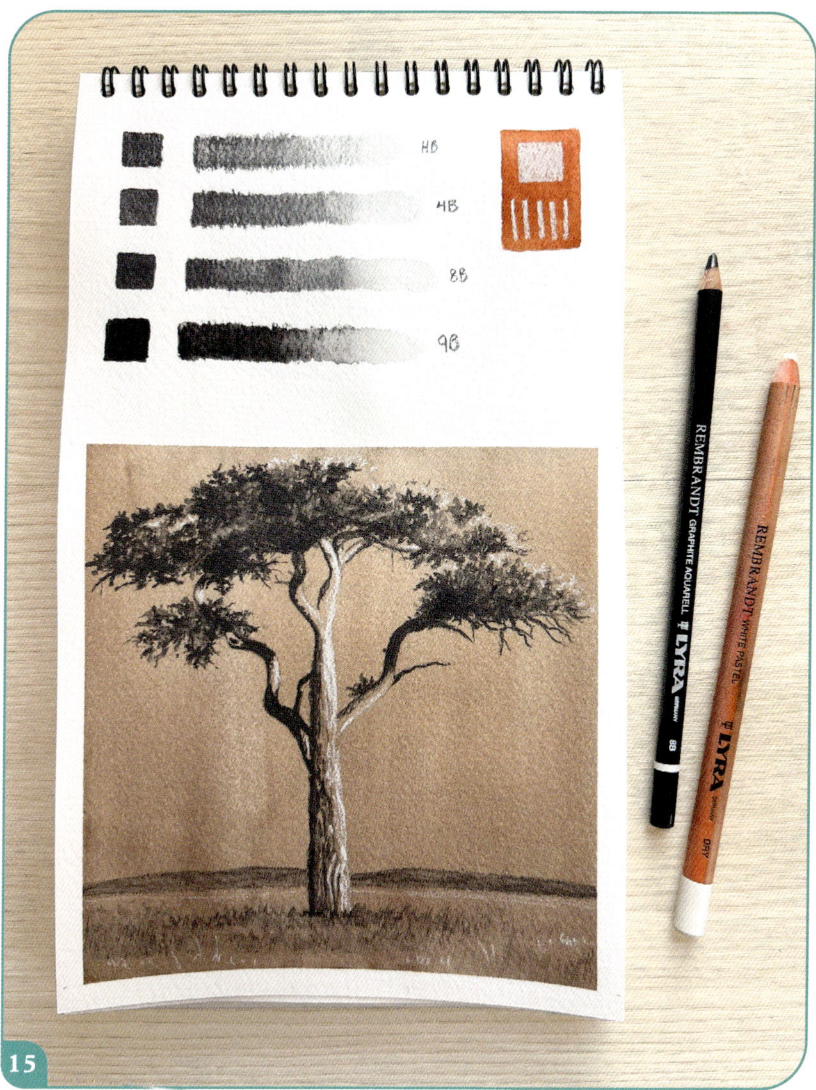

I hope you enjoyed your foray into watercolor graphite! This is a great medium for sketching and painting on the go or *en plein air* since you don't need many materials. It's also a great way to create a value and/or composition study of a scene you'd like to paint later! Make sure to analyze your painting and take note of what went well, and what could be improved next time!

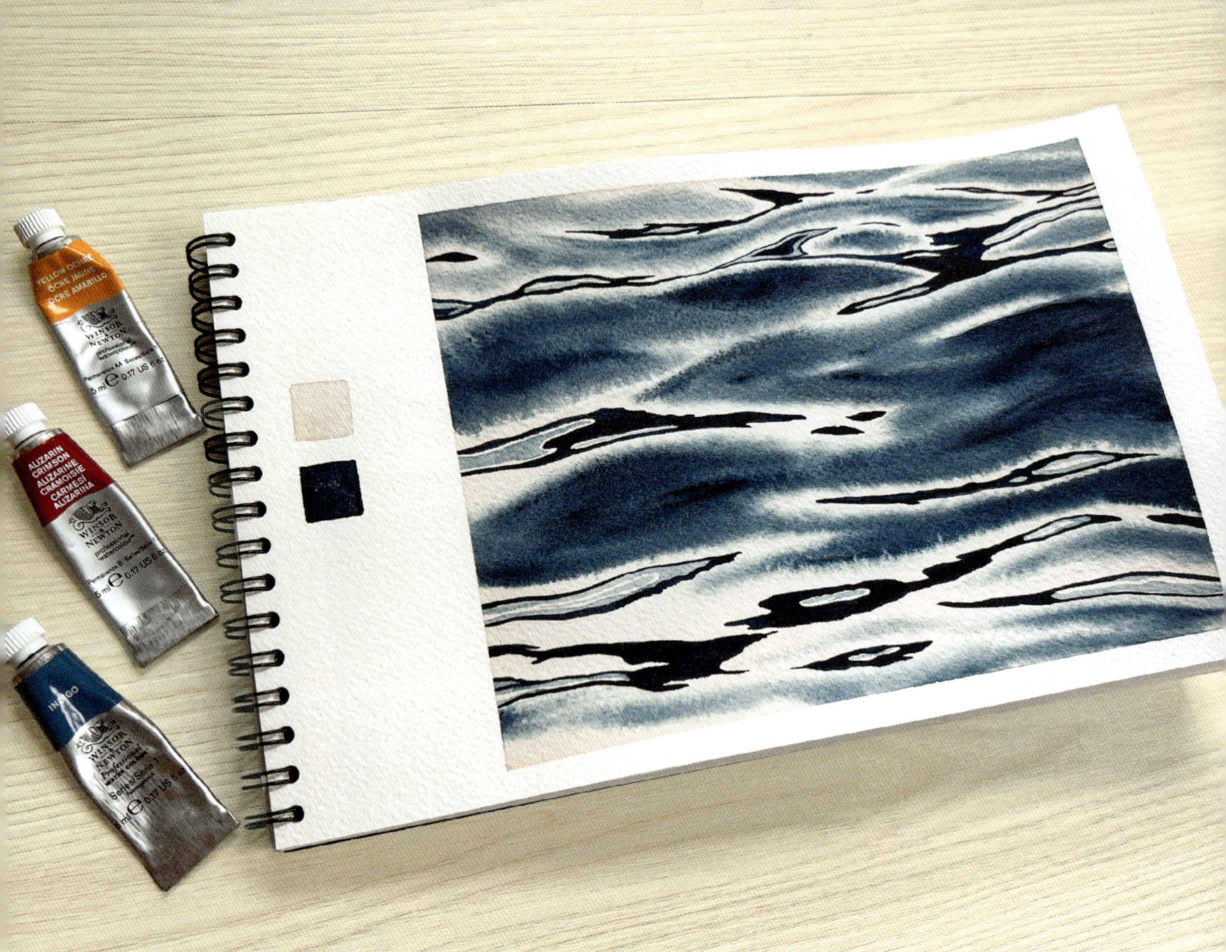

Painting Water with Water(color)

Up to this point in the book, we've painted a few different water landscapes. Today I want to introduce you to a new and super cool technique for painting water textures. I first discovered this technique through Julia Barminova (@juliabarminova on Instagram), a super talented watercolor artist who uses this technique to paint beautiful seascapes. The technique is called dry-on-wet, and

it involves brushing barely-liquid paint onto a wet paper surface to create lightly diffused brushstrokes. This technique requires some practice to get used to, and even I don't have it completely locked down yet, but I wanted to include it in this book anyway so you can give it a try. If you enjoy it, I highly recommend checking out Julia's Instagram page for more tips and tricks!

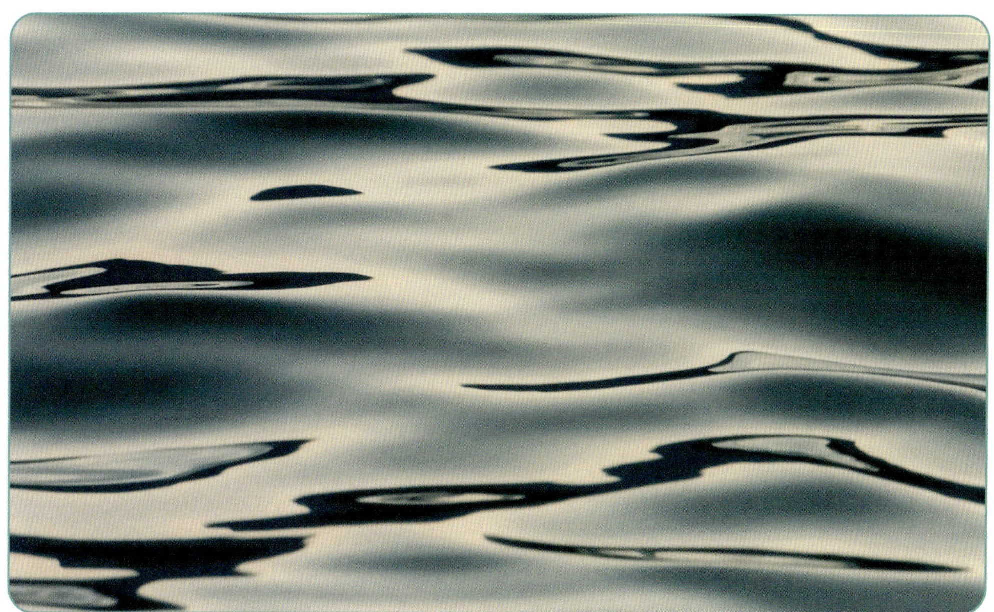

You can see the reference photo we'll use for this painting pictured here. I cropped it down quite a bit from the original reference photo so that we can focus in on just a few of the ripples and the reflections. For this project, you'll need:

» Cup of water and paper towel

» Watercolor paints: Yellow Ochre, Alizarin Crimson, Indigo

» Watercolor paper (I used a page of my Arches sketchbook)

» Optional: masking tape

» Pencil

» 1 large, 1 medium and 1 detail watercolor brush (I used a 12 round, a 4 round and a 2 round)

1   Add a drop of water to each of your colors and give them a minute to soften. In the meantime, prep your paper how you like it, taping the edges down if desired.

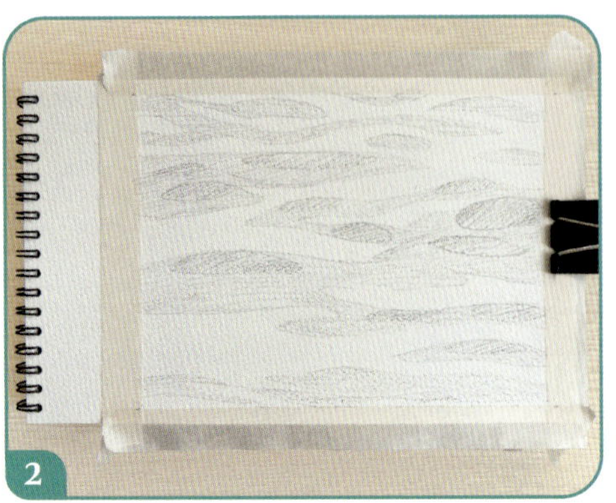

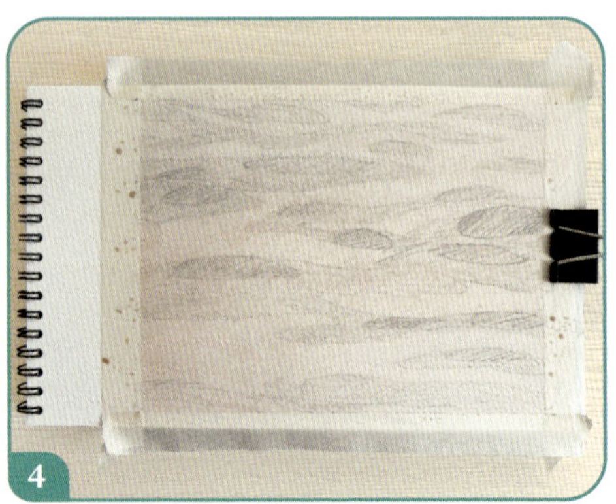

2 With your pencil, sketch out the shapes of the water ripples onto your paper. Note in the reference photo, you can see both the soft shadows of the ripples in the water and the sharp wavy lines of reflections. Right now, just focus on the shadows of the actual water and ignore the reflection details. I like to use my pencil to lightly shade in these ripple areas on my page to help me keep track of where to add the paint later.

3 Prepare your colors for this painting. You'll need to mix a super light peach color combining Yellow Ochre and a touch of Alizarin Crimson, along with a ton of water. You'll also need Indigo, but you'll need to add the least amount of water possible to it. It should be super thick on your palette and you should barely be able to move it with your brush.

PAUSE: The next few steps need to be completed while the painting is still wet, so read through Step 7 before starting.

4 Use a large brush and cover your entire paper with a generous layer of the light peach color.

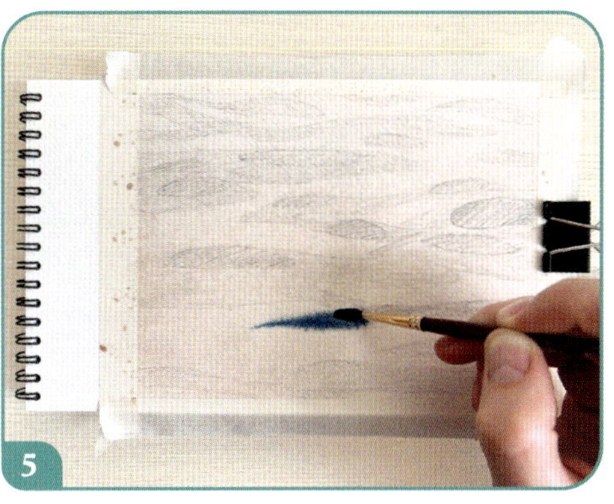

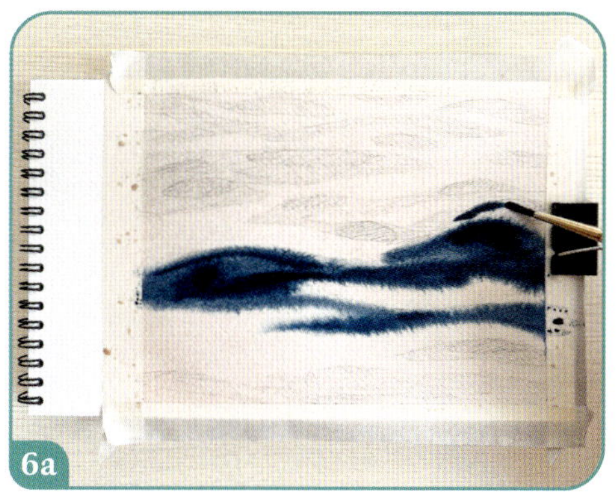

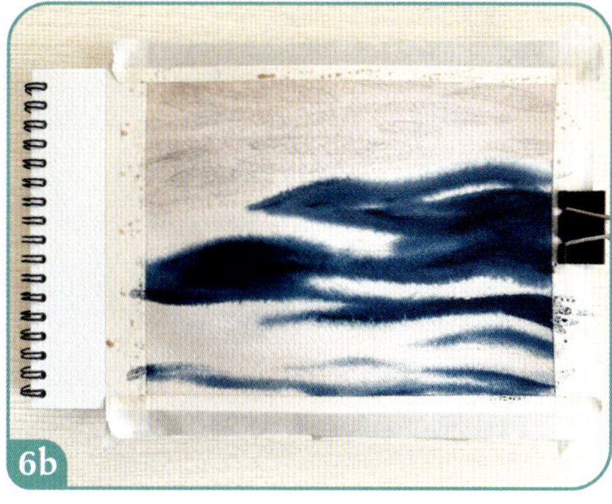

5 Switch to your medium brush and grab some barely-liquid Indigo. Swipe it into the shaded areas you sketched using smooth, sweeping brushstrokes. The paint should diffuse just slightly, but mostly stay right where you put it. Continually dry off your brush on a paper towel to avoid making the Indigo paint too wet.

TIP: You'll find if you end a brushstroke on the paper, you'll get a little starburst pattern where the brushstroke ended. To avoid this and keep the paint application smooth, try to start your brushstrokes near the center of the paper and take them toward the edge of the page, and end the brushstroke by painting right off the edge of the paper. You can't always do this, since sometimes there are ripples directly in the middle of the paper, but it's something to try to do when you can!

6 Continue painting in your ripple shapes throughout the paper, observing the reference photo to help you. Note that you can create darker areas by using more paint and by adding multiple layers, and you can create lighter areas by using less paint on your brush.

7   If you get to a point where an area has dried before you could add ripples, go back to the peach color and put down another layer in that section to re-wet it, then continue as normal. Once you've filled in all the ripples, let it dry completely.

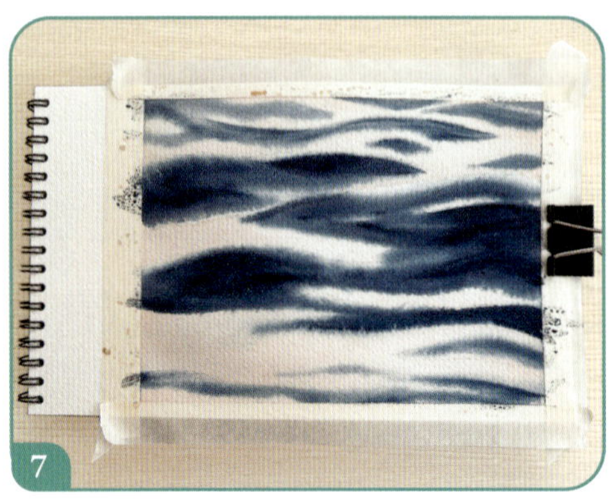

Remember Your Fundamentals: This dry-on-wet technique is very similar to the wet-on-wet technique (page 77), just with less water in the paint to give you more control. Feel free to compare the effects of this dry-on-wet technique to those you got when using the classic wet-on-wet technique to see the differences!

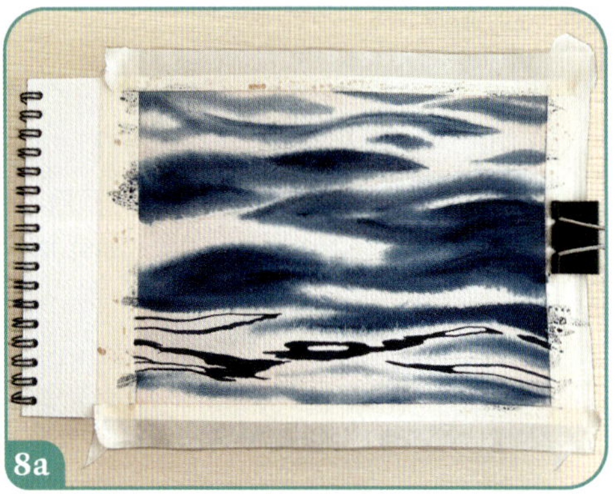

8   Add some water to your Indigo paint so that it's still dark, but now behaves like normal watercolor. Use your detail brush and add the wavy reflection shapes you see in the reference photo. The reflection shapes should be placed in the lighter spots between the darker ripples, so feel free to improvise a little bit based on where those lighter areas are on your painting. Let this dry before moving on.

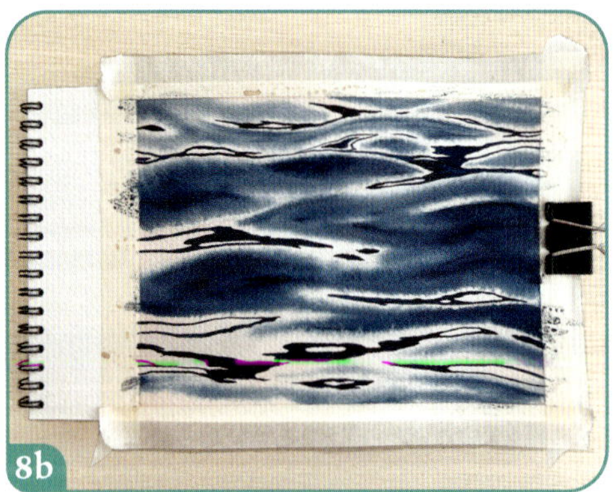

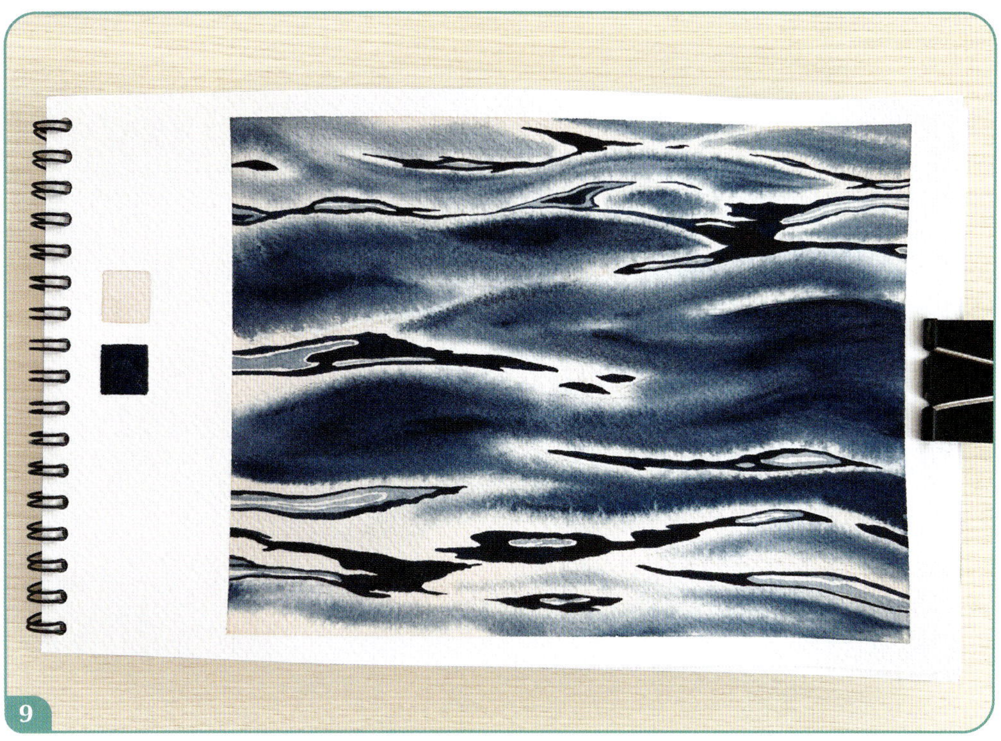

9 Water down the Indigo even more and use it to add a touch more detail inside the reflection shapes.

Once you're happy with those details, let the painting dry completely and take off the tape if you used it. Take a step back and analyze your painting. How did this technique work for you? Were you able to use the right paint consistencies to achieve both the soft shadows of the water and the sharp details in the reflection shapes? This is a tricky technique so no worries if you didn't get it on your first try (gold star for you if you did); just take note of what went well and what can be improved next time!

No Brushes Allowed!

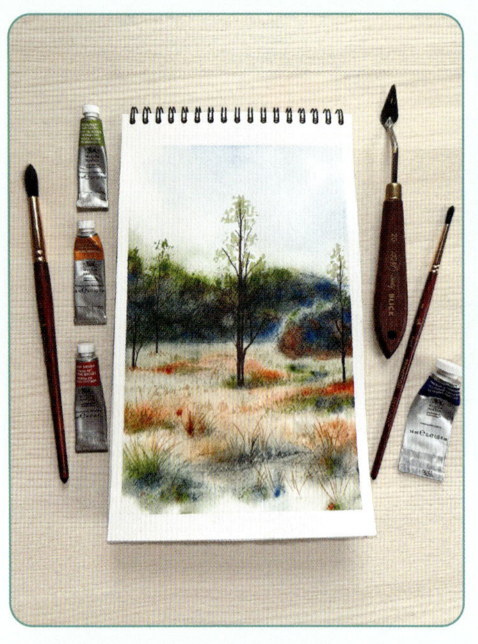

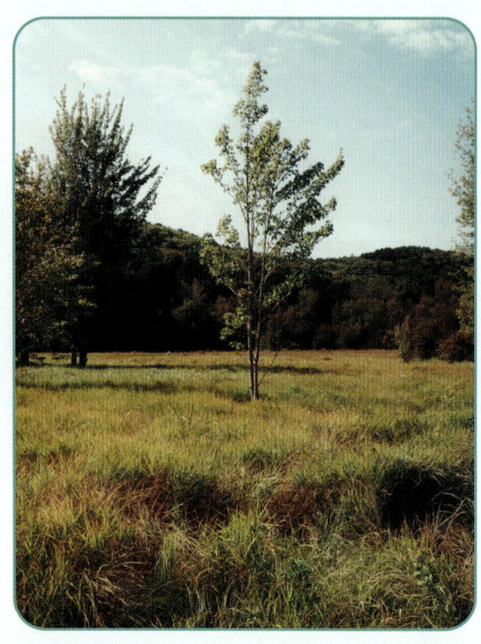

I lied; we'll be using brushes in this painting too. But we will also be using a palette knife (or a similar flat object) to give us a loose, abstract base to work off. For today's lesson, you will need tube watercolor paint. If you don't already have some and you're not interested in buying more than one color, you can absolutely do today's lesson as a monochromatic painting. Choose a dark color like Payne's Gray or Van Dyke Brown and follow the same directions, ignoring the color mixing instructions and focusing on value and detail. If you'd like to follow along with the full color version of today's lesson, you'll need four colors in tubes: Yellow Ochre, Burnt Sienna, Sap Green and Ultramarine Blue. You'll use Van Dyke Brown sparingly later in the project, but it can be in a tube or a regular pan. You'll also need a palette knife, or something that behaves similarly. You can get palette knives (including cheap plastic palette knives, which will work just fine) from any art store, or if you're in a pinch, you could use something thin and flat like a used-up gift card. We'll be using the reference photo you see pictured above for inspiration, but this painting style is meant to be loose and abstract so feel free to take liberties and make it your own!

You'll need:

» Watercolor paper (I used a page of my Arches sketchbook)

» Optional: masking tape

» Pencil

» Cup of water and paper towel

» 1 large and 1 detail watercolor brush (I used a 10 round and a 2 round)

» Small palette knife (or used gift card)

» Watercolor paints in tubes: Ultramarine Blue, Burnt Sienna, Sap Green, Yellow Ochre

» Watercolor paint in a tube or pan: Van Dyke Brown

1   Prep your paper how you like it, taping the edges down if desired.

2   Sketch the horizon line and general shape of the trees in the distance on your paper.

PAUSE: The majority of this painting needs to be done wet-on-wet, so please read through the following directions before starting so you can work quickly!

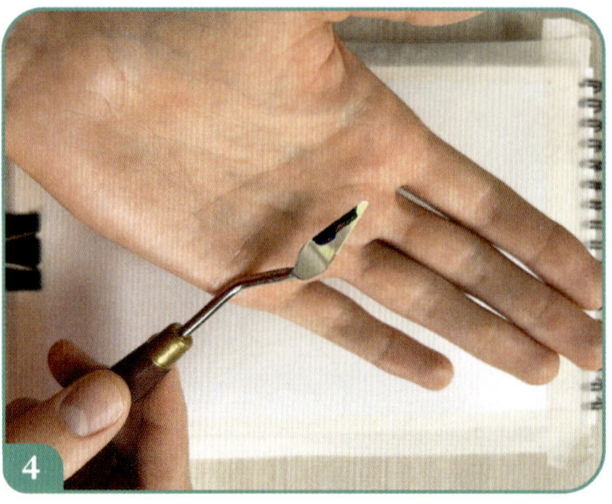

3   Using a large brush, coat your paper in a thick layer of clean water.

4   Load the edge of your palette knife with a small bead of Ultramarine Blue, a small bead of Burnt Sienna and a small bead of Sap Green.

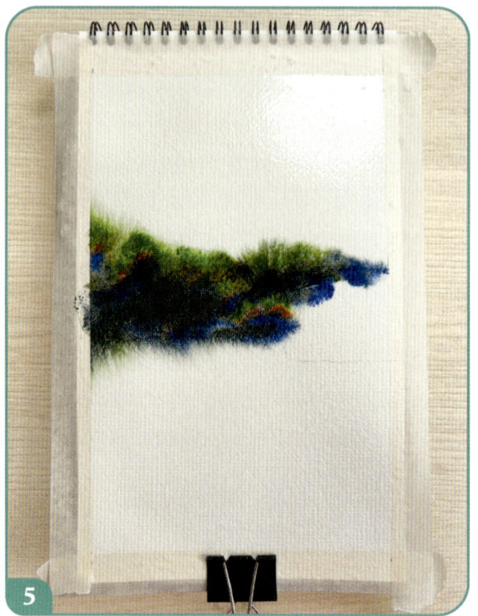

5   Scrape the paint onto your paper with the palette knife, following the tree area you sketched. Use a circular motion with the palette knife to imitate the texture of distant trees. The paint should spread out and mix together on the paper!

6   Switch to a large brush and touch it to Ultramarine Blue, then scrub in circular motions in the area above the trees to create a loose sky.

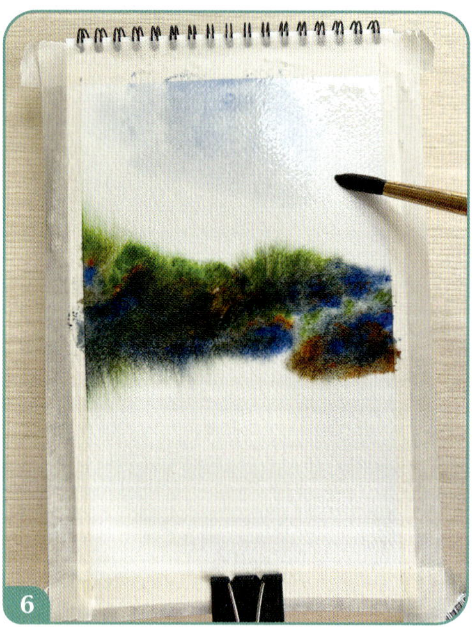

7   Load your palette knife with a small bead of Burnt Sienna and a small bead of Yellow Ochre and use horizontal scraping motions to create a field in the foreground, leaving some white spaces in between.

8   Load your palette knife with a small bead of Sap Green and a small bead of Ultramarine Blue and add some darker areas in the grass, still using horizontal brushstrokes.

Remember Your Fundamentals: Since this painting is a bit more abstract, you'll need to rely on value (page 53) to create something that makes sense. Make sure you're adding plenty of paint to the trees to create a darker value, then using lighter colors and less paint to cover the sky and grassy field sections.

9   Use the tip of your palette knife to scrape the paper and create some grass textures in the field area.

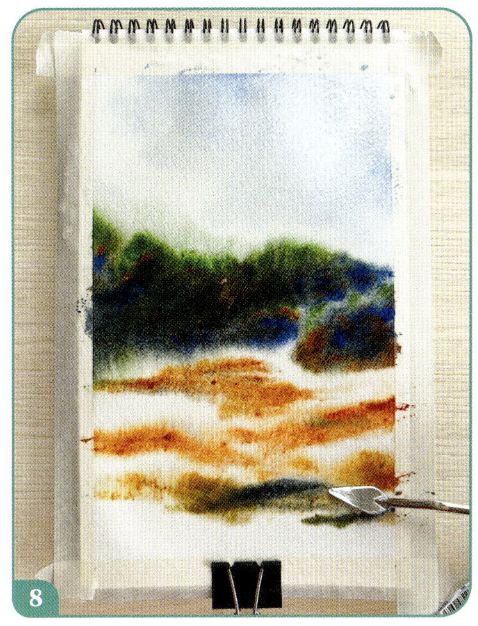

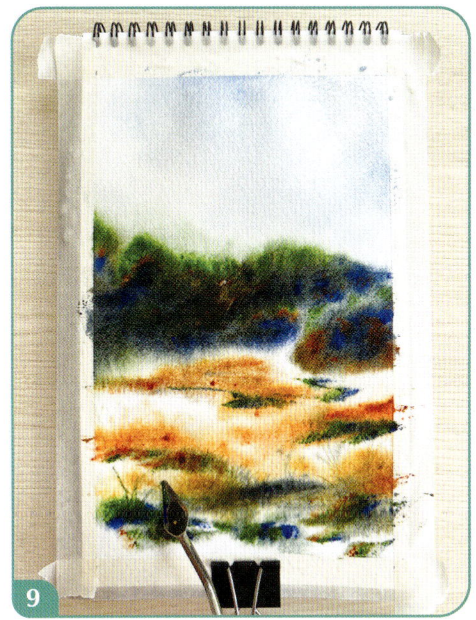

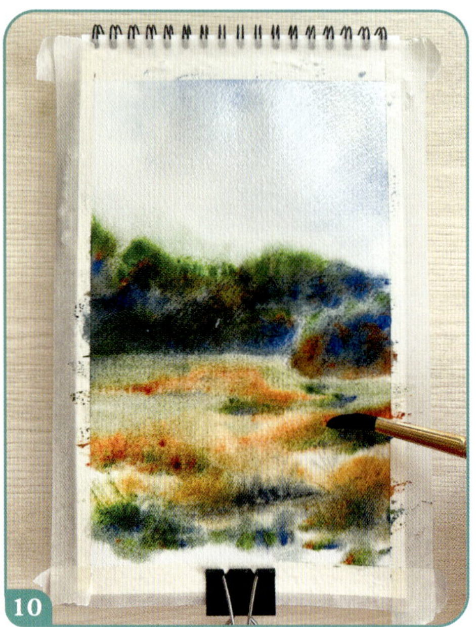

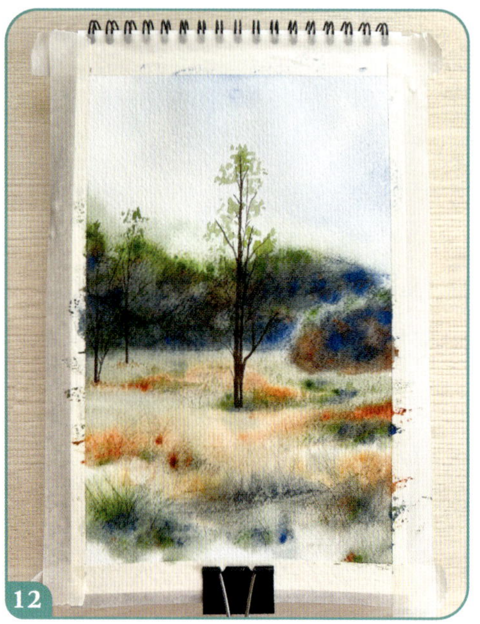

10 Switch to a clean damp medium brush and use it to blend any spots that didn't get blended enough. You can also use a completely dry brush to pick up wet paint and create highlights in the grassy field. Once you're happy with it, let it dry completely.

11 With a detail brush, mix a neutral brown (Van Dyke Brown and a little Ultramarine Blue) and add a few tree trunks throughout the field, keeping them closer to the horizon line.

12 Use watered-down Sap Green and a detail brush to add some leaf textures to each tree. I used a circular scraping motion with the side of the brush to create a more organic texture.

13 With any of the four tube watercolors (Ultramarine Blue, Burnt Sienna, Sap Green or Yellow Ochre) add some extra grassy texture to the foreground, using a super light touch with your detail brush!

Once you're happy with the final details, you're all done! Take off the tape, take a step back and analyze your work. Are you happy with the textures you were able to achieve? If viewed from a distance, does the painting look like a grassy field with trees? Make a note of what went well, along with what could be improved next time. These more abstract paintings can be tricky to control, so give yourself a pat on the back for completing this one!

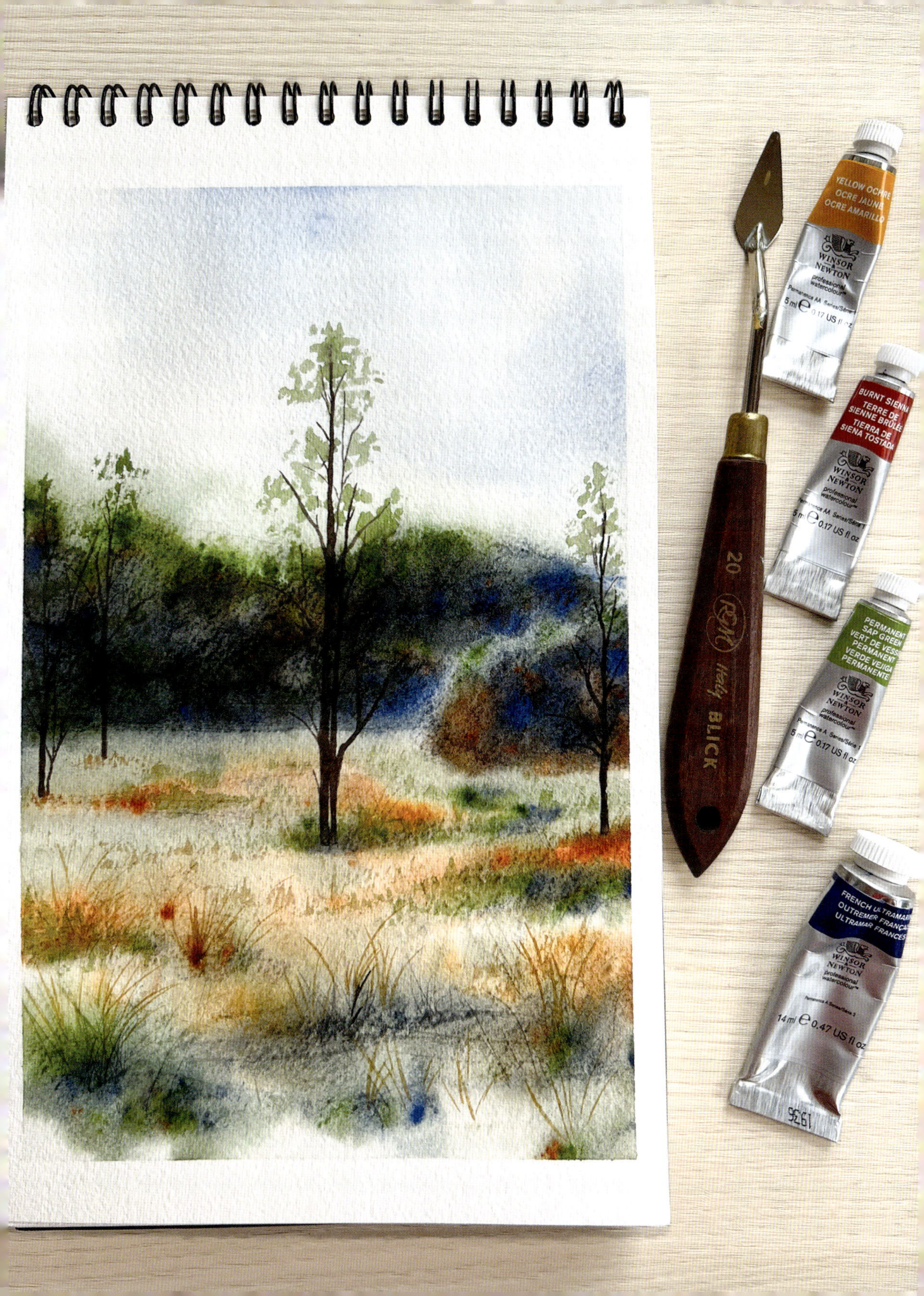

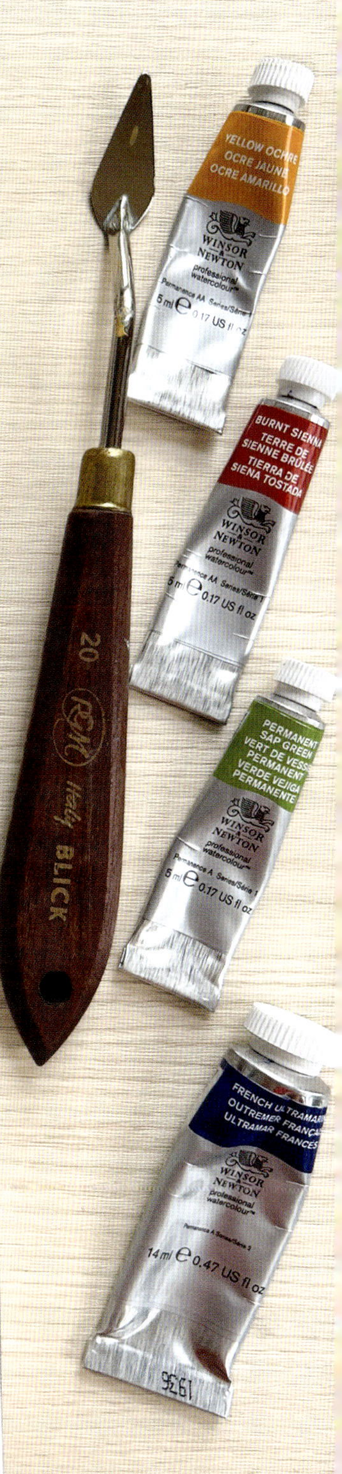

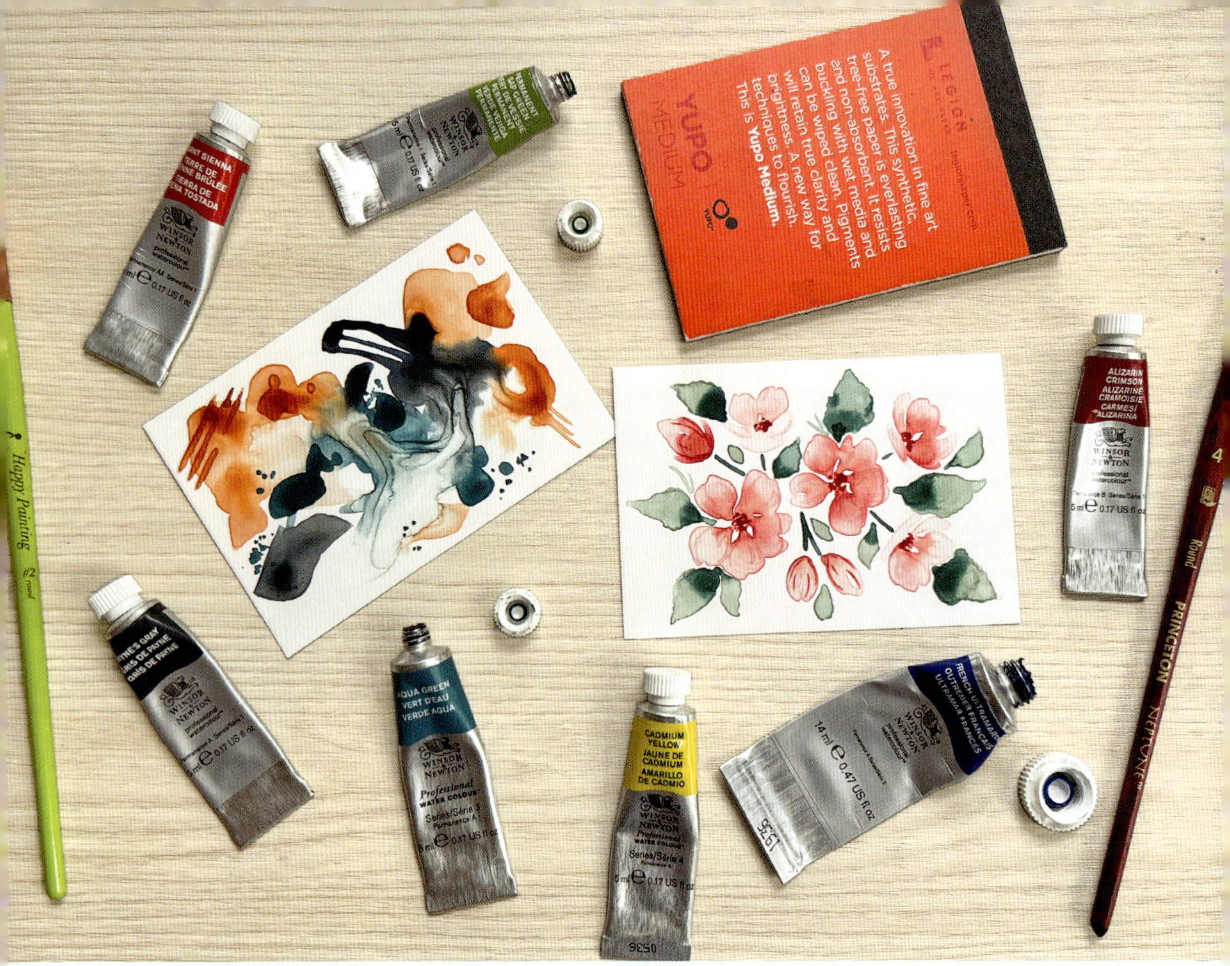

Stone(d) Paper

Let's get stoned! Today we are diving straight into the world of synthetic and non-traditional papers, meaning papers not created using plant fibers. I've personally tried out two different types, so I'll just be talking about those here, but there are plenty of other brands and varieties out there to explore if this lesson piques your interest!

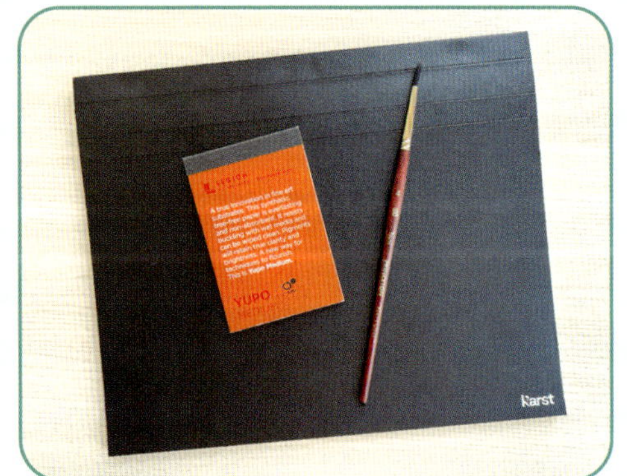

YUPO paper is a recyclable synthetic paper made by extruding plastic pellets into very thin sheets, and the result is a thick and durable paper with a slightly shiny finish. Stone paper, made by the brand Karst, is created by combining calcium carbonate (stone) with resin to bind it together into paper, and the result is a buttery and soft yet tear-resistant paper. These synthetic papers have similar qualities when it comes to watercolor—they're both waterproof, which means any wet media dries on top of the paper rather than absorbing into it. Because of this, the paper can be wiped completely clean with a wet brush and paper towel even after the paint has dried. It allows for some interesting textures and really vibrant colors, similar to the look of alcohol inks.

When I first tried out stone paper, I was inspired by the patterns the paint made when I used a hair dryer to dry it. Since the paint doesn't absorb into the paper, it just moves around on the surface until the water evaporates into the air and leaves the paint behind in concentric rings. These rings reminded me of maps with altitude lines, so I created a little series to explore this idea. You can see one example pictured here, and if this looks like something you'd like to try I published a video on my YouTube channel (@hannahartandprints) showing how I did it on September 25, 2024!

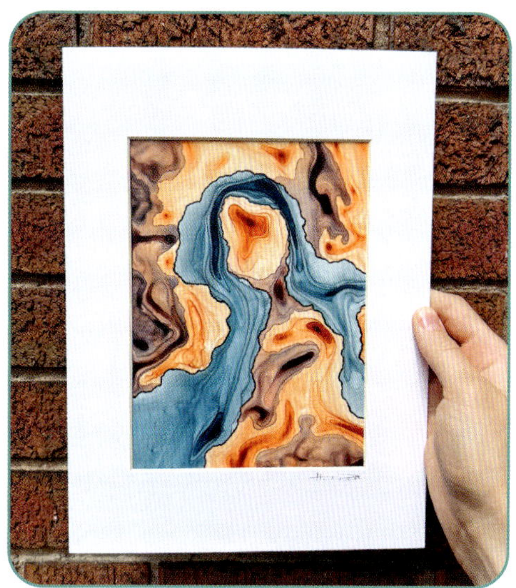

For today's lesson, you can use either YUPO paper or stone paper. I will say that YUPO paper is more readily available in most arts and crafts stores, and it is available in these mini pads like the one I used in this project for about $2, which makes it a great way to test out the medium before buying a larger pad. You can use any size paper you'd like for this lesson, and simply scale the directions up or down depending on the size of your paper. For our first experiment, we'll create an abstract painting to just test out how this paper behaves. In addition to the synthetic paper you've chosen, you'll also need:

» Cup of water and paper towel

» Watercolor paints: 3 colors (I used Burnt Sienna, Aqua Green and Payne's Gray)

» 1 medium brush (I used a ¼-inch [6-mm] dagger just to mix it up)

» Optional: hair dryer

1   Choose the three colors you'd like to use for this painting and add a drop of water to each of them, letting them sit for a minute to soften.

2   Make a puddle of each color in your mixing area, adding some water so that the paint flows easily.

3   Create some interesting shapes and textures on your synthetic paper, alternating between these three colors and allowing them to blend with each other on the page.

Remember Your Fundamentals: While I chose to use a dagger brush, you don't need a new brush to create different brushstrokes. Adjust your brush posture by shuffling your hand up or down the handle. Play with how much paint you load on your brush or how much pressure you use when you apply it to your page. While it's always fun to try out a new brush, you can also create a wide array of strokes with just one brush—and doing so keeps your mark-making (page 70) skills honed.

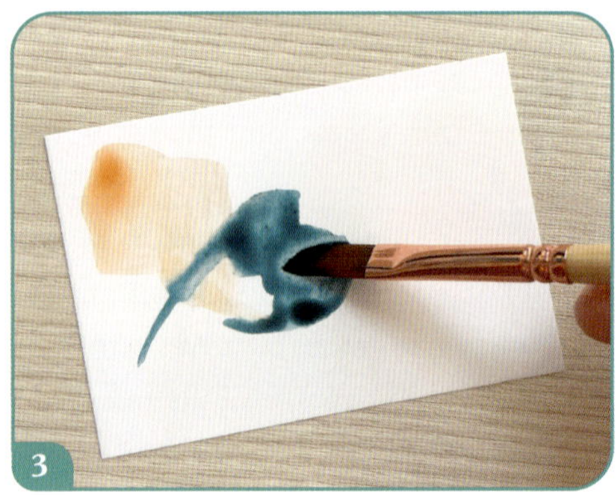

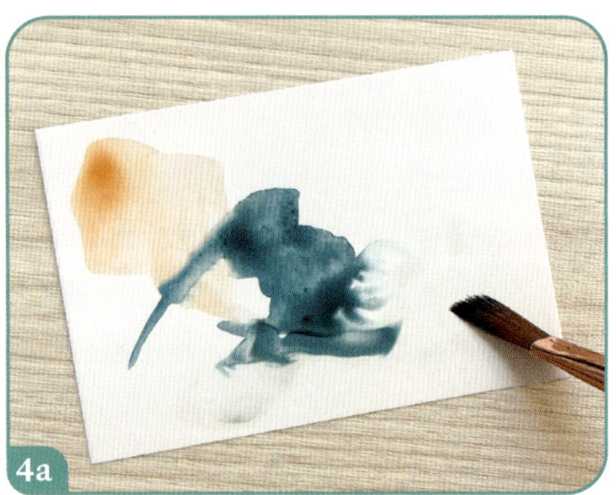

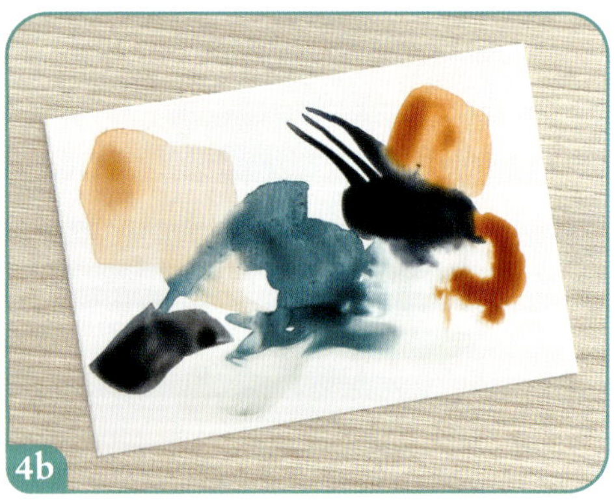

4   Introduce some clean water to the page to add even more texture and interest as the paint colors blend into the clean water.

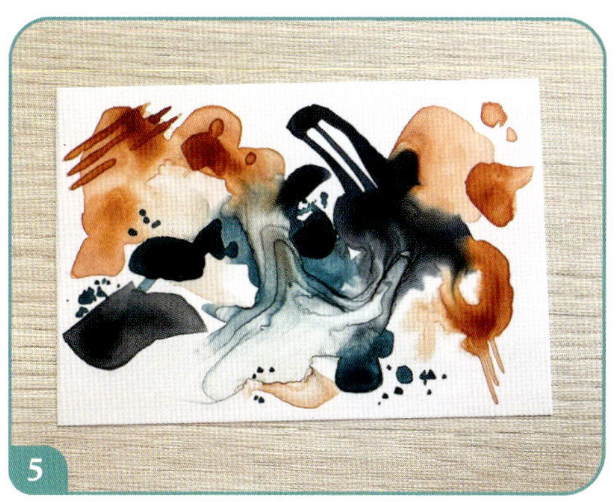

5 After the paint dries, you can add additional layers of color and texture on top. You can also experiment with lifting the paint off the paper with a clean damp brush, or with using a hairdryer to create additional textures. If you need more time to get used to this new medium, you can make as many abstract paintings as you like. Feel free to use different colors, brushes and techniques to fully explore the possibilities!

Now that we've gotten our feet wet with this new type of paper, let's try painting something a little more realistic! I love painting cherry blossoms, and they make great subjects for this synthetic paper. You'll need:

» Cup of water and paper towel

» Watercolor paints: Alizarin Crimson, Cadmium Yellow, Sap Green, Ultramarine Blue

» 1 medium brush and 1 detail brush (I used a 4 round and a 2 round)

» Optional: hair dryer

1 Add a drop of water to each of your colors and give them a minute to soften.

2 Mix a very light pink color combining Alizarin Crimson, a touch of Cadmium Yellow and plenty of water. Also mix up a more concentrated pink color, combining the same two colors and adding less water.

3 With your medium brush, create a small flower with five petals radiating from a center point. For the petals, I like to start with really light pressure at the center of the flower, then press down with my brush and use two brushstrokes to create a rounded shape for the main part of the petal.

4   Add some more concentrated pink paint to your brush and gently touch your brush to the center of the flower while the paint is still wet on the paper. The concentrated pink paint should gently spread out into the lighter pink paint in an organic way.

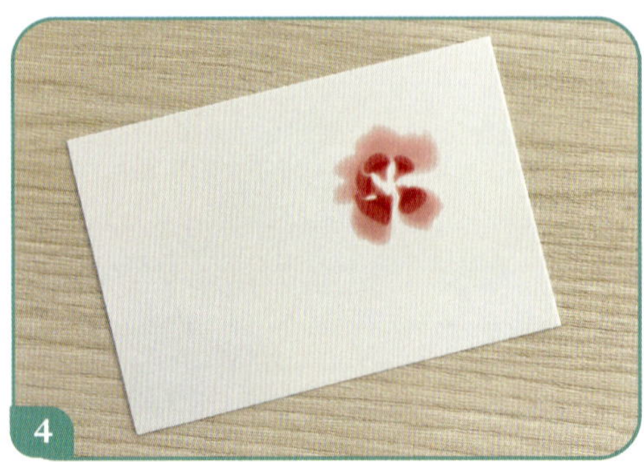

5   Add as many flowers as you want to your paper. You can create flowers facing slightly away from you by flattening the petals on one side of the flower (similar to the way we did in Expressive Florals, page 128), and you can create buds by painting a loose oval shape.

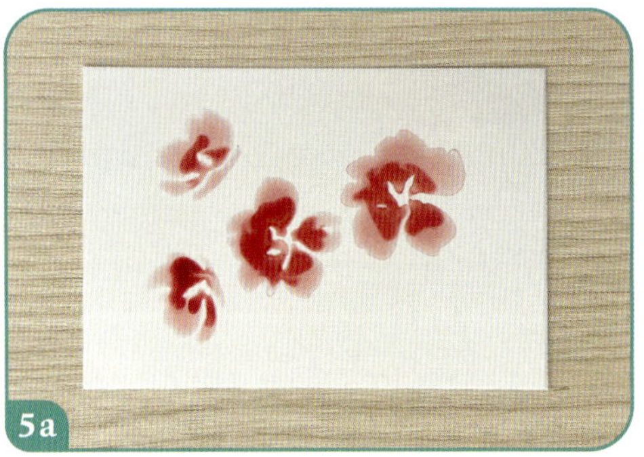

6   Let the flowers dry completely. This will take a little while, and while you can use a hairdryer, remember, you will end up with that concentric ring texture. I happened to be painting on a sunny day, so I put my painting in a sunny spot to dry and that helped speed things up.

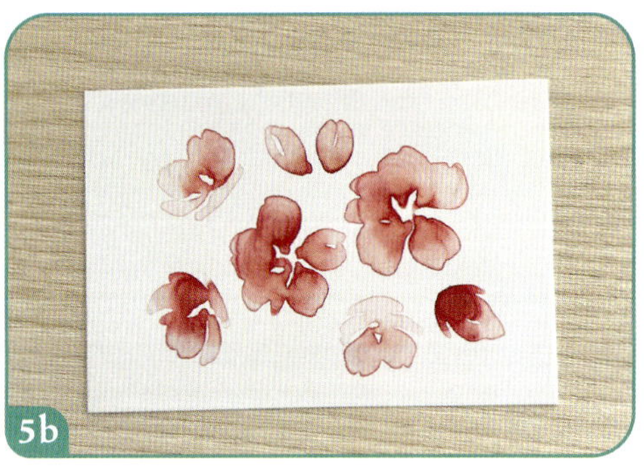

7   Create a very concentrated pink shade combining Alizarin Crimson, a touch of Cadmium Yellow and very little water. Use your detail brush to add a cluster of small dots of this concentrated pink color to the center of each flower. Add some small curved lines to the flower buds you painted, following the contours of each flower bud.

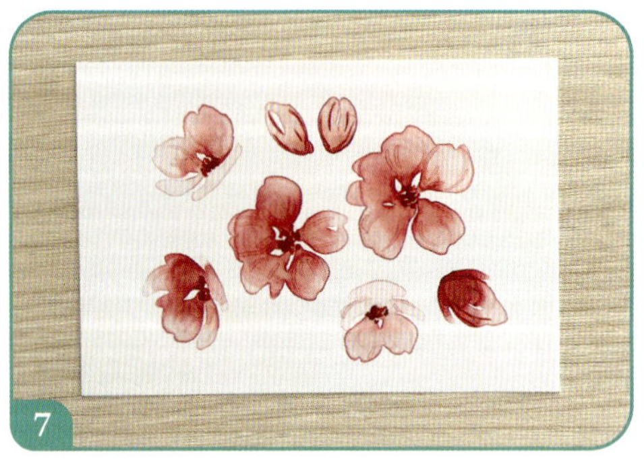

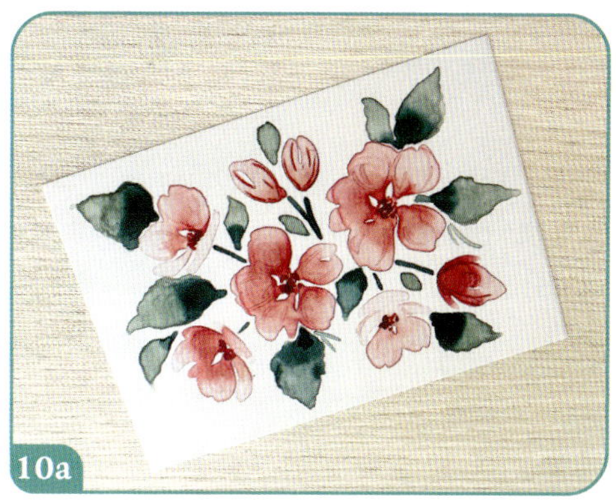

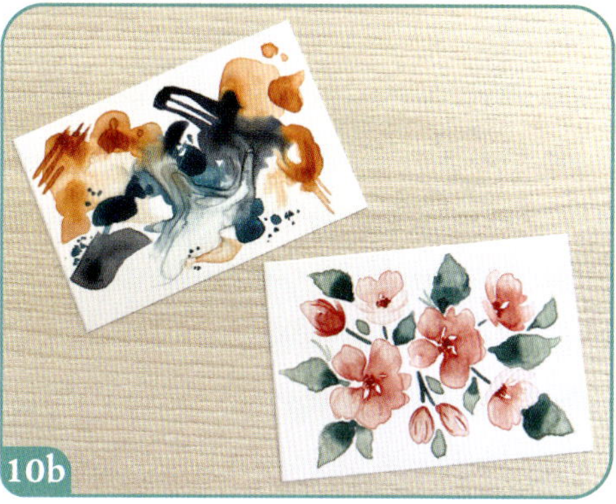

Remember Your Fundamentals: As we discussed in Colorful Language (page 59), complementary colors are especially vibrant when used next to each other. The pink and red colors in the flowers are the complementary colors of the greens we're using for the leaves, which creates effortless vibrance! You can also neutralize a color you're mixing by adding the complementary color. In Step 9, we toned down the vibrancy of the green paint by adding a tiny bit of Alizarin Crimson. This also increases color harmony throughout the painting, since Alizarin Crimson is used in every color mixture!

8   Mix a light green combining Sap Green, Cadmium Yellow and just a touch of Alizarin Crimson to neutralize it. Mix a dark green combining Sap Green, Ultramarine Blue and a touch of Alizarin Crimson.

9   With whatever brush you're comfortable with, start with the light green color and fill in the blank spaces between the flowers with stems and leaves.

10   While the stems and leaves are still wet, drop a little dark green to the base of each leaf and stem to add color variation and contrast.

I hope you enjoyed this adventure with non-traditional papers! The world is really your oyster here—there are so many ways to play with watercolors when using paper like this, so I hope you take some time to do some experimenting for yourself and see if you can come up with something new and exciting!

Glossary

1-point perspective: a technique to portray 3D objects in a two-dimensional way using one vanishing point

2-point perspective: a technique to portray 3D objects in a two-dimensional way using two vanishing points

Analogous colors: a group of colors next to each other on the color wheel

Atmospheric perspective: using different values and saturations of color to create the illusion of depth and distance in a painting

Bloom: starburst-like texture that can occur in watercolor painting, typically when parts of the painting dry much quicker than others

Cast shadow: the shadow created on the table or floor by an object, always extends in the opposite direction from the light source

Color swatch: a small patch of paint created to test the color and consistency of a paint mixture

Color theory: the study of how different colors function together

Color wheel: a circular diagram containing every visible color and its relationship to others

Complementary colors: colors exactly opposite each other on the color wheel

Composition: the position of focal points and balance of light and dark areas in a painting

Composition shapes: different ways to place focal points in a painting to make it feel balanced

Contrast: the total range of values in any painting

Cool colors: any colors in the green-blue-purple half of the color wheel, with blue being the coolest color

Core shadow: the darkest area of an object shaded from the light

Damp brush blending: placing wet paint on dry paper, then quickly blending the edges with a damp brush to soften the edges

Dry brushing: a texture created by removing most of the paint from a brush, then lightly scraping the brush over dry paper

Dry-on-wet: using barely liquid watercolor paints on a wet paper surface to create soft, slightly diffused brushstrokes

Flat wash: a smooth, even layer of paint with as little texture as possible

Focal point: a subject which draws attention in a painting

Glaze: a thin layer of watered-down paint applied to alter the color or tone of the layer(s) underneath

Gouache: an opaque, water-based paint that works well with watercolor to add highlights

Gradient: a smooth transition between two colors, or between a color and the white of the page

Highlight: the lightest point of an object, faces the light source

Horizon line: the horizontal line across a scene where "ground" and "sky" meet

Hue: an art synonym for a specific color, like green or red or purple

Layering: applying multiple thin washes in the same space to build up color and depth, letting each one dry before adding the next

Lifting: using a completely dry brush to lift wet paint from the paper to create highlights or correct mistakes

Light source: the type of light used to illuminate a scene, and the angle at which it shines down on the scene

Limited palette: creating a painting using only a small selection of colors, usually two or three

Local light: light originating from a nearby source like a fire, flashlight or light bulb

Masking: using masking fluid or masking tape to cover an area of paper to protect it from subsequent layers of paint

Midtone: the most saturated (area with the brightest color) spot on an object, usually located right at the edge between the light and dark sections of the object

Mixed media: using more than one medium to create an artwork (e.g., pen and watercolor)

Monochromatic: a painting created using tints and shades of only one color

Natural light: light coming from the sun or moon

Primary colors: colors that can't be mixed using any other combination of colors, and from which all other colors can be mixed

Reflected light: the slightly lighter area within the core shadow, usually at the opposite end from the highlight, where light from the surrounding environment bounces up

Rule of thirds: dividing a painting into thirds and placing focal points on those third lines and/or intersection points

Saturation: the purity or vibrancy of a color

Scrubbing and lifting: using a damp brush to scrub an area of dry paint for a few seconds, then dabbing with a paper towel to create a highlight

Secondary colors: colors created by mixing two primaries together

Shade: hue with black paint added

Splatter: loading a brush with paint, then tapping the handle firmly above the paper to spray droplets over the paper

Study: a quick drawing or painting meant to help the artist become familiar with the subject or a specific technique

Synthetic paper: paper made with alternative materials like stone or polymers rather than plant fibers

Tertiary colors: colors created by combining one primary color and the secondary color next to it on the color wheel

Tint: hue with white paint added (or water added in the case of watercolor)

Trompe l'oeil: a French term meaning "trick the eye," a style of painting small, everyday objects life-sized and as realistically as possible to give the illusion that the actual object is sitting on the paper

Value: the lightness or darkness of any given color

Vanishing point: a point to which all straight lines point in any object distorted by perspective

Warm colors: any colors in the red-orange-yellow half of the color wheel, with orange being the warmest color

Watercolor: a medium combining powdered pigment with water-soluble binder, allowing the pigment to be suspended in water and applied to paper

Watercolor graphite: a water-soluble graphite pencil used to create watercolor sketches

Wet-on-dry: placing wet paint on dry paper, giving you sharp details and defined brushstrokes

Wet-on-wet: placing wet paint on wet paper, creating interesting textures, gradients and soft blends

Zentangle: doodles with a variety of repetitive patterns

Acknowledgments

This book would not exist without the help and support of quite a few people. First and foremost, thank you to my wonderful family, friends and partner, Michael, for all your love and support. You people hold me together and support me in so many different ways, and I am so lucky to have you in my life. Next, thank you to my editor, Sadie Hofmeester, and all the folks at Page Street Publishing for asking me back, keeping me on track and turning my pages of rambling into a beautiful, cohesive book. Thanks to all photographers who provided photos for this book—your work is very much appreciated. A huge thank-you to everyone who has supported me as an artist—all of you who have purchased a piece of my art, watched my content online or supported *Watercolor Wanderlust*, you are the reason I get to continue to live my dream life. Finally, thank you to you, my friend, for reading this book and sharing your creativity with me.

About the Author

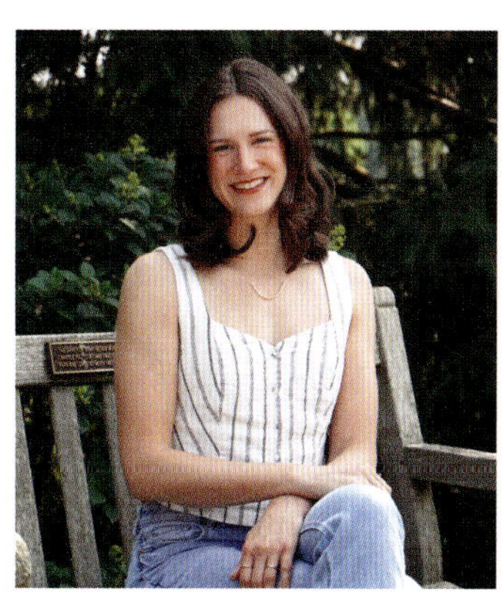

Hannah M. Pickerill is a professional artist and social media creator born and raised in Seattle, WA, and now based in Cincinnati, OH. Her work is mainly inspired by landscapes, but she dabbles in other subjects like architecture, animals and still life. She is a multidisciplinary artist proficient in watercolors, gouache and oil paint. She has a passion for teaching and loves inspiring others to pick up a paintbrush and get creative. In her spare time, she trains in Brazilian Jiu Jitsu and Muay Thai, loves to read and loves to travel.

Watercolor Boot Camp is her second watercolor book; Hannah is also the author of *Watercolor Wanderlust*, published in 2024.

Index